The *Alliance Israélite Universelle*
and the Jewish Communities
of Morocco: 1862–1962

SUNY Series in Modern Jewish History
Paula Hyman and Deborah Dash Moore, Editors

The *Alliance Israélite Universelle*
and the Jewish Communities
of Morocco: 1862–1962

MICHAEL M. LASKIER

State University of New York Press

ALBANY

Published by
State University of New York Press, Albany

© 1983 State University of New York

For information, address State University of New York Press, State University Plaza, Albany, N.Y., 12246

Library of Congress Cataloging in Publication Data

Laskier, Michael M., 1949-
    The Alliance israélite universelle and the Jewish communities of Morocco, 1862-1962.

    (SUNY series in modern Jewish history) (Pirsume ha-Makhon le-ḥeker ha-tefutsot)
    Revision of thesis (Ph.D.) — University of California.
    Bibliography: p. 355
    1. Jews — Morocco — History. 2. Alliance israélite universelle. 3. Morocco — Ethnic relations. I. Title. II. Series. III. Series: Pirsume ha-Makhon le-ḥeker ha-tefutsot.
DS135.M8L37 1982   305.8'924'064   82-5892
ISBN 0-87395-656-7   AACR2
ISBN 0-87395-655-9 (pbk.)

Publications of the
Diaspora Research Institute
TEL-AVIV UNIVERSITY

EDITED BY

Shlomo Simonsohn

Book 45

State University of New York Press

ALBANY

*To My Parents Haya and Abe
and to my Grandmother Pnina Lieder*

Contents

x   Contents

Tables

Illustrations

Acknowledgments

This book, an outgrowth of a doctoral dissertation presented at the History Department of the University of California, Los Angeles, was rewritten and revised under the auspices of the Diaspora Research Institute and the Department of History of the Jewish People, at Tel-Aviv University. I would like to express my sincerest gratitude to Professor Shlomo Simonsohn, the Institute's and the department's head, for his generous and unfailing assistance in all areas, including costs and co-publication with the State University of New York Press. My gratitude goes as well for Dr. Yehuda Nini of the Department of History of the Jewish People at TAU for his support. I would like to thank the State University of New York Press and its editors, Professors Paula Hyman and Deborah Dash Moore, as well as Nancy Sharlet, the production editor, for publishing the work as part of the SUNY Press Modern Jewish History Series.

I thank Professors Nikki R. Keddie, Malcolm H. Kerr, and Amos Funkenstein of the University of California, Los Angeles, for their assistance during the preparation of the doctoral thesis.

Numerous other people played direct and indirect roles in this project. In the United States, the advice given to me by Professor Norman A. Stillman of the State University of New York at Binghamton was quire useful at different stages of the research. In France, my gratitude goes to *Alliance Israélite Universelle* president Jules Braunschvig, the organization's former secretary-general, the late Eugène Weill, and the organization's chief of services, Léon Benaroya. Yvonne Levyne, head librarian, and Georges Weill, chief archivist at the AIU library and archives gave invaluable help. The staff at the *Quai d'Orsay* archives and at the *Centre des Hautes Etudes sur l'Afrique et l'Asie Moderne* were also very helpful, as was the staff at the *Institut National d'Etudes Demographiques*. Several people, especially Professor Haïm Zafrani of the University of Paris VIII, provided data based on firsthand experiences in Morocco. Finally, the staff at the *Bibliothèque Nationale* supplied primary and secondary sources regarding French and Spanish Morocco.

In Israel, I am grateful for the advice, comments, interviews, and other assistance offered by Dr. Michael Abitbol, Dr. Issachar Ben-Ami, Dr. Shalom Bar-Asher (the latter encouraged me to undertake this study in the first place), Robert Attal — all from the Hebrew University of Jerusalem. I thank as well Dr. André Chouraqui, Mordechai Soussan, Hanania Dahan, Rabbis Ishaq Rouche, David Ovadia, and Albert Hazan; Meir Knafo, Professor Simon Schwarzfuchs of Bar-Ilan University, and Elie Elmaleh, the former AIU delegate in Israel. More recently, the staff at the Jerusalem-based Zionist Archives and at the American Jewish Joint Distribution Committee facilitated my research.

Last, but certainly not least, I am indebted to the AIU (*Ittihād*) delegate in Morocco, Elias Harrus, for vital data on the schools. Without his help, many gaps would have remained. The literature on ORT, furnished by David Alberstein, ORT's chief of operations in Switzerland, enabled me to analyze the contributions made by the ORT-AIU towards the promotion of vocational training.

Whatever merit there is in this work, it must be shared by all those who made its completion possible. For the errors, failings, and opinions expressed, I alone am responsible.

MICHAEL M. LASKIER

Tel-Aviv University

Introduction

The purposes of this study are (a) to analyze and document the educational, cultural, social, and political activities of the *Alliance Israélite Universelle* (AIU) in the Moroccan Jewish communities from the creation of the organization's first school (Tetuan 1862) until 1962, when after one hundred years of activity, despite emigration to Israel, France, and the Americas, its schools were still quite active under the arabized title, *Ittihād Maroc*. These activities underwent considerable evolution in various stages between 1862 and 1912 (the precolonial period), between 1913 to 1945, and during the period since, when the work of the AIU was supplemented by a variety of European and American Jewish organizations. I have recorded and analyzed these changes in order to explore the implications of reform within the communities; (b) to document as much as possible the history of modernization within the communities in these critical years; and (c) to relate the subject to the broader issues of government during the protectorate and immediate postindependence periods, as well as to Jewish-Muslim relations in the colonial process.

The *activities* of the AIU in the Jewish communities of the Middle East and North Africa is a subject that began to attract scholars in the recent past. To this point (1982) some recent scholarly studies on the AIU's political, educational, and extraeducational activities are Paul Dumont, "La condition juive en Turquie à la fin du xixe siècle," *Les Nouveaux Cahiers* 57 (1979), pp. 25–38; Joan Gardner Roland, *The Alliance Israélite Universelle and French Policy in North Africa: 1860–1918*, Ph.D dissertation, and Paul Silberman, *An Investigation into the Schools of the Alliance Israélite Universelle: 1862–1940*, Ph.D dissertation, New York University 1973. To these may be added the interesting theoretical study written recently by Georges Weill on the aims of the AIU: "Emancipation et humanisme: Le discours idéologique de l'Alliance Israélite Universelle," *Les Nouveaux Cahiers* 52 (1978), pp. 1–20. Of these, Roland's analysis on the political ties of the AIU with the French political establishment, as well as with the French administration in Algeria and Tunisia, and later in Morocco, is

1

especially interesting and thorough, relying extensively on the archives of the AIU and of the *Quai d'Orsay*. This study provides excellent groundwork for additional studies on North Africa and on Middle Eastern countries, for the understanding of the mutual aspirations of France and the AIU to promote French cultural and political values among the Jews until the end of the First World War. It also provides sufficient background to assess the changes in French policy after 1918 when the colonial functionaries carefully sought to alter their policy vis-à-vis the Jews in accordance with the political realities on local scenes. Finally, though a solid study on Franco-AIU relations, Roland's thesis, based on a variety of political considerations, could not possibly concentrate on social, educational, and political factors influencing the Jews in the three Maghrib countries, a considerable subject that must be researched separately.

Less recent studies that placed emphasis on the AIU and its work in the Jewish communities of the Muslim world which, are also noteworthy, include: André Chouraqui, *L'alliance israélite universelle et la renaissance juive contemporaine: 1860-1960* (Presses Universitaires de France, 1965); Doris Bensimon Donath, *L'evolution de la femme israélite à Fès* (Faculté des Lettres no. 25, Aix-en-Provence, 1962) and *Evolution du judaïsme marocain sous le protectorat français: 1912-1956* (Paris: Mouton and Co., 1968); Narcisse Leven, *Cinquante ans d'histoire: l'alliance israélite universelle* (Paris, Librarie Félix Alcan, 1911-1920, two volumes); and Rabaud, "L'Alliance Israélite au Maroc," (Bordeaux, Faculté d'Histoire et de Géographie 1953. [unpublished manuscript]). Donath's works are excellent sociological and theoretical studies. They are not historical studies, nor are they based on archival work. They are indispensable for historians specializing in the comparative social and cultural evolution of Jews and Muslims. On the other hand, both Chouraqui's and Leven's works are based more on inside information rather than on scholarly research, for both men were closely affiliated with the AIU, the latter having been one of its founders. Chouraqui's book is somewhat general, though it outlines some of the main aspects of the AIU's ideological orientations and its relationship with other Jewish organizations in the Mediterranean-basin communities. Leven's study is far more instructive to the historian, well written, and truly interesting. Nevertheless, it covers too much ground, surveying *all* the organization's activities and, naturally, it does not offer an objective analysis. Furthermore, it stops at 1910, the year marking the fiftieth anniversary of the AIU. I did not consult Rabaud's study, because I was unable to obtain a copy.

It is expected that European, and Israeli scholars will undertake further studies on the AIU's activities to provide a better understanding of the important Jewish communities of the Arab and Muslim world.

In undertaking this task in January 1976 in partial fulfillment for the doctorate in the field of Modern Middle Eastern History at the University of California, Los Angeles, I collected archival data, interviewed former students and teachers, and consulted newspapers, manuscripts, statistical abstracts, articles, and books. Of these sources the archival material is especially important, notably the archives of the AIU, the *Quai d'Orsay*, the Zionist archives of Jerusalem, and the archives of the JDC (American Jewish Joint Distribution Committee).

The AIU archives

The AIU archives on Morocco in the *Bibliothèque de l'Alliance* (Paris) are primary. I consulted the files of categories *B* (Communities), *E* (Schools), and those files separated from the above categories (i.e., without file number or unclassified for unexplained reasons), leaving aside categories *C* and *F*, which contain materials on political aspects of the AIU unrelated to this study. The files of categories *B* and *E* give a fairly extensive picture of the educational and extraeducational work of the AIU, as well as vital data on the situation of the Jews in a country that on the one hand was sinking into anarchy, while, on the other hand, opening itself up, ever so reluctantly, to European colonial penetration. Prior to 1939 the teachers were not always of Moroccan background but originated from Europe or from the Turkish communities of Izmir, Andrinople, Constantinople, or from Salonika and Rhodes in Greece. Though they frequently painted a daily or weekly picture of the internal communal setting, sometimes in rather full reports, their training in Western culture often biased their views of traditional local lifestyles. The Moroccan *indigènes*, be they Jews or Muslims, were portrayed at times as "primitive souls" and as "uncultured," while the rabbis were in some cases referred to as "reactionaries" or "ignoramuses," simply because they either refused to enlist greater community support on the AIU's behalf, or because they had accepted the AIU slowly, and with utmost caution. Interestingly, the teachers' criticism of the rabbinic elite was stronger during the colonial era than before 1912, when the AIU was struggling to become an institution in the Moroccan communities. Before 1912 with a few exceptions, the teachers displayed greater caution in their dealings with traditional leaders in order to win support. Afterwards, they were less hesitant in pushing forward reforms or criticizing the rabbis. In fact, some of the Moroccan-born members of the AIU revealed similar tendencies and would describe the rabbis and other elements in derogatory terms. Consequently, the archives must be consulted carefully and with the knowledge that information and analysis is mixed with personal and subjective views.

The *Quai d'Orsay* archives

These archives, categories *A.E. Maroc* I.403 and 405 as well as *Série Administrative-C 142dr2*, are particularly important for information about the cultural penetration of the AIU between 1897 and 1914, especially into Morocco's coastal towns. These archives reflect the reaction of the most prominent French consuls and legation heads to the development of the school network and discuss the potential benefits that France could derive from these cultural activities. French concern in these archives is with the spread of colonial culture in competition with other colonial-cultural influences.

These archives, too, are sometimes marred by biased views on the *indigènes*, for some consuls and legation heads, be they French, British, Spanish or Italian, saw in Moroccans inferior beings in need of "cultural rejuvenation."

The Zionist archives

These archives shed significant light on the political dynamics of Moroccan Jewish society since 1897, on AIU-Zionist competition for influence in the society, and on the activities of Zionist representatives from Europe and Palestine who were determined to cultivate local leadership, indoctrinated by the Zionist idea.

The most important of these archival files are the series *S5* (Organization Department) and *Z1,2, :Z1* = The Zionist Office in Vienna; *Z2* = The Zionist Office in Cologne; *Z4* = The Central Headquarters of the World Zionist Organization in London. These include important correspondence during the years 1897–1955 with representatives of the Zionist societies in Morocco, most of whom were affiliated with mainstream Zionism. They shed considerable light on the social, economic, and political status of Moroccan Jewry prior to emigration. Like the AIU and *Quai d'Orsay* archives, the Zionist documents reflect subjective views.

The archives of the American
Jewish Joint Distribution Committee (JDC)

These archives contain vital data—statistics, program director's reports, budgets, correspondence with various Jewish and non-Jewish organizations, and with governmental and nongovernmental agencies—on the activities of the JDC in Morocco since the end of the Second World War. The JDC, which promoted food, clothing, welfare, loan, and other social, economic, and cultural programs after 1945, collaborated closely with the AIU. It became a major organization in Morocco, supported by American Jews. It financed and subsidized the work of local or outside Jewish groups dedicated to fighting poverty and disease. These archives, which have only recently become available, are invaluable.

The most relevant archival files contain the correspondence between the JDC offices in Morocco and its offices in Geneva. The files consulted are classified in boxes, numbered thus: 9(c), 10(a); 10(b); 232(b); 233(a); 233(b); 247(b); 263(b); 330(a); 330(b); 402(b); 420(c); and 421(a). Despite some bias and preference by the JDC local directors for one Jewish organization over another, or occasional inclination to be highly critical of AIU teachers and educational programs, the JDC archives are surprisingly objective, much more so than other archives discussed above.

The nine chapters in this work cover one hundred years of modernization and evolution of the *Alliance*. The first chapter paints a brief picture of the history of Moroccan Jewry. Several recent studies dealing with the pre-1860 period, emphasize the historical *roots* of these communities and its prominent rabbinic elite.[1] My purpose here is not to provide an exhaustive survey of the earlier periods, but rather to provide the reader with the understanding that this Jewry had a rich background, long predating the effects of colonial and Western culture. The chapter surveys the ethnic composition of the Jewish Community, the communal structure, the political status of the Jews, their socioeconomic stratification, and their beliefs and customs.

In the second chapter I concentrate on the political roles of the members of the AIU, as well as of the Paris headquarters, in pressuring the Moroccan authorities and the European consuls to better the status of the Jews; and the cultural penetration of the AIU and the interest manifested by the European powers in its schools for the spread of modern ideas among Jews. In this chapter I stress the growing political significance of the AIU and emphasize the fact that the raison d'être of the organization went far beyond educational goals.

The third chapter is a study on the challenges confronted by the AIU in obtaining legitimacy for its presence among Jews of all social classes and the rabbinic elite, in widening its influence, and in establishing its schools. The chapter shows how the AIU became more popular in the coastal and port communities, whereas its influence penetrated much more slowly — with perhaps minor exceptions — into the interior. It was during the 1862–1912 period that the crucial process of institutionalization within the communities took place, facilitating the subsequent official recognition of the AIU by the colonial systems that established their bases in the country.

The fourth chapter accentuates the precolonial educational role of the AIU in the communities, the type of education offered, the reforms undertaken, and the extraeducational tasks of its members. Most important, however, the chapter emphasizes the impact of modernization on the Jews and the transformation that occurred within elite Jewish society in the wake of AIU activities on the eve of the era when France and Spain set up protectorates.

The fifth chapter introduces the reader to the colonial period and to the efforts of the AIU to (a) lobby and plead before the French authorities for the improvement of the judicial status of the Jews; (b) preserve its influence in the communities; (c) continue the promotion of French culture in northern Morocco which, since 1912, came under Spanish colonial influence, and in Tangier, which became an International zone after 1923; and (d) confront, together with the Jews, the anxieties of Vichy presence and the challenges of the immediate post-1945 period.

The sixth chapter reveals that alongside messianic longings for Zion, Moroccan Jews, certainly among the most educated ones, were gradually influenced by political and secular Zionism. Moreover, as modern Zionism penetrated the communities, AIU teachers were pressured to promote cultural Zionism together with French culture. Generally, the chapter shows periodic struggles between *Alliancistes* and Zionists before 1939 and the changes that occurred in the political position of the AIU vis-à-vis the Zionist idea after the Second World War.

The seventh chapter analyzes (a) AIU educational and sociocultural factors which accentuate its educational as well as extraeducational role in Jewish society after 1912 and until Moroccan independence in 1956; and (b) effects of education on the Jews during that period as compared with the precolonial period. This chapter is undoubtedly the most important in this study, for it demonstrates the magnitude of the changes that occurred in connection with modern education, changes initiated by the AIU and other Jewish organizations that were active in Morocco since 1945.

The eighth chapter is comparative analysis of Jewish and Muslim educational development. My purpose here is to delve into (a) the problem of comparative educational representation in modern schools; (b) colonial educational policies and the reactions of the *indigènes* to these policies; and (c) the problems of social conflict between Muslims and Jews that were aggravated as a direct result of Western and colonial penetration. The role of the AIU in this situation is quite relevant.

The ninth and final chapter enters into the immediate postcolonial period when the position of the Jews, the AIU, and other organizations undergo vital transformations as a result of reforms in education. For the Jews this is a period of social, cultural, and political readjustment. To a large segment of this group it is a period for reflection about their future in Morocco and for considering alternatives, including emigration, which had begun before 1956.

In all these situations, and throughout the period under study, the AIU was a major force, a vital part of modern Moroccan Jewish history.

Notes

1. For some of the best studies, see: Shalom Bar-Asher, ed., *The Taqanot of the Jews of Morocco* (Jerusalem, Zalman Shazar Center, 1977); Jane Gerber, *Jewish Society in Fez* (Leiden; E. J. Brill, 1980); Norman A. Stillman, *The Jews of Arab Lands* (Philadelphia, The Jewish Publication Society of America, 1979).

CHAPTER I

Background of the Activities of the *Alliance Israélite Universelle* in Morocco: The Traditional Jewish Society

At the time of Moroccan independence the Jewish communities there were by far the most important in the Muslim world. Moreover, they ranked among the world's largest along with North American, Soviet, French, Argentinean, South African, and British Jewry, and were estimated at between 210–240,000. The Moroccan Jewish communities, like their counterparts elsewhere in the Muslim world, were and still are neglected by scholars. H. Z. Hirschberg, who pioneered in the writing of scholarly studies concerning Maghribi Jewry, deplored the treating of this diaspora as a backwater of Jewish history, with only a handful of scholars giving the Jewish periphery the attention it deserves.[1] Only recently has Moroccan Jewry received serious attention from scholars who recognized the importance of the population that has dwelt in the area for 2,300 years.

1. The Maghribi Jewish Communities before the Advent of Islam

The recorded history of the Maghrib begins with the founding of Carthage in 813 B.C. For 667 years, until its fall to the Romans, Carthage shaped North Africa into its own Semitic mold; not even the Romans were able to uproot the Oriental civilization left by the oldest and most tenacious colonizers of the Mediterranean, the Jews and Phoenicians of Palestine.[2] The number of Jews who left Palestine with the Phoenicians after 586 B.C., when the destruction of the Temple in Jerusalem took place under Nebuchadnezzar, is difficult to ascertain. It is known, however, that the Jewish population in the Maghrib was numerically strengthened in A.D. 70, the date of the second destruction of the Temple and the city of Jerusalem by Titus. While many of the survivors fled to Babylonia, a significant number of the Jews sought refuge in North Africa. Until the fall of Car-

thage to the Romans (146 B.C.), the Jews, in partnership with the Phoeni-
cians, placed North Africa under Semitic influences. Later, under the
Romans, the state religion became Christianity. The Romans were succeeded
by the Vandals, the Vandals by the Byzantines, and the Byzantines by the
Arabs. In the areas which became Algeria and Tunisia, there were also the
Turks, representatives of the Ottoman Empire.

The Punic and Jewish impact on the region apparently had far-reaching
consequences. In fact, the major source on the spread of the Punic language
in North Africa is Saint Augustine; his writings confirm that the Berbers,
the earliest inhabitants of North Africa, were speaking Punic several centuries after the fall of Carthage to the Romans. Semitic culture, then, had
become deeply rooted among the indigenous population and, as André
Chouraqui points out, the similarities of Hebrew and Punic were bound to
bring about, right from the start, a deep association of Jews and Berbers in
the Maghrib; Hebrew and Punic were sister languages. Modern research
has confirmed the ancient traditions by showing that Hebrew and Punic
shared a common ancestry; these similarities explain the extraordinary extent of the spread of Jewish beliefs in North Africa that prepared the
ground for the acceptance of Christianity and eventually of Islam.[3]

Under the *Pax Romana*, Judaism in the Maghrib entered a new phase.
The Romans allowed the Jewish faith to organize under a *nāsī*, a patriarch
resident of Palestine, who was both a spiritual and temporal leader. Hierarchy reached into every community through the primates who headed each
province and through the local heads of the communities, thus foreshadow-
ing to some degree the later developments of the Christian hierarchy. Each
community was headed by a religious assembly in which full Jews, pro-
selytes, and semiproselytes shared equally, and was governed by an administrative council, usually of nine members, elected by the community.
The council directed the finances, supervised the religious organization of
the town and represented the interests of the community before the courts
and the authorities. It distributed relief, decided on the construction of the
synagogues, schools, and libraries. The synagogues were the center of all
Jewish activity, of prayer, preaching, study and justice. Jewish communities were granted a large measure of autonomy, of which they were
temporarily deprived only during the worst of their struggles against the
Romans.[4]

Details on the spread of the Jewish faith among the Berbers are scarce.
We learn from Hirschberg's guess that it is impossible to assume that the
conversion of many Berber tribes to Judaism took place in the Byzantine
period; if it had, the Church Fathers would certainly have decried it and
warned of the danger it spelled for Christianity. On the other hand, we cannot assign it to the period of acceleration of the islamization of the Berbers,
that is, from the tenth and eleventh centuries onwards.[5] The time during

which many Berber tribes, mentioned by Ibn Khaldūn, might have adopted Judaism, narrows down to the two or three hundred years between the defeat of the Byzantines and the consolidation of Islam; that is, between the eight and tenth centuries.[6]

Prior to the advent of Islam in North Africa, at the time of Roman and later of Byzantine rule when the Christian church was supreme in the region, the position of the Jews was highly precarious. In the interval between Roman and Byzantine rule, during the vandal occupation of North Africa, the Jews enjoyed a short respite. The Vandals who conquered North Africa from the Romans in A.D.430, supported the Arian heresy, denying the coeternity, consubstantiality and, therefore, the divinity of Jesus, and hated the Roman Empire with utmost passion.[7] They were destroyers and despoilers in their war against the Catholics, whom they hounded and whose churches they destroyed.[8] Further, the Vandals freed the Jews from the oppressive laws of the *Pax Romana* and granted them freedom of religious expression. Yet these privileges were of relatively short duration. When the Byzantines defeated the Vandals in A.D. 553, the old persecutions resumed, especially after the Byzantines restored the authority of the Catholic church. This situation lingered until A.D. 642 when the Arabs conquered North Africa.

The Arab conquest of North Africa and the defeat of the Byzantines was only half the problem. The real resistance had only begun. Despite the conversion of the Berbers to Islam, the Berbers' resistance had not been easily broken. The tensions between the Arabs and the native Berbers endured into the eleventh century, ending only after the Berbers, now Muslims, had put up a protracted struggle.[9]

2. The Status and Evolution of the Jews under Arab Rule

The penetration and consolidation of Islam in North Africa brought about a comprehensive overhauling of the structure of its society. As in all territories which came under Islamic jurisdiction, the Jews and Christians were classified as a "protected people" or *dhimmī*s. The term *dhimmī* as applied in the Sacred Law of the *sharī'a* and in the *Quar'ān* designates the Christian and Jewish subjects of any Muslim ruler. Like most of the Sacred Law, the principles upon which the non-Muslims are to be dealt with by Muslim rulers evolved in the early centuries of Islam. However, they have their roots in the attitude of the Prophet Muhammad himself to the other religions with which he was acquainted, and to the problem of opposition to his mission. H. A. R. Gibb and Harold Bowen argued this point well, saying that the Prophet was acquainted with five religions: the Christian, the Sabaian, the Zoroastrian, and the polytheistic cults of Arabia; but the Jews and Christians had a special place in his concept of the world: unlike the polytheists, they at least had books of their own to excuse them for not receiving him and were thus the "People of the Scripture."[10] Therefore, it was established that whereas on the conquest of new territory by Muslims, polytheists must accept Islam or die, the People of the Scripture would be permitted to practice their religion.

What did this mean? It outlined the basic tenets under which Jews and Christians would become tolerated infidels.[11] By the term of his contract with the *dhimmī*s, the Muslim ruler was supposed to guarantee their lives, liberty, and property, and was responsible for their freedom of religious practice. The *sharī'a* laid down the conditions by which the Muslim ruler would be willing to protect these minorities. The *dhimmī*s undertook to pay the special poll tax known as *jizya* and the land tax called *kharāj*. Generally speaking, in comparison with the Muslims, the *dhimmī*s were at a disadvantage legally and juridically. For instance, their evidence was not accepted against that of a Muslim in a *qāḍī*'s court. The Muslim murderer of a *dhimmī* did not suffer the death penalty and a *dhimmī* could not marry a Muslim woman, whereas a Muslim could marry a *dhimmī* woman.[12] Further, *dhimmī*s were obliged to wear distinctive clothes so as not to be confused with true believers, and they were forbidden to ride horses or bear arms.[13] Finally, though their churches and synagogues were at times converted into mosques, the Jews were usually not permitted to build new ones. They could merely repair those that had fallen into decay.

The Jewish organizational apparatus underwent profound changes in the period since Muslim rule over North Africa. The Jews were granted administrative autonomy over their communal institutions, including the rabbinic courts that deliberated over crucial judicial matters with the exception of cases involving legal disputes between Jews and Muslims, in which case the *sharī'a* court took charge. In Morocco most communities had chief rabbis who served as spiritual guides and presided over the synagogues and rabbinic courts. In some cases the rabbinate was hereditary. In the Jewish community, the chief rabbi and rabbi-judges, *dayyānīm*, were the most powerful forces representing the religious elite, with the chief rabbi possessing both judicial and executive power. In communities such as Larache, Mazagan (El Jadida), Casablanca, and the rural areas known as the *bled*, Jewish notables rather than rabbis were sometimes the most powerful. For a long time these communities did not have rabbinic courts or councils of prominent citizens and in the case of religious courts, were represented by the courts of Fez, Marrakesh, or Tangier.

The prominent citizens, whose power was partly determined by the degree of their wealth, were assembled in councils composed of seven to ten members elected by the communities, although some councils, notably in Tangier, had fifteen members. A community council was known in Hebrew as a *ma'amad* or, in the case of the northern communities of Spanish ancestry, as a *junta*. What role did the community councils play in the welfare of these communities? Their task was to maintain and administer community budgets, contribute to charities, and aid the economically impoverished. Council members, elected by their communities, included a treasurer — responsible for the administration of community-owned baths and buildings — and an individual responsible for the collection of the *jizya* and *kharāj* taxes. The latter, known as *shaykh al yahūd*, did not merely levy taxes on behalf of Muslim rulers. He represented Moroccan Jewry before government officials on all or most matters pertaining to Jews. Only taxes over kosher meat purchases were collected by citizens other than the *shaykh al-yahūd*.[14]

In Fez, the community's resources included the *nedava*, money provided by wealthy notables for impoverished Jews before holidays and feasts, strikingly similar to the *zakāt* in Islam; the *heqdēsh*, revenues which were derived from pious organizations similar to the foundations in Islam known as *waqf* of *ḥubus*, which served as indispensable sources for the financial maintenance of rabbinic schools and synagogues; and the *gerzuma*, a tax from which revenues were collected on the sale of kosher meat.[15]

Regarding educational institutions and their role in Moroccan Jewish society, whereas Muslim children attended primary schools known as *kuttāb*s or *msid*s, the Jews attended primary rabbinic schools known as *talmūdē tōra* and *ṣlā*s. The *talmūdē tōra* were largely subsidized by the community and its wealthy elements and served children from impoverished homes. The *ṣlā*s were attended by children from the wealthier strata. Similar to the Islamic *msid*s, whose graduates received advanced education at the *madāris* (sing. *madrasa*), the rabbinic school graduates continued to study at a *yeshīva* (pl. *yeshīvōt*). Although more will be said later about the rabbinic schools, it is noteworthy that the *yeshīvōt* were training schools for the formation of the rabbinic elite which included *dayyānīm, shōhatīm* (ritual slaughterers) and *mōhalīm* (who performed circumcision).[16]

Under Muslim domination of North Africa, the Jews spoke Arabic. The Jews of Spanish ancestry who left Spain after 1492 used the Castilian tongue. In the *bled*, particularly of the Atlas mountains and the Ante-Atlas, the Jews spoke Arabic but many knew Berber, needed for communication with the Berber tribes. Of the Jews who emigrated to Israel during the 1950s many knew both Arabic and Berber.

The Arabic and Spanish spoken by the Jews was supplemented during the late Middle Ages by vernaculars known as Judeo-Arabic and Judeo-Spanish. As Arabic spread among North African Jewry, the homily at the synagogue, both oral and written, was in that language. It was studded with sayings and passages from sacred writings, which were translated into Arabic and allowed to be briefly rendered in Aramaic by the homilists.

These usages led to the emergence of a special language, a mélange of Arabic, Hebrew, and Aramaic.[17] When writing Arabic, the Jews used Hebrew script. Only in exceptional cases, as when one of the parties to a contract was a Muslim, did they use Arabic characters. The adoption of their own vernacular was a deliberate self-segregation from the Arab-Muslim majority (Syrian Christians likewise used their own alphabet when writing Arabic).[18]

Similarly, the descendants of the Spanish Jews who retained their Castilian culture deviated to an extent from the Spanish of their ancestors. They spoke Judeo-Spanish, which included a variety of Hebrew words and Biblical verses. However, it was apparently a purer Spanish than the vernacular spoken by the descendants of the Spanish Jews who settled in Turkey.[19]

Linguistic separations were accompanied by segregation of residential quarters. While the Jews enjoyed certain measures of communal autonomy, the separation between the two native populations were quite apparent. With the exception of Tangier, Mazagan, Agadir, Safi, and several communities in the *bled*, the majority of the Jews were confined to special quarters known as the *mellāh*. The first ghetto was created in Fez by the sultan in 1438 following an outburst of violence against the Jews,[20] a commonplace phenomenon in the fourteenth century. The part of town in which they lived before this date (Old Fez) was thus abandoned for New Fez next to the *dār al-makhzan* (government administrative center).[21]

The removal of the Jews from Old Fez to the *mellāh* was meant for their own protection against fanatics.[22] Was this the only reason? According to Norman Stillman, despite the fact that the *mellāh* was founded for the protection of the Jews and not as a punishment, the Jewish sources make it quite clear that the Jews themselves viewed their confinement to the *mellāh* as a tragedy, a sudden and bitter exile; it only increased their sense of isolation and marginality; during the sixteenth and seventeenth centuries the *mellāh*s were founded with the express intent of ostracism rather than protection.[23]

It appears that the etymology of the word *mellāh* was based on the Muslim rulers' inclination to grant Jews salty and nonproductive land. Kenneth Brown says that the *mellāh* of Salé, like other Jewish residential quarters, was so named because it was a former salt marsh.[24] Stillman, on the other hand, points out that the word *mellāh* was perhaps based on the legend that it was a place where Jews originally salted the heads of executed criminals for public display[25] and, if either one or both etymologies are valid, then it emphasizes the connotation of outcast.

Despite the isolation and segregation of the Jews from the Muslims, there have been discussions among scholars on their degree of coexistence. Larry Rosen and André Chouraqui paint a generally rosy picture of Jewish-

Muslim relations, contending that despite occasional abuse and humiliations the Jews maintained positive and amicable contacts with the Muslims.[26] Stillman, however, points out the limitations of the Jews in various professions and their inferior judicial status,[27] a phenomenon that comes across in this study, too. Moshe Shokeid takes the middle-of-the road approach, contending—based on social anthropological research and interviews with Moroccan Jews in Israel—that the political and economic situation of the Jews varied from region to region, and that additional research is necessary.[28] On the economic side, at least, Jewish-Muslim relations were often positive. We know of cases in which Muslims, in business transactions, loaned money to Jews and vice versa, and we know that Jewish peddlers who went from village to village to sell their products often stayed overnight at the homes of Muslims.[29]

The position of the Jews in pre-Almohad Morocco was apparently free of major abuses. According to Hirschberg, "We find no factual complaints [prior to 1150] of excesses, coercion, or malice on the part of the authorities."[30] After the ascendce of the Almohad ruler Abū Yūsuf Y'aqūb al-Mansūr (1184–1199), however, the Jews of North Africa began to encounter humiliations: many were forced to convert to Islam and had to wear the *qalansuwa*, a cap of strange and ugly shape, reaching down to their ears.[31] Roger le Tourneau corroborated this description: "The Jews, who officially had been converted to Islam but who were suspected of secretly practicing their own religion, were compelled to wear special and rather ridiculous clothes so that they were easily identified by the Muslims."[32] At the same time, Jews were not the only victims of Almohad cruelty; the Muslim *mālikī* school of Sunni Islam was banned in Almohad North Africa and its leading works were burned in the public squares.[33]

Despite the repressive policies of the Almohads, the relations between the Jews and the Muslims generally remained cordial. After the fourteenth century, the abuses perpetrated against the Jews intensified. While the Muslim authorities, save the Almohads, might have been sympathetic to the Jews, they were often unable to restrain their functionaries. Working behind the backs of the sultans, the governors (*pashas* and *qā'ids*) and military functionaries exploited the political weakness of their rulers and extorted money from the Jews; and they often forced them to sell their goods and pay exorbitant taxes.

Among the Berbers, abuses against the Jews were also common. However, Muslim Berber peasants, too, were often mistreated by their chieftains. In the anarchic areas of the *bled*, the Jews frequently paid protection money to the Berbers in order to remain secure.

There was little the sultans could do to remedy the situation because the country often was roughly divided into two geopolitical regions: *bled al-makhzan* and *bled al-sība*. The former included areas under the control of

Figure 1. Two elderly Jews outside their home in the *mellāh of Safi, 1949*

the sultans, mostly the large urban centers and certain small towns. The latter was under the control of Berber chiefs hostile to the Moroccan authorities. The Atlas mountains in the south and the Rif areas of the north effectively were dominated by dissident tribal culture. The Jewish communities of these areas, like the Muslim peasants, lived in a feudal atmosphere.

Humiliations included the use of the bastinado, particularly during the Sherifian period (1553 onwards). The *pashas* and *qā'ids* would often use it on the Jews or impose on them forced labor. Again, though the Jews were not the only ones humiliated, as Muslims were subjected to similar abuses, their European coreligionists pressured the *makhzan* to remedy the situation. These abuses, attributed in large part to anarchy in the country, to political and administrative decentralization, and to the fact that the *mellāhs* proved to be ineffective shields of protection against uprisings and dissidence, were making life for the Jews intolerable. In Meknes alone the *mellāh* was sacked during the years 1703, 1720, 1728 and 1790.[34] Even though the Muslim masses were involved in these activities, upon the instigation of a mutinous soldiery or a rebellious governor, there is ample evidence that Jews took refuge in the homes of Muslims during riots.[35]

The position of the Jews may have deteriorated further under the rule of the Sherifian sultans: the Sa'adians (1550 to 1660) and the 'Alawids (1666 to the present). It was during this period, and well into the nineteenth century that the number of *mellāhs* increased in Morocco. In assessing the conditions of the Jews under Sherifian rule, Stillman perceptively pointed out that:

> Moroccan Jews took refuge from the harsher realities of their life in the fervor of their religiosity. There were strong currents of kabbalistic mysticism, messianism, and religious Zionism in Moroccan Judaism. There was an important Maghrebi Jewish community in Palestine from the sixteenth century on. A considerable number of Moroccan Jews also found solace from the vicissitudes of their existence in *mahya*, their potent anise-flavored brandy. Like their Yemenite brethren, Moroccan Jews were hard drinkers. Many travelers to both communities commented on the widespread alcoholism. The parallel is not at all fortuitous. For these two countries were by far the strictest in the Arabic-speaking world in their interpretation and implementation of the laws pertaining to *dhimmīs*, who in both instances were exclusively Jews.[36]

The Sherifian sultans did not always spare the Jews from forms of discomfort, either. For example during the reign of Sultan Mawlāy Ismā'īl (1672-1727), the Jews of Meknes, then the seat of the sultanate, were ousted from their *mellāh* and were offered instead a terrain remotely isolated from the Muslim population.[37] A similar case occurred in Tetuan a century later.

Before 1807, the Tetuan *mellāḥ* was situated in the center of town next to the Arab quarter. The same year, Sultan Mawlāy Sulaymān decided to build a huge mosque over a vast terrain which included part of the *mellāḥ*. Consequently, he ordered the Jews to evacuate the quarter and instead, offered them new land. The sultan then issued a *ẓahir* (edict) which was presented to prominent Jews who promised to obey the *ẓahīr* and implement it as soon as possible; subsequently the *qā'id*, 'Abd al-Rahmān al-A'shāsh, and the town's notables[38] proceeded to become familiar with the new land. They examined it thoroughly and distributed it to the Jews.[39] The distribution was carried out in the presence of the *qā'id* and construction of houses and shops began during the month of *muharram* in the year 1225 of the Islamic era.[40]

In the intellectual sphere, Maghribi Jews made significant contributions to the cultural advancement of Judaism. It was in Fez, one of the oldest Jewish communities in Morocco, where Jewish intellectual development was bustling. In addition to great rabbis, poets, and scholars, there were Hebraists and philologists such as Dūnash b. Labrāt ha-Levi, Juda Hayyūj and David ben Abraham al-Fassi, who lived in Fez during the late ninth and early tenth centuries.[41] The fame of Fez in Jewish eyes was permanently established during the eleventh century by Rabbi Isaac b. Jacob ha-Kohen Alfassi, known acrostically as "Rif" and sometimes simply called Ha-Alfas. Although born in Lucerna, Spain, he made his main contribution during his sojourn in Fez.[42] Alfassi was known for composing a code known as *halakhot* in a form of an abridged Talmud. Being mainly interested in practical concepts, he omitted debates with tractates, and even whole tractates, which had no practical significance in his days, while gathering elsewhere those parts of them that were nevertheless of interest to him; at the same time, he followed the order in which the tractates are arranged in the Talmud.[43]

The *yeshīvōt* and rabbinic intellectualism of Fez during the Middle Ages attracted important Jewish thinkers to Morocco. Maimonides did not hesitate to settle in Fez in 1159. He even sent his children about that time to pursue their studies there.[44] Among the Jewish philologists and a native of North Africa's Tiaret, was Ibn Quraysh. He settled in Fez during the ninth century and became one of the most renowned Hebraists in the Jewish tradition. Ibn Quraysh was known as the Father of the Hebrew Grammar; he developed a new approach to the study of this subject through comparison with other Semitic languages, with special emphasis on Aramaic. He, moreover, widened his field of study by drawing on Persian, Berber, and Arabic, and was known to have quoted the *Qur'ān* quite extensively.[45]

Another renowned scholar, Juda Hayadi, living in Fez around the year 1000, spent considerable time in making comparative linguistic studies of

Hebrew and Arabic. He was thoroughly familiar with the grammatical structure of both Semitic languages and his works were widely acclaimed as authoritative by the great Jewish scholars of Spain.[46]

An important addition to Fez intellectual circles was Abraham ben Salomon of Ardutiel who was expelled from Spain in 1492. His major work was the *Sēfer ha-Qabbalah* (The Book of Tradition), a contribution to and a continuation of the work of Abraham Ibn Daud. This contribution became significant to Kabalists and mystics.

In modern times, however, intellectual fervor began to subside as a result of the growing inability of the *yesīvōt* to cultivate a large number of rabbis and scholars.[47] The quality of educational institutions declined markedly over the years and, while some would argue that the arrival of Spanish refugees since 1492 added a new intellectual impulse, they are mistaken, for these elements were not prominent people, such as court dignitaries and great religious scholars. Rather, they were members of the middle class: merchants, agents, and craftsmen.[48] Indeed, it was in the commercial sphere that the Castilian and Portuguese Jews made their contribution to North Africa.

After the expulsion from Spain, Spanish Jews helped mold Fez into a reputable commercial metropolis which, for many years, served as a vital center for international trade. At that time the Portuguese conquered the coastal towns of North Africa and, rather ironically, whereas the Portuguese expelled Jews from their country, they did not hesitate to employ them in North Africa as their commercial agents. Their knowledge of Portuguese, Spanish, and national customs helped the Jews become intermediaries between the Portuguese conquerors and the Muslims.[49] Further, the trade routes from Europe to the Indies passed through the Jewish centers of Spain and the Maghrib, a commercial link which was strongly reinforced by a cultural relationship.[50]

The ability of the Castilians after a period of economic and social acclimation to contribute their commercial expertise did indeed help revitalize Jewish social and economic life. These refugees were actually Europeans living in exile, signifying the beginnings of this region's first serious encounter with Western ideas. At the same time, one must not overlook the benevolence of the Banū Waṭṭās dynasty in Morocco (1472–1553), which granted asylum to the Jewish refugees. The rulers of Morocco adopted the same policies as the Ottomans and opened their gates to the inflow of refugees, essentially because of their own hatred of the Christians for harassing the Moors in Spain.[51] In Morocco, the sultans viewed the new arrivals with approval. The latter eventually founded communities of their own, mainly in Fez, Meknes, Debdou, Tangier, Tetuan, Salé, Arzila, Larache, Rabat, and Safi.[52]

The relations between the new arrivals and the indigenous Jews were initially quite harmonious. The Castilians, known by the Hebrew term of *megōrāshīm*, the ones expelled, brought with them a culture and mentality which differed from the customs of the *tōshvīm*, the indigenous Jews. Only in Tunisia the harmony between the two elements was not destined to survive and frictions developed there. The Tunisian *tōshāvīm*, on observing that the *megōrāhīm* had different rites and rituals, seated them in special parts of the synagogues.[53] It is due to policies of this sort that led to the fundamental segregation between the two communities; eventually, when the newcomers were significantly reinforced by new arrivals from Livourno, they established themselves in separate factions apart from the *tōshāvīm*.[54]

The Moroccan sultans employed the Castilians in distinguished commercial and diplomatic positions, for they recognized their talents in the area of finances and negotiations. This feeling was shared by the Algerian and Tunisian authorities, so much so that the monopoly over international trade was mainly in Castilian hands. No import - export transaction was handled without the Jews; the sultans of Morocco, the deys of Algeria and the beys of Tunisia, did not believe French merchants who contended that breaking the monopoly of the Jews over commerce would bring them more business directly from France.[55]

At the court of the Wattāsids in Fez, great influence was wielded by Spanish refugees like Jacob Rosales and Moses Abūtām. In 1537, another Jew, Jacob Roti, undertook an official mission for the sultan of Fez and served as his advisor in foreign affairs.[56] Roti traveled on diplomatic missions for the sultan to Portugal and handled extremely delicate political negotiations at a time when the Portuguese occupied key Moroccan towns.[57]

The eighty years which marked the rule of the Wattāsids reflected violent struggles for power between them and their Sherifian Sa'adist archrivals. One immediate consequence of the struggle was the gradual shrinking of Wattāsid territory in the interior. This accompanied the Portuguese military penetration of the coastal towns. When the Sa'adists finally defeated the Wattāsids in 1553 and ascended to power, they concentrated their efforts in diminishing Portuguese presence as well. Sa'adists military assaults at the beginning of the seventeenth century weakened the Portuguese military machine, and their hold over the Moroccan coastal towns was crumbling. At the same time, the commercial initiative gradually passed from the Portuguese to the Dutch. Once again, the Jews were the major commercial emissaries for the sultan at the Hague.[58]

In Mogador (Essaouira), the Jewish community became commercially important as Jews extended their economic activities to include towns in the interior and much of the south. Within the Mogador community the Jews were not strictly confined to the *mellāḥ*. Jewish merchants dwelled alongside Muslim and European merchants in the quarter known as the *qasba*. It was in this residential section that the Jews were relieved of restrictions and freely mingled with the general population.[59]

Yet, the growing weakness of the central authorities led to a significant deterioration of Jewish rights. Further, the Jews lived on the margin of public life and could not serve in the army, police, and administration. These disadvantages were so widely admitted that, when the European powers first became actively involved in the political fate of Morocco, numerous Jews sought and obtained foreign protection under the title of *protégés*. However, the ones who did obtain this status were usually employed in European diplomatic legations, consulates, and commercial houses. Ordinary Jews, like Muslims, rarely had access to such privileges. The impoverished Jewish masses often hated the wealthy members of their own community and viewed them as "Jewish lords" who lived in vast homes whose tables were loaded with the best meats and wines from Europe; and it was this stratum that was respected but feared by the Muslims.[60]

Turning to the composition of the Jewish communities in mid-nineteenth century Morocco, the following classifications need to be discussed:[61] (1) *Jews whose mother tongue is Spanish* — descendants of the Jews exiled from Spain in 1492 or those who left Spain for Morocco already in the 1390s. They retained their Spanish language and culture and transmitted to their

Figure 2. A talmūd *tōra* in Marrakesh

children the culture of medieval Spain. They mostly lived in northern Morocco (Tangier, Tetuan, Elksar, Larache, and Arzila); their presence was also quite visible in the coastal towns of Casablanca, Mazagan, Mogador, Safi, and others. The Castilians were more receptive to European ideas and their manners and customs differed from the rest of the Jewish population. They practiced monogamy. Their segment of the population offered the prime candidates for banking and commercial employment, and their family names included the following: Nahon, Toledano, Pinto, Pariente, Laredo, Elmaleh. (2) *The Judeo-Arab group*—this segment of the Jewish population was divided into three categories. First, the descendants of the Jewish population which settled in Morocco long before 1492; they accompanied the Phoenicians of Syria-Palestine in their journey to North Africa. Second, the descendants of the Castilians who had forgotten their Spanish language and assimilated the Judeo-Arabic culture and vernacular. They did retain such Spanish family names as Serero, Serfati, Verdugo. Their communities were located in the interior (Fez, Meknes, Sefrou, Marrakesh) and in the coastal towns. Third, Jewish Berbers who became arabized and who lived in the interior. They also constituted the majority of the Jewish population of the western coastal towns and spoke Judeo-Arabic. They practiced polygamy on occasions as well as bigamy. They customarily gave their daughters in marriage at a very young age. (3) *The Judeo-Berber group*—there is scant information available on this group. They were found mostly in the Atlas mountains and in the Rif mountains in the north. This group was often multilingual: they spoke Judeo-Arabic among themselves but used Arabic and Berber in relations with the Berbers.

The socioeconomic class level of Moroccan Jewry may be divided into the following categories: (1) *Upper and Middle Classes*—which included the merchantile elite, composed mostly of Spanish Jews who engaged in busy commercial enterprises in the coastal towns. They were mostly descendants of the *megōrāshīm* from Spain, enjoyed either consular protection from one European power or another, or were the sultan's merchants (*tujjār al-sultān*),[62] that is, they carried out commercial activities in the name of the sultan, and with his money and blessings, or as intermediaries in international commerce between the *makhzan* and Europe. (2) *Lower-middle classes*—which included the grocers, peddlers, goldsmiths, tailors, shoemakers, fruit and vegetable merchants, and the various artisans. Many of the artisans acquired their profession on a hereditary basis.[63] (3) *Poor and unemployed*, who lived off communal charity.

The AIU archives shed some light on the composition of the population. In Tangier of 1873, the artisans were mainly shoemakers, tailors, and goldsmiths.[64] In Fez, the artisans included goldsmiths, gold thread spinners, wine-makers, glass product manufacturers, and precious metal workers; it was estimated in 1882 that there were 15,000 Jews in Fez out of a

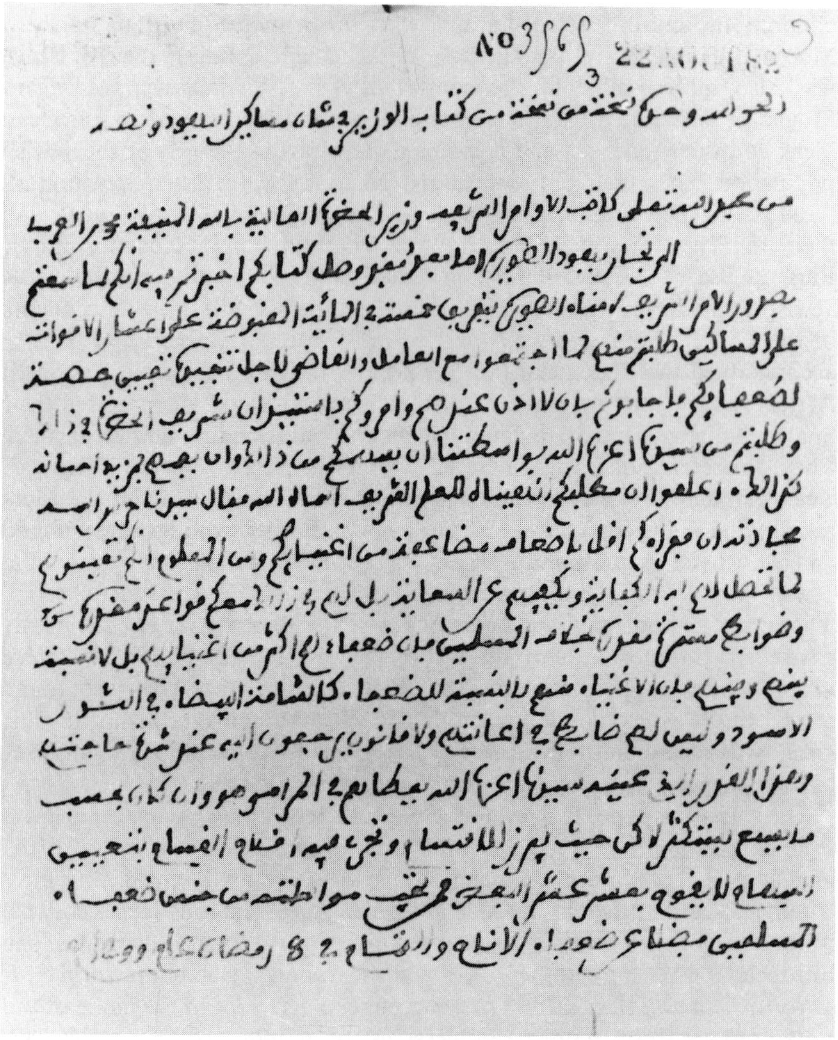

Figure 3. A letter from the Moroccan government to Jewish merchants in Mogador, 1882.

total population of 100,000.[65] It appears, however, that these figures of the AIU are too high. In 1877, only five years preceding the above estimation, Joseph Halévy, an Orientalist, found between 8,000 and 10,000 Jews out of a total population ranging between 30,000 and 40,000.[66] On the eve of the French protectorate, Amram Elmaleh, then AIU director in Fez, estimated the Jewish population at 10,000 prior to the sacking of the *mellāh* by mutinous Sherifian troops (April 17, 1912) and, afterwards, when Jews fled to Meknes and the coastal communities, at 7,500.[67] Le Tourneau came close to the Elmaleh figure, at 8,000.[68]

In Meknes, there were 6,000 Jews living in 250 houses in 1901; most of them were artisans: goldsmiths, shoemakers, small-scale merchants and shopkeepers. They were mainly descendants of Spanish Jewry who had neglected their Spanish culture and language in favor of Judeo-Arabic.[69] Out of thirty families interviewed by an AIU representative, most were Spanish descendants and had family names like Albo, Gozlan, Azagne, Pariente, Castro, Verdugo, Bibasse and Toledano.[70] In 1897, there were 3,000 Jews and 600 Europeans in Casablanca out of a total population of 25,000, most of the Jews being small- and large-scale merchants.[71] According to the AIU representative, Casablanca was developing rapidly and attracting European commercial activities.[72] Parallel to this development, the Jewish population in Casablanca was growing due to migrations mainly from Tetuan, southern Morocco, and the interior in search of lucrative commercial activities. It was predicted that Casablanca would become the most important Moroccan metropolis — all the more reason why AIU schools ought to be opened there.[73]

This data, though important, is incomplete, for the AIU did not extend its educational network outside the major towns prior to 1912, and in the Atlas mountains the AIU did not open schools until the late 1920s. All in all, there were probably no less than 100,000 Jews in Morocco at the turn of the century.

Regarding customs and attitudes of Moroccan Jewry, some basic points may be noted. First, like their Muslim neighbors, Jews believed in a variety of superstitions. Such beliefs were prevalent in the south, where the rabbis were often powerless to control them. Superstitions arose partly from centuries of Jewish interaction with the rest of the population. Moroccan Arabs, Berbers and Jews all included many devout believers in the evil eye and in demons. Seldom could a house be built in certain communities until the blood of a sheep had been sprinkled on the foundations — an obvious carry-over from Punic antiquity.[74]

The veneration of saints was another manifestation shared by both Jews and Muslims. Jewish saints were divided into three basic categories: saints who were known and venerated throughout the country, usually rabbis from Palestine who died in Morocco; saints whose fame and popularity was confined to a particular region; lesser saints, venerated only on a strictly local basis.[75] The saints' tombs became objects of veneration of great magnitude to the extent that pilgrimage to them was like pilgrimage to holy shrines. It was widely held by followers of the saints that the latter could heal the sick, the wounded, and the blind, and cure the insane.

As we noted earlier, mysticism was yet another current which gained popularity among the Jews. In the Middle Ages, Spain served as the vital center for the development of the Kabala, from the thirteenth century onwards. All Kabalistic traditions were attributed to Rabbi Shim'ōn b. Yōhay, a disciple of Rabbi Akiva Meir of the second century. The Zohar sometimes achieved equal sanctity with the Bible, the Talmud, and the Mishna, and gave meaning and importance to the smallest Talmudic prescriptions. Between the two extremes of good and evil, between election and rejection, human life was a contest whose stake was the eternal salvation of the soul, of the community of Israel and of the world; conscious submission of the Divine Order brought about *dvekut*, a mystic adherence or communion with God in which lay redemption and the source of salvation.[76]

Doubtless, the expulsion from Spain helped intensify the Jewish mystical world. The victims turned to mystical hope in order to escape the reality which they were compelled to face in Catholic Spain. When many of the exiled arrived in Morocco, their thoughts were imbued with mystical tendencies. As Chouraqui notes, "Their uprooting brought about a spiritual glow which was diffused among the communities that received the messengers of the new enlightenment. Consequently, Kabalistic ideas came to exert a profound influence on Maghribi Judaism.[78]

It was within these communities that the *Alliance Israélite Universelle* commenced its social, cultural, and political activities after 1860. Its educational representatives were sympathetic to the way in which the Castilians respected monogamous marriages, and were unsympathetic to the customs of interior and southern Jewish communities, where young girls were married off in their early teens. Immediately upon the creation of its first school in Tetuan in 1862, the AIU launched vigorous campaigns against what it regarded as anachronistic. Several of the schools' members were often too critical of the "degree of civilized manners" of the indigenous population, an attitude of superiority endemic among the Christian missionaries in the Middle East and North Africa.[78]

Notes

1. H. Z. Hirschberg, *A History of the Jews in North Africa*, vol. I: *From Antiquity to the Sixteenth Century* (Leiden: E. J. Brill, 1974), pp. 9–10.

2. André Chouraqui, *Between East and West: A History of the Jews in North Africa* (Philadelphia: The Jewish Publication Society, 1968), p. 7.

3. Ibid.

4. Ibid., pp. 15–16.

5. Hirschberg, *A History of the Jews in North Africa*, p. 145.

6. Ibid.

7. Chouraqui, *Between East and West*, p. 27.

8. Ibid.

9. Ibid., p. 37.

10. Hamilton A. R. Gibb and Harold Bowen, *Islamic Society and the West* (London: Oxford University Press, 1957), vol. I, pt. II, pp. 207–208.

11. Ibid., p. 208.

12. Ibid.

13. Ibid.

14. Doris Bensimon Donath, *Evolution du judaïsme marocain sous le protecorat français: 1912–1956* (Paris: Mouton and Co., 1968). pp. 16–17.

15. Roger Le Tourneau, *Fès avant le protectorat: etude economique et sociale d'une ville de l'occident musulman* (Casablanca, 1949), p. 269.

16. Chouraqui, *Between East and West*, p. 62.

17. Hirschberg, *A History of the Jews in North Africa*, p. 153.

18. Ibid., p. 155.

19. Manuel L. Ortega, *Los Hebreos en Marruecos* (Madrid, 1934), p. 197.

20. Norman A. Stillman, *The Jews of Arab Lands* (Philadelphia: The Jewish Publication Society of America, 1979), p. 79; Narcisse Leven, *Cinquante ans d'histoire L'alliance israélite universelle, 1860–1910* (Librarie Félix Alcan, Paris: 1911), vol. II. p. 92.

21. Stillman, *The Jews of Arab Lands*, p. 79; Y. D. Sémach, "Une chronique juive de Fès: Le Yahas Fès' de Ribbi Abner Hasserfaty." *Hespéris* 19, fasc. 1–2 (1934), p. 91.

22. Ortega, *Los Hebreos en Marruecos*, p. 125; Stillman, ibid.

23. Stillman, pp. 80–81. He bases his information on Jacob Toledano, *Nēr ha-Ma'arāv: Hū Tōledōt Yisrā'ēl be-Mārōqqō* (Jerusalem, 1911), p. 44. The latter cited unspecific chroniclers. Stillman also bases his information on ha-Ṣarfatī, *Yahas Fès* in Sémach, "Une chronique juive," *Hespéris* 19, p. 91.

24. Kenneth L. Brown, *People of Salé* (Cambridge, Mass.: Harvard University Press, 1976), p. 228.

25. Stillman, p. 91.

26. See André Chouraqui, *Between East and West*; and Larry Rosen, "Muslim-Jewish Relations in a Moroccan City," *International Journal of Middle East Studies* 3 (1972), pp. 435–449.

27. Moshe Shokeid, "Jewish Existence in a Berber Environment. "*Pe'amim* 4 (Winter 1980), p. 61 (in Hebrew).

28. Ibid., pp. 60–71.

29. Shalom Bar-Asher, "Social Ties between Jews and Muslims During the Eighteenth Century," in Shmuel Almog, ed., *Antisemitism through the Ages* (Jerusalem: Zalman Shazar Center, 1980), p. 232 (in Hebrew).

30. Hirschberg, *A History of the Jews in North Africa*, pp. 200–201.

31. Ibid., p. 201.

32. Roger Le Tourneau, *The Almohad Movement in North Africa in the Twelfth and Thirteenth Centuries* (Princeton, N.J.: Princeton University Press, 1969), p. 77.

33. Ibid.

34. Bar-Asher, "Social Ties between Jews and Muslims," pp. 230–231.

35. Ibid.

36. Stillman, *The Jews of Arab Lands*, p. 85.

37. Hirschberg, *A History of the Jews in North Africa*, p. 310.

38. Those who accompanied the *qā'id* to the area destined to become the new *mellāh* were the Jewish notables and members of the *'ulamā'*.

39. Muḥammad Dāwūd, *Ta'rīkh Titwān* (Tetuan, 1965), vol. III, pt. II, pp. 238–239; Issac Benchimol, "Les juifs de Tétuan," *Bulletin de L'alliance Israélite Universelle* (BAIU) 13 (1888), p. 82.

40. Dāwūd, ibid.
41. Hirschberg, *A History of the Jews in North Africa*, p. 310.
42. Ibid., p. 347.
43. Ibid. p. 350.
44. Chouraqui, *Between East and West*, p. 87.
45. Ibid., p. 83.
46. Ibid.
47. Joseph Halévy, "Sur l'état des écoles dans les communautés juives du Maroc," *BAIU*, le sem. (1877), p. 58.
48. Hirschberg, *A History of the Jews in North Africa*, p. 418.
49. Ibid., p. 419; Stillman, *The Jews of Arab Lands*, p. 82.
50. Chouraqui, *Between East and West*, p. 87.
51. Gibb and Bowen, *Islamic Society and the West*, vol. I, pt. II, p. 219.
52. Chouraqui, *Between East and West*, p. 89.
53. Ibid., p. 93.
54. Ibid.
55. H. Z. Hirschberg, *Me-Ereṣ Mevō ha-Shēmēsh* (Jerusalem, Goldberg Press, 1957), p. 23.
56. Hirschberg, *A History of the Jews in North Africa*, p. 412.
57. Ibid.
58. Hirschberg, *Me-Eres Mevō ha-Shēmēsh*, p. 163.
59. Ibid., p. 164.
60. Halévy, "Sur l'état des écoles dans les communautés juives du Maroc," p. 55.
61. Moïse Nahon, "Les israélites du Maroc," *Revue des Etudes Ethnographiques et Sociologiques* 2 (1909), p. 260.
62. Michael Abitbol, "Une elite economique juive au Maroc precolonial: les tujjār al-sulṭān," in Michael Abitbol, ed., *Judaïsme d'Afrique du Nord aux xixe - xxe siècles* (Jerusalem: Institut Ben-Zvi, 1980), pp. 26–34.
63. Agriculture in the nineteenth and twentieth centuries was not popular in the Jewish communities, though in the *bled* there were Jewish manual and agricultural laborers.
64. Samuel Hirsch to the AIU, Tangier, May 5, 1873, Archives AIU, LIV.E (coles), 894. The Jewish population of Tangier was estimated by Hirsch in 1873 at 5,000, while the total pupulation of Tangier was estimated at 15,000. In the coastal town of Safi, he found 2,000 Jews; in another coastal town, Mazagan, Hirsch found 3,000 Jews who constituted no less than twenty-five percent of the population, mostly involved in commercial activities.
65. Salomon Benoliel to AIU, Fez, October 15, 1882, Arch.AIU.VI.B.27.
66. Halévy, "Sur l'état des écoles dans les communautés juives du Maroc," p. 59.
67. Amram Elmaleh to AIU, Tangier, July 12, 1901, Arch.AIU.XVI.E.248(c).
68. Le Tourneau, *Fès avant le protectorat*, p. 259.
69. Abraham Ribbi to AIU, Tangier, July 12, 1901, Arch.AIU.V.B.24. Meknes was the only Jewish community that owned its own *mellāh*; usually the homes within the *mellāh*s and much of the terrain was either the property of the Muslims or of wealthy Jews who collected rent. This community was financially better off than many others.
70. Ibid.
71. Ribbi to AIU, Tangier, May 28, 1897, Arch. AIU.V.B.24.
72. Ibid.
73. Ibid.

74. Chouraqui, *Between East and West*, p. 69.
75. Ibid., p. 73.
76. Ibid., p. 104.
77. Ibid., p. 105.
78. See, for instance, Benoliel to AIU, Fez, October 15, 1882, Arch. AIU.VI.B.27.

SECTION I

THE JEWISH COMMUNITIES AND THE *ALLIANCE ISRAÉLITE UNIVERSELLE* BETWEEN 1862 AND 1912

CHAPTER II

The Political Activities of the *Alliance* in Morocco Before the Protectorate Era

1. Political Emancipation and the Emergence of the AIU in Morocco: Some Background on the Nature of its Activities

"L'*Alliance* n'est pas seulement le plus beau fleuron de gloire du judaïsme contemporain, elle est toujours pour les juifs opprimés du monde entier une mère vigilante et devouée" Abraham Ribbi, on the occasion of the fiftieth anniversary of the AIU

During the first half of the nineteenth century Western European Jewry were determined to aid their less fortunate coreligionists. Although they were themselves in an inferior status for centuries following the dispersion, the age of the Enlightenment and a series of European revolutions elevated their position among Christians. Most of them began taking their place besides their fellow countrymen. It appeared that the Jews and Christians were leaving their conflicts behind once and for all.

The French Revolution and its aftermath generated a new spirit of self-confidence among liberated Jews which served as a guide for Jewish actions not only in Europe, but in dealing with the problems of their brethren elsewhere. In the postrevolutionary era, on an equal footing with their Christian compatriots, the Jews assimilated European culture and ethics. It was in this assimilated atmosphere that the Jews could present grievances to their newly elected organizations.

Initial political and institutional strength in France was inspired by the *Consistoire Central des Israélites de France* headquartered in Paris which had branches throughout the country. As the supreme Jewish representative body, the *Consistoire* was originally organized by Napoleon in 1808 and consisted of several rabbis and lay members who governed the Jewish congregations, and who served as intermediaries between the French government and the Jewish communities. Similarly in England, the Jews were represented by the Board of Deputies of British Jews, founded in 1859 and whose most influential member, Sir Moses Montefiore, was the renowned fighter for Jewish rights.

The earliest action launched by European Jews on behalf of their brethren occurred in 1840 when a Capuchin friar in Damascus, Father Tomas, disappeared, and, at the instigation of Ratti Menton, an Italian serving as French consul, the blame for his disappearance was laid upon the Jews. A case of ritual murder was made out and subsequently, in conjunction with the Catholic clergy, the instigators were successful in organizing activities which led to the torture and imprisonment of many Jews. The tale of the event reached Europe and led to meetings of protest, inducing Montefiore, Adolphe Crémieux, and Salomon Munk (both of the *Consistoire*) to travel to see Muḥammad 'Alī of Egypt, who governed Syria at the time, to obtain redress from him. Their efforts succeeded in halting the anti-Jewish activities. This intervention had two implications: it revealed the lobbying strength of these Jewish leaders, and it set the pattern for future intervention of European Jewry on behalf of their counterpart in the Muslim world.

Until 1860, the Jews of England and France had been represented by the Board of Deputies and the *Consistoire*, respectively. However, there was room for the diversification of political activities, and a multiplicity of organizations began to flourish, notably the *Alliance Israélite Universelle* in Paris (1860), the Anglo-Jewish Association in London (1870), the *Wien Allianz* (1873), and the *Hilfsverein der deutschen Juden* in Berlin (1901).

On May 17, 1860, several idealistic French Jews — businessmen, political activists, and members of the free professions — founded the AIU in Paris. They included the illustrious Narcisse Leven, a lawyer who was actively involved in French municipal politics, Eugène Manuel, a celebrated poet, and a dozen other young distinguished or rising professionals of mid-nineteenth century France. Certainly the most important member of the newly created organization was Adolphe Crémieux, an antimonarchist lawyer who from 1848 onward advocated a Republican government. In 1870 Crémieux became Minister of Justice while serving as AIU president at the same time. He is widely known for his lobbying efforts to obtain French citizenship for Algerian Jewry, a process which resulted in the collective naturalization of Algerian Jews as French citizens in 1870. The naturalization decree was named after him.

The decision to create the AIU, though certainly a move to diversify Jewish political activities outside France, was partly hastened by the controversy of the Mortara Case, a case of the abduction of a Jewish child by Catholic conversionists. On the night of June 23, 1858, Edgardo Mortara, aged six years, son of a Jewish family in Bologna, Italy, was abducted by the Papal police and conveyed to Rome. The boy had been secretly baptized five years earlier in an irregular fashion by a Christian domestic servant, who thought that he was about to die. The parents vainly attempted to get their child back, and the case caused a universal outcry. Napoleon III was among those who protested against the infringement of religious freedom and parental rights; Sir Moses Montefiore went to Rome in 1859, in the hope of obtaining the child's release. But the case had a wide impact among young French Jewish intellectuals who, partly owing to the case, created the AIU a year later. In 1870 the child was free to return to his family and religion; but he refused. Edgardo Mortara eventually became a canon in Rome and professor of theology.

The Mortara affair, and the advocacy by AIU intellectuals of religious freedom and rights set the organization's activities in motion already in 1860 though, ironically, on behalf of Christians, as the first activity. During the occasion of the AIU's founding, the Maronite Christian community of Syria was in danger of being slaughtered by the angry Muslim population which resented the Maronites' elevated socioeconomic status, their ties with the West, and France in particular, and their overt insolence vis-à-vis the Muslim masses. Adolphe Crémieux himself urged the French government to intervene in Syria and protect the Maronites, of whom 11,000 men, women and children were slaughtered.

The AIU was created in order to aid Jews and Judaism in three ways: The first was "working toward the emancipation and moral progress of the Jews." While not stating that education was the basic motivation behind emancipation and moral progress, the first aim defined the educational sphere. Moral progress signified the need to combat disease, poverty, ignorance, and to acculturate the Jews in the tradition of French secular education. For that purpose the AIU established schools which served as vehicles for the Jews to absorb the concepts of equality, fraternity, and liberty.

The instrument to transmit ideas from *métropole* was the French language. In the eyes of the AIU French constituted the most important and effective instrument for the dissemination of modern civilization. Nevertheless, the AIU did not advocate total emulation of French secular culture, for its leaders realized that blind imitation of ideas emanating from the *métropole* would encounter fierce opposition among tradition-bound Jews. Therefore, from the outset, the AIU attempted to strike a balance between profane learning, embodying progressive Western ideas, and the sacred traditions and education of the Jewish communities.

The second goal was "lending effective support to all those who suffer because of their membership in the Jewish faith." It referred to the need for allocating the necessary funds to help Jews in distress around the world, and more importantly, to inform European leaders and their diplomatic representatives in countries where Jews were harassed, to urge that action be taken. Further, this meant that the AIU had to alert the leaders of the countries involved, such as Morocco, where the injustice occurred, and possibly wrest concessions from them to remedy the situation. The third aim was to awaken Europe to the Jewish problem. It called for "encouraging all proper publications to bring an end to Jewish sufferings." Whereas the second category called for quiet negotiations and diplomatic action, the third stressed the utilization of AIU and other periodicals to influence public opinion.

The information on the abuses perpetrated on the Jews was obtained by the AIU in Paris through regional committees in the countries where the organization had schools. In addition to fund raising, these committees, composed of influential members of the communities, also established intimate ties with European diplomatic representatives. Thus, the latter could be informed about the conditions of the Jews and act upon information submitted by AIU representatives. The school directors, too, played a decisive role in alerting European consuls to abuses. These educators often combatted injustices themselves by taking independent action.

In his memoires, Leven deplored Moroccan Jewry's exposure to excessive taxations, and the bastinado; he was particularly touched by the humiliating measures by which the Jews were forbidden to ride horses and were recruited for forced labor.[1] The problem of forced labor and the use of the bastinado also were common in the Sherifian Empire and in Persia during the reign of the Safavid and Qajar dynasties. However, these punishments were not confined to Jews alone. Yet European Jews were concerned about their coreligionists, and in 1863 the Board of Deputies dispatched Montefiore to Morocco where he met the Sultan Muḥammad IV. The latter granted Montefiore a decree in February 1864 which forbade the continuing application of humiliating practices. Although the abuses continued virtually unchallenged, only to be regularly combatted by the AIU in later years, Montefiore's achievements set in motion the diplomatic lobbying efforts of Anglo-French Jewry on behalf of the local Jews, bringing these matters before European politicians, consuls, and European public opinion through the press—a phenomenon that encouraged Moroccan Jewish leaders to report abuses. This policy sometimes placed the *makhzan*'s representatives on the defensive.

One classic example of this is found in the correspondence between Montefiore and Abraham Corcos, the leading figure of the Jewish community of Mogador and an affluent merchant. In one letter which was published in the *Times* of London (July 1864), following the enactment of the Montefiore decree, Corcos wrote to Montefiore concerning the situation of the Jews in the Haha province near Mogador, relevant to a problem which surfaced:

Esteemed Sir, I take upon myself the painful task of communicating to you a most deplorable event which has very recently occurred in the vicinity, within a few hours ride from [Mogador].

A poor Jew named Joseph Ben Eish M'Sellim, a resident of this town, while traveling for his usual occupation of petty trading in the adjoining province of Haha had occasion to present himself at the residence of the Governor of the province to prefer a complaint to the Chief in command respecting some money which he said he had been robbed of and lost. It appears that the Khalifa or Deputy Governor Sidi Houssein (acting in place of the Governor of the province, Hadj Abdalla who was absent) did not credit the said Jew's story, and under the impression that his statement was false, ordered him to be punished with the lash, which was so severely applied that the poor Jew was left dead on the spot, and some hours afterwards his remains were buried there by some Jews sent from hence to bring the body of the deceased to this town for internment but which was refused by the Khalifa.

I shall not attempt at present to describe to you the whole of the details of this shocking, cruel affair, which have come to my hearing, as it would be difficult to do so, perhaps, with all truth and correctness. I am, however, happy to inform you that the Resident Consuls, including myself, have taken up this affair properly and seriously, and have each made their report to the Consul-General and the European Ministers at Tangier, with the object of obtaining from the Court of the Sultan a thorough investigation into this horrible tragedy, with due reparation and security for the future against repetition of such totally unjustifiable conduct on the part of the Sultan's chiefs in command in the different parts of the Empire; and I feel persuaded that His Imperial Majesty will not only cause strict inquiry about this melancholy matter, but will likewise take all possible means to prevent the recurrence of similar disgraceful conduct on the part of his different Governors in the country.

I think it right to mention that the said province of Haha has for a great many years been ruled by its present Governor, Hadj Abdalla, who, though considered a very strict and severe chief, showing but little mercy to delinquents of all classes, at some time the province is quiet and comparatively orderly, and due protection is afforded for travelers, traders, strangers, and property, and during the disasters of the bombardment of Mogador by the French some time ago, and the more recent troubles caused by the Spanish war with the Empire the Jews of this place were all received everywhere in Haha and their person and property protected, and were all well treated as far as possible to be done under the strict surveillance, and by the voluntary desire of the ruling Governor, Hadj Abdalla, and much to his credit. Mogador is situated in the province of Haha, and its inhabitants could scarcely expect in such times as described to obtain equal security and protection in any other of the surrounding province, where there exists greater confusion and misrule.

I wish to remove any impression that may erroneously be felt that your late visit to this country is the cause or in any way connected with disasters similar to the occurrence above described; on the contrary, the recent edict of the

Sultan, published on the occasion of your visit to his Court, has undoubtedly produced the most beneficial results, and without which at the present moment the position of the Jews in this Empire might be far worse. I feel, however, confident the good effects of the edict in question will increase tenfold in the course of time.[2]

The political efforts of Anglo-Jewry and the AIU also showed remarkable signs of progress in the case of Persia. Persian Jews, from the time of the Safavids, were forcibly converted to Islam in considerable numbers. They, too, were humiliated by the vexing measures of the bastinado and forced labor.[3] When Nāṣir al-Dīn Shah embarked for Europe in 1873, the leaders of the Anglo-Jewish Association decided to confront him. At the AJA's suggestion, a vast petition drive was planned to present the Shah with demands that he start protecting his Jewish subjects. However, the most effective reception took place in Paris on July 12, 1873, when the Shah met with members of the AIU Central Committee. The following are passages from the discussion launched by Crémieux with the Shah:

Sire, the *Alliance Israélite Universelle*, represented by its Central Committee, is deeply touched by the honor which you have paid it in calling it to this special audience. Sire, all the Jews, even the least enlightened, know—what all Persian Jews know—that, among the people with whom their history is mingled, the Persian people, filled with generous sympathy, brought the Jews back into their beloved Palestine, under the protection of the immortal Cyrus, who showed himself constantly their faithful protector, after having been their liberator. And, yet, Sire, from the kingdom of Persia there have been coming desolating reports about the oppression which has afflicted the Jews in your states. Sire, we cannot believe it.[4]

The Shah, much moved, assured Crémieux that he protected all his citizens and, moreover, showed special attention to non-Muslims.[5]

The results of the meeting had positive consequences for Persian Jewry. Under the façade of diplomatic niceties, Crémieux made it plain to Nāṣir al-Dīn that the abuses perpetrated against the Jews in his empire must be terminated. The Shah, perhaps more sensitive to European public opinion than any of his predecessors, apparently understood the hints and instructed his minister to correct the injustices.[6] Indeed, the conditions of Persian Jewry improved somewhat, temporarily, during the 1870s.[7] Equally significant was the Shah's consideration to permit the AIU to open schools in his empire.[8]

In the Middle East, North Africa, the Balkan regions and Eastern Europe, the AIU engaged in a broad range of activities. The organization's actions were warmly welcomed by the Jews of the Russian Empire, including Poland. These Jews saw in the AIU representatives miracle workers, out to solve all their problems. On numerous occasions the AIU addressed itself to the plight of the Jews in Czarist Russia, long before the pogroms of the 1880s. When emigration of Russian Jews to the United States and Western Europe was judged in the Jewish world as the solution toward ending Russian Jewry's sufferings, the AIU played a preponderant role: in defiance of the Czar, and through its agents in Russia, the AIU encouraged illegal Jewish emigration to the United States and Europe.

These and other actions prompted financial support for the AIU, and earned it the reputation as a major force struggling for the emancipation of the Jews. Consequently, wealthy philanthropists like the Hirschs made generous financial contributions to the AIU, enabling it to intensify its activities. Until the emergence of the Zionist movement at the turn of the century, the AIU held the incontestible title as the chief advocate of Jewish emancipation and solidarity. Ironically, the organization's strength even proved worrisome to its leaders, for anti-Semitic folklore proclaimed that the AIU was the secret Jewish world government.

2. The Political Situation in Morocco, 1860–1912: Background Analysis to the Politico-Educational Activities of the AIU in the Sherifian Empire

At the time the AIU opened its first school in Tetuan of northern Morocco (1862), the country had already been victimized by European political, economic, and military colonial penetration. The French occupation of Algeria (1830) had set in motion a series of events that gradually undermined the traditional economic and military systems in Morocco and led to the emergence of a new precolonial setting.[9] And although Moroccan sultans, including Mawlāy 'Abd al-Raḥmān (1822–1859), had tried to block European encroachment, thus maintaining Morocco's traditional independence, it was in vain. Whereas the French, particularly Foreign Minister Théophile Delcassé, had set up since 1900 a complex strategy which aimed at securing Morocco for France, known as the strategy of "peaceful penetration," through bilateral loan agreements, internal reforms with French advice and supervision, and through reinforcement of commercial and other economic ties,[10] they, like their chief colonial archrivals, the British, did not hesitate to consider, at times, military options. Lesser powers, such as Spain, had pursued similar strategies.

At first, between 1830 and 1845, the Moroccans were not overtly concerned about French and other European colonial intentions. Edmund Burke III observed convincingly that the implications of the French presence in

Algeria since 1830 were for a long time not grasped by the Moroccan elite.[11] Even the French victory at the Battle of Isly (1844) on the Algerian-Moroccan border between Moroccan and French Algerian troops—instigated by the French in response to Moroccan support of, and the granting of a place of exile to, 'Abd al-Qādir, the famed Algerian anti-French resistance leader and French bombardment of Mogador (1844)—produced few echoes in Moroccan political circles.[12] Since the defeat occurred on the eastern frontier of the Sherifian Empire and France refrained from following up its victories Moroccans were not compelled to recognize the full extent of their military inferiority.[13]

Nevertheless, subsequent efforts by Britain and Spain to penetrate the empire proved far more worrisome than the military debacle at Isly. Under constant political maneuvering and even threat of military action by Britain's minister in Tangier, Sir John Drummond Hay, Sultan Mawlāy 'Abd al-Rahmān was compelled to sign an agreement in 1856 that gradually facilitated European economic penetration of his empire. Britain was granted a most favored nation treaty which served as the model for similar agreements with Spain and other European powers. The agreement included such privileges in favor of Britain as: (1) the elimination of state monopolies except those on arms, ammunition, and tobacco; (2) the setting of duty on all imports which would be handled mostly by British merchants, at ten percent, which meant a reduction ranging from ten to twenty percent, without reducing duty on exports; (3) British subjects would be able to have court power to try cases in which a British subject was the defendant.[14]

In 1859–60, under Sultan Muhammed IV (1859–1873), the Moroccan army was soundly defeated by the Spaniards. It all began when the Anjara Berber tribesmen from the Rif mountains in northern Morocco attacked and seized the *San Jose*, a Spanish ship. Fearing that the treaty of 1856 was a British design to dominate the country to the exclusion of all other European powers, the Spaniards found an excuse to invade Tetuan after the sultan had refused to pay indemnity for the ship. A military confrontation took place between Spanish and *makhzan* troops, a confrontation which ended in the ignominious defeat of the latter, the occupation of Tetuan until 1862, the payment of war indemnities to Spain, and, most importantly, Spanish procurement of economic and political concessions. The Spaniards withdrew from Tetuan only after they had obtained a separate Spanish-Moroccan commercial treaty which included permission to install Spanish missions throughout Morocco. The treaty was signed in 1861 and contained much the same guarantees as had the Anglo-Moroccan treaty of 1856.

What was the significance of these treaties? First, they enabled the embryonic European colonies of the pre-1850 period, usually composed of businessmen and international merchants, to open commercial houses and to become larger through immigration. The European population of the ports in 1850 was just 389; in 1872 it was 1,650; in 1877, 2,860; in 1886, 3,500; and in 1894, 9,000.[15] Second, and most tragically, the inevitable result of the lowering of customs duties on European imports was to open the Moroccan market to a flood of cheap manufactured goods and to hasten the decline of the Moroccan artisanry; in 1830, for instance, the town of Salé was able to support hundreds of textile workshops making a variety of woolen and cotton items. By 1880, as a result of the importation of cheap Lancashire cottons, many artisans had been forced out of business.[16]

It was during the reign of Mawlāy 'Abd al-Raḥmān, and until 1856, that the *makhzan* sought to challenge the power of European merchants operating in Gibraltar, Tangier and Mogador, for the latter aspired to gain strong influence over internal commerce and to upset the traditional agricultural and artisanal economy. This was done by nominating local Jewish merchants, the *tujjār al-sulṭān*.[17] These Jews, being the loyal sultan's merchants for many years, mainly in the years 1848 to 1856, controlled all the major imports—sugar, coffee, tea, metals, gunpowder, and tobacco—and such vital exports as wheat, hides, cereals, and wool—items which became government monopolies at the time, resulting from the *makhzan*'s fears of the political and social consequences of European penetration.[18] But with the passage of time and granting of commercial treaties by the *makhzan* to Europeans, the Jewish merchants' privileges were declining. Many of them sought consular protection from the European powers as the latter widened their diplomatic representation in the coastal towns.

Third, the Spanish-Moroccan treaty enabled the Spaniards to strengthen the few Catholic missions in the country and to extend them beyond northern Morocco. There were similar efforts by the British through Protestant missions in Mogador, especially since 1875, revealing strong, though unsucessful, efforts to spread Christianity among Jews.[19]

Another serious encroachment into Moroccan sovereignty was the protection, or *protégé* system that became widespread following the Franco-Moroccan treaty of 1767. Until the mid-1850s the system, which offered judicial and political privileges to Moroccans, enabling them to escape the *makhzan*'s political jurisdiction, functioned properly. Yet the ensuing increase in the volume of commerce with Europe, the need for Moroccan commercial agents, known as *simsārs*, mainly among Jewish merchants, to serve as intermediaries between the Muslims and the growing European community, led to the rapid undermining of the system by all manners of abuses.

In 1863, Muhammad IV tried with the help of Béclard, the French *chargé d'affaires*, to obtain the total abolition of the system. But the French would not hear of this. Instead Béclard signed that same year an agreement with the sultan limiting the number of protected commercial agents in each port to two. The British and the Spaniards, too, supported the agreement, but in practice ignored it like the French.

When Mawlāy Ḥasan came to power in 1873 he understood that, the cause of the *makhzan*'s loss of authority at home and abroad was in part due to an abusive protection system, granted to a privileged elite of Muslims and Jews. To curb the abuses he called on the major powers to convene a conference and, indeed, such a conference was held in Madrid in 1880. The conference reviewed the position of the *protégés* and foreign nationals, mostly *simsārs* and consulate agents (interpreters, advisors, vice-consuls), but did little to alter the status quo.

The war with Spain, resulting in Moroccan payment of huge indemnities; a series of treaties with Europe unfavorable to local economic interests which influenced the balance of trade in favor of the Europeans; the ability of Europeans after 1860 to obtain tax and legal immunities; the growth of the consular networks; the beginnings of intensive cultural penetration through European-style education; the granting of consular protection to Moroccans; the growth of the European colonies; and a prolonged agricultural slump particularly in the years 1878–1884[20]—all helped to transform the old Morocco and to deprive her of the independence she enjoyed for so long.

There were strong reactions in Morocco to these developments, even within *makhzan* circles. These included during Sultan Mawlāy Ḥasan's reign (1873–94), military reforms to rid the army of many of its traditional recruits from tribal areas, and to deprive tribal chiefs (the recruiters of this soldiery) from favors and positions in the *makhzan*; and it meant equipping a modernized army with sophisticated weaponry.[21] However, this step, during Mawlāy 'Abd al-'Azīz's reign (1894–1908), including administrative and tax reforms, required the aid of European advisors, and proved to be a strain on an already drained economy. They could not be effectively implemented.

The dependence on British advisors and on other Europeans meant that the latter could intervene in Morocco's internal affairs. So much so, that in 1900 French troops from Algeria occupied the western Saharan oases of Tuat, the latter having been occupied by the Sa'adians in the sixteenth century and considered Moroccan by the sultanate. Eventually an agreement was reached between the Moroccans and the French for the establishment there of frontier posts for the collection of customs and defensive purposes.

Economically, 'Abd al-'Azīz was in at least as much trouble as his predecessors. To confront his problems head on, he began borrowing substantial loans from France, Britain, and Spain. On December 31, 1901, after lengthy negotiations with the French government, the sultan obtained a loan of 7.5 million francs at six percent interest from a consortium of eleven French banks headed by the *Banque de Paris et des Pays-Bas*, a consortium which collaborated closely with the *Quai d'Orsay*.[22] This loan was regarded by the French banks and the *Quai d'Orsay* as the opening wedge of a long-term process which could place the Moroccan treasury completely in the hands of French finance.[23] Other loans were signed in subsequent months and years, with France, and served Théophile Delcassé's strategy of peaceful penetration: through major and successive loans, as Burke III indicated, the *makhzan* would be conditioned to look to France for financial assistance in the modernization of the country.[24]

Morocco, in economic decline partly because of additional agricultural slump (between 1900 and 1904) and unable to pay its debts, became increasingly dependent on the consortium of banks headed by the *Banque de Paris et des Pays-Bas*. In the absence of loan repayment, these banks and their allies at the Ministry of Finance in Paris, tended to impose stiff terms such as the creation of a debt commission, the creation of a Moroccan state bank, and close supervision over Moroccan customs revenues.[25]

It should not be forgotten that despite French economic inroads, the British were still enjoying economic respectability in the country, the result of Drummond Hay's successful negotiations that led to the Anglo-Moroccan treaty of 1856. But the French were resolved on neutralizing all European interests in the country and had done just that through a series of agreements signed with the powers.[26] Between 1900 and 1912 France succeeded in removing Italy, Britain, and Germany from the arena of colonial rivalry. France agreed with Italy that the latter should have a free hand in Libya while the Italians had to agree to a hands-off policy regarding expansion in Morocco; the *Entente cordiale* of 1904 between Britain and France resulted in a French decision to renounce her claims to Egypt and in return received a British promise to "forget" Morocco; and in 1911, a Franco-German agreement was signed which gave Germany two strips of territory in the French Congo with access to the Congo River and, in return, Germany agreed to a French protectorate over much of Morocco. As for Spain, she agreed with France in 1904 to share spheres of influence in Morocco, an agreement that was transformed into a formal treaty in later years, defining the geographical boundaries of French and Spanish territorial influence.

A conference held in Algeciras (1906), attended by the European powers, granted the French (and Spanish) considerable power over the Moroccan economy, enabling them to intervene in the country's internal reforms more than Britain had done previously. During this crucial meeting an international control body was established, deminated by the French. It had the power to intervene in the economic life of the country. A special port police force was created to insure security for European interests; and though composed of Moroccan personnel, it was headed by Frenchmen and Spaniards.[27] A state bank (*Banque d'Etat*) was created, dominated by representatives of the consortium headed by the *Banque de Paris et des*

Pays-Bas. It became the sole financial agent of the Moroccan government, and was to negotiate all future loans, rendering the *makhzan* prisoner of the Paris banking establishment for its continued existence.[28]

Therefore, by 1906 Moroccan sovereignty faced enormous economic, military, and political challenges. But the worst was yet to come, for the systematic French penetration after Algeciras brought Moroccan Muslim resentment to the boiling point. The resentment was manifested in the form of popular protests and in tribal and military unrest throughout the country. The French proceeded by occupying Oujda;[29] and following anti-European manifestations in Marrakesh and riots in Casablanca (1907), resulting in the killing of Europeans, the French government sent to Casablanca's coast the cruiser *Galilée*,[30] and a French expeditionary force. French troops were now in Casablanca, whereas major portions of the adjacent Chaouia plain were occupied under the command of Generals Drude and d'Amade. In 1907–1908 anti-European feelings extended to include anti-Jewish manifestations in Oujda, Casablanca, and Fez.

The French military moves only heightened tensions. Mawlāy 'Abd al-'Azīz was increasingly regarded by the religious elite (*'ulamā'*), tribal chiefs, the soldiery, merchants and, interestingly, by his brother Mawlāy 'Abd al-Hafīz, as a ruler who placed his empire in foreign hands. From the sale of *makhzan* properties in 'Abd al-Hafīz's charge, some money was raised as early as 1906 to finance a campaign aimed at overthrowing 'Abd al-'Azīz; and loans were obtained from Josué Corcos, the wealthy head of the Marrakesh Jewish community.[31] But to finance a popular revolt 'Abd al-Hafīz needed additional funds which he managed to procure in Germany, a power that prior to 1911 sought to neutralize the French penetration of Morocco. Having secured his loan, he held a series of talks at Marrakesh with tribal leaders from around the country.[32] 'Abd al-Hafīz also procured the support of substantial segments of the country's *'ulamā'*: they gave legitimacy to his leadership for a holy revolt (*jihād*) against his brother.[33]

With the combined support of these dynamic forces 'Abd al-Hafīz forced his brother 'Abd al-'Azīz to abdicate in 1908 and ascended to the sultanate in Fez. And though he managed to obtain French recognition of his sultanate in 1909 despite their strong misgivings about his personality, he failed to fulfill the demands of his supporting coalition to abrogate the Act of Algeciras, to restore Morocco's territorial integrity, and to evacuate French troops from Casablanca and Oujda.[34] Instead he became more deeply entangled in the web of political dependence on the very France he challenged during his revolt against 'Abd al-'Azīz. 'Abd al-Hafīz tried to moderate the radicality of his supporters, to tone down their militancy, and consistently sought to allay the fears among Europeans that he was a fanatic.[35]

Increasingly, the former coalition that brought 'Abd al-Ḥafīẓ to power turned against him once it was certain in their minds that he continued his brother's policy of subservience to the French. Additional French interference in the internal functioning of the *makhzan* only weakened 'Abd al-Ḥafīẓ and led to anti-French and anti-*makhzan* rebellions in 1911 and 1912, requiring additional French military intervention to prop up a crumbling central authority. Morocco was now mature for a colonial takeover. On March 30, 1912, Mawlāy 'Abd al-Ḥafīẓ signed the Treaty of Fez establishing a French protectorate over Morocco. On November 27, 1912, the French and the Spaniards signed an agreement formalizing their division of Morocco into territorial spheres of influence. Most of the country came under the jurisdiction of a French protectorate while northern Morocco, Tangier excluded, became a Spanish zone. Tangier became an International zone in 1923. Within a year after the signing of the treaty in Fez, the French removed 'Abd al-Ḥafīẓ from the throne and replaced him by his brother Mawlāy Yūsuf. The French were now an integral part of Morocco's destiny. Having penetrated Algeria in 1830, and having established a protectorate over Tunisia in 1881, they now completed their North African venture.

It was in the midst of this interesting and politically tumultuous times, the mid-nineteenth century until 1912, that the AIU not only entered the Moroccan scene, but widened its activities. In fact, the growth of the European presence since 1860 enabled the AIU to open schools, even if *makhzan* officials did not always approve. Moreover, the schools were supported politically by the major powers. And given the importance of the commercial treaties, the creation of European banks, post offices, and commercial houses, the AIU schools fortified their role as the most important agent for the preparation of an educated Jewish elite of clerks, interpreters, and *simsārs* to confront the new realities and economic developments of the post-1860 period. The AIU, then, was part of the colonial evolution.

3. The Pioneers of the AIU

The efforts of the AIU on behalf of Moroccan Jewry beginning in 1862 were initially fortified through the work of the above mentioned regional committees, which were instrumental in raising funds to maintain and extend the organization's early schools. These committees encouraged prominent members of the Jewish community to participate with the Central Committee in supporting the embryonic educational projects. In this task the committees obtained considerable assistance from the European consuls, especially in Tetuan, Tangier, and Mogador. The arrival of AIU teachers from Europe after 1862 significantly outweighed the importance of the regional committees, as the educators established amicable relations with the consuls and were not less effective as fund-raisers.

The teachers dispatched to Morocco during the organization's formative years originated from Alsace and other parts of Europe, a phenomenon that changed only after 1870, when the graduates of the AIU Paris training school[36] were alumni of the organization's primary schools in the Sherifian and Ottoman Empires. During the 1860s, as the AIU did not train its own teachers, it was urgent to seek qualified educators who would be willing to make sacrifices in Morocco for the Jews. The AIU found such candidates in the European Jewish communities.

The early teachers and directors were remarkable missionaries. Though, unlike their Protestant and Catholic counterparts, they had a secular mission, they nonetheless paid some attention to Jewish education. While they set out to disseminate French language and culture, these pioneers tried to strike a balance between the profane and the sacred in their educational policies.

In their political efforts on the Jews' behalf, the European teachers of the AIU and their successors could rely heavily on European diplomatic agents. This was clearly the case in the coastal towns where legations and consulates existed. The number of consulates representing Europe increased after 1856, owing to developing European political and economic interests in Morocco. Yet, whereas these consulates extended their influence largely into the coastal towns of Tangier in the north, Mogador in the south, and Casablanca in the west, such representation was weak or nonexistent in the interior and much of the south.[37] In these areas it was extremely difficult for the AIU to organize schools. Why was the interior or the south so unpenetrable for the Europeans and the AIU? The division of Morocco into government controlled and uncontrolled areas shows where success was most likely. Even towns like Fez and Meknes—within the *makhzan*'s domain—were prey to Berber attacks. The Berbers would attack these towns, murdering, looting, and kidnapping. The fear for the well-being of the teachers by the Central Committee, and the concern of the Europeans for their diplomatic agents, slowed Western advancement into anarchy-prone areas.

During the 1860s and early 1870s the AIU teachers, operating from Tetuan, Tangier, and Mogador, were determined to fight injustices. They were critical of the *dhimmī* concept of the "protected people," which applied to non-Muslims. For them, the protected status initiated by a Muslim ruler symbolized mere gestures of toleration rather than concrete solutions to existing abuses. Dr. Bernard Lévy, the founder of the boys' school in Tangier, was quite critical of conditions within the empire. Lévy's formula for action implied an immediate intervention on the part of European capitals in

Morocco's internal affairs. His prescription was twofold: first, the Paris organization had to awaken Western European public opinion to bear pressure on the *makhzan* to improve the protection of the Jews; second, the AIU, given its influence in French political circles, had to obtain for him, Lévy, the position of consular agent so he could share in the responsibility of defending the Jews.[38]

The AIU did not go along with Lévy's demand, doubtless because they feared that he was contemplating the buildup of his own career. Further, such a request could easily have aroused the suspicions of the *Quai d'Orsay*, and might have undermined the organizations position in Morocco. On the other hand, Lévy faced no opposition from Paris over the need for European intervention. The AIU was aware of the realities of the time: the sultan was either too weak to cope with a solution to abuses and anarchy, or simply had no inclination to take bold action. Lévy contended that the argument depicting the sultanate as weak and politically impotent in face of rampant anarchy, was not completely accurate; that European political pressure would compel the *makhzan* to restrain the rebellious regional governors,[39] the rural *qā'ids* and the urban *pashas*.

Lévy's views were shared by M. Gogman who served as the Tetuan boys' school director from 1866 to 1876. He was known for his uncompromising views and did not hesitate to defy both the Central Committee and the European consuls in his actions. He strongly resented the fact that the Jews were confined to ghettos and attributed a considerable portion of the assassinations and pillaging to *makhzan* functionaries.[40] A wave of assassinations in 1867 compelled Gogman to recruit soldiers from the *makhzan* in order to protect the Jews and enable them to conduct business activities; he accused Aymé d'Aquin, then French Minister in Tangier, of negligence over the Jewish question.[41] It seems, however, that in his accusations, Gogman went too far, as d'Aquin was rather helpful to the AIU in its drive for influence amid the Jews. Yet Gogman, apparently set in his ways, decided to take independent action contrary to formal procedures: he considered taking into his home Jews who sought refuge and, perhaps in defiance of French diplomacy, placing the French flag over his home to symbolize a refuge station or a second French consulate.[42] Be that as it may, it is doubtful that the AIU or the French legation in Tangier would have tolerated this development. For want of information it is impossible to determine whether Gogman carried out his idea.

Others among the European teachers of the AIU interpreted the political scene somewhat differently. Maurice Caplan, who preceded Gogman as director in Tetuan, was less inclined to blame the sultan. He was uncertain if political pressure from Europe would bring concrete results. Caplan contended that arbitrary acts were the fault of *makhzan* functionaries who conspired against the sultanate.[43] While arguing that the school directors ought to listen to Jewish grievances, Caplan believed that there was little the sultan could do in light of anarchy.[44] Curiously, he sounded a note of caution. Not denying that Jews suffered from abuses, he reported that they were increasingly cognizant of political efforts undertaken in their favor. To avert unhappy repercussions, Caplan urged the AIU to clarify to the Jews that they should never overestimate the extent of such efforts, that they abandon theories that the Rothschilds are in command of armies and battleships, and, most of all, the Jews had to understand that obedience to the sultan as well as refraining from insolence towards the Muslims was crucial for their security.[45]

These views, too, carried considerable weight in AIU leadership circles, for the AIU could not show irresponsibility in delicate matters. The independent actions of idealistic yet overzealous teachers, could jeopardize the small but developing school network. After all, it was the generosity of the European powers and their assurances of protection that enabled the AIU to enter Morocco in the first place. Such important backing from Paris, London or Rome could not be forfeited and hence restraint was essential. At the same time, the concern shown by the teachers for the political future of the Jews earned the AIU immeasurable respect within several communities. The letters that poured into the Paris headquarters, expressing gratitude for this concern, were many.[46]

Although the Muslims were vulnerable to abuses imposed by *makhzan* functionaries, and their social and economic conditions were in many cases worse than the Jews', the latter not only suffered from abuses, but were barely tolerated as subjects of the sultanate. Only Jewish *protégés* had political advantages. As Leland Bowie noted in his study of the consular protection system in Morocco, it involved a special judicial status to which Western legations and Europeans elevated Moroccans to employment in foreign businesses, legations, and consulates.[47] The *protégés* by enjoying full consular protection, exercised a number of privileges: they were exempt from military duty;[48] they were exempt from Moroccan judicial authority; and they were exempt from the payment of the *jizya*. In other words, these individuals enjoyed the benefits of aliens residing in Morocco, while at the same time, they did not possess foreign nationality.[49]

Whereas the European legations concentrated their diplomatic efforts on behalf of the wealthier strata, the AIU was most active for the unprotected masses, reminding Europe of its traditional commitment to oppressed minorities, in the spirit of the French Revolution and human rights. For Muslims who were overcome by injustice the situation was markedly different: unlike the Jews, the Muslims did not have a "big brother" in Europe to look after their well-being. The AIU, and other European Jewish associations, seized on the Jewish problem because it was, politically, inherent in its mission.

4. The Political Strategies and Actions of the Central Committee and the Schools on Behalf of the Jews

In spite of growing political unrest and the determination of the AIU to look after the Jews, its leaders were obliged to alert the communities that insolence on their part toward the Muslims would serve as a catalyst for hostilities. This warning came in 1874 in a written declaration addressed to Moroccan Jewish leaders by Adolphe Crémieux and Secretary General Isidore Loeb. The following selected lines of the declaration are noteworthy:

> The Central Committee of the *Alliance Israélite Universelle* has heard about the hardships which you encountered and has decided to remove them in recalling the sayings of our fathers that all of Israel is responsible for each other . . . . As more evil acts committed against you will multiply, so will the mercy of your brothers living among the Goyyim. Did your [brothers in Europe] not always contribute money to the eradication of misery and for the removal of obstacles in the way of their coreligionists? We set out and created schools . . . in order to water the children of Israel with the wisdom of the Torah. Despite what numerous people have told us: that there was no hope of redemption for you, we said in our hearts that we should do the utmost . . . . In our success [on your behalf] we will recall . . . all of which the righteous among the Goyyim have done for our brethren, and it is our constant and daily duty to thank the rulers of Europe and their [diplomatic] representatives . . . who stood by us on all occasions and everywhere. Also, your rulers are commended, for they never refrained from listening to your prayers and rescued the righteous from the wicked . . . . However, we ask of you one thing and hope that you heed this for our sake and yours: Please do not incur the wrath of your compatriots . . . . Most of all . . . refrain from saying in the ears of the people things which will displease them and cause anger on their part toward you . . . . [This could] reduce sympathy for you on the part of the sultan and his advisors . . . . They will then say about you: what a disgraceful and arrogant people these Jews are. Therefore, remember the sayings of our Fathers that "wisdom is often the ability to remain silent," and do refrain from boasting about the help [you are getting] from foreign governments and of deliverance from afar. May, the lips of those who boast [of such help] be silenced.[50]

The reasoning in the minds of the declaration's authors was probably this: it seems that they worried—because of reports they received from school directors—that Moroccan Jews believed, or wanted the Muslims to believe, the AIU and wealthy European Jews had means at their disposal which could rescue them from every crisis. The Central Committee probably sought to clarify to the Jews that heavy reliance on the AIU would compel the Muslims and the Europeans to think that the organization was abusing its power and thus its presence in Morocco would be resented. On the one hand, the politics of caution was a realistic appraisal of the organization's capacity in coping with the intricate problems of intervention. On the other, it would not be difficult to understand that certain leaders of Moroccan Jewish society resented these "instructions." Jewish leaders saw in the AIU a potent political force capable of achieving concrete results on their behalf without delays. They did not believe that by merely being obedient to the sultan, positive results would ensue.

At about the time when the Crémieux-Loeb declaration was presented, the AIU formulated its political strategy. In Morocco the policy of the AIU after 1874 can be divided into two areas: first, fighting for the preservation of the *protégé* system at a time when it was rumored that the *makhzan* aspired to substantially alter it; second, protecting the Jewish masses who had no official consular protection.

Dealing with the first category, the Sultan Mawlāy Ḥasan argued justifiably that the *protégé* system presented a serious challenge to his sovereighty and its excesses could not continue unabated. On the other hand, one could argue that the system was a necessity; that there was no irregularity in individuals enjoying the benefits of aliens while, at the same time, not possessing foreign nationality. Yet, on the other hand, it was highly irregular to grant consular protection with no properly defined limits, and the number of appointed *protégés* increased beyond control.[51] The sultan realized that the abuses of this system had to be curbed because, in addition to these privileges, consular protection often covered the wives, children, and even cousins and distant relatives.[52]

The AIU, France, Italy, and even the United States among others, believed it was unwise to abolish or substantially alter the protections. They advocated the maintenance of the system, stressing the need for cautious reforms. The British, the Spaniards, and, to some extent, the Austro-Hungarians, supported the sultan's aspirations over the matter. During considerable deliberations over the system in Madrid (1880) the powers who favored the system's preservation argued, as far as the Jews were concerned, once the protections would be completely lifted or substantially altered for a fortunate elite, the perilous conditions of all the Jews could be exacerbated.[53]

In support for the maintenance of the protections, the AIU found an ally in Anglo-Jewry. Whereas the British government supported the sultan, the Anglo-Jewish Association and the Board of Deputies joined forces with the opponents of the reforms. Contrary to the will of their government, they declared that no time should be lost and no effort spared in endeavors to prevent the withdrawal of the consular protections as contemplated by Drummond Hay and other representatives of the powers; that every effort should be made to induce the powers to direct their representatives in Morocco to continue their benevolent protection of the Jews.[54] And in mid-

May 1880 a deputation from the AJA and the Board of Deputies waited on Earl Granville, British Secretary of State for Foreign Affairs, at the Foreign Office, to ask for the retention of the protections. Among the leaders who attended were Serjeant Simon, Arthur Cohen, J. M. Montefiore, A. G. Henriques, F. D. Mocatta, A. Löwy, and Léopold de Rothschild: perhaps the most powerful representatives of Anglo-Jewry. Introducing the leaders Serjeant Simon said:

> The principles of protection no doubt your Lordship is aware is of long standing, and indeed goes back as far as the twelfth century when the settlers from the southern countries of Europe took their place upon the coasts of Morocco. In their establishments there consuls were appointed who watched the subjects of the different countries to which they belonged. According to international law the household of the representatives of those countries would be entitled to protection through the consuls. Through commotions in the interior, relations were considerably distrubed, and at length their was no regular protection through two or three centuries. But on looking back to the treaties on the subject, I find that as the treaty of 1767 between France and Morocco so by the treaty of 1856 with England, a treaty of commerce and navigation, not only were British subjects trading there placed under consular protection, and not only were special reservations under the treaty made, but your Lordship will find on referring to the treaty itself, in clauses 14, 17 and 20 an express distinction between the subjects of Her Majesty and other persons enjoying consular protection. That could only have arisen from long usage or the example of other countries. Whatever may have been the origin of the treaty rights between other countries and Morocco, they were defined and put in practice by express treaty provision. I can give your Lordship the express terms if you wish it, but I think I have quoted them almost verbatim, where some of the articles provide for the full protection of all subjects of Her Majesty. Article 7 provides that "subjects of the Queen or any other persons under her protection" — the same words as in Article 20 — are in the same position as the persons in the household of the consul — on the principle that the household of the ambassador is entitled to the protection of his own country, and is not subject to the law of the country if it is a foreign land. Here is an express provision in the treaty between Great Britain and Morocco so late as 1856, no doubt still in operation. We are quite aware and sensible of the inconvenience of having consular protection of foreign subjects against their own government when we are asking Her Majesty's Government to continue this special protection . . . . But, independently of the treaties to which I have referred and the long usage, I may remind your Lordship that the principle of this usage is not confined to Morocco; it has existed ever since the Turks were implanted in Europe . . . . Under these circumstances I hope your Lordship will see that the request we make now to Her Majesty's Government is not contrary to known usages which in process of time have come to be considerably extended in their application.[55]

Speaking specifically of the Jews Simon added:

> We do not ask Her Majesty's Government to give the Jews of Morocco any immunity, but we do say Great Britain has treaty rights, and we do ask the British Government not to abandon the Jews of Morocco . . . . With regard to the abuses which it is said this system of privileges is open to, I am aware that it is said that the right to protection is bought and sold by Consular representatives, and that those who enjoy Consular protection have an immunity from taxation. This may be so, and there are evils no doubt, but they are only abuses of the system, and do not touch the system itself. The question is whether it is a necessary and a right thing to afford protection. The British, the French, and the Spanish Governments have, by their various treaties with Morocco, shown that they think it is a right thing to afford protection . . . .
>
> The Jews . . . are also a great civilizing factor [in addition to their importance in commerce], and if consular protection is withdrawn they will be left entirely at the mercies of the ignorant, fanatic, and barbarous Moors. Again, in the case of Moorish subjects, they need not be exempted from payment of the taxes due. The revenue of the country would be protected by specific protection as the groundwork of the treaty. We ask your Lordship, as the representative of Her Majesty's Government, to consider the necessity and importance of retaining, at least, and, if possible, of extending this protection to Moorish subjects to the Jews and non-Mahommedans generally in Morocco. We ask, as regards the Jews, that this should be done, and we say it would be best done by treaty.[56]

Simon and the delegation outlined three points, supported by the AIU, that (a) special courts be established, open to all non-Mahommedans, at which their testimony would be received as valid; (b) provincial and local authorities should be deprived of the right of inflicting the bastinado or of keeping people imprisoned without trial; and (c) it should be declared unlawful to compel non-Mahommedans to walk barefoot or to impose on them other personal indignity.[57]

Earl Granville, in reply retorted over the protections, saying:

> It appears that there are great abuses connected with these irregular privileges; they are bought and sold and got by fraud and exercised most unjustly, and this practiꞓe does excite such a feeling of animosity against the Jews there that it injuriously affects the position of the great bulk of the people. The instructions have gone out and they are in accordance with what has been the opinion for some time of the Foreign Office. All I can say is that we can fairly deal with this; we cannot undertake in any way whatever to reverse the instructions or say that the meeting shall be one for the extension of these privileges instead of for the consolidation of the irregularities connected with them.[58]

Of the Jewish organizations, the AIU did the following: the Central Committee took immediate action by dispatching to Madrid two of its most influential members, Charles Netter and Emanuel F. Veneziani, to lobby on behalf of the Jewish *protégés*. Already a month before the Madrid Conference, the AIU sent the French foreign minister a memorandum[59] pointing to the humiliations suffered by the Jews in the empire at the hands of government functionaries; it enumerated many incidents between 1862 and 1880 in which Jews were exposed to beatings and deaths. The memorandum shows that the AIU seized the opportunity to discuss injustices committed against *protégés* and non-*protégés* alike, for the memorandum stated that:[60] humiliations of all sorts were continuously inflicted on the Jews by local authorities; in the interior they were obliged to wear different clothes from the rest of the population; if at all allowed to leave their quarters, they could do so only barefooted; and they were often forced to work on Saturdays; if they refused to obey these commands, they were in danger of execution.

The AIU contended that owing to the ongoing internal crisis in the country there was no need to aggravate matters by lifting the protections. At least an elite should be permitted to lead a tranquil life: "The protection of a foreign power enables a certain number of Jews to escape the common misery and engage in commercial transactions without fear for themselves and those who live under their dependence."[61] The insertion of the "commercial" argument was doubtless intended to convince the French to uphold the protection for several thousand Jews, which would benefit the colonial interests of the *Quai d'Orsay*. Otherwise European commercial interests in Morocco would be imperiled. To strengthen the argument, the memorandum was worded so as to explain the impact the abolition of the system could have on the economic front:

> Morocco in part owes its *protégés* its industrial and commercial activities with Europe. All of the European travelers who visited Morocco, are in accord on the premise that the services rendered by the *protégés* are essential to the country. In certain towns the *protégés*, through their proper initiatives and financial resources, contribute to public works, road construction, building bridges, etc. They also contribute to the economic development of the coastal towns.[62]

The memorandum also pointed to an abominable crime which took place in Fez on the eve of the Madrid conference. Early in 1880, a seventy-year-old Jew had been killed and his body burned without serious protest on the part of the Moroccan government; the only action taken to cool tempers was to indemnify the victim's family.[63] This affair was certainly food for thought in the mind of the French foreign minister on his way to Madrid.

Finally, the memorandum pointed to the illegalities perpetrated against the Jews, and claimed that the Sherifian establishment was unable to adhere to past written promises: that at different stages in history, the sultans of Morocco published edicts promising peace and security for the Jews in the empire; a decree by the sultan in February 1864, granted to Sir Moses Montefiore, affirmed that all Jews living in the empire must be on equal footing with the Muslims; that no Jewish merchant or artisan would be forced to work against his will; in 1874 the new sultan affirmed his obligations to the decree, but these were merely gestures which brought no constructive results, for they have been continuously violated by the governors.[64]

The sultan, for his part, was concerned about the efforts of the AIU and European public opinion, and at the conference his foreign minister, Sidī Muhammad Bargash, read the *makhzan*'s statement on the matter:

It has come to our knowledge that certain Jews, our subjects, have repeatedly complained to their brethren in Europe and to foreign representatives in Tangier, that they do not succeed in obtaining justice for their complaints against murders, robberies, etc. They pretend that the governors show indifference in securing for them satisfaction from the persons who attack them, and their demands never reach our Sherifian Majesty, unless it be led by the interference of these persons, the Jews residing in Europe, and the foreign representatives. Our Sherifian will is that they obtain justice without the intervention of the powers or of their representatives, because they are our subjects and our tributaries, having thereby the same rights as Muslims before us, and all outrages upon them are prohibited by our religion; therefore, we enjoin them to accept the complaints of any Jew who will state that he does not receive justice before a governor, and give us knowledge of the same when thou will not find means to give him redress. We have sent orders in the same spirit to the governors of the towns . . . and of the rural districts, that they give communications of the same to the Jews, and at the same time we have warned them that if any of them do oppose, or place any difficulty in the way of a Jewish complaint arriving to thee, we shall punish them severely. We order them to treat their affairs with all due fairness, and to conceal from none of us arbitrary acts of the governors against them, because all men are equal before us in matters of justice.[65]

This was obviously an effort, for the benefit of the representatives of the powers in Madrid, to convince everyone that Mawlāy Hasan was master of his house. While downplaying complaints of humiliations directed against the Jews by governors, the sultan nevertheless was inclined to concede that problems did exist. However, his inability to offer concrete solutions for an orderly society only enfeebled his diplomatic stance.

As the conference was drawing to an end, the *makhzan* capitulated over the rights of the *simsārs*, many of whom were Jews, and thus one could well argue that the efforts of the AIU and Anglo-Jewry were fruitful. Further, the powers after tense deliberations, agreed to continue granting protections to Muslim and Jewish consular agents, though on a reduced scale. Protection was to include Moroccans and their families serving legations and consulates as organized by the French treaty of 1767, the English of 1856, and the Spanish of 1861. This included exemption from taxes, military service, and native tribunals. Foreigners, too, retained the right to hold immovable property. On the issue relevant to naturalization, a rather complicated policy was formulated: "Every Moroccan naturalized abroad who shall return to Morocco must, after a period of residence equal in time to that which was legally to obtain naturalization, choose between his complete submission to the laws of the Empire and the obligation to leave Morocco."[66] Nevertheless, a qualification was attached to this: "unless it was proved that the foreign naturalization was obtained with the consent of the sultan."[67]

Perhaps the most vocal figure at the conference was Britain's Drummond Hay. He did not care to please the Jews, and did his utmost to strengthen Mawlāy Ḥasan's position at Madrid. Ironically, it was Drummond Hay who originally challenged Moroccan economic and political isolation through the Anglo-Moroccan treaty of 1856, a policy which exposed Morocco to aggressive colonial influences in the first place. But Britain's policy was to oppose such privileges as granting consular protection in significant numbers to the affluent and educated of Moroccan society, most likely out of fear that the other powers would encroach upon the strong colonial base which Drummond had built for her. Drummond Hay was mostly concerned with France because the latter had a power base in Algeria, had made colonial headway in Tunisia, and was liberally granting consular protections in Morocco: a policy that was bound to augment French colonial gains.

Drummond Hay was particularly displeased by Jewish influence at the conference, and did not hesitate to warn Anglo-French Jewry that their proclamations and meddlings would prove counter productive. Having once referred to Moses Montefiore as "an overzealous philanthropic,"[68] he now struck a rather pessimistic note, forecasting that the continuance and extension of irregular protection to a limited number of wealthy Jews has not, and will not, aid in mitigating the oppression of the Jews in the interior; undue pressue on the sultan for the sudden abolition of the degrading measures to which the Jews were subjected, or for removing their disabilities and placing them on an equal footing with the Muslims, could lead to the intensification of the Muslims' hatred towards the Jews, and would culminate in a catastrophe.[69]

Drummond Hay's suggestion that the Jews display patience until the propitious time came for them to be equal with the Muslims, did not acquire sympathy in European Jewish circles. The latter were convinced that the sultan was either unable or unwilling to avert a catastrophe one way or another, and they had told Drummond Hay how they felt on more than one occasion. To a significant extent, their position was justified, for not long after the conference ended, the abuses continued to multiply. On the other hand, the continuation of the protections, which was envisaged by Drummond Hay as a future catalyst for anti-Jewish sentiments, may have aided the abuses and encouraged their perpetrators.

In addition to the AIU, the Jews found a particularly worthwhile friend in the Italian minister at Tangier, Stefano Scovasso, who, during the 1870s and 1880s, devoted his time to upholding Jewish rights and to maintaining the protections. A close friend of the AIU, he continuously resisted limiting the number of irregular *protégés* and had been increasing them in Tangier in violation of every existing treaty; and, upon his return to Tangier in May 1880, Jews, encouraged by his support for the protections, hastened to the shores to greet him, shouting "Viva Scovasso, Viva el Protector."[70]

Between the time the conference ended and the inauguration of the protectorate era, the AIU received complaints from the rabbis and notables in Morocco of further abuses committed against them. The complaints centered mostly around the sufferings of the Jewish masses and not the *protégés*, and they varied from town to town. In Demnat, a small southern town in the Atlas mountains, the Jews were exposed to undue humiliations by the local *qā'id* who instigated the abuses. Owing in part to the efforts of the Fez boys' school director, Salomon Benoliel, the French Minister at Tangier, L. C. Féraud, was informed of the situation in Demnat and contacted the sultan over the matter. Féraud's intercession led to the issuance of two *zahīrs* advocating cessation of the abuses.[71]

From the contents of the *zahīrs* — for the year 1885 — we can discern the nature of the abuses in Demnat. Jews, for instance, were compelled to buy goods against their will;[72] they were recruited for work without receiving wages;[73] they had to give away their animals (probably farm animals) without receiving pay;[74] and they had to give up some of their most precious products: in the case of leather goods, they had to practically give them away.[75]

However, these and other *zahīrs* often were ineffective, as the sultans were simply unable to enforce them. The letters by rabbis and prominent community members were quite moving. They came from the most remote communities, where the sultan, even if he had the power, would not have been able to curb the abuses. For example the leaders of the Jewish community of Ouezzan in the interior wrote to the AIU in 1908 complaining that they were forced to work without pay; their synagogue was destroyed; they were subjected to harassments and arbitrary arrests; they were forbidden to perform their religious duties; and, among other abuses, they were burdened with taxations.[76] The community leaders felt helpless and were unable to find a solution to their miseries. They had written to the AIU because they had heard from other Maghribi Jewish communities that the AIU always came to the rescue and thus they pleaded in the name of their community that the AIU intervene in order to remedy the situation.[77]

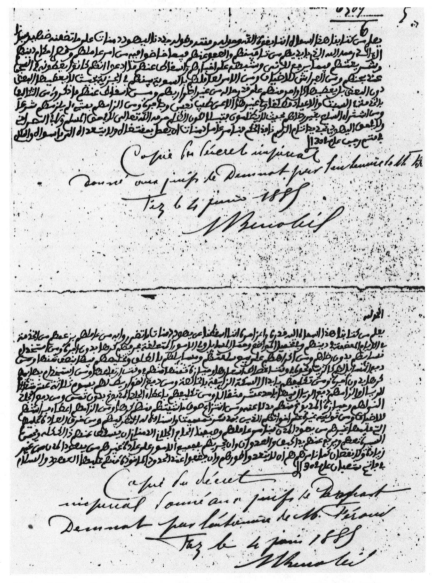

Figure 4. Two sultanic *zahīrs* concerning the Jewish community of Demnat, 1885

Similar and perhaps more severe letters came from the larger and better-known communities, as seen in the case of Marrakesh. In 1893, the leaders of that community complained to the AIU above several *makhzan* soldiers who had forcefully taken the wife and children of a Jew. The latter converted to Islam, apparently under pressure. The woman and her children were in panic and hence community leaders sought to redeem her and the children. Their efforts were fruitless.[78] On another matter, Marrakesh leader reported in the same letter that a Jew was beaten to death by a Muslim; they made it clear that in view of their situation the AIU was an important force for bettering their status.[79]

There is no archival evidence of action taken by the AIU specifically in Ouezzan and Marrakesh. However, the organization in Paris and its

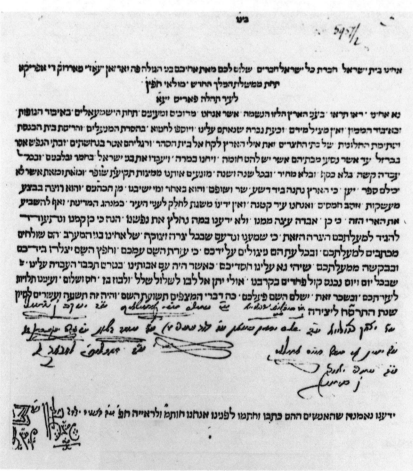

Figure 5. A letter of the Ouezzan community seeking the aid of the *Alliance*, 1908

teachers usually attended to the most pressing of problems. Not only did they alert the Europeans but attempted to end abuses by working directly with the *makhzan*. During the first decade of this century, the AIU successfully contacted the *makhzan*, wresting far-reaching concessions from them. Indeed, after Mawlāy 'Abd al-Hafīz's ascendance to the sultanate, a political honeymoon developed between the AIU and the *makhzan*. It all began in October 1908, when the sultan's influential *wazīr* (minister), Sī

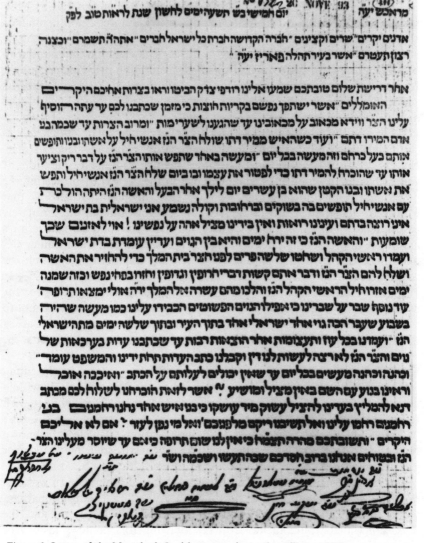

Figure 6. Letter of the Marrakesh Jewish community to the *Alliance*, 1893

Madanī al-Glāwī, whose politically influential family of southern Morocco provided the *makhzan* with governors, administrative agents and, at times, *wazīr*s, was contacted by AIU president, Narcisse Leven. Glāwī was appointed by the sultan to transform Marrakesh into a stable *makhzan* stronghold, particularly since political and military unrest plagued the town after the preceeding year. Through the efforts of Josué Corcos, president of the Marrakesh Jewish community, the AIU established this contact. Leven's contacts with Glāwī through correspondence dealt with the harassment of the Jews and their degradation; it also informed the *wazīr* that its Marrakesh schools closed down following nation wide unrest, and demanded that they be reopened.[80]

On October 26, 1908, responding to Leven, Glāwī committed himself to offering a brighter future for the Jews and, in addition to giving green light for the Marrakesh schools' reopening, he encouraged the AIU to develop its educational network, downplaying rumors in Europe that Mawlāy 'Abd al-Hafīz was a fanatic.[81]

What was the significance of this particular contact? The *makhzan* was certainly aware of unfavorable European opinion to the prevalence of anarchy in Morocco, before and after the revolt, and the occupation of Casablanca and Oujda by French troops, on the pretext of protecting the developing European colonies, was a case in point. Realizing that Morocco's Jews had an ally in the AIU, an organization that was intimately associated with the *Quai d'Orsay*, Glāwī may have sought the organization's assistance in projecting a better image of the sultanate in European circles and the press, dispelling notions of Sherifian fanaticism. It should be remembered that France recognized the *Hafīẓīyya* sultanate only in 1909. In 1908, however, the *makhzan* was still seeking broader recognition for the regime in Europe, and counted on every possible source of support, not to mention European loans to rebuild the ravaged country in the revolt's aftermath. Hence, by accomodating the AIU and other European elements, the *makhzan* could gain support.

Glāwī honored his commitment to Leven. While entrusted by the sultan to bolster the *makhzan*'s influence in the south and Marrakesh, Glāwī had allowed the Jews to move freely among the Muslims. Meanwhile Jewish tailors worked for the *wazīr*s.[82] The exorbitant taxes imposed on the Jews of Taroudant, in the Ante-Atlas, caught his attention. Glāwī let it be known to the local *qā'id* that unless the Jews were better treated, he would face grim consequences.[83]

The AIU, for its part, no doubt realized that an accomodation with the *makhzan* would give it greater flexibility in expanding its educational network, and would create a friendly atmosphere between itself and the *makhzan* which would facilitate direct lobbying for the Jews instead of through Europeans.

The independent political role of the school directors on behalf of the

Jews deserves some attention. Their reactions to the abuses were analyzed above. However, these teachers did not hesitate to act in face of challenge. A rather central figure in this category was Amram Elmaleh, director of the boys' school in Fez, educated at the AIU schools of Tangier. He was famous for his dynamic appeal for Jewish rights, which earned him the reputation as a hero. Upon his arrival in Fez (1909), Elmaleh learned that a considerable number of Jews were occasionally compelled to work in the royal stables and the *makhzan's* gun depot without receiving pay. This was certainly a serious violation of the Montefiore decree granted some forty-five years earlier by the sultan, challenging unorthodox labor practices. Yet there had been so many deviations from this and other decrees that intensive lobbying efforts were necessary.

In Fez, Jews were recruited by the governor to transport barrels of gunpowder to the ordnance factory where these barrels were opened, weighed, and the gunpowder dried; in the royal stables Jews were required to clean the animals, carry dead beasts to a remote corner of the Fez countryside, and bury the carcasses of animals belonging to the sultan; they used to return home without pay, living off charity. To terminate the abuses, Elmaleh called on Glāwī, reminding him of the Montefiore concessions, formally calling for the abolition of unorthodox labor practices; and he insisted that European Jewry would not tolerate the continuance of cruelty perpetrated against their coreligionists.[84] The tactic was effective, for it was quickly decided that wages be paid to the Jewish laborers; and Glāwī issued a warning to the governor not to allow such irregularities in the future.[85] It also seems that the bastinado disappeared once and for all from the list of abuses in Fez, for such violations were not reported after 1909.

Concerning other irregularities, Elmaleh was equally insistent for immediate reforms. For instance, the sultan's chamberlain, whose acts of cruelties towards the Jews of Fez were notorious, had gone unchallenged. On Yom Kippur in 1909 the chamberlain threw into jail all the Jewish butchers because they refused to make him a present of lungs from the animals which they butchered, for the sultan's cats. According to the *Jewish Chronicle*, it appears that Elmaleh's efforts before Glāwī were successful: the prisoners were released at once.[86] However, the powers of the chamberlain were not curbed. On the following day, while the Jews were still observing High Holiday, he sent soldiers to assemble the goldsmiths to whom he wished to entrust some work. The Jews refused on grounds of religious obligations, and with memories of the previous day's arrests, the goldsmiths quickly sought refuge in Elmaleh's school. And he refused to let them go.[87]

Through Elmaleh's efforts before Glāwī the Jews of Fez began leading a more tranquil life. Where Montefiore laid the foundations, Elmaleh provided continuity of policy, a reality demonstrated in a statement made by Glāwī to the rabbis and lay leaders of Fez:

It has come to our attention that the director of your *Alliance* school has several times written in your favor to the public authorities. I am charged by my master to tell you that you will never again have to suffer injustices at the hands of the *makhzan*, forced labor will no longer be imposed on you, and your Sabbaths and festivals shall be respected.[88]

In Rabat, the director of the AIU schools, Joseph Conquy, proved indispensable for the political security of the Jewish community.[89] In May 1903, the *Zair* Arab tribe attacked the town. Directing their violence on the population, they also damaged the already weak walls of the *mellāḥ*. These walls required repair, a task which the town's authorities apparently refused to undertake; when all Jewish communal efforts to achieve the desired concessions failed, Conquy succeeded in enlisting the support of the Spanish consul; within days work began toward repairing the walls.[90]

In a more difficult situation, David Benzaquen and his wife, Brazilian *protégés*, were attacked by a group of Muslims while crossing from Salé to nearby Rabat. Conquy claims that a group of Muslim workers barred the couple's entrance to the Jewish quarter.[91] Push came to shove and Benzaquen and his wife were roughed up but managed to escape; subsequently, several of the Muslims in explaining their conduct to the *qāḍī*, accused Benzaquen of making insulting comments about Islam; the authorities then ordered Benzaquen's arrest, despite the protests of the Brazilian vice-consul.[92]

One can well imagine that Benzaquen might have aroused anger in the first place by demeaning their religion. It is acknowledged that *protégés* and foreign nationals tended to display arrogance toward the less privileged, assuming that they could rely on the consulates to bail them out of trouble.[93] On the other hand, the Benzaquen affair triggered unrest in Rabat: for several days Muslims attacked, humiliated, and beat up Jews; to end the unrest, Conquy approached the European consuls in Rabat; the latter provided him with their representatives whom he led on a march to the governor's house where he related the events to the governor and insisted on immediate protection for the Jews; immediately afterwards the *makhzan* dispatched soldiers to the *mellāḥ* and protected its inhabitants from further violence.[94] Benzaquen's fate is not known, though the status of foreigners and *protégés* was strictly related to the consulates.

In conclusion, from these selected examples it is evident that the efforts of the AIU in Paris and Morocco were important in affording *temporary relief* to Jews from political humiliations. In Morocco which was still in the pre-Colonial period at the time, the AIU played a preponderant role as the protector of the Jews, by constituting the most indispensable body informed of their sufferings. In all efforts on the Jews' behalf, the AIU relied on its European and *makhzan* connections. Aware of the *makhzan*'s deep concern with its image in the West, particularly considering its financial dependence on European economic markets, investments, and loans, the AIU probably exploited this weakness to pressure the Moroccans—directly and indirectly—to improve the conditions of their Jewish subjects, at least in areas under *makhzan* jurisdictions as opposed to the *sība*. Notwithstanding, great leaps forward leading to political emancipation did not take place before 1912. Temporary relief was certainly essential, as were the efforts to uphold the Montefiore concessions. However, the inability to lobby for a host of legislative reforms favoring the Jews, rendered the AIU's accomplishments in the political arena unfinished.

5. The *Alliance* and the Politics of Precolonial Cultural Penetration

The Relations of the *Alliance* with the European Powers

We have seen that the presence of the AIU in Morocco was the result of multiple efforts on the part of Anglo-French Jewry and European diplomatic representatives. Already in 1861, a representative of the AIU, the renowned Orientalist, Joseph Halévy, and James Picciotto of the Board of Deputies, met with Tetuan's Jewish leaders. The meeting took place through the efforts of Emmanuel Menahem Nahon, the Jewish French consul since 1849. As a result of his mediation, the following agreement was reached: the schools would be subsidized by the AIU, the *Consistoire Central*, and the Board of Deputies; the AIU would send teachers for French and general education while the community would supply the rabbis for Hebrew and Judaic studies. The rabbis' salaries became the responsibility of the community; the schools would be administered through a director appointed by the Central Committee, though the *junta* would have power of decision making over matters pertaining to Jewish education; finally, the community would participate with the AIU in finding suitable buildings for the schools and by paying a portion of the rent.

The boys' school, being the first AIU institution ever, was inaugurated on December 23, 1862, in the presence of community lay and rabbinic leaders, the *pasha*, members of the European consular corps, and a number of Spanish Catholics. The latter came to Morocco in large numbers in the wake of the Spanish occupation of Tetuan and expressed approval of sending their children to the newly founded school.[95] During the inauguration, Chief Rabbi Isaac ben Oualid opened the meeting, thanking the Central Committee for the creation of the school and praising the Board of Deputies for its role in the event; he addressed himself to the *junta*, reminding them of the sacrifices which its members must make for the school's progress. Following the chief rabbi to the podium, Hermann Cohn, the first

AIU teacher and director in the Sherifian Empire, spoke about the benefits of a modern education, gave a brief account of the AIU's raison d'être, and thanked the Board of Deputies and the Tetuan *junta* for their efforts.[96]

The school developed rapidly within a year of its inception, with one hundred and sixty youths attending its classes; an additional one hundred and forty were waiting to attend but were unable to register due to the lack of space.[97] Between 1862 and 1912, the AIU educational network extended to most of the towns in the north, south, the interior, and the coastal areas in the west, where large communities dwelt. The support and encouragement which resulted in the educational expansion of the AIU was largely attributed to the activities of the European consuls, for these representatives envisaged in the AIU an indispensable force for the intellectual regeneration of the Jews and for enhancing European cultural influence in the empire. One might ask if the powers saw in the AIU a boost to their influence collectively. After all, it was predominently French.

The powers' representatives were inclined to believe that since they encouraged the development of the school network they could in return use the AIU to further their political ends. Though realizing that the French character of the schools could not be completely altered, they were willing to settle for a program that would embody a multilingual education representing their languages and cultural heritage collectively. As we shall see, the AIU was reluctant to play cultural host for all the European powers, and though offering a diversified program,[98] was selective, gearing its policies to meet local Jewish aspirations. The French representatives, for their part, opposed vehemently any encroachment on the schools.

The extent of cordiality between the representatives of the powers and the AIU is noteworthy. During the sixties and seventies of the last century, the AIU established intimate ties with the French consul in Mogador, Auguste Beaumier, the Spanish consul in Tetuan, Ramon Lon, and Aymé d'Aquin, the French minister in Tangier. These representatives were among the most zealous collaborators with the AIU in the often difficult task of consolidating the influence of the schools within the communities. In the port town of Mogador, Beaumier considered the popularization of the AIU as one of his most vital missions, and in 1866, addressed his pleas to the Central Committee decrying the lamentable conditions of the Jewish masses, encouraging the organization to create schools. Though the AIU appeared willing, Beaumier encountered insurmountable obstacles in the community because community leaders turned down his initial request for a French-type school.[99] However, he was not discouraged. When the leaders told him that Mogador was a British commercial stronghold and that there already existed a school founded by the Board of Deputies, Beaumier retorted that an additional institution would only accelerate intellectual progress.[100] Within several months Beaumier succeeded in opening an AIU boys' school in the *qaṣba* quarter. In that part of town Jewish merchants lived alongside Muslim and European businessmen.[101] Yet, despite the progress made by the school, the pro-British Jewish leaders preferred a curriculum modelled on the English school system and consequently, the AIU school was forced to close. After painful negotiations between Beaumier and Jewish leaders, the school reopened in 1875 just prior to the consul's death. However, it soon closed down once again and was reopened in 1888 permanently.

In Tetuan, the Spanish consul became an indispensable intermediary between the Jewish community and the AIU. The consul, Ramon Lon, was a major source of inspiration for the schools and, writing to Crémieux in 1871, he expressed his appreciation for the great humanitarian services performed by the AIU on behalf of the Jews. During his tenure in Tetuan, he had the advantage of witnessing the progress made by the schools for Jewish youths: young men, who were at one time condemned to a lamentable and obscure life, graduated from the AIU and found lucrative employment in Morocco and elsewhere.[102]

Ramon Lon was particularly impressed with the efforts to educate the girls, a phenomenon which did not exist in pre-1862 Morocco, and found that of the one hundred and thirty-seven pupils attending the girls' school in Tetuan, forty-eight were capable of reading and writing French and would be easily integrated into any *lycée* in Europe.[103] Notwithstanding, Ramon Lon warned that the AIU would face an uphill struggle for recognition in most communities because (a) Jewish youths, in his opinion, had to be "cleansed" of their impurities by bathing in European progressive ideas; (b) the schools had to struggle against outdated ideas and to do so, needed the protection and support of Europe; (c) the school directors, having access to the synagogues, to the homes of Jewish families, and to the streets of the *mellāḥ*, had to fiercely challenge archaic customs in both the classroom and the community at large; (d) there was ill will and negligence on the parents' part who viewed the essence of secular education with great disdain and insisted on heavy doses of religious education; (e) the indifference, if not outright hostilities of the rabbis to secular education, constituted another obstacle; and (f) the religious schools directed by the rabbis of Tetuan were attended by hundreds of pupils exposed to fanaticism and superstitious learnings.[104]

Ramon Lon's conception of local cultures was certainly patronizing and typical of European attitude in the preoccupation with the "civilizing mission" and "moral conquest." His position towards the rabbinic schools was analogous to the strategies of the French. They, too, wanted to see the old institutions disappear, for they saw in the latter an obstacle to their cultural penetration among Jews. By encouraging the AIU to challenge the rabbinic schools and minimize their importance, the representatives of the powers attempted to use the AIU for their own interests at a time when European educational institutions in Morocco were relatively scarce or unpopular. The AIU, on the other hand, adhered to an educational policy advocating retention of Jewish learnings and averting hostility from the rabbinic establishment toward their schools. Most teachers realized that if the AIU was to become popular, then patience and caution were of utmost necessity. Their position was justified because Jews, though eager to receive the benefits of AIU political lobbying, were nevertheless apprehensive about "abandoning" their youths to European educators.

In several communities, however, the AIU could afford to be less cautious in its policies, depending on the outlook of community leaders. Further, several communities were economically more important than others and hence could help the schools become better institutionalized in their midst. In the economically developing communities, the Jews were more eager to welcome the schools, for it meant giving their youths a modern education that could provide them with ample employment opportunities. This can be deduced from Maurice Caplan, teaching in Tetuan during the mid-1860s. Comparing Tetuan and Tangier, he envisaged correctly that the schools in Tetuan would eventually face obstacles within the Jewish community whereas in Tangier the AIU could look forward to fruitful activities: The Jews of Tangier were not as economically impoverished as their counterparts in Tetuan. Even among the poorer segments of the Tangier community, one could engage in commercial activities of this strategic commercial port and consequently, the AIU there was destined to play an important role in preparing employees for European commercial houses. There were numerous migrants in Tangier from other parts of the country, seeking lucrative employment due to the developing trade activities and, therefore, they too were sending their children to the AIU schools. In Tetuan, on the other hand, there was hardly any important industries or commercial activities, and local Jews were in fact leaving the town, contributing to the eventual decline in school enrollment.[105]

If the AIU had expected to face serious encounters in the north, there were greater challenges in the interior. Unlike Tetuan and the key coastal towns, the political situation in Fez, Meknes, or Sefrou was far less stable in view of political unrest and European reluctance to open consulates. Therefore, the AIU found it impossible during its first years of activities to become established in these communities.

An earnest attempt was made by the French minister in Tangier, Aymé d'Aquin, to help the AIU extend its network to the community of Fez as early as 1866. During one of his deliberations with the Tangier school director, Bernard Lévy, d'Aquin promised to confer with Fez Jewish leaders on the occasion of his meeting with the sultan. Through d'Aquin, the AIU succeeded in paving the road toward contacting the forgotten Jews of the interior.[106] Upon his arrival in Fez, d'Aquin assembled the members of the community council and briefed them on the history of the AIU and its aims.[107] He explained to them that their social and political conditions would improve through the efforts of the AIU and pleaded with community leaders to support the creation of schools in Fez.[108]

Although d'Aquin's efforts led to the establishment of a channel of communication between the AIU and the Fez community, it required an additional seventeen years to create a school. In 1883, when Salomon Benoliel opened the boys' school, it was possible largely because Spain had already opened a consulate in Fez and other European powers were following suit.

Encouragement for the AIU's efforts came from Italy's Scovasso. Being a devout champion of Jewish rights, he urged Moïse Fresco of the Tangier boys' school to concentrate on educating the Jews of the interior. He was acutely aware of the realities of the time: the AIU needed considerable funds for its projects while the Jews of the interior, suspicious of the organization's intentions, did not make significant financial sacrifices to meet educational goals.[109] Scovasso, moreover, did not conceal his misgivings about having French as the language of instruction, and claimed that Spanish was far more relevant in several major communities where the Jews were of Castilian ancestry. Fresco vehemently opposed, on the grounds that French had become an indispensable language for the transmission of Western culture among the Jews, their *langue adoptée*.[110]

In advancing this argument, Fresco obviously displayed a tinge of chauvinism, portraying French as the absolute vehicle for the spread of modern concepts. On the other hand, one wonders about Scovasso's intentions. Though the need to teach Spanish as language of instruction was rejected by the AIU, Scovasso was doubtless aware of the fact that Spanish was not at all neglected by the schools in the north. Perhaps realizing that AIU institutions, despite their French character, were not financially bound to the French government, Scovasso may have felt that the organization ought to be more flexible in its educational offerings and emphasize other European languages to a greater extent.

In 1884 David Cazès[111] was sent to Morocco by the Central Committee on a fact-finding mission, in part pertaining to the question of the schools and European political rivalries. The mission completed, Cazès observed that the European ministers in Morocco knew that the schools were neutral — political and national rivalries had no place there — and besides, the schools were the object of sympathy from all the European ministers, for they understood that the AIU has only one aim: social and intellectual pursuit among the Jews through education.[112]

Despite the Cazès observation, however, the AIU found it increasingly difficult to stay out of big power rivalry. The representatives of the powers began pressuring the AIU in the mid-1880s to develop the school network.

They were aware of Moroccan Jewish eagerness to collaborate with the Europeans, an orientation that could render immense services to the economic and political advancement of the major political powers. By applying the pressure tactic on the AIU to open additional schools, an even greater number of European-educated Jews would emerge, versed on those fields most important to the powers' undertakings. To realize their aspirations, the consuls launched intensive appeals to the AIU Central Committee. Therefore, in 1886, for example, M. Craveri, French vice-consul in Casablanca, pleaded in his and the community's names for a school, and indicated that Casablanca was a rapidly developing town that would become the most important commercial center of the Moroccan coast; and that the Jewish population was 3,000 strong but deprived of modern education; he practically begged the Central Committee to open a school in order to spread knowledge of French among the Jews.[113]

Several years later Craveri's successor, M. Collomb, made a similar appeal, urging the AIU to open a school as soon as possible.[114] One might deduce that the French encouraged the AIU to extend its network for the propagation of French. At the same time, however, the school directors were willing to go along with the expansion of the network because it would enable them to absorb many youths enrolled at the rabbinic schools, and it would attract the youths of the European communities in the ports. Hence, shortly after a girls' school was founded in Casablanca, the directress urged the AIU not to ignore the fact the European colony of Casablanca was composed of diverse elements and nationalities, for given the growing prestige enjoyed by the AIU in Morocco, it was probable that the Europeans would send their children to its schools.[115]

In light of this, it is possible to concentrate on the reactions of the powers to the presence of the AIU, with case studies confined to France, Italy, Germany, and Spain.

French Reactions to the Influence of the AIU: 1900–1912

Of the European powers, France was the first to organize a small network of secular-modern type schools. The first serious efforts date back to 1894 when the *Alliance Française*[116] opened its schools in Tangier, receiving subsidies from the French administration in Algeria. After 1900, the French legation in Tangier, not completely satisfied with the results achieved by these and other *Alliance Française* schools scattered throughout the country, decided to sponsor schools known as *écoles franco-arabe*. However, between the time when the Franco-Arab schools were created and until any noticeable progress was made through its program, the French considered the AIU as its most vital cultural ally.

In 1902, G. Saint-René-Taillandier, the French minister at Tangier, reported about the existence of AIU schools in different parts of the country, modelled on the curriculum of the *métropole*. Ranking among the founders of the Franco-Arab consular schools, Saint-René-Taillandier observed that while it would be ideal to attract Muslims to French schools, their parents were indifferent to the idea.[117] The following year he praised the AIU schools for spreading French culture. At the same time, however, he did not conceal his bitterness with AIU policies that catered to other interests: teaching Hebrew, Arabic (at times), Spanish, and English. Though Saint-René-Taillandier knew that the teaching of Hebrew and Spanish, the latter being the language of Jews of Spanish ancestry, was justified, the same could not be said for English which was not so important.[118]

The bias on the part of the French to the offering of English education at the AIU, was politically motivated, Saint-René-Taillandier's statement was still in the spirit of the pre-*Entente cordiale* era when France and Britain were competing for geopolitical and cultural influence. Nothing could be farther from the truth than to suggest that British influence in Tangier or in any other coastal town was minimal. In fact, the British enjoyed a respectable degree of commercial influence in most of these towns before 1904, particularly in Mogador, owing in part to their dealings with the Jews.

In any case, Saint-René-Taillandier felt that the AIU schools were the most efficient instruments for disseminating French cultural influence among the Jews, especially in view of Muslim "indifference" to secular education. He found that AIU graduates constituted the only indigenous element speaking French, and it was this group that introduced French into the empire's commercial circles and which served as the chief intermediary between Europe and Morocco.[119] He therefore urged that France "must continue to regard with utmost sympathy the activities of the *Alliance*, hoping that its schools advance French culture among the Jews. It may also be that these schools might achieve a victory by diminishing the influence of the rabbinic schools, on the one hand, and the Spanish and British schools, on the other."[120]

Surprise at the progress of the AIU schools was expressed by numerous French travelers to Morocco. One Frenchman, Dr. Mauran, toured Morocco in 1909. Devoting some attention to his book on the AIU, Mauran, though not specific, found two prevailing intellectual currents in the Moroccan Jewish communities: the reactionaries, composed of archtraditional conservative rabbis and community leaders, and the progressive elite, headed by the alumni and agents of the AIU, who disseminated the ideas of the *métropole*.[121]

The support for the AIU, however, was not accompanied with financial subsidies in the preprotectorate era. Yet, the number of Frenchmen who visited the schools was growing as were the suggestions for subsidies. When General d'Amade, whose forces occupied Casablanca, realized the importance of the schools, he informed the AIU that he would use his influence before the French government to obtain subsidies so the network could expand its activities.[122] D'Amade considered the Jewish communities as an important element for future French presence in the empire and presumed that helping subsidize the AIU would constitute a sound investment for French cultural and political influence.[123] As we shall see, the French did eventually grant subsidies for the schools.

Italian and German Interests in the AIU Schools: 1890–1912

Toward the end of the nineteenth century, both Italian and German consuls expressed genuine interest in the AIU schools. They were as convinced as the French that the Jewish population, which at the time was estimated at 100,000, would facilitate their penetration of the country. In 1890 the Italian legation in Tangier had in its service a considerable number of Jewish *protégés*. Through them the Italians had hoped to rally support in the communities for extending their sphere of influence. The legation had become popular among Jews in the north largely because of Scovasso's pro-Jewish sentiments. To realize their aspirations, Italian diplomats began urging Jewish *protégés* to propagate Italian language and culture in the communities. One method applied by the *protégés* was to pressure the AIU into adding Italian to the program, and this was very much the case in the coastal towns where the Italians were eagerly seeking commercial influence. Once AIU graduates, imbued with Italian language and culture would enter commerce, they could render great services for Italy.

The pressure for such arrangements was especially pronounced in Tangier, where the school directors often complained about this to the Central Committee. In June 1890, for instance, Abraham Ribbi of the boys' school complained that the AIU existed amidst political rivalries. Several members of the *junta* are Italian *protégés*; the honorary president of the community, Joseph Toledano, and other influential members are serving as interpreters at the Italian legation; they insist on introducing Italian into schools.[124]

The Central Committee would not hear of this. Secretary Loeb rejected the pro-Italian plea for several reasons. First, too many languages were already taught at the Tangier schools. In this community Hebrew, French, and Spanish were taught comprehensively while the Board of Deputies financed an English language course.[125] Second, Italian had no practical advantages in Morocco: it was not widely spoken in the coastal towns, where French and English were the prime commercial languages.[126] Finally, the AIU would not tolerate efforts by several powers to make the schools bear the brunt of political interests.[127]

This did not seem to discourage the pro-Italian efforts. In 1891 these elements sought financial subsidies from the Jewish community of Rome for the language course, and it was suspected that the Italian legation was the culprit in the whole affair.[128] However, the AIU refused to succumb to Italian pressures and the proponents of the measure had to drop the matter.

If Italian influence worried the AIU, German interests in its network caused greater apprehensions. Since 1875 the Germans were resolved on extending Imperial influence into the Sherifian Empire. They, too, believed that political expansion would have to be accompanied with cultural activities. To assist them in their aspirations, German consulates granted protection to influential Jews, much to the dissatisfaction of the French.[129] Moreover, Jewish commercial houses and representatives worked with German importers and exporters—especially in Tangier—during the third quarter of the nineteenth century. A Jew by the name of Azancot represented in Tangier the Gerdzen and Ruschhaupt commercial enterprise of Hamburg; Bengio represented the Schuback und Söhne of Hamburg; Semtov and A. H. Cohen, the Georgi of Leipzig; Coriat as well as Jacob and Isaac Laredo were agents of Atlas Linie and the German Lloyd maritime insurance company; H. A. Toledano, represented the Viktor Sperling of Leipzig.[130] In 1890 there were forty-three Germans, mostly merchants, in the port towns whereas in 1904, one hundred eighty-seven.[131] Yet on the whole, German efforts to win Jewish support soon became a thorny problem for the school directors. German agents were accused by the AIU of intrusion into the affairs of the schools and for insisting that German be taught. Once again, the AIU responded saying that German influence in the empire was not sufficiently significant for German to be taught at the AIU, and burdening the youths with unnecessary languages could lead to superfluous education.

In 1906 there appeared a lengthy article in *Kölnische Zeitung* by August Hornung, a German journalist, after his visit to the interior and coastal towns. Describing his visit on behalf of the Imperial government, Hornung was pleased to find AIU schools in a fervently Islamic town like Fez; he observed that Germany could exploit these schools to further its interests and, ironically enough, was angered by French and British efforts to use the AIU for political ends; he accused the AIU of catering to the latter by offering French and English in the programs; he referred to anger expressed by the French consul at Casablanca for offering English at the AIU, while the latter insisted that this was justified on the grounds of impartiality between Britain and France.[132]

Hornung's grievances were rather apparent: if the AIU permitted the teachings of English in the schools, despite French protests, then the Central Committee of the AIU would be in a position to offer German, too. The intent of the report caused anxiety in French Jewish circles. In its prestigious journal, *Archives Israélites*, the editor commented that if French is taught in the schools of the AIU in Asia and Africa, it is because the Jews prefer it; if German was given preference by Moroccan Jews over French, there would be no reluctance in integrating it into the curriculum.[133]

The Germans, however, did not relent easily. Though they opened a boys' school for members of their Tangier colony, it enjoyed a limited influence and thus the AIU was still needed. Much of the attack was directed by Hornung through his German newspaper, the *Deutsche Marokko-Zeitung*, which he founded in Tangier and edited from 1907 on. He made a major appeal, in one article, to the AIU and the Jewish community, urging them to welcome German influence in their midst, and attempted to dispel the notions made by the AIU to the Jews that only the French were humanitarians. Germans, too, were concerned with Jewish rights and often displayed greater concern on their behalf than either the French or the British. He cited the examples of Fez and Casablanca during the riots of 1908, hailing the German consul in Fez for being the envoy who looked after the Jews; according to Hornung, the German consul in Fez placed Jewish *protégés* of France and Britain under his protection.[134] In Casablanca, too, the representatives of the powers did not much care for the fate of the Jews once the *mellāh* was sacked. The Germans, claims Hornung, made certain that destitute Jews could board the German steamship *Arkadia* and reach safety.[135]

Having done so much for the Jews, Hornung signaled that some sincere gratitude was owed to Germany.[136] And he strongly intimated that German humanitarianism could be better understood culturally, with the AIU schools serving as vehicles for that purpose; he then called for impartial educational policies and the training of AIU members from the Paris normal school in Bonn, for the purpose of acquiring German linguistic and cultural background.[137] Once again, the AIU disregarded the suggestion. By 1910 when the Hornung article was written in Tangier, Morocco was clearly becoming a zone of French and Spanish influence, and German pleas were less convincing.

Spanish Quest for Influence

As seen above, Spain's influence in the Sherifian Empire acquired considerable momentum following the conquest of Tetuan. The Spanish military occupation was accompanied by the introduction of the Spanish printing press[138] and the opening of Catholic missions, the educational quality of which was not on par with the AIU schools. Consequently, the more progressive elements of the Spanish colony sent their children to the AIU. One teacher in Tangier observed that while it went without saying that the majority of the youths in the schools were Jewish, a new phenomenon had emerged: Spanish Catholic parents had a better tuition-paying record than their Jewish counterparts.[139] But there were political reasons, too. The Moroccan towns were populated by Spanish Socialists and anarchists who loathed reactionary and clerical institutions like the Catholic schools, and for them the AIU symbolized a progressive and liberal alternative.[140]

The Spanish consuls concerned themselves with the AIU, too. Similar to the French and British consuls, they would periodically inspect the progress made by the schools. Thus, for example, Adriano de Rotondo, Spain's consul in Casablanca, inspected the schools, examined the children in Spanish, and heard a recital in Spanish of a translated Haggadah of Passover; he then tested their knowledge of Spanish history and geography.[141] To explain the motive behind the policy, the school director contended: "Both Spain and France are competing in order to attract and win over the Jewish population to their side. In this situation, our schools are the *points de mire* in the realization of their aspiration."[142]

With time passing, the Spaniards suspected that the AIU was increasingly catering to French cultural interests and hence, the enthusiastic support for the schools, reminiscent of the Ramon Lon days, was diminishing. In the years immediately preceding the Spanish protectorate, the opposition to the AIU was becoming quite intense. Much of the discontent centered in the north, mainly in Tetuan, Larache, and Elksar. Alarmed by opposition from Jewish community leaders, among others, the Elksar boys' school director warned in 1911 that an increasing number of Jews, among them Spanish *protégés*, wish to appease Madrid, for Elksar was to become part of a future Spanish protectorate; these Jews, along with Christians and Muslims, had shown their disdain for the schools, accusing the teachers of being French agents.[143] Having assembled all the community leaders, the director (Albert Benaroya) declared that he understood that several of them saw the schools as purely French; however, it was essential to realize that the AIU does not politicize; its unique aim was to eradicate misery; if the AIU was here to establish schools; it was for the purpose of educating the children and guiding them in the path of the Jewish heritage.[144]

European Cultural Penetration and the Reaction of the AIU

When the AIU first opened schools in Tetuan, Tangier, and Mogador, other educational efforts were attempted by Europeans. In Mogador the AIU had to contend with the schools founded by the Board of Deputies in the *qaṣba*.[145] After years of protracted struggles, the AIU consolidated its position within the community without arousing the anger of its sister organization. On the contrary, the AIU worked closely with the Board schools, even subsidizing to a large extent a girls' school opened by the Anglo-Jewish Association (1886) in the *mellāh*.[146] Eventually, upon the request of the latter association, French was taught in its schools by AIU teachers.[147]

Whereas the Anglo-Jewish Association girls' school survived until 1917, the Board institutions closed long before. In 1907, the last Board school relinquished its influence in Mogador. In explaining the circumstances behind the move, the correspondent of the *Jewish Chronicle* in Mogador offered political reasons: "Three years ago I showed in these columns how the language that the children should learn had by necessity become French. Current events are justifying these views."[148] Current events signified the diminution of British influence in their commercial bastion of Mogador after the signing of the *Entente cordiale*. The creation of the French protectorate several years later clearly confirmed the trend.

Of the powers represented in Morocco, France was the most successful in creating a durable educational network, either through the *Alliance Française* or the consular schools. Moreover, as the AIU disseminated French education in Morocco, the French had a clearcut "cultural" advantage over their European rivals.

The AIU, however, did not always welcome the French additions. Its representatives were often critical of these schools on the grounds of mediocrity or out of fear of challenge to their own growing cultural predominence within the Jewish communities. In 1901 Ribbi noted that the *Alliance Française* extended its educational network to Morocco since 1894, with the first school opening in Tangier, while additional schools were created in Fez, Elksar, and Arzila.[149] Three years later Ribbi related that the representatives of the *Alliance Française* in Elksar and Arzila intended to educate Moroccans with no political strings attached; but in Tangier and Fez, both important cultural centers, these schools were to disseminate French culture and attract Muslims to the side of France.[150]

The strategy applied by the *Alliance Française* to win Muslim support, especially in Tangier, was to give the schools a quasitraditional character and to offer tuition-free education; in Tangier the school was directed by Caddour Benghabrit, working for the French legation, and was given the title *madrasa* (Muslim religious school) which was elegantly carved on stone in Quranic Arabic. The school was not popular, largely attended by Algerian youths, most of whom children of consular and legation employees.[151]

One of the distinguishing characteristics of the *Alliance Française* was its Algerian teaching staff, doubtless a policy to attract Muslims to the school. Ribbi's reaction to the intellectual standards of the schools was mostly negative:

Our youths who frequent the schools of the *Alliance Française*[152] receive a mere touch of modern education. Oh, how superficial this education really is! The result of education in these schools will lead to intellectual decline as was the case with Jewish children in Algeria who attended these schools.[153]

Although we do not have information on the curricular activities of the *Alliance Française* schools, it is certain that in its "Muslim" schools there existed a dual program of sacred and profane education. This was the case in Tangier and Fez, where Quranic studies and Arabic occupied a respectable place in the curriculum.

Where the *Alliance Française* schools failed to attract youths, the French legation tried to pick up. In Tangier the French minister, Henri Regnault, became the chief architect of the consular schools, and his efforts led to the creation of a French *lycée*, later named in his honor. The Tangier *lycée*, founded in 1908, constituted the cornerstone of modern secondary education which, however, included Arabic studies, English, and Spanish. In addition, courses were offered in bookkeeping and accounting, all of which led to the *baccalauréat*. Once opened, *Lycée Regnault* attempted to recruit students of diverse ethnic and national origins and, almost inevitably, Jews were well represented.

Added to the important creation of the *lycée*, Regnault concentrated his efforts on the elementary educational level. Already in 1902, under Saint-René-Taillandier a few Franco-Arab and ethnically mixed schools were in existence. Under Regnault (1907–1912), the network extended to the major coastal towns[154] and to the south. Thus, when the protectorate era was inaugurated, there were probably a dozen consular schools in Morocco. And while there is no data on enrollment, it is doubtful if these institutions were widely attended.

Despite his lack of high regard for the early French schools, Ribbi did not conceal his apprehensions about their eventual challenge to the AIU. He sensed a trend developing among privileged Jews to sending their youths to these schools and stressed that the wealthier elements were placing their children at the Perrier school[155] whereas the poorer families sent their children to the AIU.[156] Although some *évolués* sent theirs to legation-sponsored schools, the AIU, claimed Ribbi, offered an excellent program: modern education that was as comprehensive as the one offered at the Perrier school or even *Lycée Regnault*; and like the *lycée* French, English and (sometimes) Arabic were offered; the English teacher at the AIU was the best in town; and the AIU enjoyed a clear-cut advantage over these schools by teaching Hebrew and Jewish studies.[157]

By affirming that Hebrew was taught exclusively at the AIU, Ribbi apparently expressed concern over losing pupils to the legation schools. However, his apprehensions were hardly justified, for with the inauguration of the protectorate era the AIU became popular in all the major communities and among the diverse social and economic strata. In conclusion: Did the AIU succumb to the desires of the national powers to use the schools to further their political and cultural interests? It appears that the school directors were indeed selective in allowing various European languages to dominate educational activities. The Italian and German experience is very much a case in point. At the same time, the AIU introduced Spanish and English language and literature into some of the schools, fulfilling local needs and aspirations. It would be folly to deny AIU collaboration with France in the precolonial period, for much of the educational training at the schools was geared to French commercial and business acitivity after graduation. Nevertheless, it would be inaccurate to suggest that the AIU had intentionally sided with France in order to facilitate her colonial penetration, a theory cherished by well-informed, modern-day Moroccan nationalists.

On the eve of the protectorate era, the AIU had twenty-seven schools in the country.[158]

Notes

1. Narcisse Leven, *Cinquante ans d'histoire: l'alliance israélite universelle* (Paris: Librarie Félix Alcan, 1911–1920), I: 156.
2. *Times of London* (August 17, 1864), p. 12.
3. Hanina Mizrahi, *Tōledōt Yehūdē Fāras ve-Meshorerehem* (Jerusalem, 1966), pp. 34–35.
4. *BAIU*, 3e sem. (1873), p. 85; Walter Fischel, "The Jews of Persia, 1795-1940," *Jewish Social Studies* 12.2 (April 1950), p. 131.
5. Ibid.
6. Ibid.
7. Mizrahi, *Tōledōt Yehūdē Fāras*, p. 45: Fischel, "The Jews of Persia," p. 131.
8. Mizrahi, *Tōledōt Yehūdē Fāras*, loc. cit.
9. Edmund Burke III, *Prelude to Protectorate in Morocco: Precolonial Protest and Resistance, 1860-1912* (Chicago: University of Chicago Press, 1976), p. 20.
10. Ibid., pp. 68–70. Tangier was the European and diplomatic capital of Morocco, the center of the European legations to which consulates throughout the country were subordinate.
11. Ibid., p. 20.
12. Ibid.
13. Ibid.
14. Jean-Louis Miège, *Le Maroc et l'Europe* (Paris: Presses Universitaires de France, 1961-1963), II: 331; Burke III, *Prelude to Protectorate*, p. 23; Kenneth L. Brown, *People of Salé: Tradition and Change in a Moroccan City, 1830-1930* (Cambridge, Mass.: Harvard University Press, 1976), p. 120; Jamil Abun-Hasr, *A History of the Maghrib* (Cambridge, 1971), pp. 289-290.
15. Miège, *Le Maroc et l'Europe*, II:474; III:260; IV:285; Burke III, *Prelude to Protectorate*, p. 24.

16. Burke III, *Prelude to Protectorate*, p. 23; Brown, *People of Salé*, pp. 120-121.

17. For an analysis on the sultans' Jewish merchants, see Michael Abitbol, "Une elite économique juive au Maroc precolonial: les tujjar al-sultan," in M. Abitbol, ed., *Judaïsme d'Afrique du Nord aux xixe - xxe siècles* (Jerusalem: Institut Ben-Zvi, 1980), pp. 26-34.

18. Ibid.

19. Miège, *Le Maroc et l'Europe*, II: 462-467; see also his "Les missions protestantes au Maroc, 1875-1905," *Hespéris* 43 (1955), pp. 153-192.

20. Burke III, *Prelude to Protectorate*, p. 24; Miège, *Le Maroc et l'Europe*, III: 443-446.

21. Burke III, *Prelude to Protectorate*, pp. 31-33.

22. Ibid., p. 56.

23. Ibid.

24. Ibid., p. 69.

25. Ibid., p. 71.

26. Ibid., pp. 69-70, 172.

27. Ibid., p. 87.

28. Ibid.

29. Ibid., p. 92.

30. See, for instance, André Adam, "Sur l'action du Galilée à Casablanca en août 1907," *Revue de l'Occident Musulman et de la Méditerranée* 6 (1969), pp. 9-21.

31. Burke III, *Prelude to Protectorate*, p. 103.

32. Ibid.

33. Ibid., pp. 106-113.

34. Ibid., pp. 116-128.

35. Ibid., p. 125.

36. *Ecole Normale Israélite Orientale* (ENIO), founded in Paris (1867).

37. In the interior towns like Fez, Sefrou, and Meknes, there was no European consular representation prior to 1882. In the south, even important towns like Marrakesh did not have consular representation on a significant scale until the end of the nineteenth century.

38. Bernard Lévy to AIU, Tangier, June 22, 1864, Arch.AIU.V.B.24.

39. Lévy to AIU, Tangier, May 4, 1864, Arch.AIU.V.B.24.

40. Gogman to AIU, Tetuan, July 16, 1867, Arch.AIU.LXXVII.E., no file number.

41. Ibid.

42. Ibid.

43. Maurice Caplan to AIU, Tetuan, April 3, 1865, Arch.AIU.LXV.E.993.

44. Ibid.

45. Caplan to AIU, Tetuan, April 30, 1865, Arch.AIU.IV.B.24.

46. See, for instance, Moses Benchimol to AIU, Tangier, August 24, 1864, Arch.AIU.IV.B.24.

47. Leland Louis Bowie, *The Protégé System in Morocco: 1880-1904*, Ph.D. dissertation (Ohio State University) 1970, p. 12.

48. Jews did not serve in the army, nor were they recruited as policemen.

49. Bowie, ibid.

50. Adolphe Crémieux and Isidore Loeb to the Moroccan communities (1874). Quoted in David Ovadia, *The Jewish Community of Sefrou* (Jerusalem, Center for Research on the Jewish Communities of Morocco, 1974), I:280-281, in Hebrew.

51. Bowie, "The Protégé System," p. 12.

52. Ibid., p. 17. See also Jean-Louis Miège, "La bourgeoisie juive du Maroc au xixe siècle," in *Judaïsme d'Afrique du Nord aux xixe - xxe siècles*, p. 31. According to Miège there may have been as many as 4,000 Jewish *protégés*.

53. On a similar position held by the AIU, see: Benoliel to AIU, Larache, June 15, 1879, Arch.AIU.XX.E.321.

54. Anglo-Jewish Association," *The Jewish Chronicle*, October 17, 1879, p. 7.

55. "The Jews in Morocco: Deputation to Earl Granvile," *The Jewish Chronicle*, May 21, 1880, pp. 11-12.

56. Ibid.

57. Ibid.

58. Ibid.

59. On the memorandum see *BAIU*, mensuel, mai 1880, pp. 127-130.

60. Ibid., p. 128.

61. Ibid.

62. Ibid., pp. 128-129.

63. Ibid., p. 129.

64. Ibid.

65. "The Jews of Morocco," *The Jewish Chronicle*, July 30, 1880, p. 6.

66. Bowie, "The Protégé System," p. 49; quoted from the conference's protocol #11, meeting of June 24, 1880.

67. Ibid., pp. 49-50.

68. Miège, *Le Maroc et l'Europe*, II:567.

69. "Morocco," *The Jewish Chronicle*, November 12, 1880, p. 10.

70. "The Morocco Conference," *The Jewish Chronicle*, May 28, 1880, p. 7.

71. For a copy of the *zahirs* see p. 55.

72. Benoliel to the AIU, Fez, June 4, 1885, Arch.AIU.XIII.E.215(a); sultanic edict for Rajab 1302, in Arabic.

73. Ibid.

74. Benoliel to AIU, Fez, June 4, 1885, Arch.AIU.XIII.E.215(a); sultanic edict for Shaban 1302, in Arabic.

75. Ibid.

76. Letter of the Jewish leaders in Ouezzan to AIU, sent through the Larache boys' school director, July 12, 1908, Arch.AIU.XX.E.324, in Hebrew.

77. Ibid.

78. Jewish community leaders in Marrakesh to AIU, Marrakesh, November 20, 1893, Arch.AIU.XXXIV.E.582(a), in Hebrew.

79. Ibid.

80. "Israélites du Maroc," *BAIU*, ler sem. (1909), pp. 78-87; Narcisse Leven to Sī Madanī al-Glāwī, p. 82; letter dated October 16, 1908.

81. Ibid. Sī Madanī al-Glāwī to Narcisse Leven, pp. 83-84.

82. Ibid. Nissim Falcon to Narcisse Leven, December 4, 1908, p. 86.

83. Ibid., pp. 86-87.

84. "Morocco," *The Jewish Chronicle, July 23, 1909*, p. 9.

85. Ibid.

86. "Morocco, *"The Jewish Chronicle*, October 15, 1909, p. 9.

87. Ibid.

88. "Morocco," The Jewish Chronicle, December 24, 1909, p. 9; Amram Elmaleh to AIU, Fez, December 7, 1909, Arch.AIU.XV.E.248(a). The Glāwī statement in Fez was made on December 6, 1909.

89. A significant number of school directors and teachers obtained French citizenship. Among them were Amram Elmaleh and Joseph Conquy. Others included those who enjoyed consular protection.

90. Joseph Conquy to AIU, Rabat, June 21, 1903, Arch.AIU.XXXIX.E. 685(a).

91. Ibid.

92. Ibid.

93. Ibid. On this point see a similar analysis by Norman A. Stillman, "L'experience judeo-marocaine: une point de vue revisioniste," in *Judaïsme d'Afrique du Nord aux xixe - xxe siècles*, p. 21.

94. Joseph Conquy (above, note 90).

95. Emmanuel Menahem Nahon to AIU, Tetuan, December 24, 1862, Arch. AIU.VI.B.25.

96. Ibid.

97. Ibid.

98. Hermann Cohn to AIU, Tetuan, November 17, 1863, Arch.AIU.VI.B.25. Other languages were taught at the AIU. In fact, in Tangier and Casablanca English was taught for two essential reasons: (a) the Board of Deputies contributed subsidies for the schools; and (b) English was an indispensable medium for communication in the coastal towns, where it often served as the commercial language par excellence. Prior to 1880 English was taught at the AIU school in Tetuan.

99. Y. D. Sémach, "L'oeuvre scolaire de l'alliance israélite," *Paix et Droit*, 12, no. 3, mensuel (mars 1932), pp. 8–9.

100. Ibid., p. 9.

101. In Mogador the *qasba* section of towns represented wealth and contact with the European cultural and commercial world. In addition to this quarter, there existed a *mellāh* for the Jews and a *madīna* for the Muslims.

102. Ramon Lon to AIU, Tetuan, December 29, 1871, Arch.AIU.LXXVII.E. no file number.

103. Ibid. In 1871 one hundred and fifty-seven youths attended the boys' school, whereas one hundred and thirty-seven attended the girls' school, founded in 1865.

104. Ibid.

105. Maurice Caplan to AIU, Tetuan, October 30, 1865, Arch.AIU.LXV.E.993.

106. Bernard Lévy to AIU, Tangier, July 15, 1866, Arch.AIU.VI.B.25.

107. Ibid.

108. Ibid.

109. Moïse Fresco to AIU, Tangier, March 8, 1886, Arch.AIU.LIII.E.874.

110. Ibid.

111. David Cazès was born in Tetuan and was educated at the boys' school; later he attended the ENIO in Paris, sponsored by the AIU, and was noted as the architect of the AIU educational network in Tunisia.

112. David Cazès, "Rapport sur les écoles de l'alliance de Tanger et de Tetuan," *BAIU*, sem.(1884–1885), pp. 49–50.

113. M. Craveri to AIU, Casablanca, March 20, 1886, Arch.AIU.III.E.49.

114. M. Collomb to AIU, Casablanca, January 23, 1889, Arch.AIU.III.E.49.

115. V. Benzaquen to AIU, Casablanca, October 31, 1900, Arch.AIU.IV.E.86.

116. The *Alliance française* has promoted in the past and continues to promote French education; it has established schools in the colonial possessions of France since the latter half of the nineteenth century, but elsewhere, too.

117. G. Saint-René Taillandier to Théophile Delcassé, Tangier, January 6, 1902, A. E. Maroc.I.405.
118. G. Saint-René Taillandier to Delcassé, Tangier, January 6, 1903, A. E. Maroc.I.405.
119. Ibid.
120. Ibid.
121. Dr. Mauran, *La société marocaine* (Paris, 1909), p. 180.
122. General d'Amade to AIU, Casablanca, January 16, 1909, Arch. AIU.III.E.49.
123. Ibid.
124. Abraham Ribbi to AIU, Tangier, June 25, 1890, Arch.AIU.LVI.E.934(a).
125. Isidore Loeb to Ribbi, Paris, July 9, 1890, Arch.AIU.LVI.E.934(a).
126. Ibid.
127. Ibid.
128. Ribbi to AIU, Tangier, June 8, 1891, Arch.AIU.LVI.E.934(a).
129. M. Cambon to Stephen Pichon, Berlin, August 12, 1907, A. E. Maroc. Série administrative. 142 Dr2. *Alliance Israélite Universelle.*
130. Pierre Guillen, *L'Allemagne et le Maroc* (Paris, Presses Universitaires de France, 1967), pp. 406–407.
131. Ibid., p. 480.
132. Jacques Bigart to Pichon, January 6, 1906, A. E. Maroc. Série administrative. 142Dr2. *Alliance Israélite Universelle:* 1897–1907.
133. H. Prague, "La question de Maroc et le patriotisme juif," *Archives Israélites* 67, no. 7 (février 15, 1906), p. 50.
134. August Hornung, "Deutschland und die Tactigkeit der Alliance Israélite Universelle in Morokko," *Deutsche Marokko-Zeitung*, Dritter Jahrgang, no. 265 (1910), p. 2. ("Der Deutsche Vertreter Dr. Vassel verschob daraufhin seine Reise um einen Tag, auf den Sonntag, sodass die deutschen, Französischen und englischen jüdischen Protegirten unter seinem Schutze reisen konnten."
135. Ibid.
136. Ibid.
137. Ibid.
138. Muhammad Dāwūd, *Ta'rīkh Titwān*, V, pt. 3, p. 379.
139. Salomon Benoliel to AIU, Tangier, June 5, 1904, Arch.AIU.LI.E.835.
140. Ibid.
141. Israël Pisa to AIU, Casablanca, May 12, 1907, Arch.AIU.VII.E.148.
142. Ibid.
143. Albert Benaroya to AIU, Elksar, November 20, 1911, Arch.AIU.XI.E.181.
144. Ibid.
145. In 1912 the AIU had three schools in Mogador: a boys' school in the *qasba*, a girls' school in the same quarter, and a boys' school in the *mellāh*. Eventually around 1890, the Board of Deputies created a boys' school in the *qaba* next to the Anglo-Jewish Association girls' school founded in 1886.
146. Stella Corcos to AIU, Mogador, May 12, 1902, Arch.AIU.E.602, in English.
147. Ibid.
148. "Morocco," *The Jewish Chronicle*, December 6, 1907, p. 11.
149. Ribbi to AIU, Tangier, July 25, 1901, Arch.AIU.LVII.E.935(c).
150. Ribbi to AIU, Tangier, February 28, 1904, Arch.AIU.LVII.E.935(d).
151. Ibid.

152. In Arzila, a town in the north, the *Alliance Française* school (coeducational) was attended by Jewish youths only. Some fifty of them were enrolled there after the AIU was reluctant the extend to that community its educational influence. (Ribbi, ibid.).

153. Ribbi, ibid.

154. Franco-Arab schools were created in Tangier, Casablanca, Mazagan, Rabat, and Mogador.

155. The Perrier school was perhaps the first legation-sponsored school in Tangier. This institution was founded in 1902 and named after its first director. More shall be said about the school below.

156. Ribbi to AIU, Tangier, January 21, 1910, Arch.AIU.IV.E.935(e).

157. Ibid.

158. France probably had a Franco-Arab school in every major port; Spain, Catholic missions, mainly in the north; there were several English schools, too.

CHAPTER III

The *Alliance* and the Struggle for Recognition within Moroccan Jewish Society

When the AIU entered Morocco in 1862 and opened schools in the major communities of the Sherifian Empire, its task was far from simple. It is true that the Jewish communities were eager to benefit from the political lobbying efforts of the organization on their behalf, but they were at first less disposed to help the schools flourish. In fact, the period preceding 1890 witnessed strong currents of opposition to modernization envisaged by the AIU.

The less than rapid adaptation to change in many Moroccan communities originated from old traditions. But sometimes, the opposition to the AIU was derived from the more intellectually oriented. Interestingly, some of the so-called *évolués* were also *protégés* of political powers, Jews who served the consulates and legations. The latter tended to support the languages and educational systems of the European powers they represented. They tried unsuccessfully to pressure the AIU to diversify its educational offerings, often seeking to please their European employers. Such tendencies, at times, erupted into full-scale confrontation between these elements and the AIU, causing the latter to threaten to close the schools.

Nevertheless, the most effective challenge to the AIU drew its inspiration from the traditional elites of rabbis and community leaders. Even in the more progressive communities of the ports and coastal towns, these influential people sometimes presented insurmountable obstacles to the schools, and, consequently, the AIU opened and closed schools with startling frequency during the first three decades of activities.

In order to neutralize the opposition of the traditionalists, it was necessary for Jewish culture to be disseminated in the classroom without neglect of secular education. At the same time, it was essential that Moroccan Jews be made to understand that overreliance on traditional education, offered at the rabbinic schools, was not appropriate to modern times. The AIU contended that in the absence of a sound secular education, which included the sciences, intellectual emancipation would fail. Nevertheless, in

order to fortify its influence, the AIU needed to exercise discretion in relations with the rabbis to make them feel that they were an integral part of the
schools' operation, dispelling notions that the AIU was alien and
undemocratic. This was sometimes difficult to achieve, for several school
directors, notably the ones who came from Europe, and the Ottoman Empire, refused to make political and educational concessions, or they belittled
local cultures.

A major concession, however, was made by the AIU in most communities from the outset: the maintenance of a balance of authority over
the schools. The Tetuan schools, as was pointed out above, were administered jointly by the AIU and the community. The latter provided
funds, recruited the rabbi-teachers for the AIU, helped find suitable school
buildings, and determined the amount of tuition. Eventually, this arrangement applied to most communities, though initially even these accomoda-
tions were viewed by the traditionalists with utmost suspicion. Although
they took an active part in administering the schools, the rabbis and lay
heads of the communities feared that their power might be challenged by
the AIU directors. Yet, as we shall see, not all rabbis and notables placed
obstacles in the way of the schools. With the passing of time, an increasing
number of these leaders rallied to the side of the AIU.

Opposition to the schools originally came into focus in Tetuan and
Tangier, the starting point for the organization's educational network.
Beginning in Tetuan, there was vociferous antagonism toward M. Gogman,
AIU school director, whom the rabbis accused of de-Judaizing their youths.
Gogman, on the other hand, complained that the greatest obstacles to the
schools were a handful of intransigent and intolerant rabbis who continuously pressured the parents not to send their youths to these centers of
impiety.[1] Gogman, however, was happy to reveal that the chief rabbi, Isaac
Nahon, offered his blessing to the schools. When Gogman appealed for
Nahon's intercession to neutralize the opposition of several rabbis, the latter
responded that he was in favor of seeing the community's youths frequent
the AIU schools.[2] Yet he did not think that there was much he could do to
weaken the opposition.[3] Writing to Crémieux, Nahon expressed his appreciation for the secular mission and for the advantage of European
language education.[4] Nevertheless, the chief rabbi hinted that the AIU had
to remain patient and cautious if it wanted to win genuine support for the
schools.[5]

In 1874 the opposition to the schools mounted with the death of Isaac
Nahon and the emergence of Samuel Nahon to the chief rabbinate. Strained
relations between Nahon and Gogman nearly led to the permanent removal
of AIU educational presence in Tetuan. Gogman found the rabbi to be
superstitious and a believer in the Zohar.[6] Certainly no fervent Talmudist
himself, Gogman indiscreetly interpreted Nahon's beliefs in theosophical

concepts as an anachronism and belittled him; when Nahon praised the Kabalist Shim'ōn b. Yōhay as a great figure in Jewish history, the director impetuously accused the rabbi of ignorance.[7]

From the that point on Gogman was at odds with the religious establishment, and if this was not bad enough, an additional incident made things worse. During a Hebrew lesson given by the director in June 1874, Nahon entered the classroom, apparently without advance warning, demanding that Gogman not use Kleine's grammar book in his lessons; Gogman appeared to have lost his cool and added an insult to the previous injury: "Klein knows Hebrew one hundred times better than you," he snapped; it appears that this was the straw that broke the camel's back: within a month, the boys' and girls' schools were forced to close down for several months.[8]

While it is difficult to discern who the real culprit was in the absence of Nahon's response in the archives, it is clear that the behavior of the director was questioned. Already in 1873, Drummond Hay informed Crémieux that the rabbis and Elders of Tangier had transmitted to him most deplorable accounts of the moral character of Monsieur Gogman, and that he, Drummond Hay, was of the opinion that retention of this person as director of the school in Tetuan would be most injurious to the welfare of that community; that it would be preferable to allow the youths to remain without education than for them to have such a man as an example.[9]

It is plausible that additional occurences may have contributed to the crisis. Once the school reopened — late in 1874 — and Gogman was reinstated as director, an editorial appeared in an Algerian newspaper, *L'Echo d'Oran*, in his defense, suggesting that Gogman was accused by the *junta* of teaching the youths about the rotation of the earth and informing them that there was no magic and that chemistry and physics were indispensable for the mind.[10] Such accusations may have been common in some communities; however, one cannot rule out that possibility that Gogman himself was behind the editorial, trying to clear himself of all wrong doing.

In Tangier Gogman's contemporary, S. Cohen, chose to pursue a more cautious line based on accomodation with community leaders. Becoming increasingly aware that full recognition for the AIU could not be achieved automatically, Cohen, who considered education and communal affairs to be an integral part of his public and private life, asserted that to antagonize the community would isolate the AIU and its personnel from the people, an error which he did not wish to commit.[11]

Yet in Tangier, too, problems had emerged. Warnings were expressed by Dr. Bernard Lévy after he had created the boys' school in 1864, that community leaders were challenging the authority of the teachers and openly interfered with the school's functioning.[12] According to Lévy, the rabbis and leaders attempted to reduce the secular school to a mere rabbinic school by significantly diminishing the European language program, and he did not hesitate to attribute partial responsibility to the Paris leadership. He wrote in 1865:

> You [the Central Committee] have treated the community leaders too gently. This is why they abuse the civilizing mission. You have confined the financial administration of the school largely in their hands and now they are contributing to the sacreligious act of interference in the school's affairs. If you continue in your laissez-faire policy towards the community leaders, I can promise you that in six months from now there will no longer be a school in Tangier.[13]

These were hardly prophetic forecasts. Perhaps the laissez-faire attitude of the AIU towards the community, if indeed there was one, was not conducive to the progress of the school. However, not only did the school remain open six months later, but a girls' school opened in 1865 as well. It appears that the AIU at the time could not alienate the rabbis in Tangier by curbing their administrative power. Once the AIU was more firmly entrenched in the community, efforts were made to minimize their role in the schools. Twenty-two years after the Lévy prediction, the boys' school finally closed down. The circumstances which led to the closing of the school, as related by the representative of the AIU alone, are complicated.

Rivalries in Tangier reached the boiling point during the mid-1880s between Moïse Fresco, then school director, and members of the community council, the *junta*. In 1885, Fresco attributed all the school's problems to a handful of influential rabbis and to Yahya Benassayag, a prominent leader.[14] Based on Fresco's account of the events, Benassayag was displeased with the boys' school because the AIU placed greater emphasis on profane than on sacred education, allotting little time for Hebrew and Judaic studies.[15] The community was particularly angry with the director for teaching the youths that rain was produced not by God but by vapor which forms clouds; Benassayag allegedly proclaimed that the youths were told that Moses did not part the Red Sea but instead was able to pass through because of the low water level: "It is like saying that God does not exist!" Benassayag supposedly answered; Fresco responded that he was not guilty of the accusations but insisted that the AIU was not a rabbinic institution and would not be transformed into one.[16]

Upon request from the *junta* twelve months later that more Hebrew be taught, Fresco suggested that the *talmūd tōra* within the AIU[17] become detached from the secular program and then the youths could attend two separate institutions: the AIU for secular learnings and the *talmūd tōra* for the sacred.[18] There is no evidence that the *junta* welcomed the plan. However, the Central Committee in Paris probably went along with Fresco's scheme, for he had funds at his disposal to implement it.[19] Sometimes early in

March 1887, he rented a building and detached the boys' school from the *talmūd tōra*.[20] Upon hearing of the event, community leaders were understandably enraged and mounted a fierce campaign against the director. So much so that Fresco grimly expected serious encounters, but insisted, Tangier was in need of a good lesson; the AIU had to clarify to the Tangerinos that they were in need of the AIU and not the other way around.[21]

The new school was in trouble. On March 17, Fresco reported that the *junta* had done everything conceivable to ensure that he had no pupils left; that the parents were called before the rabbis to refrain from sending their youths to the school; that they told them that the school is a center of atheism, and that their youths ought to attend the now separated *talmūd tōra*; that once the boys' school closed down French and general education would be offered in the traditional school.[22]

It seems that numerous parents supported the anti-AIU drive, mostly out of fear of defying the rabbis. Thus attendance at the AIU boys' school had dropped from two hundred pupils in early March 1887 to fourteen on March 14, to seven on March 16, to five on March 17.[23] The rabbis called for a *herem* (ban) on the school, and threatened to enlist all available support to disrupt AIU activities.[24] Fresco, similarly, threatened to enlist all available support to protect the school.[25] Unwilling to let the ship sink, he continued to direct a school attended by five pupils. On May 16 he had better news: attendance had risen to forty-one, an indication that the opposition was perhaps weakening.[26] Yet the Paris headquarters decided that the school was surviving on borrowed time and ordered the director to have it closed down. The school reopened in late 1887.

Interestingly, nothing was said about the girls' school which remained open throughout the crisis. A plausible argument for the continued existence of the school can be attributed to the fact that Hebrew and religious education in the formal sense of the word was not deemed as essential as for the boys. On the other hand, it appears that the boys' school faced opposition for yet another reason: the conflict between Fresco and Tangier leaders seemed to have rested on personality clashes and mutual indiscretion.

In November 1887 the boys' school reopened under a new director. To avert future clashes, Moïse Fresco was relieved of his duties and replaced by David Haym who succeeded in establishing an agreement with the community. It appears that the *junta* regretted the loss of the school and, consequently, during the negotiations for its reopening, the community gave in to virtually all the conditions imposed by the AIU. The agreement stipulated that:[27] the boys' school would be directed and administered by the AIU and not the *junta*; the school director would deal directly with the parents over the process of admitting their youths to the school, not the *junta*; the amount of tuition would be determined by the director, not the *junta*; and the community would be commissioned with the task of providing the AIU with the rabbinic personnel for Hebrew studies in the school.

These stipulations clearly defined the demarcation lines of influence, for some time, between what the *junta* and the AIU could or could not do. And one thing is certain: the AIU through its members—mostly teachers and directors of Turkish and Greek origins—had the upper hand in challenging the community leadership. Though these concessions did not automatically signify the end of ideological rifts between the two, they never again escalated into open hostility.

The attitude of Jewish leaders in Tangier toward the AIU underwent profound changes in subsequent years. In 1899, Mordechai Bengio, then chief rabbi, informed the boys' school director, Abraham Ribbi, that owing to the AIU the youths successfully procured lucrative commercial and administrative employment.[28] Moreover, Bengio conceded that the secular subjects, like the sacred, had to be taught at the schools.[29] Backing his assertion Bengio observed that it is well to combine Torah studies with some worldly occupation, for the energy taken up by both of them keeps sin out of one's mind.[30]

A similar situation developed in Tetuan during the years which followed the 1874 crisis. Samuel Nahon was still the spiritual head of the community, but he appeared to have undergone a change of heart about the AIU. In 1889 when Ribbi directed the boys' school in Tetuan, he met with a friendly Nahon. The latter requested that the AIU devote not less than two hours daily to Hebrew and informed Ribbi that the Central Committee had to understand the importance of tradition and quality Jewish education.[31] Yet to demonstrate his support for the schools Nahon acknowledged the importance of secular education, affirming that "half the time should be allotted to your [education] and the other half to God (*ḥesyō lākhem ve-ḥesyō la-Shēm*.[32]"

In Mogador, the AIU had opened and closed schools during the formative years of activities owing not less to pro-British sentiments among the notables than to rabbinic opposition. Yet despite the various opposition forces, the AIU had a most loyal ally. He was Joseph De A. Elmaleh, the chief rabbi, who ranked among the most venerable in modern Moroccan history. Elmaleh belived that the AIU was a vital agent for emancipation, and he corresponded with Crémieux to inform the AIU of the lamentable conditions of Moroccan Jewry.[33] He challenged the organization's president to help the Mogador community help itself through extensive education for girls, and was in favor of teaching them a trade.[34] A similar phenomenon applied for other communities of the coast, where rabbinic support was more easily obtainable.

Although the full extent of the opposition is not known, it is clear that the schools' popularity had increased in most communities before 1912. This was partly due to the steady decline of British influence in the coastal towns at a time when the French were making serious inroads into Morocco. French had become more important as the language of commerce and hence the AIU schools began to achieve greater prominence. In Mogador, the support for the AIU came even from the fiercest of its opponents, namely Reuben Elmaleh, who served as community president. He had been in the forefront of the opposition to the schools largely because of his intimate commercial and political ties with Britain. After nearly a generation as community president and opponent of AIU,[35] Elmaleh finally waved the white flag of surrender and explained in 1908 that most of the youths who graduated from the AIU in Mogador found employment rather easily as bank clerks at the French *Banque d'Etat*, in the various European post offices, and as representatives of European commercial enterprises; that all of these firms gave preference to the AIU graduates in their recruiting process.[36]

In Mazagan, a western coastal town, the AIU was urged since 1877 to create a school in the community, where, similar to Tangier but unlike Mogador, the Jews mingled to some degree with the Muslims due to the absence of a *mellāh*. In October 1877, the chief rabbi, Joseph Samuel Abulafia, wrote to Crémieux asking him to introduce intellectual stimulation into the community by creating a school, for he feared that Jewish children, roaming the streets, would become assimilated with the Goyyim.[37] In addition to sacred learnings, Abulafia encouraged Crémieux to introduce secular education and the study of European languages. The AIU did not make any commitments in Mazagan before 1900.[38]

Judging from this evidence, we find that the coastal communities were more receptive to the presence of the AIU than the communities of the interior. Unlike the interior and parts of the south, the Jews of the coastal and port towns came in more frequent contact with European commerce and ideas and hence were more willing to welcome the eduational doctrine of the AIU. Further, the religious intensity of the Jews of the interior was greater than that of the Jews in the coastal and port communities.

Looking into two examples in the interior, Fez, and Meknes, we find that Jewish traditionalism, similar to that of Islam, was firmly rooted in the lives of the Jews. It was in Fez that the rabbis, leaders, and the masses were suspicious of foreign concepts and often regarded their importation with contempt. While in Tetuan and Tangier the rabbis and leaders clashed with school directors, opposing overemphasis on secular education, even threatening to close the schools, they originally welcomed the schools' presence and, for the most part, the educational doctrine of the AIU. Despite conflicting interests, and personality clashes, the AIU and community leaders cooperated in financing the schools and expanding their size. Not so readily in the interior, especially in Fez and Meknes.

Although the AIU had to postone the creation of schools in Fez until the early 1880s due to Berber tribal unrest and the lack of consular representation—hence the absence of political security—Fez Jewry also displayed indifference to the creation of the schools and reluctance to collaborate with the Central Committee in promoting and maintaining them. Only years later, just prior to the establishment of the French protectorate, did the Jews show greater concern for the schools.

When Salomon Benoliel founded the boys' school in Fez (1883), the beginning was difficult. And if opening a boys' school was a difficult task, then the creation of a similar institution for girls was, for the time being, out of the question. The rabbis were still firmly opposed to this development, preferring, it not encouraging, young girls to marry in their early teens; he warned that if the school is to survive in Fez, the curriculum would necessarily have to gear the youths toward a sound Jewish education.[39] The morning school prayers, too, were meticulously observed by the director under the watchful eyes of the rabbis, so as not to arouse ill feelings.[40] However, regardless of such measures, the religious establishment in Fez remained suspicious of the secular teachers to the point where the rabbis found the liberal-minded director to be an atheist.[41]

Despite the foreseeable problems, Benoliel sensed that in due time the community would come around to recognize the importance of the AIU and would abandon their rabbinic schools, where in 1882 alone, some nine hundred and forty-five children received, in his opinion, a mediocre and pedagogically outdated education.[42] He predicted that the AIU would ultimately spark a revolution that will lead to intellectual enrichment through the dissemination of European languages and ideas.[43]

Enrollment in the Fez boys' school in the 1890s increased steadily and a girls' school was opened in 1899. Community support for the AIU eventually included rabbinic backing. In September 1903 Jacques Valadji, boys' school director, asserted: "In one of the synagogues where I lectured on the *Alliance*, the influential rabbi, Vidal Sarfatī, praised the schools. He then urged the congregation to send their children to our schools in significant numbers."[44] Several months later Valadji managed to win over rabbis Raphaël Abensur and Shlomo Aben Danan, whose importance rivaled Rabbi Sarfatī's.[45]

In Meknes, where Jewish orthodoxy was virtually uncontested and where religion was so deeply rooted in everyday life, the AIU encountered much criticism. A boys' school was created in the *mellāḥ* in 1901, but not before several previous efforts to do so failed. In 1901, the school's opening was achieved through Ribbi's efforts. It was directed by Jacques Valadji who, from the start, predicted that its survival would be brief, for the prevailing mood of indifference to secular education in the community was quite apparent.[46] He complained that he had hardly any support or encouragement

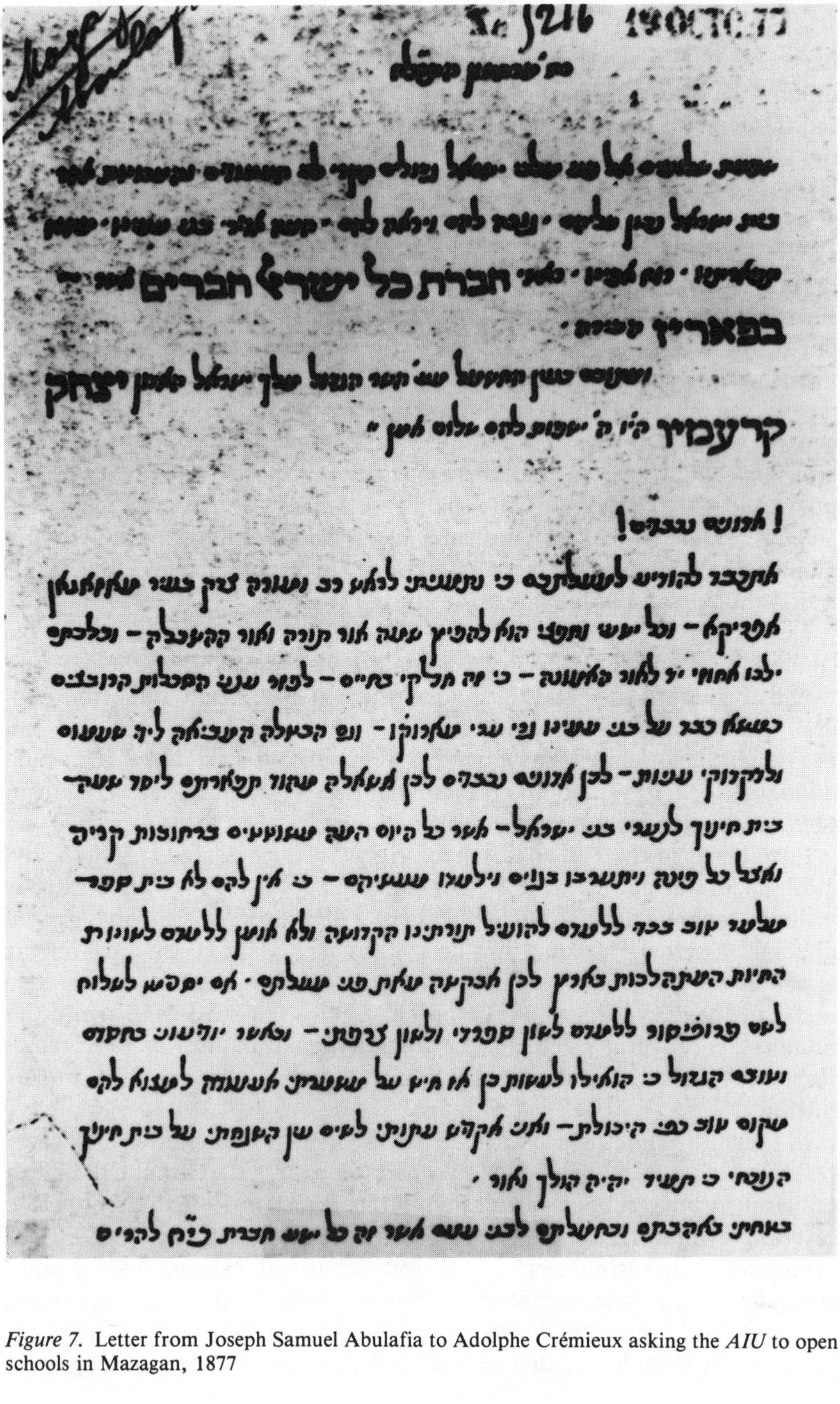

Figure 7. Letter from Joseph Samuel Abulafia to Adolphe Crémieux asking the *AIU* to open schools in Mazagan, 1877

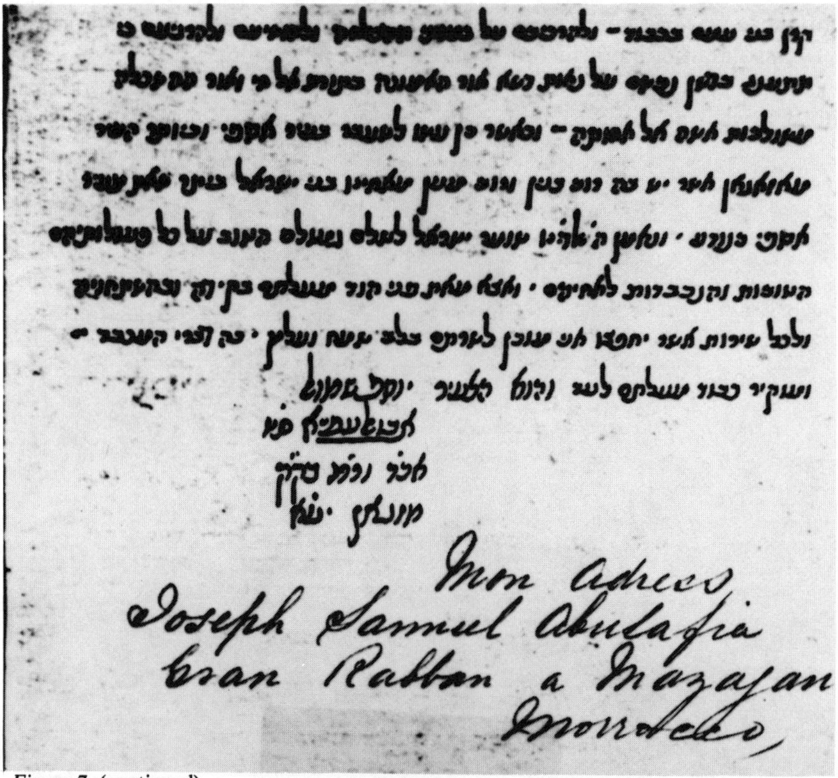

Figure 7. (continued)

from the parents or the leaders, whose council had been dissolved and whose powers were curbed by the rabbis.[47] The situation became precarious in 1903 due to the rabbis' dissatisfaction with the educational program, and the community's reluctance to share the financial burdens of maintaining the school. Consequently, as Valadji had predicted all along, the school closed its doors until 1912, when it was reopened upon the community's request.

Notwithstanding the setbacks in Meknes and other problems encountered elsewhere in the interior, the first decade of the twentieth century witnessed the rising star of the AIU in most communities. The importance of the French language and the training of the youth for lucrative employment in Mogador are two factors which were already pointed out. Speaking for Morocco as a whole, Albert Saguès, director in Casablanca summed up the situation well in 1909: the French political inroads into Morocco in recent years, the multiplication of business and commercial exchanges, the establishment of European merchant communities, the establishment of new financial enterprises all worked to the advantage of the AIU. As French influence was becoming predominent in the empire, the AIU was in process of consolidating its influence in the Jewish communities.[48]

Jewish communities which had AIU schools by 1900, usually preferred both boys' and girls' schools. We know that in Tangier, Tetuan, and

Figure 8. Teachers from the past: Abraham Pimienta

Mogador girls' schools were welcomed from the very beginning (there was an AJA girls' school in Mogador). However, the interior communities, particularly Fez, Meknes, Sefrou, and Marrakesh eventually welcomed such institutional innovations with no less enthusiasm. This was in view of the growing importance and demand for educating the girls. In 1912, on the eve of the protectorate, of the fifteen communities endowed with AIU schools, twelve had both boys' and girls' schools.[49]

The rising importance of the AIU is further indicated by the many demands of even the most geographically remote Moroccan communities that the AIU endow their *mellāhs* with schools. Analyzing the data for 1913, we can confirm that the Jewish communities not only welcomed the schools, but often surpassed the AIU in the contribution of subsidies to

Figure 9. Abraham Ribbi

maintain them, with the exception of the secular teachers' salaries, granted by the Central Committee. This was a clear indication of communal recognition (see table 1).

The tabulated data available in the bulletins of the AIU (table 2) for the period 1872 to 1912 confirms that the schools developed and that (a) enrollment rose from 995 in 1872 to 5,036 in 1912; (b) whereas only 310 girls were

Table 1. Alliance Enrollment and Schools' Subsidies (in francs)

Town	Number of AIU pupils	Local annual subsidies	AIU annual subsidies
Azemmour	164	2,124.00	3,306.15
Casablanca	557	21,683.70	7,290.00
Elksar	212	4,770.40	5,110.65
Fez	340	13,884.30	9,547.20
Larache	325	9,713.45	7,748.00
Marrakesh	413	6,768.70	10,675.00
Mazagan	260	7,959.60	6,269.00
Meknes	184	4,379.85	6,400.00
Mogador	785	4,423.50	8,050.00
Rabat	235	3,984.55	4,200.00
Safi	303	8,111.90	5,300.00
Tangier	674	31,930.00	11,300.00
Tetuan	697	14,806.00	6,105.25

SOURCE: *Bulletin de l'Alliance Israélite Universelle,* semestriel, 1913, p. 122.

Table 2. Years of School Network Expansion

Town	1872		1875		1878		1897	
	Boys	Girls	Boys	Girls	Boys	Girls	Boys	Girls
Azemmour	–	–	–	–	–	–	–	–
Casablanca	–	–	–	–	–	–	281	–
Elksar	–	–	–	–	–	–	–	–
Fez	–	–	–	–	–	–	164	–
Larache	–	–	55	–	45	–	–	–
Marrakesh	–	–	–	–	–	–	–	–
Mazagan	–	–	–	–	–	–	–	–
Meknes	–	––	–	–	–	–	–	–
Mogador	–	–	105	–	100	–	130	–
Rabat	–	–	–	–	–	–	–	–
Safi	15	–	–	–	–	–	–	–
Sefrou	–	–	–	–	–	–	–	–
Settat	–	–	–	–	–	–	–	–
Tangier	360	120	285	116	372	30	386	238
Tetuan	310	190	365	125	254	110	295	266
Total: (By Sex)	685	310	810	241	771	140	1256	504
Total: for both Sexes:	995		1,051		911		1,760	

SOURCE FOR 1872: "Notes sur les écoles fondée par l'Alliance en Orient et en Afrique" *Bulletin de l'Alliance Israélite Universelle,* semestriel, (1872) pp. 132–134.

SOURCE FOR 1875: "Écoles primaires et apprentis," *Bulletin de l'Alliance Israélite Universelle,* semestriel (1875) pp. 38–45.

SOURCE FOR 1878: "Détails sur les écoles," *Bulletin de l'Alliance Israélite Universelle,* semestriel (1878) pp. 21–23.

SOURCE FOR 1897: "Écoles préparatoires et primaires," *Bulletin de l'Alliance Israélite Universelle,* semestriel (1897) pp. 104–120.

Table 2 (continued)

Town	1901 Boys	1901 Girls	1905 Boys	1905 Girls	1907 Boys	1907 Girls	1912 Boys	1912 Girls
Azemmour	–	–	–	–	–	–	80	52
Casablanca	295	161	256	141	365	214	332	198
Elksar	–	–	–	–	–	–	103	–
Fez	103	80	175	82	218	95	276	127
Larache	128	67	159	105	213	122	285	–
Marrakesh	116	61	350	117	187	70	297	108
Mazagan	–	–	–	–	121	100	139	115
Meknes	61	–	–	–	–	–	174	50
Mogador	148	–	350	117	748	150	596	161
Rabat	–	–	–	117	76	–	107	111
Safi	–	–	–	–	148	66	134	74
Sefrou	–	–	–	–	–	–	65	45
Settat	–	–	–	–	–	–	75	–
Tangier	298	246	335	262	339	322	290	331
Tetuan	242	280	182	312	272	341	261	450
Total: (By Sex)	1391	895	1807	1253	2687	1480	3214	1822
Total for both Sexes:	2,286		3,060		4,167		5,036	

SOURCE FOR 1901: "Statistiques des écoles et de l'apprentissage," *Bulletin de l'Alliance Israélite Universelle*, semestriel (1901) pp. 128–141.

SOURCE FOR 1905: "Table des écoles par pays: Maroc," *Bulletin de l'Alliance Israélite Universelle*, semestriel (1905) p. 116.

SOURCE FOR 1907: Arch. AIU. Maroc. XLII.E.717(b). Rabat. October 18, 1929.

SOURCE FOR 1912: Arch. AIU. Maroc. XLII.E.717(b). Rabat. October 18, 1929.

enrolled in 1872 the figure was nearly six times larger in 1912; (c) in 1872 the AIU had five schools in Morocco, in 1912 there were twenty-seven schools. Moreover, the expansion of the network is best seen in the period beginning with 1897, when both the number of youths and schools—notably in the north, west, and the interior—grew steadily. In the pre-1897 era, the schools and their clientele did not progress as steadily, owing to the opening and closing of schools, political instability, desertions of young people from the schools to aid their impoverished families, migrations, emigration, and long-term absence from the schools. Enrollment shifted back and forth in this period. Moreover, for various reasons, the AIU did not create schools in key towns like Casablanca before 1897, despite local readiness to participate in the task. The progress since 1897 confirms earlier assertions that the AIU did emerge as a powerful and recognized force around 1900. Yet despite this important progress, the AIU did not succeed in undermining the strength of the rabbinic schools before 1912.

We know that some parents preferred to send their youths to both the rabbinic and the AIU schools simultaneously. Others sent theirs to the traditional schools first and only when the youths, in their judgment, acquired sufficient religious training, were they permitted to enter the AIU.

There was yet the category of youths whose parents refused to send them to the AIU altogether. The latter two categories gave added strength to the rabbinic schools.

Figure 10. Moïse Nahon

Let us look at the data on comparative enrollment. In the Nahon reports for 1906, on Fez, Rabat, Tetuan, and Mogador, the only available data on the subject, we find that (a) in Fez, 218 youths attended the AIU boys' school whereas 306 attended the rabbinic schools;[50] (b) in Rabat, 150 youths attended the boys' school whereas 240 attended the rabbinic counterparts;[51] (c) in Tetuan, 175 youths attended the AIU boys' school whereas 250 attended the traditional schools called *esnoguitas*;[52] (d) in Mogador,

310 attended the boys' school in the *qasba*, and there is no data for the boys' school in the *mellāh* created at about that time; as for the rabbinic institutions, 125 attended the *qasba* schools and 350 attended the ones in the *mellāh*.[53] In Mogador there were 475 at the rabbinic schools, 310 at the AIU.

Figure 11. Salomon Benoliel

It seems that the Nahon statistics are incomplete and cover perhaps *some* of the rabbinic schools, for in Fez alone, a vital traditional Jewish center, there were hundreds of youths enrolled in rabbinic institutions. Yet even the partial data suggests that the rabbinic schools were better attended than the AIU. Only in the protectorate era did the trend of youth enrollment favor the AIU over all other schools. The pre-1912 period set the stage for this enormous expansion.

Figure 12. Adèle Israël

Notes

1. Gogman to AIU, Tetuan, December 29, 1871, Arch.AIU.LXXVII.E. no file number.
2. Ibid.
3. Ibid.
4. Isaac Nahon to AIU, Tetuan, March 29, 1872, Arch.AIU.VI.B.25. (in Hebrew).
5. Ibid.
6. Gogman to AIU, Tetuan, July 10, 1874, Arch.AIU.LXXVII.E. no file number.
7. Ibid.
8. Ibid. The girls' school headed by Gogman's daughter closed down, too.
9. John Drummond Hay to AIU, Tangier, May 12, 1873, Arch.AIU.XXVII.E. no file number.
10. Gogman to AIU, Tetuan, December 29, 1874, Arch.AIU.LXXVII.E. no file number.
11. S. Cohen to AIU, Tangier, May 12, 1873, Arch.AIU.LII.E.858.

Figure 13. The founding of the *AIU* schools in Mazagan, attended by Europeans, Jewish and Muslim leaders, 1907

12. Bernard Lévy to AIU, Tangier, May 14, 1865, Arch.AIU.LV.E.903.
13. Ibid.
14. Moïse Fresco to AIU, Tangier, November 30, 1885, Arch.AIU.LIII.E.874.
15. Ibid.
16. Ibid.
17. Apparently the community-sponsored religious school in Tangier became part of the AIU boys' school at an undisclosed date and constituted a school within a school.
18. Fresco to AIU, Tangier, November 21, 1886, Arch.AIU.LIII.E.874.
19. Ibid.
20. Fresco to AIU, Tangier, March 3, 1887, Arch.AIU.LIII.E.874. There is actual evidence that the AIU had at its disposal a building to which it had intended to move in February 1887, but it was not clear if the community would have agreed to separate the *talmūd tōra* from the new school. See Fresco to AIU, January 31, 1887, Arch.AIU.LIII.E.874.
21. Fresco to AIU, March 3, 1887, ibid.
22. Fresco to AIU, Tangier, March 17, 1887, Arch.AIU.LIII.E.874.
23. Ibid.
24. Ibid.
25. Ibid.
26. Fresco to AIU, Tangier, May 16, 1887, Arch.AIU.LIII.E.874.
27. Ribbi to AIU, Tangier, November 20, 1889, Arch.AIU.LVI.E.934(a).
28. Ribbi to AIU, Tangier, July 13, 1899, Arch.AIU.IV.B.24.
29. Ibid.
30. Ibid. Bengio quoted the statement by Rabban Gamliel, son of Rabbi Judah ha-Nasi (Pirqē 'Avōt 2,2).
31. Ribbi to AIU, Tetuan, May 10, 1889, Arch.AIU.LXXI.E.1044(c).
32. Ibid.
33. Joseph De A. Elmaleh to AIU, Mogador, January 28, 1875, Arch.AIU.III.B.14. (in Hebrew).
34. Ibid.
35. Reuben Elmaleh was particularly fond of the Board of Deputies schools before coming to support the AIU.
36. Reuben Elmaleh to AIU, Mogador, March 25, 1908, Arch. AIU.III.B.14.
37. "Goyyim" may refer to either Christians or Muslims: in this case, reference is to the latter.
38. Joseph Samuel Abulafia to AIU, Mazagan, October 19, 1877, Arch.AIU.II.B.10.
39. Benoliel to AIU, Fez, October 31, 1888, Arch.AIU.XIII.E.214(b).
40. Ibid.
41. Ibid. Benoliel wrote in dismay: "Ne peut-on pas être réligieux sans être athée?"
42. Benoliel to AIU, Fez, October 15, 1882, Arch.AIU.VI.B.27.
43. Ibid.
44. Jacques Valadji to AIU, Fez, September 9, 1903, Arch.AIU.XIX.E.307.
45. Valadji to AIU, Fez, December 9, 1903, Arch.AIU.XIX.E.307.
46. Valadji to AIU, Meknes, July 22, 1903, Arch.AIU.XXXII.E.561.
47. Ibid.
48. Albert Saguès to AIU, Casablanca, January 30, 1909, Arch.AIU.VIII.E.155.
49. *BAIU*, semestriel (1913), p. 122.

50. Nahon to AIU, Tangier, June 28, 1906, Arch.AIU.LV.E.913.
51. Ibid., June 15, 1906.
52. Ibid., March 22, 1906.
53. Ibid., May 1, 1906.

CHAPTER IV

The *Alliance* and Its Sociocultural Influence on Moroccan Jewry

1. The Educational, Social, and Cultural Basis of the Schools: Ideologies and Actions

Some Light on the Early Educational Experiment: 1862–1903

When the AIU established its embryonic educational network, there was no clearly defined program for its schools. The archives, include lists of courses offered, but not information on the precise nature of the curriculum and its duration in number of years. Certain essential points, however, seem quite clear. No primary school certificates were issued by the AIU or any other educational institution in Morocco before 1909; that time the French legation under Regnault's patronage, launched a primary school certification program. Prior to 1912, the AIU schools were purely elementary without any efforts by the Central Committee to develop a postprimary educational program. It was in 1903 that the AIU published its first official manual under the title of *Instructions Générales Pour les Professeurs* and only after that date can we determine the correlation between the AIU schools in the Balkans and the Muslim world on the one hand, and the French educational curriculum of the *métropole*, on the other.

In Tetuan, which symbolized the cornerstone of early AIU activities, the schools offered the following program in 1873:[1]

Boys' School	Girls' School
French	French
Arithmetic	Arithmetic
European Geography	European Geography
Biblical History	Biblical History
Hebrew	Hebrew
Spanish	Spanish

From this embryonic program we learn several things: first, no local Moroccan history and geography were taught in the early years of educational activities; second, Spanish was taught to meet local needs in a community which was overwhelmingly of Castilian ancestry and where Judeo-Spanish was spoken; third, Literary Arabic, was not taught; fourth, the program did not include English, though it was offered in the years immediately following the creation of the school; finally, considering that girls' schools were still few to begin with, in Morocco of the 1870s, the girls' school curriculum, besides profane education, included courses in Hebrew and Judaic studies. Until 1862, only the boys went to school, the rabbinic ones, to become versed in the knowledge of prayers and to prepare for the Bar Mitzvah at the age of thirteen.

The Tetuan school of the 1870s appeared to have offered only some of the courses taught in the schools of the *métropole*. Subjects such as moral education, object identification lessons,[2] singing, drawing, and penmanship, were absent from the curriculum.

It is questionable whether much attention was focused on French language and literature during the formative years of AIU activities in the north, because of the presence of a sizable portion of Jews of Spanish ancestry. In 1863, only scant attention was paid to French in Tetuan while Spanish was the language of instruction; gradually French instruction became more important.[3] Similarly in Elksar, in 1879 French grammar was absent from the curriculum.[4]

It has been indicated that the AIU introduced English and Spanish into the curriculum of the northern and coastal towns where they bore direct political, economic, and cultural relevance. English courses were offered at the AIU in Tangier, Casablanca, Mogador, and, temporarily, in Tetuan. This program was subsidized by Anglo-Jewry through the Board of Deputies and fed British aspirations for political and cultural influence in the strategically vital coastal towns. For AIU graduates in Tangier, Casablanca, and Mogador, knowledge of several European languages — English, French, and Spanish — was a great asset: it enhanced their role as effective commercial intermediaries between the Muslims and the Europeans.

A reasonably well-balanced program was offered at the Fez boys' school during the 1880s. It was there that the AIU applied its activities to meet local traditional needs while, at the same time, offering courses which were taught at the schools of the *métropole*. In 1884, the program in Fez had the following features:[5] (a) early morning prayers before class; (2) lessons in arithmetic between 8:00 and 10:00 A.M.; (3) French language, composition, and penmanship between 11:00 A.M. and noon; (4) Arabic grammar and literature, accompanied by translations of texts into French, between 1:00

and 2:00 P.M.; (5) Jewish education and Hebrew, taught by the rabbis who were salaried by the community. They taught biblical history, the *haftārōt*[6] (sing. *haftāra*), *gemārōt* (sing. *gemārā*)[7], biblical recitals, and their translations into Judeo-Arabic.[8]

Unlike some of the early schools, the Fez institution taught French from the outset. Other languages such as Spanish were not included in the curriculum, not a surprising phenomenon considering that while Fez Jews were of Spanish ancestry, they had forgotten their Spanish and were influenced by Judeo-Arabic culture. English did not serve a purpose primarily because Fez was not essential from the commercial point of view. Further, given the already mentioned Berber unrest, there was no influx of Europeans coming to the interior and thus commercial activities were inevitably discouraged.[9] Indeed, unlike the coastal towns, Fez could hardly boast of thriving European colonies in the preprotectorate era and consequently, even though French was taught at the boys' school in 1884, it did not serve a significant purpose, for with whom could the children converse?

The reports on the AIU schools since 1884 provide insight into the courses taught. For instance, the history program at the Tangier boys' school in 1886 was divided into the medieval, modern, and contemporary periods. For the medieval period, the pupils were taught about the information of European city-states, the exploits of Charlemagne, the medieval emperors, and the Hundred Years' War.[10] For the modern period, the accent was placed on the military conquests of the Spaniards and the Portuguese, the Renaissance, the Protestant Reformation, France under Louis XIV, the English revolts, the Russian Empire, the Prussian Hohenzollern family, the Indies, the United States, and the partition of Poland.[11] For the contemporary period, emphasis was put on the French Revolution and its impact. Some attention was shifted to the Ottoman Empire, the Sherifian dynasty as well as nineteenth-century Egypt.[12]

It was Eurocentric to expose the youths to events relating to the Hundred Years' War, the Prussians, and the partition of Poland. Such events were remote from their surroundings. On the other hand, one could argue that progressive notions of the French Revolution and human sufferings in the Russian Empire which included the Jews, were relevant, for they promoted Jewish solidarity with their coreligionists in other parts of the world.

One should not automatically reproach the AIU for underplaying the importance of Moroccan history and culture. The teaching of the history of the Moroccan people was not effectively represented in the curriculum of all Moroccan schools, traditional or modern. This anomaly may be attributed to the unavailability of historical literature suitable for children at the elementary school level. Perhaps in the more intellectually advanced Qarawīyīn University of Fez, more emphasis was placed on Moroccan history within the greater context of Islamic culture. Nevertheless, the AIU made some sincere efforts to teach local history based on limited data.

In 1894, for example, the directress of the Tangier girls' school prepared lessons on Moroccan history. In view of the absence of books on the subject she wrote compositions on the backgrounds of the Berbers and Arabs and distributed them as reading material.[13] Similarly, Isaac Benchimol, a Moroccan-born teacher in Tangier reported in 1890: "I am thinking of preparing a study on the traditions and customs of the Arabs. The reason for this stems from the need to educate the Jews of this country about their Muslim neighbors of whom they know little."[14] Indeed, whereas the Jews knew spoken Arabic (*darija*), they hardly knew the *fuṣḥa*, literary Arabic.

Arabic was not taught systematically and regularly at the AIU schools,[15] for there were few qualified individuals capable of offering such a program. From the archives, one may conclude that during the preprotectorate period Arabic was temporarily taught in Fez, Tangier, and Casablanca. The problems of teaching Arabic were threefold: first, there were not enough qualified Arabic teachers among the members of the AIU; second, while the AIU tried to recruit qualified teachers from the *makhzan*, few Muslims were eager to teach in Jewish schools; third, very often the parents gave preference to the learnings of European languages, for they felt that in view of Morocco's exposure to Western influence, these language rather than Arabic would benefit their children in finding lucrative employment.

At the Fez boys' school Arabic was offered to a selected number of youths whose parents were favorably disposed to the idea.[16] The director taught the course himself in 1888 for quite some time, but was replaced by a Muslim who served as a consular agent for France.[17] Moïse Nahon, an ENIO graduate and native of Tangier, emerged as the most firm advocate of Arabic education at the AIU. In 1892, while serving as assistant-director in Tangier, Nahon reported that when he directed the Fez school (1889–1892), he personally taught Arabic. Believing that Arabic education ought to be expanded, he structured a similar program in Tangier.[18] As part of the program, Nahon used the Arabic text of *Arabian Nights* and strongly urged the Central Committee to send him Arabic literature and grammar books to develop the program.[19]

His insistence on teaching *fuṣḥa* was based on his desire to bridge the ethnic gap between Jews and Muslims; he firmly believed that Arabic would contribute immensely toward that goal.[20] Nahon was also in love with the language, impressed by its melodic tones and similarity to Hebrew.[21]

In Casablanca, the boys' school director, Samuel Daniel Lévy, promoted Arabic education in 1900 upon assuming direction. He found a qualified teacher in the community to offer the course 5½ hours weekly[22] in order to disseminate the written language. Lévy's intention to promote Arabic was tied to European commercial interests in Casablanca: the youths had to be versed in that language so they could engage in written correspondence with Muslim merchants. According to Lévy, Jewish merchants in Casablanca had carried out business transactions with Muslim merchants from the interior.[23]

Until 1903 most school directors had a free hand in preparing the curriculum, with little interference from the Paris headquarters. However, much of this changed in 1903 when the AIU published its teachers' manual, setting the rules for the structural composition of the educational program.

The Formalization of the Secular Program: 1903-1912[24]

As the 1903 manual (*Instruction Générales Pour les Professeurs*) shows curriculum was tailored to fulfill the requirements prescribed by the French public school system. Generally, it was in accordance with the seven-year program of the *métropole*, evolving around the outline shown in table 3. Though, theoretically, the elementary model applied to most AIU schools, this was not the case in Morocco where, with the exception of Tangier, the schools were on a six-year basis with only one upper year instead of two, prior to graduation. Similar to the elementary school program in France, the AIU curricular model can be seen in table 4.[25] The exceptions to the French model curriculum were the offering of biblical and postbiblical history; the continuation of the mixed foreign language programs which included Spanish and English; and the teaching of Hebrew and, occasionally, the language of the country, in which case Arabic was taught.

Table 3. The Curriculum Structure: 1903

AIU Classes[a]	Designation in French	Designation in English
Fifth	Preparatoire	Preparatory
Fourth	Elementaire I	Elementary 1st Year
Third	Elementaire II	Elementary 2nd Year
Second A	Moyen I	Middle 1st Year
Second B	Moyen II	Middle 2nd Year
First A	Supérieure I	Upper 1st Year
First B	Supérieure II	Upper 2nd Year

SOURCE: Paul Silberman, *An Investigation of the Schools Operated by the Alliance Israélite Universelle from 1862 to 1940*. Ph.D. dissertation submitted to the School of Education of New York University, 1973, p. 49; *Instructions Générales Pour les Professeurs*. Paris, 1903, p. 84.
[a]Some of the elementary schools of the AIU in Morocco and elsewhere had, prior to the preparatory level, a kindergarten program as well.

Table 4. The Subjects Taught at the AIU: 1903 (Hours per Week)

Subjects[a]	Grades 2-3		Grades 4-7		Grades 2-7	
	Mini-mum	Maxi-mum	Mini-mum	Maxi-mum	Mini-mum	Maxi-mum
Post-Biblical History	0	0	1	2	1	2
Biblical History	1	2	1	2	1	2
Hebrew	5	10	5	10	2	2
French Reading	6	10	5	8	4	5
French Language	6	6	5	6	4	4
Arithmetic	2	3	3	4	2	2
Geography	2	3	2	3	1	1
History	1	2	2	2	1	1
Science	1	1	1	2	1	1
Object Lessons	2	3	2	3	2	2
Penmanship	2	3	2	2	2	2
Language	5	10	5	10	4	5
Singing	1	1	1	1	1	1
Drawing	0	0	1	2	1	1
Physical Training	1	2	2	2	1	1

SOURCE: Silberman, p. 91; *Instructions Générales*, pp. 49–50.
[a]Sewing, knitting, embroidery and manual education was offered in some of the schools of Morocco, though not all of them.

The offering of biblical and postbiblical history was considered a unique innovation by the Central Committee, brought into the program of the AIU at a time when such courses were nonexistent in the curriculum of the European Jewish schools.[26] As for biblical history, it was supposed to have been taught by the rabbis from the kindergarten to the fourth grade and included the best-known biblical stories which were narrated to the children or translated to them from the text; during the first two years, some of the most important historical events through the fall of the Kingdom of Israel and Juda were taught; in grades two to four, the material was supposed to cover the dispersion of the Jews by the Romans and the moral and literary greatness of the Jewish Prophets; some basic notions about the Talmud were essential parts of this program.[27]

The teaching of postbibilical history was theoretically reserved for the school directors rather than for the rabbis. The AIU covered the postbiblical program in either one or two years, surveying the following: the Babylonian captivity, the period of the Second Temple, the Roman conquest, the age of the Talmud, the origins of Christianity, the pre-Islamic *jāhiliyya* period and the emergence of the Prophet Muhammad.[28] It included the contribution of the Jews to literature and medicine, the Jews in

Spain and their golden age, French Jewry, Rashi,[29] the Spanish Inquisition and the expulsion of Castilian Jewry as well as Jewish life in Europe. Finally, it dealt with the Renaissance, the Protestant Reformation, the influence of the Jewish Bible on Protestantism, the Jews in the Ottoman Empire, the *Haskala* movement and Jewish enlightenment, the French Revolution and its aftermath, the rapid integration of French Jewry into the general society, and the emergence of the *Alliance Israélite Universelle*.[30] As to supplementary languages, mainly Spanish, English, and the occasional teaching of Arabic, it is doubtful whether the course schedule structure of the manual was strictly adhered to.

The 1903 manual did not include vocational and agricultural training; nor did it speak about the creation of evening courses. These programs were usually independently structured by the school directors. Already in the preprotectorate period, the AIU set up a number of manual workshops in various Jewish locations (see below). The evening course programs were more widespread and easier to organize, particularly with the penetration of Europeans into the country. This development aroused the desire of Jews to learn European languages and acquire a general education, whatever their age.

Thus, for example, in 1904 the director of the Marrakesh boys' school created an evening course which offered French, arithmetic, Jewish history, hygiene, penmanship, and geography.[31] Two years later, out of sixty students attending the courses there were merchants, tailors, glass manufacturers, grocers, and European post office employees; their ages varied between fifteen and forty-five, an interesting cross-section of the professionally active elements of the Marrakesh community.[32]

The formalization of the curriculum in 1903 was not accompanied by any kind of a certification program. Instead, the AIU relied on noncertified graduation examinations conducted by consular representatives, European businessmen, and scholars. Only in 1908, after the French legation in Tangier decided to promote certification programs for its schools, and had come to consider the AIU schools an important force in the propagation of French, the CEPE (French primary school certificate) was introduced into the AIU and the Sherifian Empire for the very first time. Regnault, the French minister, believed that this process would help institutionalize French cultural influence in Morocco and had the *Quai d'Orsay's* blessings.[33]

The AIU, however, though not firmly opposed to the presentation of its own candidates for the certified examinations, did not believe that the project was particularly beneficial, and Secretary Jacques Bigart contended that the AIU schools were not designed to prepare youths for an elementary certificate; he, moreover, feared that a certification program initiated by the French legation could infringe on the schools' curriculum as prescribed in the teachers' manual of 1903.[34] Yet it quickly appeared that there was no cause for anxiety: the French legation apparently found that the candidates of the AIU schools were highly qualified. So much so, that the excellent performance displayed by these candidates during various examinations, helped boost the prestige of the AIU in the eyes of the French.

The CEPE examination was first launched by the French legation during the second half of 1909 with the participation of the AIU and consular-sponsored schools.[35] The examination, conducted by the legation, and confined to Tangier and Casablanca, was by no means a "popular" program, for the candidates who were permitted to register belonged to two basic categories: those originating from French families residing in Tangier and Casablanca; and Europeans and "assimilated" elements, which included Jewish and Muslim *protégés* whose parents had intimate ties with the European legations. This category did not only confine itself to the *protégés*. Some Moroccan Jewish youths, who were neither *protégés* nor naturalized citizens of a European power, participated in the examination.[36] How they came to be accepted for candidacy is not known.

The 1909 examination was divided into two parts, the written and oral sections. It began with a written dictation followed by a composition in French; questions were raised by the examiners based on the contents of the dictation and composition to judge the candidtates' analytical aptitude. This was supplemented with two or three questions in arithmetic and the metric system. Subsequently, the candidates were examined in history, geography, moral education, and on elementary notion of the sciences and their application.[37] For the girls there was an examination in dress design and needle work, while for the boys there was an examination in drawing and geometrical designs.[38] Table 5 describes the examination plan.[39]

The results of the examination were transmitted to the French legation by members of the examination commission, composed of Henri Regnault, an inspector of French education, consular functionaries from the French legation, the president of the *Alliance Française* in Tangier,[40] and members of the French colonies in Tangier and Casablanca.[41] The best-written compositions in French were those submitted by the candidates of the AIU and ranked on the level of nine and ten on the scale.[42] All in all, thirty-two candidates presented themselves for the certification examination sessions in both towns: twenty-one of them were Jewish (from the AIU), eleven were European Christians, and only two were Muslims.[43]

As for the performances of the candidates of the AIU in Tangier and Casablanca, the coeducational Perrier school of Tangier, and the Petermann coeducational school of Casablanca, the following is noteworthy: whereas 80 percent of the AIU candidates from Tangier passed the examination (eight of the ten candidates), 75 percent of the Perrier school (six of the eight candidates) were successful; in Casablanca, 100 percent of the

Table 5. CEPE Examination: 1909

	Course Description	Time Allotted for the Examination	Maximum Grade Given
The Written Examination	Ortography:		
	(a) Dictation	20 Minutes	5
	(b) Questions on the Dictations	" "	5
	Arithmetic	One Hour	10
	Composition & Analysis	" "	10
	Dress Design & Needle Work (for females)	" "	10
	Design & Drawing (for males)	" "	10
The Oral Examination	Reading & Recitation	1/4 Hour	10
	History & Geography	1/4 Hour	10

AIU candidates (eleven pupils) passed, while 66 percent (two of the three candidates) of the Petermann school performed successfully.[44] What is more, the data indicates that the Muslim candidates were underrepresented, which raises some room for speculation: were the French unconvinced that Muslims did qualify for educational certification? Did they not consider Muslims "progressive" or "assimilated" even among *protégés*? It appears that the 1909 and subsequent preprotectorate examination sessions were rather selective. The French legation appeared to have adopted a policy of attracting candidates from elements most sympathetic to French presence in Morocco: the Jews and the European residents.

For the Jews, the CEPE was no ornament, for this diploma served as a valuable passport for AIU graduates to secondary education in the *lycées* of France and Algeria on the one hand, and the newly established *lycée* of Tangier, on the other. It enabled them to develop into an elite nourished by an emerging French cultural presence. For their part, the French were impressed by the AIU and the elite it was creating and consequently they encouraged the organization to develop its own network of postelementary education.

The AIU and the Strategy of Secondary Education

Through AIU representatives in Tangier, the French legation urged the Central Committee to develop a program known in France as the *cours complémentaire*, representing a form of postelementary program that followed the primary school certificate. The *cours complémentaire* actually served as the first cycle of the French high school (*lycée*) level and led, after four years, to the diploma of *brevet elémentaire*. The fourth year of the *cours complémentaire* was the equivalent of the eleventh grade of an American high school.[45] Then followed an additional three years which completed the second cycle of *lycée* education and led to the *baccalauréat*, certifying the completion of secondary education.

Those who completed the four-year cycle of the *cours complémentaire* could cease their studies and find employment in administrative positions, particularly during the protectorate period. Those who did continue to attend the second cycle at the *lycées*, obtained the *baccalauréat* and sometimes continued their higher education in France.

French encouragement of the AIU to create *cours complémentaires* was the beginning of a process which materialized only during the first two decades of the protectorate era.[46] While in 1911 the French legation in Tangier and their *lycée* attempted to structure a *cours complémentaire* program in the AIU schools in that town, all efforts were abortive.[47] It was intended to be a three-instead of a four-year plan; moreover, the program was based purely on the French curricular model, not focusing attention on Muslim civilization or Jewish education; too much consideration was given to French Algeria and French colonial expansions in the Muslim world in both the history and geography programs.[48]

The *Ecole Normale Israélite Orientale*: A Teachers' Training School.

It has been noted that during its formative years the AIU recruited Europeans to teach in the Moroccan schools. Since the mid-1860s, however, the AIU decided to create a normal school which would draw its teachers among the graduates of the primary schools. In 1867, when the AIU schools already stretched throughout Morocco and much of the Ottoman Empire, an institution for these schools' graduates was created in Paris, known as the *Ecole Normale Israélite Orientale* (ENIO), and it started to train youths from Turkey, Greece, Palestine, Morocco, Iraq, and Bulgaria. In Morocco, a sizable portion of the teaching staff came from the Middle East and did not enable their Moroccan counterpart to halt this trend for quite sometime.[49]

The ENIO was created owing to the generous contributions made by European Jewish philanthropists, and was divided into a girls' institution, known as *Institut Bischoffsheim* and a boys' division, known as *Ecole d'Auteil*.[50] The curriculum for both divisions was based on a four-year program leading to the *brevet supérieur*. While some of the school's graduates preferred to obtain the advanced *brevet*, others obtained the elementary counterpart after two years and were dispatched to teach in the primary schools of the AIU. However, to become a director or directress of a school an advanced rather than an elementary *brevet* was required, and it was not at all uncommon for teachers to return to the ENIO to complete the four-year program.[51]

The Moroccan-born graduates of the ENIO found it a valuable experience to spend several years in Paris, their first direct encounter with French civilization. However, the AIU faced numerous obstacles in bringing Moroccans to study in France, for unlike the more assimilated Jewish communities of Turkey and Greece, the Jews of Morocco were initially apprehensive about sending their children to France. Those who did frequent the ENIO, were exposed to the historic landmarks and intellectual circles of the *métropole*; they were usually chosen by the school directors among the most gifted youths.[52] Eventually, the ENIO graduates—Moroccans and other Middle Eastern Jews—emerged as an integral part of the elite of the AIU and contributed substantially to the social and political welfare of Moroccan Jewry.

The admission to the ENIO rested on the choice and recommendation of the school directors, while the selection of the female candidates depended largely on parental consent, as the latter were reluctant to send their daughters to Paris and thus the number of girls who went to France was rather small at first. Those who did go to Paris usually reacted favorably and became strongly attached to French culture.[53]

The Moroccans reacted favorably to their training at the ENIO. For example, Salomon Benoliel, reminiscing about his experience in Paris, noted that while undergoing training he breathed the air of liberation, was in contact with new ideas, and experienced quickly the shock produced by new intellectual trends of Paris during the 1870s, all of which were lacking in Morocco.[54] In 1888, as boys' school director in Fez, Benoliel promised to reduce parental and communal opposition to sending their children to Paris, and argued that since the ENIO enhanced his career, he would promote the institution in Morocco.[55]

There was yet another obstacle in the way of sending candidates to the ENIO. Once the parents agreed to send their children to France, they were often financially handicapped and did not have the means to pay for travel expenses, for according to the 1903 manual, the candidates for the ENIO, who could be no less than fourteen years old, had to have their parents finance the trip to France, while the AIU would provide the trainees with dormitory facilities, food, and clothing.[56] Nevertheless, deviations from the rule became common due to the large number of trainees from Morocco originating from humble socioeconomic backgrounds and, therefore, the AIU allocated funds to finance the trip of outstanding youths.[57]

At the ENIO trainees were exposed to the idea of Jewish solidarity, to human rights modelled on the French revolutionary concept of *droit de l'homme*, and to philosophical aspects of education necessary for teachers planning to serve Jewish communities. In short, they were trained in a secularly oriented normal school, one which opened for them avenues to French and European civilization and culture, yet they received training with emphasis on Jewish social work and Jewish pride, a phenomenon which was totally absent in other teachers' seminaries of the *métropole*. (Table 6 outlines the ENIO program.)

Upon completion of training, the young teachers were assigned to posts in the Mediterranean-basin countries. It has been suggested that native Moroccan teachers did not enjoy in their own communities the same level of prestige as their counterparts recruited from the Ottoman Empire who were teaching in Morocco. Therefore, Moroccans were intentionally selected to teach in countries other than their own, usually in the Middle East where, moreover, being separated from their families was a source of strength as opposed to weakness.[58] This argument is only partly true. In the first place, the archives attest to the great respect bestowed on indigenous teachers: Salomon Benoliel, Amram Elmaleh, Samuel Daniel Lévy, Moïse Nahon, Isaac Benchimol are only few examples. They were respected because of their roles as protectors of the Jews and as outstanding and progressive

Table 6. ENIO Program for 1913-1914

First year	Hours	Second year	Hours	Third year	Hours	Fourth year	Hours
Hebrew	4	Hebrew	3	Hebrew	2	Hebrew	2
Jewish History	2	Jewish History	2	Jewish History	1	Jewish History	1
French	7	French	3	French	3	French	1
History	2	History	2	History	2	Literature	1
Geography	2	Literature	1	Literature	1	Literature	2
The Sciences	2	Geography	1			Economic Geography	1
Arithmetic	5	Sciences	2	Geography	1	History	1
Geometry	2	Arithmetic	2	Sciences	2½	Ancient History	1
Drawing	2	Geometry	2	Psychology	2	History of the Orient	1
Music	2	Drawing	2	Arithmetic	3	Sciences	2
Penmanship	1½	Music	1	Geometry	2	Gymnastics	1
Gymnastics	2	English	1	Drawing	2	Geometry	1
		German	1	Music	1		
		Spanish	1	Gymnastics	1		
		Gymnastics	1	English	2½		
				Spanish	2		
				German	2		
				Arabic	2		
Total weekly	33½	Total weekly	25	Total weekly	32	Total weekly	15

SOURCE: André Chouraqui, *Cent ans d'histoire: l'alliance israélite universelle et la renaissance juive conemporaine (1860–1960).* Presses Universitaires de France, 1965, p. 457.

leaders. Second, with the passing of time, the AIU increasingly recruited Moroccan-born Jews into the ENIO in order to train them to teach on their native soil. To avert challenges to their authority, the Central Committee sometimes preferred to employ Moroccan-born teachers in towns other than their own, in places where they were less known but where their influence could develop.[59] In the long run, Moroccan and non-Moroccan teachers alike were equally judged by their communal activities and contributions.

2. Jewish Traditional Education

One of the most crucial problems facing the AIU was the continuous struggle waged by its teachers with the traditional schools. Whereas certain members of the rabbinic establishment initially expressed their reaction to the AIU by characterizing its schools as "centers of impiety," the organization's teachers referred to the *talmūdē tōra* as "centers of reaction," where intellectual expression and independent thinking was deliberately absent from the educational program. The youths frequenting these schools were described by the AIU as lacking all qualities of innovation, where biblical verses were recited along with the rabbi-teachers without the accompaniment of textual interpretation, and where Hebrew was taught without a sound grammatical basis. The AIU, moreover, considered the rabbi-teachers to be intellectually underqualified for their tasks.

In the traditional Jewish schools of Morocco, the AIU discovered crowded rooms in synagogues packed to maximum capacity with children sitting on the floor in a circle with their rabbi in the center. The representatives of the AIU contrasted the overcrowded classrooms with the spacious modern schools, contending that the youths did not respect their rabbis since the latter lacked proper authority over them; and they pointed out with some resentment that while parents conceded that French should serve as an essential medium of communication, the youths were often sent to the rabbinic schools first before transferring to the AIU. Consequently, numerous children entered the AIU schools in their teens.[60]

However, AIU teachers sometimes tended to oversimplify their assessment of the *talmūdē tōra* and showed blind indifference to the importance of the traditional milieu. In depth exposure to European education and pedagogy at the ENIO, particularly among Turkish and Greek teachers, often rendered them insensitive to old customs and institutions. Realistically speaking, the rabbinic schools were extremely vital to the Moroccan communities from the point of view of education and acculturation, even if they needed pedagogical and curricular renovation. The latter were divided into two types of institutions:[61] (1) *talmūdē tōra* — situated in community-sponsored buildings and attended mostly by underprivileged youth, including orphans; (2) *ṣlās* were not tuition-free and were analogous to the *ḥadārīm* that dotted the Jewish communities of Eastern Europe. The youths who frequented these two categories of schools were usually between the ages of three and thirteen, and it was the parents' responsibility to pay the rabbi-teachers' salaries. To these one may add that the affluent preferred to pay a rabbi who served as a tutor to their children in the privacy of their home; he taught them the prayers, and Hebrew and Judaic studies.[62]

The educational program of these schools consisted of: reading the letters of the Hebrew alphabet aloud (the letters were carved on stone or wooden boards and displayed by the rabbi-teachers); reading the Hebrew vowels; combining the letters of the Hebrew alphabet for the purpose of articulating words correctly; and articulating the word without spelling it.[63] This was usually begun after two or three years, once the children were able to read from the printed text.

After an additional three years, the children entered the next level known as *al-ʿabrān*, intensive Hebrew education, which included the studying of the *teʿāmīm* or cantilation.[64] Here the pupils were divided into two groups: the first group learned the graphic signs of the cantilation in a melodic tone, while the second group was required to study biblical chapters, analyze them, and translate biblical passages; the translations were done in either Judeo-Arabic, Judeo-Spanish, and sometimes in Judeo-Berber, depending on the geographical location of the communities and their makeup.[65]

The major aims of elementary Jewish education were to give the youths an understanding of synagogue culture, to guide them in the Jewish traditions, and to prepare them for the Bar Mitzvah and manhood.[66]

Although rabbinic schools were for boys, girls were still required to know and observe the traditions. Much of their education was obtained in the household, where their mothers and the elder women taught them to observe *kashrūt* and other important procedures in the preparation for Jewish holidays, the *Shabbāt*, and various festivities.[67]

Rabbis and members of the religious elite attended the *yeshīvōt* were served as sacred normal schools and for the formation of religious leaders, the financial maintenance of which rested on to philanthropists and funds available to the community councils.[68] The teachers at the *yeshīvōt* were usually the most reputable rabbis, and it was customary to name a *yeshīva* after its most venerated educators.[69] It was from the *yeshīvōt* that generations of rabbis and community servants emerged, and included the members of the religious and intellectual corps, the *mōhalīm*, the *shōhatīm*, and the *dayyānīm*, the Jewish tribunals' judges.

In addition to the study of the functions of circumcision, the slaughter of meat, and Jewish Law, the *yeshīvōt* provided extensive education on the oral and written Torah, its Rashi interpretations, Talmudic tracts, the

Shulḥān 'arūkh,[70] and on a variety of aspects relevant to Jewish holidays and customs.[71]

The teachers of the *talmūdē tōra* and *slās* were usually not part of this elite. They often did not even frequent *yeshīvōt*, a fact which partly strengthened the allegation of AIU teachers that they were not adequately prepared for their task. In comparing the status of the rabbi-teacher with that of his AIU counterpart, it should be stressed that the position of the former was quite tenuous. He lived in extreme poverty and frequently seized the first opportunity to desert his post for more lucrative employment in another sector of the economy. Though often employed for the AIU as well as for the religious schools, the rabbi-teacher never enjoyed the level of prestige gradually acquired by his ENIO-educated counterpart among the Jews as a community leader and protector, as a mediator in local disputes, and as a reformer.

3. Educational and Sociocultural Ideas and Activities of the AIU

The Ideology of Education

The AIU schools in the Middle East and North Africa based their ideological tenets on several crucial factors. In the 1903 instructions manual, four basic tenets were prescribed for the teachers. In the first place, the idea was to instruct less and teach more. The flooding of the youths' minds with an overabundance of factual material was counterproductive. Instead, students were expected not merely to learn facts but to draw conclusions from them by understanding their significance. Object lessons, for example, required them to apply their creative capacity to interpret the materials.[72] This innovation, creativity, and analytical interpretation were important to the teaching process.

The second tenet urged that education be patterned in such a way as to elevate the spirits of the youths, to make them feel that they were in a friendly atmosphere, where the teachers were like substitute parents.

Third, the very presence of the secular school imbued in the tradition of European education signified the need to eradicate bad habits, selfishness, exaggerations, superstitions, unlimited lust for material goods, and excessive pride. According to the AIU manual, these factors were viewed as common attributes of Mediterranean Jews.[73] This was obviously the main purpose of the French colonial advocacy of the need for a civilizing mission among Muslims, Jews, and Christians of the Middle East and North Africa: the need to conquer their minds "morally."

Finally, the AIU considered the inculcation of the virtues of love for country, humanity, truth, and respect for public property as a vital mission.[74] This last tenet included the promotion of Jewish solidarity, an *esprit de race*, but also of religious toleration toward non-Jews. As for Jewish solidarity and religious toleration, the AIU made significant inroads. In many cases the teachers broke the barriers which prevented Jewish solidarity by urging Moroccan Jewry to help their less fortunate coreligionists. Thus we learn that even the most economically impoverished communities collected funds for Russian Jewry before and after the pogroms of the 1880s and 1905.[75]

Moïse Nahon wrote in 1896 that the community of Tangier was ideologically divided into the categories of traditionalists, who frequented the old schools, and the progressives, their modern secular counterparts.[76] The traditionalists conceptualized the modern world in medieval terms. They were less inclined to open their eyes to reformist ideas concerning the toleration of non-Jews. In Nahon's view, the AIU served as a catalyst in Tangier and elsewhere in Morocco for developing new outlooks fo toleration among the youths.[77] Nevertheless, this process was not always successful. The mutual and age-old Jewish-Muslim-Christian animosities were prevalent in places like Tetuan, where members of the three religions could be found in substantial numbers: Jews of Castilian ancestry, Muslim Arabs and Berbers from the Rif, and Spanish Catholics. Nahon, who in 1906 inspected the Jewish schools in Tetuan, observed that he was unpleasantly surprised to hear from the youths attending the AIU that they must be proud of being Jewish because their Sabbath is more important than the Catholic Sunda ; that God prefers Jews over all people and the Messiah will appear to redee n the Jews and only the Jews.[78]

In more prog ressive communities, the teaching of toleration had become more efficacious with time. Whereas the traditionalists were often too prejudiced to come in contact with Muslims and Christians, save perhaps for business reasons, the graduates of the AIU were more inclined to do so. In Tangier the results were far better than in Tetuan, and Nahon explained in 1896 that while it was once common to never pronounce the name of a stranger without heaping on him unkind comments, Tangier witnessed a process whereby Muslims, Christians, and Jews had the best of relations, particularly when members of the three faiths were alumni of the AIU.[79]

Tangier, however, was a special case, for there were no physical barriers between Muslims and Jews. As no *mellāh* existed, and as graduates of the AIU collaborated closely with the teachers to bridge ethnic and social gaps by maintaining amicable ties with the population, the work of the AIU was greatly facilitated. Part of this success was attributed to the AIU's open-door policy for youths of all religions. In 1906, of the three hundred youths attending the boys' school and three hundred and twenty attending the girls' school, forty Catholics were enrolled in the first institution and forty in the second.[80]

From time to time Muslim youths, too, were represented at the AIU, notably in the coastal towns. Most of them, however, despite an open-door policy, chose not to attend, and only a handful, youths coming from affluent families, welcomed the schools. Nevertheless, the absence of discriminatory practices earned the teachers respect in the Muslim world. One expression of support was voiced by Shāhīn Makāryūs, a Christian intellectual living in Egypt during the first decade of the twentieth century. Makāryūs admired the integrational policy of the AIU, asserting, moreover, that it prevented religious questions and beliefs from interfering with the educational process (*bi-qat' al-naẓr 'an masā'il al-i'tiqādāt al-dīniyya*).[81]

In another area, the AIU attempted to remove the Jews from the confines of their local atmosphere through the modern school. Attention focused on youths living in unsanitary and crowded *mellāḥ*s, to free them of ghetto culture and its insulated atmosphere[82] by removing them from the rabbinic schools and by increasing their contacts with nature. The teachers argued that the rabbinic schools offered a set of rigid and complex religious practices, leaving no time for the youths to play and inhibiting their contacts with nature. The youths saw narrow streets and filth but rarely trees, flowers and animals.[83] To escape this atmosphere, they needed worthwhile distractions in the colorful Moroccan countryside and the benefit of physical and vocational education.[84] Further, while in the traditional school youths spent countless hours bending over interminable and incomprehensible texts,[85] in the modern school they were temporarily freed from their *mellāḥ* culture through reading French literature suitable to their age, notably Jean de La Fontaine's fables, dealing with nature, trees, animals.[86]

However, AIU teachers were not unanimously in agreement on this point, for some of them realized that La Fontaine's fables were reflections of a sophisticated society ruled by Louis XIV and hence not always applicable to the children of the *mellāḥ*. Interestingly, Israël Pisa, director in Casablanca, explained this position eloquently in 1906, contending that in Morocco education had to differ from education in the developed nations: the young should not be taught about their counterparts in France, who belonged to the affluent bourgeoisie, and enjoyed pretty clothes and pleasant games; they would be better off learning about the somber conditions of their coreligionists in the Russian Empire, with whom they shared unfavorable conditions. Familiarizing them with their counterparts in far away lands would surely contribute to Jewish solidarity.[87]

Promotion of Cultural Activities

The policies of the AIU included the creation of school and community libraries, and the encouragement of school theatrical plays based solely on

European cultural traditions. Beginning with libraries, the director of the AIU in Tetuan observed in 1876 that he created the first French library ever to exist in this community and urged the Central Committee to send additional literature. Among the works available at the new library were Zeller's *Histoire d'Italie*; Fleury's *Histoire d'Angleterre*; Duruy's *Histoire Universelle*; Dauban's *Histoire des temps Modernes*; Schwab's *Histoire des israélites*, and Duruy's *La Révolution de 1848*.[88] In the literary section, the works included *Oeuvres de Molière* and *Oeuvres de Lamartine*.[89]

In Casablanca, when Moïse Nahon founded the AIU school in 1897, he created a French library just as he did in Tangier during the early 1890s, which included the following works: Bert's *Deuxième année d'enseignement scientifique*; Reinach's *Histoire des israélites*; and Hoeffer's *Histoire de l'Afrique*.[90] When Samuel Daniel Lévy assumed direction of the school in 1900, he expanded the library to include such works as Bianconi's *Maroc*, Corneille, *Théâtre*, Graetz, *Histoire des juifs*, and Zola, *Paris*.[91]

These and other works were sent by the AIU headquarters or through generous contributors in the French Jewish community and the French consuls in Morocco. At the same time, works in English were sent to Tangier, Casablanca, and Mogador, where the AIU taught English, by Anglo-Jewry through the AJA and the Board of Deputies, or through such figures as Drummond Hay who supplied the Tangier schools with works of Shakespeare.[92]

The promotion of theatrical plays was an undertaking that helped propagate European, mainly French and Spanish culture, among the Jews. The teachers directed and produced these plays while the youths performed, mostly before a mixed audience composed of the Jewish and European communities. During the nineteenth century, the plays served an important purpose: at the time there were relatively few Europeans in Morocco and when the latter settled the urban centers of the north and the western coast, they longed for cultural events, so they would attend the *soirée théâtrale* programs promoted by the schools. The plays were largely based on such literary works as Ratisbone, *Dieu Fait Tout*, Victor Hugo, *Les pauvres gens*, and Bertin, *C'est la faute au Homard*.[93]

Philanthropy and Social Reforms

The AIU encouraged its graduates to form alumni associations. The latter began to flourish in the preprotectorate period to supplement the activities of the school directors. Its members, under the guidance and auspices of the AIU, sponsored philanthropic and social action on a large scale, and together they succeeded in creating and financing food and clothing programs for the community's poor.

To illustrate, in 1885 the AIU in Tetuan was the major contributor of funds for youths coming from poor homes, providing them with food and clothing.[94] In the coastal towns and the interior, the AIU allocated considerable sums of money to aid the poor: in 1905, therefore, the Central Committee voted thousands of francs to be distributed among needy youths in Marrakesh, Mazagan, Azemmour, Mogador, and Casablanca.[95] It was also in 1905 that the AIU adopted a policy of active participation in the feeding of indigent youth, whether they attended the AIU schools or their rabbinical counterparts.[96] At times, these activities extended beyond the schools to include the communities at large once they were afflicted by a variety of disasters ranging from Berber unrest to hunger and starvation. Thus, in 1903 the Jewish community leaders of Debdou, a small town in the south, appealed to the AIU for emergency relief following local unrest that left the Jews hungry and, in some cases, homeless. Despite the absence of an AIU school in Debdou, the Central Committee channeled the needed funds to the Debdou victims through Abraham Ribbi in Tangier.[97]

This activity was accompanied by much-needed sanitary education in the community, where, especially in the unhealthy *mellāhs*, disease was common. In Mogador, the director of the boys' school applied special head creams to contain ringworm prevalent among the youths.[98] Similarly in Tetuan, Ribbi, who directed the schools in 1887, organized an antismallpox vaccination program, and owing to his efforts, there were only a few people afflicted by smallpox in the *mellāh*.[99] The teachers' devotion to the communities in this sense compared with the efforts of the Christian missionaries of the Middle East and Africa. They developed the reputation of physicians and healers, especially in the pre-1912 period when qualified physicians were rare. In 1906, when visiting Rabat, Nahon observed that Joseph Conquy, the AIU director, served as that community's physician who was awakened at all hours of the night to rescue the sick and the disabled and, during a typhus epidemic, Conquy saved many lives through immunization programs.[100]

Social reforms became a pivotal factor in the activities of the AIU not merely within the confines of the classroom, but equally in the area of extraeducational policy. This was certainly the case regarding the status of the women. In Morocco, the Jewish family was patriarchal, the father being the central dominating figure, exercising authority over all members of the household. Family arrangements, marriages included, were his responsibility, and under his guidance the daughter was married, usually through his intercession with the groom and his family. This process was implemented without seeking the bride's consent.

In the household, the role of the women was largely confined to bearing children and housekeeping, responsibilities which often began early. Unlike the northern communities, where the Castilians were more inclined to grant the woman important responsibilities, or in the rural *bled* of the southern

Atlas, where the women were actively involved in agricultural pursuits and the artisan crafts, the Jews of the interior and parts of the south believed that the man was the most useful member of the family, for he worked and earned money. Further, it was in the interior that girls were usually married in their early teens, and those among them who were unmarried at the age of fifteen or sixteen were characterized as old maids.[101]

To counter child marriages among girls, the AIU sought ways to create as many girls' schools as possible, to keep girls in school until their middle and late teens. In Fez, Claire Benchimol, a directress, contended in 1900 that the way to stop child marriages and prevent the continuous emergence of *mères enfants*, was to keep them in school as long as possible despite parental resistance to the idea.[102] She envisaged that the AIU would be more effective among the girls of poor homes than among those of the affluent strata, for already in 1900 when the girls' school was in existence for only one year, Benchimol discovered early that poorer girls attended school regularly whereas their wealthier counterparts were absent more often.[103] Although the latter paid their tuition while the poor girls did not, they often deserted the school for marriage. Being wealthier, they were prime candidates for marriage and did not remain single for long.[104]

To further combat child marriages effectively, the AIU promoted conferences and dialogues with the leading rabbis of Morocco, urging them to adopt rigorous measures against this practice, notably in Fez where the teachers played an active role in this domain. In 1897, for instance, Joseph Bensimhon, boys' school director in Fez found that the Jews considered the abrogation of child marriages contrary to the Jewish religion. He spoke with the chief rabbi, Shlomo Aben Danan, on this matter, outlining various options to challenge the practice.[105] Aben Danan, however, suggested that the intervention of the AIU and the chief rabbis of France and Palestine would doubtless have a positive effect on the community, since Fez leadership respected the advice of their coreligionists in Europe and Palestine and consequently, this should serve as a solution.[106]

Aben Danan's attitude indicated that even an influential rabbi was either afraid or unwilling to challenge the practice in his community. Rather than bring the issue in front of the rabbis and community council and risk a confrontation, he referred it back to Bensimhon, advising outside intervention. On the other hand, Aben Danan was characterized as the culprit by a directress in Fez who, in 1907, accused the rabbi of consenting to the marriage of one of her pupils to his nephew; and Aben Danan himself was about to marry off his son to a girl not yet in her teens.[107]

To reinforce local AIU activities, the organization's leadership in Paris intervened against child marriages. In 1903 Secretary Bigart wrote to Mordechai Abensur, an influential Fez rabbi, urging that the Jews do away completely with the practice and pointing out that the most renowned

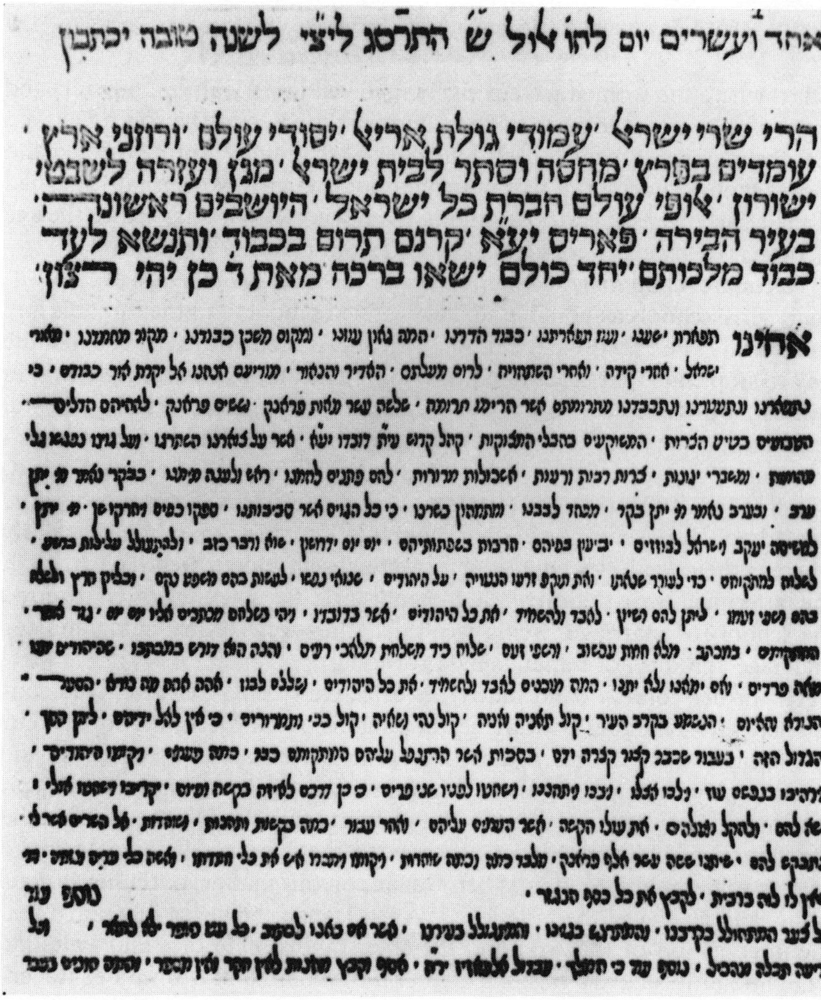

Figure 14. The Debdou letter of Community leaders, thanking the *Alliance* for economic assistance to the community's poor, 1903

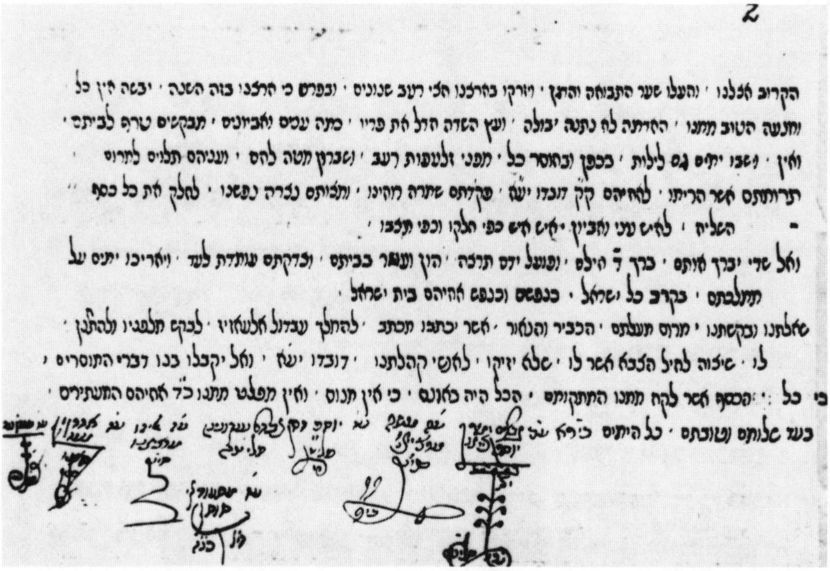

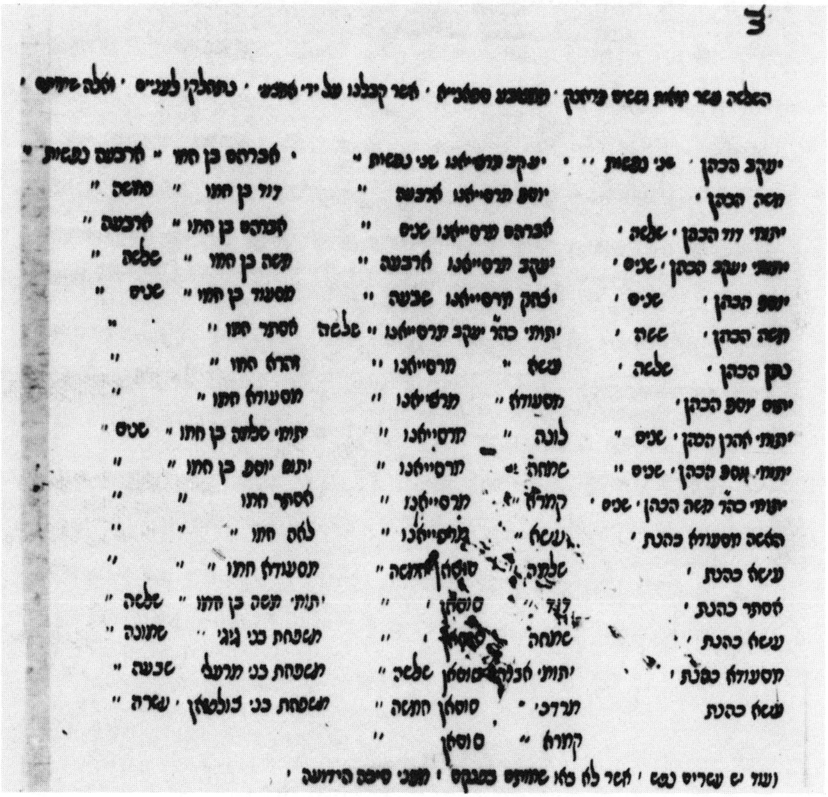

Figure 14. (continued)

טפשת שלומים · וברכות מרומים יחולו של ראם ראשי אלפי
ישראל · בחורי פרי מערים שליון · פנות צבאות קרושים ·
חברת כל ישראל · אימת ה' קשמרים · וכאגה פמן קשארידסי· יחיו
חיי שוב · ועשם מושד אכבר

· **אדונים יקרים !**
אחר שפעת התיים והשלום ·
המן קערות · ותשואות

יון יון · אנו עמבים מול פן תדידים של עוב לבב · ורוח נדכתף ·
והסגוחים שלנו · בכן התהלה כמטבנו תרע בזה המן · כי אספתו
צרות רבות ורשות · וקשה מבלל הצ תרעב האיום והנורא· הן
מצב חפרין כים קשה · יון עשב יוקר הקשרים · אשר לא היא
מעולמים · כי טפקי הפשר בכל דבר · עד לאשור · הקמת קרוב
לשלפה בליון · לליאשא אימן · פמן יין קרוב לפפה בליון ·
כשר תמאה בליון · וכל הקשרים קובפל של חד חמם · ורין
הקומן מספיק לכלכל גרוינו · ופם אטי כיתינו לאלים ולרבים·
וברשוינו הרעב הולך וחזק מאר · וכמו עשר בנפשינו · כי נפף
תזיונינו · ותלאות לבינו · אשר שמו מספר · אם כל אנמי יאור מי
אחור · פאקיס יגדלו · ולהבל ארוך יפותלו · לא ימורו את כל
התלאה אשר מצאתנו · לכן שמו פנט כחלמים · ופטכנו פיתה לפני
ידידינו אהובינו · מסיו **יעקב** ואלארנ ה'ו · המשארל בכל
עוו ותשומות · כהצלית · את נערי בן ישראל · בצלית
השודפ · והפלגו תשנה לפנו · לשפוך שימנו לפני גדולי עולס ·
רחמנים בנ רחמניס · ויהי כראותו צרת נפשינו · וירא ארץ
שאינו · וחת לחצגו · נבמרו רחמיו אלינו · שכך נקון לחם בשדנו
וישע אל מצלות כיב צוק מחסורינו · יגמלהו ה' כצדקו כ"ר

Figure 15. The leaders of the Fez Jewish community thanking the *Alliance* for contributions for providing food and eliminating hunger caused by a drastic rise in the cost of living, 1903

Talmudists were fervently opposed to such policies.[108] Despite the combined efforts of the teachers and the Central Committee little progress was made before 1912 to weaken the practice. Only during the protectorate period did the AIU made headway in this direction, with wider community support.

By structuring vocational programs such as sewing and dressmaking in workshops annexed to the schools, the AIU tried to improve the situation of the girls. The Central Committee followed this policy due to considerable and consistent pressure from the directresses.[109] Generally, though notions pertaining to educating the girls won gradual adherence even in the interior, Ribbi, when he visited Meknes in 1901 claimed that Jews had said: "If a man teaches his daughter Torah [it is] as if he teaches her [something] improper." (*kol hammelamed bittō Tōra ke'illū melamedāh tiflūt*).[110]

Education and Migration

The promotion of Jewish solidarity by the AIU, was partly reinforced by the schools' policy of struggling against communal disunity in Morocco.

This problem became particularly acute during the second half of the nineteenth century, when the AIU first extended its influence to the Sherifian Empire.

After 1850 there was a gradual but steady migration of Jewish families from the interior and the south to the coastal towns, a development that emerged from the need for the Jews of the inland communities and the rural *bled* to find refuge in towns with a European political presence. This search for security was understandable: the Jews sought to escape the arbitrary authority of the *qā'ids*, on the one hand, and the feudal or semifeudal arrangements imposed on them by Berber chieftains, on the other. Moreover, despite certain lesser migrations from the south to Fez and Marrakesh, economic insecurity for both Jews and Muslims in the interior and the south encouraged both elements to seek better living and employment opportunities in Tangier, Mogador, Casablanca, and Rabat. In these important coastal and port towns these Jews also aspired to take part in commerce, encouraged by the emerging European economic presence. It was there that economic transactions could not be easily hampered by tribal tensions.

Tetuan, a most important community, lost much of its wealthy population, who relocated in Tangier and Casablanca.[111]

Migrations coincided with the penetration of the AIU to Morocco, and as migrations clustered Jews of diverse backgrounds into different communities, the schools served as an important unifying force of elements otherwise indifferent to each other. Indeed, the migration from one town to another was found to have considerable effect on the place where the Jews settled. For example, in Settat, seventy-five kilometers from Casablanca, the Jewish population in 1910 was divided into two categories: the Jews who were native of Settat, mostly shopkeepers and small merchants, and the *shleuh*, (sing. *shilhī*), Jews who in recent years migrated to Settat from the Atlas mountains, and claimed to be descendants of Hebrew tribes that came to Morocco before the start of the Christian era.[112]

In Settat, however, the Jews were apparently not getting along well. In the first place, the *shleuh* spoke Judeo-Berber; the original inhabitants of Settat, on the other hand, spoke Judeo-Arabic.[113] The two groups became so segregated from each other that they dwelled in two separate *mellāh*s, demarcated by a major street.[114]

A more familiar problem existed between the Jews of southern Morocco, the Castilians, and the Jews of the Judeo-Arabic and Judeo-Berber culture, scattered throughout the interior, the south, and the coastal towns. Once again, linguistic barriers and diverse customs of the various migrants constituted an obvious obstacle to the integrational process. The Spanish Jews looked down on the rest, insisting on their cultural superiority.

Given these circumstances, the AIU focused its attention on the promotion of unity among the heterogeneous Jewish elements, and by preaching the need for Jewish solidarity, the AIU helped integrate the youths of the migrants with local youths. The best sources on the subject are Moïse Nahon's inspection reports from 1906, when he was entrusted by the AIU with the task of determining the schools' progress. During his tour of Marrakesh Nahon observed that the Jews, who though largely of Spanish ancestry had forgotten their Spanish and were assimilated into the Judeo-Arab scene, were recently supplemented with migrants from the *bled* of the Atlas, notably from Kasba Tadla.[115] They invaded Marrakesh and the coastal areas, contributing to the heterogeneity of the student body in the recently created AIU schools and, according to Nahon, the numerical importance of the Judeo-Arab-speaking Spanish Jews was diminishing in favor of the *shleuh.*[116] He stated that the Marrakesh schools were the rallying points in which the diverse elements united under one roof. He also pointed out that of two hundred eighteen youths at the boys' school in 1906, only one hundred and eight were natives of Marrakesh; sixty-two were *shleuh* of migrant parents; and forty-eight were born in the *bled* prior to migration.[117]

During his tour of Fez, Nahon found that the Jewish community in 1906 consisted of 1,528 families with 700 youths of school age;[118] the AIU schools were attended by youths of recent Jewish migrants from Debdou, Sefrou, Taza, and Tafilalt, most of whom were of Berber backgrounds.[119] However, the dominant element of Fez Jewry remained the Spanish ancestors who assimilated Judeo-Arab culture and vernacular. The schools, in Nahon's opinion, were instrumental in unifying these elements under one roof despite the deep-rooted differences among them.[120] The idea was to involve the AIU schools as centers for integrating the younger generations, minimizing their cultural and ideological differences.

In Tangier, where the AIU's activities mirrored the success of the school network, the town was relatively unimportant before 1850 in so far as Jewish numerical representation is concerned. Since then, however, the community increased in size significantly, partly as a result of the influx of migrants. The latter came to Tangier seeking military, political, and economic security in the presence of the Europeans. As a direct effect of this influx, the AIU schools were so to speak, invaded by youths of migrants from the interior. In 1906, the girls' school had one hundred thirty-nine pupils of Spanish ancestry while seventy came from other communities; the boys' school had one hundred fifty-four pupils from Tangier while one hundred twenty were born to migrant parents, recent arrivals.[121]

In Rabat, another attractive center for migrants, the schools were composed of migrants from Fez, Meknes, Marrakesh, the Atlas *bled*, Salé, Boujad, and northern Morocco, mainly from Tetuan.[122]

In Casablanca and Mogador, migration trends were particularly pronounced. In 1906 Nahon discovered in Casablanca that the schools were frequented by only thirty-four children of Casablanca parents, while seventy-five were migrant youths from the north, twenty-three from the Atlas, twenty-six from Marrakesh, forty-four from other parts of the interior, and eighteen from unspecified places.[123] An important development occurred: by sitting together in the same classroom the diverse elements developed the habit of speaking French, and it was this language that united them and helped eliminate linguistic and communication barriers, thus contributing to the reconstruction of the community for future generations.[124]

In the short run, however, the difficulties of integration were far from over in the case of Casablanca. The biggest obstacle involved the Castilians from the north who spoke Judeo-Spanish and the Judeo-Arabs from the interior. In 1902, the boys' school director remarked that the schools were entrusted with the task of employing a rabbi-teacher for youths from the north who was versed in Judeo-Spanish, and another who was versed in Judeo-Arabic.[125] Considering that teaching Hebrew and biblical studies often required translations of texts, the parents insisted that it be done in the language of their tradition and, to avert a crisis, the AIU in Casablanca complied.[126]

Finally, in Mogador, Nahon discovered that this southern coastal town absorbed numerous migrants from the Sūs valley in the Ante-Atlas area. Unlike migrants from the interior or from Tetuan, these elements lacked the thorough Talmudic traditions and were deprived of the great *yeshīvōt*; they could hardly boast of famous rabbinic dynasties or venerated theologians.[127] Though no data are afforded by Nahon, it appears that these Jews were well represented in the schools alongside the natives of Mogador, mostly Castilians and other migrants from the interior and the south.[128]

The Background to Vocational and Agricultural Education in the Schools

During the last three decades of the nineteenth century, the AIU explored the possibilities for introducing vocational and agricultural training into the schools. When the AIU first entered Morocco, its representatives discovered that the Jews were divided into diverse occupations, mainly artisans, small and large-scale merchants, moneylenders and peddlers. According to Eliezer Bashan's very important and thorough study on Jewish craftsmen in Morocco, there were seven types of professions which they practiced, not including commerce or finance. There were: (a) *metal workers*—including gold and silversmiths, producers of silver and gold threads used for the manufactor of clothing and shoes, blacksmiths, and weapon manufacturers; (b) *needle workers*—including tailors, embroiderers (men and women); (c) *leather manufacturers*—including shoemakers, book binders; (d) *carpenters and masons*; (e) *soap and wax manufacturers*; (f)

foodstuff producers—including agricultural laborers, farm animal supervisors, wine-makers; (g) *those providing other services*—including sanita-
tion workers, servants, and butchers.[129] The AIU sought to supplement
these professions with the modernized crafts by introducing new training
methods and to enlarge the work force by training more carpenters,
blacksmiths, and agricultural workers. Its members considered the above-
mentioned professions to be outdated. They were also ardent opponents of
peddling and moneylending. They advocated the creation of vocational
workshops (ateliers) for both sexes, as well as the need for training in
plumbing and mechanics.

Examining the occupational structure in several communities—Mogador,
Tetuan, Elksar—we find some interesting data. Beginning with Mogador,
the following professions were not practiced by Jews: blacksmithing,
masonry, pottery, matting, weaving, and tanning. All of these were
monopolized exclusively by Muslims; there were no Jewish apprentices
employed by Muslims because the latter did not welcome this.[130] Among
the actively employed Jews there were goldsmiths, copper engravers, cop-
persmiths, watch-makers, and tailors.[131]

In Tetuan the Jews in 1908 were largely classified into the following professions: *copper-engraving*—their monopoly; *coppersmithing*—their
monopoly; *tin production*—their monopoly; *goldsmithing*—their monopoly
in Tetuan and in virtually every other Moroccan region; *tailoring*—in which
they ranked among the best, some of them designing Western clothing and
importing their material from Europe; *carpentry*—largely dominated by the
Muslims; *masonry*—largely dominated by Spanish Catholics and Muslims;
the manufacture of glass products—in which the Jews had a monopoly; and
the *soft drinks and winemaking industry*, also dominated exclusively by
them.[132]

In Elksar, on the eve of the protectorate era, out of 1,367 Jews, there
were peddlers, small merchants, grocers, tailors, goldsmiths, and a handful
of carpenters and blacksmiths.[133] The remaining professions were not identified, though it may be that these included commerce and moneylending.

The AIU pressured the Paris headquarters to promote the modern vocations and those practiced by Muslims, by urging the development of
workshops annexed to the schools in most communities.[134] However, this
was not a simple task, for in order to develop workshops, a specialized
group had to be trained and the ENIO, serving as the only training school at
the time, could hardly meet these needs. In 1888, Rachel Béhar, a directress
from Tetuan, recommended that AIU graduates be trained in a Paris-based
vocational school, "I feel that you should create a special school for vocational education which, I dare say, would be more beneficial than a general
education training institution."[135] Béhar went further. She explained that
grievances were mounting in Tetuan in which parents were saying that it is

well to offer general education but it would be more valuable to teach the children a trade.[136]

Although the AIU did not establish a Paris-based vocational school similar to the ENIO, some early progress towards the creation of workshops was made. In Tangier, for example, there was a sewing and dressmaking workshop since 1873 which, in the early 1890s, was equipped with sewing machines donated by the AIU. The early success of the few workshops directed by the school personnel and local European recruits, was apparently not lasting. Nevertheless, the AIU launched an alternate program whereby the school directors served as intermediaries between their students and European craftsmen residing in Morocco, in order to enable the former to acquire apprenticeships and experience.[137] Thus, already in 1873, the Tangier boys' school placed its graduates with European carpenters, shoemakers, and painters.[138] The same phenomenon applied to the 1870s and 1880s and, consequently, these graduates obtained work as craftsmen and earned between twelve and twenty francs daily, not a small sum then, especially considering that essential consumer goods like eggs were selling for twenty centimes a dozen.[139] After 1890, however, there were new and disappointing trends that seemed to vitiate previous progress. What were these trends? Although the AIU had been effective in training workers, by the 1890s more of the schools' graduates preferred to emigrate to Latin America in order to try their fortunes there. Thus the efforts of the AIU were fruitless: whereas the AIU sought to turn out plumbers, masons, carpenters, and blacksmiths in large numbers, and despite an annual subsidy it granted for placing and supporting apprentices, the program lacked candidates.[140]

There was another reason. AIU graduates showed preference for administrative, banking, and commercial pursuits, and when the Europeans arrived in Tangier in greater numbers during the 1890s, these professions seemed more attractive. Europeans established banks and commercial houses, and the schools' graduates easily procured posts with these enterprises.[141] These graduates were especially qualified in the coastal towns, where the AIU trained students in French, Spanish, and sometimes English.

Concerning agriculture, the AIU sought to orient the Jews to work the land in significant numbers. This idea was first examined by Gogman in Tetuan during the late 1860s. When it became certain that the AIU was about to create an agricultural college in Palestine, the Mikveh Israel, near Jaffa, in 1869, hopes were raised that AIU primary school graduates in the Mediterranean-basin communities would be sent there for training. Subsequently, the Mikveh graduates, it was envisaged, would return to their native habitat as agricultural laborers and farmers.

These ideas were discussed in the 1870s by Samuel Hirsch, then director of the AIU schools in Tangier and later head of the agricultural school in

Palestine. Hirsch, however, envisaged great obstacles in the way. In August 1873, for example, the Austrian consul in Tangier who owned a plot of land outside Tetuan, expressed willingness to hand the land over to the AIU for an experimental farm school.[142] Surprisingly, Hirsch declined the offer on the grounds that aside from Jewish indifference to the profession, Jews did not have the right to own farm land and, besides, could not cultivate the land in face of tribal tensions.[143] He therefore recommended that the AIU encourage the youths to emigrate to other lands, Algeria included, where the presence of French agricultural settlers would offer them great employment opportunities; and considering that the AIU wielded some influence on the French Residency at Algiers, Hirsch remarked that it could implement this program.[144]

Hirsch's contention that political insecurity was a major consideration behind the inability to develop a local agricultural program was echoed by Secretary Bigart many years later. In 1898, when the AIU alumni association in Tangier asked of him to help them finance agricultural training programs, his response was far from encouraging: there was need for political security in the countryside as well as in other regions; that unlike Morocco, Tunisia offered a peaceful atmosphere under the French protectorate since 1881 and consequently the AIU had opened an agricultural college there in 1895.[145] The creation of the French and Spanish protectorates in Morocco (1912) enabled the AIU, after these two colonial powers pursued military pacification, to implement this program.

4. The Impact of Modern Education and the Emergence of a Westernized Elite

In addition to cultivating a westernized elite, there was another important aspect of the schools' social effects. The AIU often falsely interpreted the notion "social effect" to mean the promotion of the ideas of generosity and philanthropy, as if Moroccans were not generous. In fact, communal institutions, as already noted, were effectively designed to meet the needs of the indigent, of orphans, and of the unemployed, and societies such as *malbīsh 'arūmīm* (clothing the naked), covering most of the large communities, distributed clothing and shoes to the needy. While the archives do indeed give the false impression that without the AIU there would have been no communal charity programs, it is due to the AIU-sponsored alumni associations known as *associations des anciens élèves de l'alliance israélite universelle*, that social and charitable work in the communities was greatly increased.

What precisely was the nature of these associations and their leadership? It is clear that beginning in 1893 with the creation of the first association in

Tangier, they absorbed the membership and leadership of the schools' graduates. An alumni association had an assembly patterned on the AIU Paris Central Committee: it elected officers (president, vice-president, treasurer, secretary) and served as a vital auxiliary to the school directors in the battle against disease, poverty, hunger, and ignorance. To achieve these and other goals, the associations were generously subsidized by the AIU; with this sort of assistance, the associations could structure adult courses, create libraries, and to expand vocational training. In addition to AIU financial assistance, the alumni obtained funds by collecting dues from their membership which already before 1912 numbered several hundred active participants in Tangier, Fez, and Casablanca. By launching conferences and soirées, these associations procured additional funds that were put to use in a variety of communal projects such as feeding and subsidization of indigent apprentices, placed in European factories and workshops. In Casablanca, for instance, the alumni set up evening courses for youths coming from poor families who worked to support the household during the daytime; they placed apprentices in training programs; and they formed a mutual aid society to grant funds to AIU graduates who were determined to emigrate abroad.[146]

In analyzing the elite and occupational structure, one notes that the steady influx of Europeans, mainly Frenchmen, Englishmen and Spaniards during the 1850s became accelerated during the 1890s, a phenomenon particularly true for the key coastal towns where commercial houses were already flourishing. The Europeans who set up these enterprises were then in dire need of employees versed in European languages and customs.

It is known that the Jews, mainly those of Spanish ancestry, served as commercial intermediaries between Moroccan and European merchants. Nevertheless, these Europeans aspired to expand business activities throughout the country and therefore sought a greater number of qualified people to realize their aspirations. Realizing that even though the Muslims constituted the most important element of the population, they did not acquire the educational skills needed for employment in newly developing sectors of the economy. On the other hand, the Europeans found in the Jews a resevoir of Western-educated youths, mostly graduates of the AIU, some of whom had already obtained secondary education in French Algeria and France. They seemed to possess the necessary linguistic and cultural qualifications for commercial and administrative endeavors.

Why did the Muslims lag behind the Jews? In the first place, unlike the Jews, the Muslims were not exposed to intensive European education since 1862. Second, in the 1890s and early twentieth century the European school networks, the *Alliance Française* included, failed to attract Muslims. The Europeans argued that the reason for this anomaly was inherent in the Muslims' so-called indifference to secular education. It is more likely, however, that the latter were reluctant to send their youths to schools taught and directed by Christians, for the most part.

At the same time, the educational advantage of the Jews should not be overestimated either, for progress was not uniform. It varied from one community to another, sometimes depending on how long an AIU school had existed in a given community. In Larache, a northern coastal town, a former school director observed in 1887 that his graduates had done well for themselves: most of them procured employment in European commercial houses of the Moroccan coast; others were employed in consulates or emigrated to Latin America.[147] The same applied to most coastal communities. In Fez, on the other hand, the school director remarked in 1909 that a significant portion of AIU graduates could not find worthwhile employment.[148] He attributed the lack of progress to three basic factors: first, the isolation of the *mellāh* from the Muslim quarter discouraged comprehensive business activities; second, the absence of relations with Europeans who were rarely found in Fez, made it sometimes difficult for AIU graduates to put their newly acquired talents into proper channels; third, while emigration would have helped combat unemployment, the movement of graduates going abroad from Fez was minimal at best.[149]

Yet in Fez the situation took an impressive turn for the better several years later due to the penetration of the French military into Fez and the creation of the protectorate: time and circumstances changed everything. The community began to appreciate the activities of the AIU more than at any other time previously.[150] School graduates who owned stores in the Fez *mellāh* bettered themselves because of their knowledge of French; they communicatd with the troops, selling them merchandise in large quantities.[151] More important perhaps was the recruiting of recent AIU graduates in Fez for employment in the protectorate's administration through school directors. They were placed in the banking institutions of *Banque d'Etat, Crédit Foncier*, post offices, and in commercial houses.[152] They procured employment rather easily, especially as they hardly faced competition from the Muslims. One source indicated that before 1930 the French would practically pull the youths out of the AIU schools to offer them work in the administration.[153] The French, as expected, did not grant Jews top bureaucratic managerial positions, for in Morocco and in other French colonial strongholds such privileges were confined to French personnel. Other towns in the interior benefited from the creation of the protectorate on a level relative to Fez, notably Marrakesh.[154]

It was in Tangier, however, that the AIU displayed its greatest success in transforming the occupational structure, long before the inauguration of the protectorate era. As far back as 1883, Joseph Matalon, boys' school director, contended that of all the Jewish communities, Tangier was the most important from the economic standpoint. While there was then a large portion of impoverished Jews, there were also the affluent and middle classes that represented a growing element of Tangier Jewry. Most of the affluent dealt directly with the European merchants, and it was fertile ground for establishment of Jewish commerical houses: *Maison Pariente, Maison Benassayag, Maison Azancot.*[155] These enterprises had accumulated capital ranging between 300,000 and 500,000 francs and initiated vital exchanges with Spanish, British, and French representatives.[156] According to Matalon, the AIU schools gave Jewish commerce a major boost, and added that much of the important commercial activities in Morocco concentrated in Jewish hands. Tangier was the best port in the Sherifian Empire and offered the best access for European merchant ships. From the moral and intellectual viewpoint, the Tangier Jewish community had intimate ties with Europe. It was difficult to find young graduates of the AIU schools who did not know Spanish fluently; many of them spoke Spanish, French, and some even English. Nearly all the secretaries and employees of European commercial houses were graduates of the schools.[157]

In addition to white-collar, administrative, and commercial employment, the graduates of the AIU ranked among the pioneers who promoted the European press in Morocco. It was Spain that introduced the Spanish printing press into Tetuan during the occupation period (1860–1862). However, it was Tangier where literary and intellectual fervor emerged in the form of newspapers and journals, mostly in French, Spanish, and English. With the exception of the *Réveil du Maroc*, a French newspaper published after 1883 by Lévy-Cohen, a Jew educated in England, the newspapers and journals which appeared after 1870 were usually founded and promoted by AIU alumni. Even the *Réveil du Maroc* was later popularized by AIU members who served as correspondents and commentators.

Jean-Louis Miège in his in-depth analysis of the Moroccan press observed that the Jews pioneered in the promotion of the European press, Tangier emerging as the most important center.[158] He pointed out that it was probably the AIU that encouraged the publication of the French press, for according to the information submitted by the French legation in July 1870, the AIU promoted the publication of an unnamed journal and supplied the printing press.[159] Among the important journals that appeared after 1870 in Tangier were *Al Moghreb al Aksa* (in English) and *El Eco Mauritano* (in Spanish). *Al Moghreb al Aksa* was founded and edited by A. Pimienta, a graduate of the AIU schools and the ENIO, while Isaac Laredo and Isaac Toledano, both AIU alumni, helped publish *El Eco Mauritano.*[160] These groups frequently contributed articles to the aforementioned journals, often using their literary talent to decry their coreligionists' lamentable conditions and, as Miège remarked, given the fact that the Moroccan press was largely in Jewish hands, it was not surprising that the journals would serve as forums to express the grievances of the Jews living in the Sherifian Empire. When *Al Moghreb ^l-Aksa* noted that the Jews had shown that they know how to reap the benefits of modern civilization, that as a group who had been elevated to a higher level of social prestige, the new elite could put their feelings to the test through the press. In large part the creation of the AIU schools in Tetuan (1862) and in Tangier (1864) contributed to this evolution, for in twenty years after these institutions were founded, they helped cultivate a new generation imbued with the spirit of progress, a generation impregnated with Western ideas.[161]

In a less successful yet significant policy, the AIU urged its graduates to turn to the modernized crafts. Initially, some of these efforts, as we have seen, were fruitful. But no significant change was made in this area of the occupational structure during the period under discussion for Jews considered commerce and emigration as better alternatives for escaping poverty. Young Moroccan Jews who emigrated were mainly from Tetuan, Larache, and Elksar; some were from Tangier and fewer from Fez and Marrakesh. Many emigrants were in their teens.

In examining several locales, the emigration movement, particularly from the north already began in the 1850s or before. Following the creation of the AIU schools the youths who were determined to emigrate did so in large numbers and were better prepared than their predecessors. Having acquired a sound elementary education that included foreign languages, their employment prospects were significantly enhanced. Thus for example, the youths in Tetuan who effectively mastered French and Spanish could choose to emigrate to a Latin American country, or to French Algeria.

Looking at the available data in Table 7, sixty-five of the one hundred thirty-seven youths who left the Tetuan boys' school between 1867 – 1870 departed from Morocco while seventy-two remained in Tetuan. Of the ones

Table 7. Emigration Destination

Town or Region of Settlement	Number of Emigrants
Volo	1
Shoumla	1
Alexandria	2
Oran	45
Trieste	1
Lisbon	4
Ceuta[a]	6
Gibraltar	5
Total	65

SOURCE: Gogman to AIU, Tetuan, March 18, 1870, Arch. AIU.LXX.E.1036.

[a]Ceuta (and Melilla) though part of Morocco in the past, were annexed militarily by Spain in the second half of the fifteenth century.

who emigrated, the majority, forty-five, settled in Algeria and twenty were scattered in Greece, Bulgaria, Egypt, France, Portugal, Ceuta, and Gibraltar.[162] Although we have no data on the sixty-five migrants' professional breakdown, they were mostly employed in commercial houses, textile factories, as railroad employees, and in the transportation sector.[163] They were versed in Spanish and arithmetic. The forty-five who emigrated to Algeria, as well as the emigrants who went to Trieste, Alexandria and Ceuta, had a reasonably good command of French and were educated in geography and history. Twelve of the sixty-five AIU graduates who emigrated had a particularly strong command of French and Spanish.[164]

According to Joseph Matalon, of the four hundred seventeen youths who are known to have left the AIU boys' school in Tetuan between 1862 and 1869, one hundred eighty-two emigrated.[165] This means that more than forty-three percent of those who left the school in that period emigrated mostly to Algeria, Latin America, Europe, neighboring regions, and to the Middle East. Specifically, what was the statistical breakdown of emigration to various places? In which professions did they engage? As for the first question, we see from Table 8 that Algeria, Spain, Brazil, Ceuta, Melilla, Gibraltar, and the Canary Islands absorbed the bulk of the emigrants of the 1862–1869 period. The rest were scattered in Middle Eastern countries, the United States, England, France, and Portugal. Once scattered, these emigrants entered the employment sectors of the local economies. From Matalon we learn that of the one hundred four AIU youths who emigrated

Table 8. Emigration Destination

Country or Region of Settlement	Number of Emigrants
Algeria	104
Tunisia	1
Portugal	2
The Canary Islands	7
England	3
Ceuta	8
Melilla	9
Egypt	3
Turkey	2
Syria	1
U.S.A.	3
Spain	17
France	3
Brazil	11
Gibraltar	8
Total	182

SOURCE: Matalon to AIU, Tetuan, July 18, 1879, Arch.AIU.LXX.E.1036.

to Algeria, all of them procured employment (see Table 9). It is evident that many of them in Algeria entered traditional professions practiced by their families in Morocco, mainly small-scale commerce and the grocery business. However, twelve went into large-scale competitive commerce and five went into administrative work (including the notaries), requiring knowledge of French. Emigrants who settled in other countries found employment in economic sectors similar to Algeria (see Table 10). Matalon's data for the later period of 1877–1879 concerning Tetuan shows that of the one hundred thirty-five youths who left the boys' school, thirty-nine emigrated to Algeria, the Canary Islands, Ceuta, Melilla, Brazil, France, Portugal, Spain, and Gibraltar (see Table 11). The occupational breakdown of these emigrants is shown in Table 12.

In Tangier, the period between 1875 and 1879 witnessed the departure of three hundred fifty-three youths from the boys' school, and of that figure, one hundred five, or thirty percent, emigrated to Algeria, Spain, Portugal, and Brazil.[166] Unfortunately, we do not have breakdowns of the occupations adopted by the emigrants in their new surroundings. Nevertheless, we see a trend in the emigration movement from the north, mainly in the direction of Algeria, Brazil, and Spain. In subsequent years the emigration trends from the north, particularly from Tetuan, apparently gained addi-

Table 9. Professions of the Emigrants (Algeria)

Profession	Number of Employees
Large-Scale Merchants	12
Porters	1
Peddlers	12
Hardware Merchants	1
Fruit Merchants	8
Foodstuff Merchants	5
Bakers	2
Hairdressers	1
Ironmongers	1
Notaries	4
Administrative Agents	1
Restaurant Keepers	1
Coffee-house Keepers	1
Wool Merchants	12
Grocers	20
Cigar Merchants	1
Hotel Bell Boys	1
Shoemakers	2
Unknown Professions	18
Total	104

SOURCE: Matalon to AIU, Tetuan, July 18, 1879, Arch.AIU.LXX.E.1036.

Table 10. Professions of Emigrants (Other Countries)

Country of Emigration	Profession	Number of Employees
Tunisia	Teachers	1
Portugal	Large-Scale Merchants	1
	Wool Merchants	1
Canary Islands	Commercial Agents	1
	Wool Merchants	2
	Unspecified	4
England	Large-Scale Merchants	1
	Unspecified	2
Ceuta	Wool Merchants	6
	Haberdashers	2
Melilla	Large-Scale Merchants	1
	Wool Merchants	5
	Peddlers	1
	Unspecified	2
Egypt	Lerge-Scale Merchants	1
	Wool Merchants	1
	Unspecified	1
Turkey	Teachers	2
Syria	Teachers	1
U.S.A.	Cigar Merchants	1
	Unspecified	2
Spain	Shoemakers	9
	Grocers	1
	Large-Scale Merchants	1
	Soldiers	1
	Foodstuff Merchants	1
	Wool Merchants	1
	Unspecified	3
France	Students	2
		1 (died)
Brazil	Grocers	1
	Wool Merchants	1
	Unspecified	9
Gibraltar	Large-Scale Merchants	1
	Domestics	4
	Shoemakers	1
	Bell Boy	1
	Unspecified	1
	Total	78

SOURCE: Matalon to AIU, Tetuan, July 18, 1879, Arch.AIU.LXX.E.1036.

tional momentum. Though data are very scarce, the AIU reports indicate that emigration trends of AIU youths became increasingly accelerated during the late nineteenth century. Whereas before 1880 more emigrants from Tetuan went to Algeria and Spain, the trend during the 1880s was more towards Latin America. On the occasion of his inspection tour of the Tetuan schools, David Cazès estimated that ninety-five percent of the youths

Table 11. Emigration Destination

Country or Region of Settlement	Number of Emigrants
Algeria	24
Canary Islands	1
Ceuta	5
Brazil	1
Melilla	3
France	1
Portugal	1
Spain	1
Gibraltar	2
Total	39

SOURCE: Matalon to AIU, Tetuan, July 18, 1879, Arch. AIU.LXX.E.1036.

leaving the boys' school wound up in Latin America.[167] Writing in 1897, Nissim Lévy, then director, confirmed Cazès's earlier indication: "The emigration movement from Tetuan, particularly to Latin America, has picked up in recent years. . . . A large segment of the emigrants are rather young, in the age category of fifteen and sixteen."[168] Indeed, at the turn of the century graduates of the AIU were found in Peru where they engaged in commerce and navigation, opened stores bearing Spanish names: Toledano, Delmar, Ṣarfatī, Pinto; and in Venezuela where they helped other Moroccan emigrants to settle and build businesses as they did in Argentina.[169]

On the other hand, though the data are sketchy, we find considerably smaller emigration trends from various parts of the empire. For example, of the twenty-five graduates of the Casablanca boys' school in 1904, two emigrated to Argentina.[170] In Fez, of an unspecified number of AIU graduates in 1897, five chose to emigrate to Senegal.[171] Versed in French, they could find employment in administrative and commercial sectors in this French West African colony where military security—because of French presence—was more of a reality than in Fez, which was vulnerable to Berber invasions. This trend was encouraged by the AIU because it was felt that the French administration in Senegal needed clerks who spoke French and who could be paid less than skilled functionaries imported from the *métropole.*[172] As late as 1900 emigration trends from Fez to Senegal were still underway,[173] a trend that gained some momentum due to the allocation of funds by the AIU for Jewish resettlement.[174] Only after the French protectorate was created did emigration to Senegal stop. However, by then the schools' graduates had readily available employment in the protectorate's administration.

Two additional components: the ENIO-trained teachers and the consular employees were part of the elite. Excluding the pioneer teachers from

Table 12. Profession of Emigrants

Country of Emigration	Profession	Number of Employees
Algeria	Notaries	1
	Unspecified	5
	Students	15
	Clerks	1
	Shoemakers	1
	Grocers	1
Canary Islands	Students	1
Ceuta	Wine Merchants	1
	Grocer	1
	Unspecified	1
	Unemployed	2
Brazil	Shoemakers	1
Melilla	Student	1
	Wool Merchant	1
	Unspecified	1
France	Student	1
Portugal	Student	1
Spain	Shoemaker	1
Gibraltar	Clerk	1
	Unspecified	1
	Total	39

SOURCE: Matalon to AIU, Tetuan, July 18, 1879, Arch. AIU.LXX.E.1036.

Europe, Table 13 indicates the extent of the teachers' corps coming from diverse backgrounds. This table suggests two points: first, though the number of Moroccan ENIO graduates active in Morocco exceeded any one category of non-Moroccan teachers, the number of all non-Moroccans together surpassed the Moroccans by fifty persons. Therefore, the ENIO elite was still heavily dependent on non-Moroccans, mostly from Turkey, Greece, and Tunisia. Second, the number of ENIO graduates in general was obviously limited, and that is why the AIU had to rely on monitors. Only later, after 1930, when the number of schools increased greatly, and when a greater number of primary school graduates, both male and female, expressed willingness to study in Paris, did the number of qualified teachers, notably among the Moroccans, increase sharply. Yet despite the limited number of qualified teachers before 1912, this group made vital contributions to the evolution of Moroccan Jewry.

Among the Moroccan elite, the outstanding figures included Salomon Benoliel, Isaac Benchimol, Moïse Nahon, Samuel Daniel Lévy, Amram Elmaleh, David Cazès, Semtov Pariente, and Joseph Bensimhon. Despite their French secular education, most of them clung to their Jewish heritage, for they did not wish to emulate the West blindly. Like their Western-

Table 13. ENIO-Trained Cadres in Morocco: 1870–1912

Country of Origin	Number of Male Members	Number of Female Members	Total
Algeria	2	1	3
France	–	5	5
Gibraltar	2	–	2
Greece	4	2	6
Iran	1	–	1
Morocco	26	9	35
Palestine	2	1	3
Poland	–	1	1
Rumania	1	–	1
Russia	1	–	1
Syria	–	1	1
Tunisia	6	–	6
Turkey	12	8	20
Total	57	28	85

SOURCE: A. H. Navon, *Soixante-dix ans de l'école normale israélite orientale: 1865–1935.* Paris: Librarie Durlacher, 1935, pp. 111–177.

educated Muslim counterparts, they viewed the West as a storehouse of good and bad. They fought the early battles against child marriages in the interior, created important social and cultural institutions, and gradually acquired sufficient political power in the communities to challenge the authorities of the traditional elites.

Aside from their role as protectors of the Jews, the ENIO members' influence gradually extended beyond their communities. Lévy, Cazès, Pariente, and Nahon were sent abroad to create or enlarge AIU educational projects in Turkey, Greece, Palestine, Tunisia, and Algeria. Pariente ranked among the chief architects of the expansion of the AIU's Middle Eastern school network, while Nahon was responsible for the extension of the network in Morocco and Algeria.[175] Lévy was sent to direct projects of the Jewish Colonization Association (JCA)—a sister organization of the AIU that promoted agricultural work among Jews since 1891—at a Jewish agricultural colony in Mauricio, in the region of Buenos Aires, composed of refugees from the Russian Empire.

As for the consular employees, it is noteworthy that long before the penetration of the AIU this element was well represented in the Jewish communities. Numerous *protégés* were agents in various capacities for the relatively small consular network of the pre-1860 period which was mainly concentrated in Tangier and Mogador.[176] The Anglo-Moroccan Treaty of 1856 which set the model for successive Euro-Moroccan trade agreements, and which enabled the Europeans to expand their consular activities well beyond Tangier and Mogador, resulted in the appointment of career diplomats from Europe who, beginning with the British consulates, replaced the Jewish agents.[177] Only the small consulates of Denmark and Portugal continued to appoint consuls and vice-consuls among Jews.[178] Yet Jews were still recruited in important numbers as translators or clerks at the consulates and legations; and since the penetration of the AIU this professional component was supplemented by elements versed in French.

If the AIU cultivated a small elite in the free professions and in administrative positions, a substantial portion of its graduates still entered traditional crafts practiced by their parents. In the pre-1862 period, most youths belonged to families of artisans, small merchants, and moneylenders, occupations with the greatest numbers of workers, and they usually entered these professions on a hereditary basis, a phenomenon that was not radically altered in the preprotectorate era.[179]

The members of the modernized elite were:

(1) *large-scale merchants*, mostly Spanish Jews of the north and the west coast. Though they were active in commercial activities since the sixteenth century, the opening of Morocco to intense trade transactions with Europe already during the reign of Sultan Muhammad IV,[180] and the coming of the AIU in 1862, swelled their ranks with French or multilingual speaking agents, intermediaries and entrepreneurs, who established their own commercial enterprises. The French, English, and Spanish language training at the AIU was a determining factor in this evolution, a development that equally benefitted the *emigrant* elite, namely the AIU graduates who settled abroad;[181]

(2) *administrative employees*, a group that engaged through the activities of the AIU, included those who pursued their secondary education at the *Lycée Regnault* (since 1908), at the *lycées* of French Algeria, and at the schools of the *métropole*. They, too, were versed in European languages, particularly French and Spanish, and emerged to the fore in the period immediately preceding the protectorate era;

(3) *journalists*, a group educated at the AIU schools or at the *lycées*;

(4) *teachers*, largely composed of the ENIO nucleus; and

(5) *consular and legation personnel*, which, as in the case of the mercantile elite, was a group not created by the AIU, but which continued to function regularly owing partly to its educational efforts. These categories included social workers (AIU alumni groups), mainly men, and a new breed of community leaders. (For the Jewish population data on the eve of the protectorate era, see Table 14).

Notes

1. Gogman to AIU, Tetuan, October 8, 1873, Arch.AIU.LXXVII.E. no file number.
2. Object identification lessons were taught by the teacher who displayed certain objects; he would ask the class to identify these objects through analysis and the use of their imagination and creativity. This is how, in part, the teacher attempted to test the intensity of the children's perception.
3. Hermann Cohn to AIU, Tetuan, November 23, 1863, Arch.AIU.LXVI.E.1005.
4. Abraham Pimienta to AIU, Elksar, March 9, 1879, Arch.AIU.XI.E.191.
5. Benoliel to AIU, Fez, September 26, 1884, Arch.AIU.XIII.E.214(a).
6. *Haftāra*: the Hebrew word which denotes "conclusion," relating to the portion in the Bible dealing with the Prophets. The *haftārōt* are read in the rabbinical schools and in the synagogues immediately after the reading of the *Tōra*.
7. *Gemārā'*: the Hebrew word denoting "completion" or "perfection," referring to the second constituent of the Talmud, namely the collection of oral discussions of the civil and religious laws beginning around the year 200 B.C. These oral discussions were collected by the *Amoraim*, scholars who emerged between the years A.D. 219 and 500.
8. On the point of translating the Bible: the Jews who lived in parts of the south and the interior usually translated the biblical verses they studied into Judeo-Arabic. The Castilians of the north and those among them who settled in the western coastal towns did their translations in Judeo-Spanish. In some of the remote southern communities of the *bled*, the translations were done in Judeo-Berber.
9. Roger le Tourneau, *Fès avant le protectorat*, (Casablanca, 1949) p. 259. As late as 1909 there were only sixty-four Europeans in Fez, among them Frenchmen, Englishmen, Germans, Italians and Spaniards. This information was cited by le Tourneau from the French legation archives of Tangier.
10. Moïse Fresco to AIU, Tangier, January 1, 1886, Arch.AIU.LIII.E.874.
11. Ibid.
12. Ibid.
13. Adèle Israël to AIU, Tangier, January 4, 1894, Arch.AIU.LIV.E.897(b).
14. Isaac Benchimol to AIU, Tangier, December 15, 1890, Arch.AIU.LI.E.807.
15. The teaching of Arabic should not be confused with Judeo-Arabic, the Jews' vernacular.
16. Benoliel to AIU, Fez, February 12, 1888, Arch.LV.E.913.
17. Ibid.
18. Moïse Nahon to AIU, Tangier, May 11, 1892, Arch.AIU.LV.E.913.
19. Ibid.
20. Ibid.
21. Ibid.
22. Samuel D. Lévy to AIU, Casablanca, May 31, 1900, Arch.AIU.LV.E.132.
23. Ibid.
24. Please note that though the subject of biblical history belongs in the area relevant to traditional Jewish education, the fact that the AIU listed the course as part of its general educational curriculum, makes it part of this section's discussion.
25. It is not at all clear why the school program in Morocco, Tangier excluded, deviated from the seven-year program of the 1903 manual. Perhaps the Moroccan

authorities requested this of the AIU or it might have been worked out through an agreement with the Jewish communities themselves. In any case, one could well imagine that in Tangier only a seven-year program could suffice in view of the multiple language offerings.

26. Leven, *Cinquante ans d'histoire*. (Paris: Librarie Félix Alcan, 1911–1920) vol. II. pp.33–34.

27. Paul Silberman, *An Investigation of the Schools Operated by the Alliance Israélite Universelle from 1862 to 1940*. Ph.D dissertation, New York University, 1973, p. 30; *Instructions Générales*, (Paris: 1903) pp. 30–32.

28. Silberman, pp. 96–97; *Instructions Générales*, pp. 30–32.

29. Silberman, ibid; *Instructions Générales*, ibid. Rashi is the abbreviated name of Rabbi Salomon Bar Isaac (1040–1105) who was a distinguished French commentator on the Bible and Talmud. He wrote in Hebrew, occasionally incorporating French transliterations of words.

30. Silberman, p. 30; *Instructions Générales*, pp. 30–32.

31. Nissim Falcon to AIU, Marrakesh, May 25, 1906, Arch.AIU.XXVI.E. 398(a).

32. Ibid.

33. Regnault to Pichon, Tangier, May 23, 1908, A.E. Maroc. I. 403.

34. Bigart to Joseph Conquy, Paris, September 22, 1908, Arch.AIU.XXXI.E. 685(b).

35. Other towns were covered in subsequent years.

36. Regnault to Pichon, Tangier, September 9, 1909, A.E. Maroc. I. 403.

37. Ibid.

38. Ibid.

39. Ibid.

40. It is unclear why the *Alliance Française* did not present candidates for the certification examination.

41. Ibid.

42. Ibid.

43. Ibid.

44. Similar to the Perrier school in Tangier, the Petermann school in Casablanca was named after its first schoolmaster and was subsidized by the French legation.

45. In Morocco, as the program of the AIU primary schools was a six- rather than a seven-year program, the finaly year of the *cours complémentaire*, then, served as the equivalent of the tenth grade of an American high school.

46. Julie Cohen-Scali to AIU, Tangier, January 18, 1911, Arch.AIU.LX.E.945.

47. Ibid.

48. Ibid.

49. This presence of non-Moroccan Middle Eastern and Balkan teachers was gradually broken even in the preprotectorate era. However, on the eve of Moroccan independence the presence was decisively broken by Moroccan-born ENIO graduates.

50. *Instructions Générales*, p. 76. To this very day the ENIO is considered as one of the best secondary schools in France. It trains teachers while serving, at the same time, as a *lycée*.

51. There was another category of non-ENIO teachers known as monitors. Recruited locally, they helped solve the problems of understaffed schools. Usually, monitors had no more than a CEPE and were appointed from among the ranks of the most outstanding primary school graduates of the AIU.

52. *Instructions Générales*, p. 76.

53. Leven, *Cinquante ans d'histoire*, vol. II, p. 30.
54. Benoliel to AIU, Larache, September 19, 1877, Arch.AIU.XX.E.321.
55. Benoliel to AIU, Fez, August 3, 1888, Arch.AIU.XIII.E.214(b).
56. *Instructions Générales*, pp. 76–77.
57. Interview with Haïm Zafrani, Paris, September 20, 1976 (part II, in French).
58. Doris Bensimon Donath, *Evolution du judaïsme marocain sous le protectorat français*: 1912–1956 (Paris: Mouton and Co., 1968), p. 24.
59. Interview with Hanania Dahan, Bat-Yam (Israel), January 26, 1976 (in Hebrew).
60. Reuben Tajouri, "Les élèves israélites des écoles du Maroc," *Bulletin de l'Enseignement Public* 54, décembre 1923, p. 93.
61. Haïm Zafrani, *Pedagogie juive en terre d'Islam: L'enseignement traditionnel de l'hébreu et du judaïsme au Maroc* (Paris, 1969), p. 32.
62. Interview with Mordechai Soussan, Jersalem, March 1, 1976 (in Hebrew).
63. Zafrani, *Pedagogie juive en terre d'Islam*, p. 32.
64. Ibid.
65. Ibid.
66. Ibid.
67. Ibid., p. 78. *Kashrūt* refers to kosher dietary laws and observances.
68. Zafrani, *Pedagogie juive en terre d'Islam*, pp. 81–82.
69. Ibid., p. 84.
70. *Shulhān 'arūkh*: the codified collection and compilation of Jewish laws and ordinances relevant to crucial matters such as ritual law, marriages, and divorce.
71. Zafrani, *Pedagogie juive en terre d'Islam*, pp. 84–86.
72. *Instructions Générales*, pp. 27–28.
73. Ibid.
74. Ibid.
75. Sam Nahon to AIU, Tetuan, September 26, 1882, Arch.AIU.VI.B.25.
76. Moïse Nahon to AIU, Tangier, July 15, 1896, Arch.AIU.IV.B.24.
77. Ibid.
78. Moïse Nahon to AIU, Tangier, March 22, 1906, Arch.AIU.LV.E.913.
79. Moïse Nahon to AIU, Tangier, July 15, 1896, Arch.AIU.LV.E.913.
80. Moïse Nahon to AIU, Tangier, April 18, 1906, ARch.AIU.LV.E.913.
81. Shāhīn Makāryūs, *Ta'rīkh al-Isrā'iliyyīn*. (Cairo: Matba'at al-Muqtaf 1904), pp. 199–200.
82. Reuben Tajouri, "Les élèves israélites des écoles du Maroc," *Bulletin de l'Enseignement Public* 54, décembre 1923, p. 93.
83. Ibid., p. 94.
84. Ibid., pp. 94–95.
85. Ibid., p. 93.
86. See, for instance, Claire Benchimol to AIU, Tetuan, March 2, 1891, Arch. AIU.LXIV.E.980.
87. Israël Pisa to AIU, Casablanca, July 8, 1906, Arch.AIU.VII.E.148.
88. Joseph Matalon to AIU, Tetuan, November 26, 1876. Arch.AIU.LXX.E. 1036.
89. Ibid.
90. Moïse Nahon to AIU, Casablanca, December 8, 1897, Arch.AIU.VI.E.134.
91. Samuel D. Lévy to AIU, Casablanca, May 16, 1900, Arch.AIU.VI.E.132.
92. S. Cohen to AIU, Tangier, January 27, 1875, Arch.AIU.LII.E.858.
93. Adèle Israël to AIU, Tangier, March 5, 1891, Arch.AIU.LIV.E.897(b).
94. Haïm Hazan to AIU, Tetuan, August 28, 1885, Arch.AIU.LXVII.E.1019.

144   The Jewish Communities and the *Alliance* between 1862 and 1912

95. "Israélites du Maroc," *BAIU*, semestriel, 1905, pp. 73–74.
96. Ibid., p. 74.
97. Debdou community leaders to AIU. Appeal sent through Abraham Ribbi, Tangier, September 28, 1903, Arch.AIU.LVII.E.935(d) (in Hebrew).
98. Isaac Benchimol to AIU, Mogador, December 19, 1906, Arch.AIU.XXXIV. E.582(b).
99. Ribbi to AIU, Tetuan, December 8, 1888, Arch.AIU.LXXX.E.1044(c).
100. Nahon to AIU, Tangier, June 15, 1906, Arch.AIU.LV.E.913.
101. Donath, *Evolution du judaïsme Marocain*, p. 64.
102. Claire Benchimol to AIU, Fez, May 10, 1900, Arch.AIU.I.B.5.
103. Ibid.
104. Ibid.
105. Joseph Bensimhon to AIU, Fez, April 22, 1897, Arch.AIU.XIII.E.219.
106. Ibid.
107. Elise Cohen to AIU, Fez, June 7, 1907, Arch.AIU.XIV.E.226.
108. André Chouraqui, *Cent ans d'histoire: L'alliance israélite universelle et la renaissance juive contemporaine (1860–1960)* (Paris: Presses Universitaires de France 1965), p. 458; cited from *Instructions Générales*, p. 80.
109. V. Benzaquen to AIU, Casablanca, February 9, 1903, Arch.AIU.IV.E.86.
110. Ribbi to AIU, Tangier, July 12, 1901, Arch.AIU.V.B.24. (They quoted *Mishna Sota* 3:4)
111. Samuel V. Israël, chief rabbi, to AIU, Tetuan, October 20, 1904, Arch.AIU. VI.B.25. For data on the numerical stagnation of Tetuan, see Miège, *Le Maroc et l'Europe* (Presses Universitaires de France, 1961–1963), III:14, 36; IV:397; Burke III, *Prelude to Protectorate* (Chicago: University of Chicago Press, 1976), p. 24. Concerning Tangier and Casablanca: attracted by new opportunities in these ports and propelled by the prolonged agricultural slumps during the second half of the nineteenth century, large numbers of Muslim peasants (like many Jews) flocked to the towns. Initially, the major ports' population rose from 88,600 in 1856 to 176,000 in 1900; and the growth of Tangier, which went from 10,000 to 45,000 in the 1856–1900 period, and Casablanca, which increased in the same time period from 1,600 to 21,000 was especially notable. (Burke III, *Prelude to Protectorate*, p. 24; Miège, *Le Maroc et l'Europe*, III:461; IV:397).
112. Albert saguès to AIU, Casablanca, May 3, 1910, Arch.AIU.VII.E.155. Out of 6,000 inhabitants in Settat, 655 were Jews.
113. Saguès to AIU, Casablanca, May 3, 1910, ibid.
114. Ibid.
115. Nahon to AIU, Tangier, May 13, 1906, Arch.AIU.LV.E.913.
116. Ibid.
117. Ibid.
118. Nahon to AIU, Tangier, June 28, 1906, Arch.AIU.LV.E.913.
119. Ibid.
120. Ibid.
121. Nahon to AIU, Tangier, April 8, 1906, Arch.AIU.LV.E.913.
122. Nahon to AIU, Tangier, June 15, 1906, Arch.AIU.LV.E.913. The oldest and largest segment of the Rabat Jewish community were the local elements, mostly of Spanish ancestry who had forgotten their Spanish. This population – 242 families – was supplemented by similar Castilians from the interior, 160 families; Salé, 30 families; seventy families from Marrakesh, the south, and the Atlas (of Berber areas); Judeo-Arabs from Boujad (near Casablanca), forty families; and twenty families from the north who retained their Spanish culture.

123. Nahon to AIU, Tangier, June 10, 1906, Arch.AIU.LV.E.913.
124. Ibid.
125. M. Guitta to AIU, Casablanca, February 16, 1902, Arch.AIU.V.E.115.
126. Ibid.
127. Nahon to AIU, Tangier, May 1, 1906, Arch.AIU.LV.E.913.
128. Ibid.
129. Eliezer Bashan, "Jewish Craftsmen in Morocco in the 18th and 19th Centuries, Based on Travelers' Reports and Jewish Sources," in Abitbol's *Judaïsme d'Afrique du Nord* (Jerusalem: Institut Ben-Zvi, 1980), p. 9.
130. Isaac Benchimol to AIU, Mogador, February 22, 1894, Arch.AIU.XXXIV. E.582. The Jews also practiced certain professions which the Muslims were forbidden to enter because of religious restrictions on moneylending with interest, currency exchange, precious metal work. See Bashan, ibid., p. 7.
131. Benchimol, ibid.
132. A. Joly, "L'industrie à Tétuan," *Archives Marocaines* 11.1 (1907) pp. 374–387; A. Joly in vol. 15 (1908), pp. 146–148.
133. Albert Benaroya to AIU, Elksar, May 16, 1912, Arch.AIU.XI.E.181.
134. See, for instance, Nissim Falcon to AIU, Tetuan, December 30, 1903, Arch.AIU.LXVI.E.1010(a).
135. Rachel Béhar to AIU, Tetuan, July 12, 1888, Arch.AIU.LXIV.E.978.
136. Ibid.
137. Y. D. Sémach to AIU, Tangier, May 26, 1925, Arch.AIU.LXII.E.946(e).
138. Ibid.
139. Ibid.
140. Ibid.
141. Ibid.
142. Samuel Hirsch to AIU, Tangier, August 5, 1873, Arch.AIU.LIV.E.894.
143. Ibid. Only in the Berber *bled* and in the vicinity of Fez, Meknes, and Sefrou were Jewish agricultural laborers found. See, for instance, Bashan (above note 129), p. 18.
144. Ibid.
145. Bigart to AIU alumni association in Tangier, Paris, June 30, 1898, Arch. AIU.V.B.24.
146. Albert Saguès to AIU, Casablanca, July 22, 1909, Arch.AIU.LVII.E.155.
147. Benoliel to AIU, Fez, July 17, 1887, Arch.AIU.XIII.E.214(b).
148. Amram Elmaleh to AIU, Fez, July 12, 1909, Arch.AIU.XV.E.248(a).
149. Ibid.
150. Amram Elmaleh, "Israélites du Maroc," *BAIU*, semestriel (1913), p. 89.
151. Ibid.
152. Ibid., pp. 90–91.
153. Interview with Hanania Dahan, Bat-Yam (Israel), January 26, 1976 (in Hebrew).
154. Raphaël Danon to AIU, Marrakesh, July 1, 1912, Arch.AIU.XXV.E.394(a).
155. Matalon to AIU, Tangier, December 18, 1883, Arch.AIU.LV.E.910.
156. Ibid.
157. Ibid. Perhaps as many as three fourths of the commercial houses in Tangier belonged to Jews in 1888. See the study by Jean-Louis Miège, "La bourgeoisie juive du Maroc aux xixe siècle," in Abitbol's *Judaïsme d'Afrique du Nord*, p. 34.
158. Jean-Louis Miège, "Journaux et journalistes à Tanger au xixe siècle," *Hespéris* 41, 1er - 2e sem., (1954), p. 193.
159. Ibid.

160. Ibid., p. 200.

161. Ibid., p. 219.

162. Gogman to AIU, Tetuan, March 18, 1870, Arch.AIU.LXXVII.E. no file number.

163. Ibid.

164. Ibid.

165. Matalon to AIU, Tetuan, July 18, 1879, Arch.AIU.LXX.E.1036.

166. "Compte rendu des travaux de l'alliance israélite universelle: rapport sur les écoles," *BAIU*, sem.(1879), p. 33.

167. David Cazès, "Rapport sur les écoles de l'alliance de Tanger et de Tétuan," *BAIU*, sem. (1884–1885), p. 52. According to Cazès: L'école de Tetuan n'a pas jusqu'ici travaillé pour l'exportation . . . . Elle a fourni à l'émigration 95% des élèves . . . . L'Algérie, en effet, a reçu nombre de jeunes gens sortis des écoles de Tetuan; Oran, Mascara, Sidi Bel-Abbès, Sig, Perregaux, Tlemcen en comptent beaucoup; j'en ai rencontré à Alger, à Phillipville, à Constantine. Aujourd'hui, l'Algérie ne suffit plus à leur activité, et c'est vers l'Amerique espagnole, qu'ils se dirigent. Il y en a un grand nombre à Caracas, à Colon, à Panama, à Paramaribo, à Buenos Aires; quelques-uns se sont établis aux Etats-Unis; il y en a à New York, Baltimore, Philadelphia, etc."

168. Nissim Lévy to AIU, Tetuan, April 18, 1897, Arch.AIU.LXIX.E.1031.

169. Sarah Leibovici, "Tétouan: Une communauté éclatée," *Les Nouveaux Cahiers* 59 (Hiver 1979–80), p. 19.

170. Lazare Guéron to AIU, Casablanca, January 3, 1905, Arch.AIU.V.E.114.

171. Conquy to AIU, Fez, August 13, 1897, Arch.AIU.XIV.E.236(a).

172. Ibid.

173. Conquy to AIU, Fez, April 27, 1900, Arch.AIU.XIV.E.236(a).

174. Nahon to AIU, Tangier, June 28, 1906, Arch.AIU.LV.E.913.

175. See, for instance, Michaël Laskier, "Moïse Nahon, un intellectuel juif marocain," *Les Nouveaux Cahiers*, 61, (eté 1980), pp. 19-20.

176. Miège, *Le Maroc et l'Europe*, II:331.

177. Ibid., II: 332–333.

178. Ibid., II:333.

179. Looking into partial data we find that: Of the 417 graduates and dropouts who left the Tetuan boys' school between 1862 and 1869, 140 came under the categories of small merchants, shopkeepers, and peddlers; 65 became artisans and gardeners; only one entered farming. Matalon to AIU, Tetuan, July 18, 1879, Arch.AIU.LXX.E.1036. As for the Matalon data for 1877–1879: of the 135 youths, twenty-five became shopkeepers, small merchants, and peddlers; thirty-two were artisans and gardeners. Matalon to AIU, Tetuan, July 18, 1879, Arch.AIU.LXX. E.1036.

180. Miège, "La bourgeoisie juive du Maroc aux xixe siècle," in Abitbol, p. 30.

181. In Tangier, out of 353 youths who left the boys' school between 1875 and 1879, seventy-one became employees in European commercial houses in Tangier alone; one was employed as a commercial entrepreneur in a British firm in Rabat while two were working in unnamed European commercial firms in Elksar; another was employed as a special representative of the French maritime company, *Compagnie des Bateaux à Vapeur*. All in all, seventy-five or slightly over twenty-one percent of the youths who left the boys' school engaged in trade. ("Compte rendu des travaux de l'alliance israélite universelle: rapport sur les écoles," *BAIU* sem. (1879), p. 33). In a list of pupils from Tangier, compiled by Joseph Halévy, of the thirty-three graduates of the boys' school (presumably in 1875 or early 1876) sixteen were

Table 14. The Jewish Population in most of the Urban Agglomerations
of Morocco on the Eve of the Protectorate Era

Town	Jewish Population
Larache	2,000
Elksar	1,400
Rabat	2,000
Tetuan	6,500
Safi	2,500
Casablanca	7,000
Mazagan	3,000
Tangier	10,000
Mogador	12,000
Fez	10,000
Marrakesh	15,700
Total	72,100

SOURCE: Statistics compiled by the Elksar boys' school director (Albert Benaroya): Arch. AIU Maroc. XI.E.181. Elksar. May 16, 1912. These statistics do not include Meknes (which already in 1901 had at least 6,000 Jews), Azemmour, Salé, and Sefrou. In addition, communities of the Atlas in the south, the Rif in the north and several interior towns like Ouezzan, were not included. Nevertheless, it has been estimated that there were perhaps 110,000-120,000 Jews living in Morocco in 1912.

notaries working for commercial firms in Moroco, mainly in the coastal towns. Two notaries were abroad: one in a British commercial firm in Gibraltar, another in Manchester, England. Two were businessmen in Tangier; one was the chief representative of a British commercial firm in Rabat; and another served as a special agent for a French maritime company. All in all, twenty-one of the thirty-three pupils (63.6%) were affiliated with commerce. (Halévy, "Sur l'état des écoles dans les communautés juives du Maroc," *BAIU* sem. (1877), pp. 64-65). In a final example, Casablanca, of the twenty-five graduates of the boys' school in 1904, eight (thirty-two percent) were employed by European commercial firms in Casablanca dealing in sugar and grain. (Lazar Guéron to AIU, Casablanca, January 3, 1905, Arch.AIU.V.E.114).

SECTION II

THE JEWISH COMMUNITIES AND THE *ALLIANCE ISRAÉLITE UNIVERSELLE* BETWEEN 1912 AND 1956

CHAPTER V

The *Alliance* and the Jewish Communities in the Protectorates' Political Arena

"Il serait extrêmement désirable que le gouvernement français pût venir au secours de l'*Alliance israélite* dont le rôle est precisément la propagation de la langue française. On peut dire que l'*Alliance israélite* joue en quelque sorte au Maroc le même rôle que les missions catholiques en Orient . . . ." (Henri Regnault, French Minister Plenipotentiary in Tangier to the *Quai d'Orsay*: 1912).

It has been pointed out that Morocco was divided into three zones of influence: the French protectorate, the Spanish protectorate, and the international zone of Tangier. The latter was administered by a legislative assembly that represented the following nations: France, England, Spain, Portugal, the U.S.A., the Soviet Union, Belgium, Italy, and Holland. The assembly was established in 1924 and was presided over by the *mandūb*, representing the *makhzan*.[1]

France benefited the most from the political events that began in 1912. The March 30, 1912 treaty achieved for her the following aims: the sultan consented to French plans for placing troops throughout the French zone; he granted the French full police and military power for the restoration of public order and for Morocco's air and land defenses; he agreed that the French government would be represented before the *makhzan* by a *Commissaire Résident Général*;[2] he delegated the Resident General the power of signing, in the name of the Sherifian government, all royal *ẓahīr*s, and therefore, the Resident General was able to influence or even dictate the contents of the decrees. Without his signature the *ẓahīr*s were null and void. For his part, the Resident General merely consented to respect Islamic institutions and traditions as well as the sultan's dignity.[3]

1. Modern Education in French Morocco: Struggles and Challenges: 1912–1928

After the signing of the Franco-Spanish treaty of November 1912, the two powers embarked on a military pacification campaign between 1912 and 1934 to ensure the stability of the *makhzan* and to consolidate the economic and strategic status of their newly acquired influence. The campaign was carried out successfully, particularly under the command of the French Resident General, Maréchal Lyautey.[4] The pacification policies enfeebled the political authority of the *makhzan* and of tribal mediators (known as *murābiṭīn*) and warriors. The latter, having lost military parity with the central authorities, lost also their ability to challenge or evade the same authorities; and as the French protectorate was able to administer areas formerly in the *sība*, the importance of the *murābiṭ* as an accepted mediator in local disputes was greatly diminished.[5] Thus the central elements of the traditional system — *qā'ids*, tribes, *murābiṭīn*, and the *makhzan* — were reduced to a role of secondary importance under the protectorate.[6]

The pacification policies which enabled Jews and Muslims to walk the streets relatively unharmed, sparked important economic and political changes for the Jews in particular. David Ovadia, one of Sefrou's most renowned rabbis, observed that with the stabilization of French presence the self-confidence of the Jews increased because: (1) the Berbers were disarmed; (2) a ruling administrative unit known as *Bureau des Affaires Indigènes* was created in every rural region, commanded by an army officer to maintain law and order; (3) the Jews began serving French soldiers as community suppliers; and (4) in a short period roads were built, a modern rail system established, and new transportation facilities were put to use, enabling the Jews to extend their business activities with relative ease.[7]

Pacification and the protectorate proved to be a disadvantage to the Muslims, notably for intellectuals. The new system, more in the French than Spanish zone, alienated the educated who grouped into nationalist factions, first asking for reforms and a greater participatory role in the administrative apparatus, and then, when they were convinced that they were marginal participants, revolted and called for a total break with the system. As Kenneth L. Brown observed, the young men of Salé who attained an education and a familiarity with world politics in the 1920s were dynamic and ambitious, and not unnaturally wanted to have a voice in the affairs of government. Many had been encouraged by the French authorities to believe that by virtue of their education administrative careers would be opened to them. These ambitions and promises remained unrealized, and they began to see themselves through French eyes as second-class citizens in both political and economic terms.[8]

The position of the Jews as assessed by Ovadia was originally brought up by Yomtov Sémach[9] early in the protectorate era. After assuming the post of Tangier boys' school director in 1913, Sémach became increasingly involved in the fate of the Jews. The abolition of the *jizya* and the termination of violence, he contended, was bound to put the Jews in the path of political emancipation. In a series of articles which he wrote for *La Revue Française de Tanger*, he envisaged the solutions to Jewish problems in the context of French presence and clung to the principles of the French Revolution and the human rights declaration of 1791, which helped the Jews in France become French citizens.[10]

Sémach's argument went along the following lines: if the French Revolution and the ensuing reforms resulted in the naturalization of the Jews as French citizens, and this privilege was extended in 1870 to Algerian Jewry through the Crémieux decree, then why should this spirit not apply to Morocco?[11] Further, Sémach contended that France's role as protector of ethnic and religious minorities enjoyed a high level of historic continuity: was it not France that for centuries had rallied to protect the Christians of the Near East?[12] In his opinion, the educational activities of the AIU predating the French protectorate by fifty years, instilled the feelings among Jewish youths that France was their *patrie adoptée*[13] and accentuated the importance of the westernized elite cultivated by the schools, an element that would collaborate and strengthen the protectorate.[14] The Jews, then, were highly qualified to serve French interests and consequently deserved special privileges.[15]

Sémach was obviously insensitive to possible negative reactions that would emanate from Muslim political circles, but he was looking out for Jewish interests. He realized that once the French, strengthened their colonial influence in the country, and once the Muslims become educated in European ways, pressure on the protectorate to employ Europeans and Muslims could deprive the Jews of numerous privileges:[16] they would no longer be in great demand. To obtain privileges for the Jews early in the protectorate period was a sacred priority for Sémach.

The French were well aware of Jewish support of the protectorate system and of pro-French policies espoused by the AIU. Indeed, after 1912, the French legation in Tangier called on the *Quai d'Orsay* to collaborate closely with the Jews through stimulating the AIU network of schools with financial assistance.[17] Lyautey, visiting Marrakesh in 1913 with Josué Corcos, the former ally of Mawlāy 'Abd al-Ḥafīz and Sī Madanī al-Glāwī, and accompanying Raphaël Danon, then AIU director in town, expressed willingness to grant subsidies for the schools and asserted that Jewish and French interests are one and the same ("*Votre intérêt est le nôtre*"); he promised to inaugurate a new era based on justice for all people.[18] This was also a time when the Resident General received letters from Jewish leaders

بسم الله

(الخاتم الشريف)

يعلم من كتابنا هذا الاتحاد العربي ... أول أن العثمانيه على جماعة ...

...

٢٥ رجب الفرد سنة ١٣٣١ هـ الموافق ٢٤ يونيو سنة ١٩١٣ م

الفصل الأول

...

الفصل الثاني

...

الفصل الثالث

...

الفصل الرابع

...

الفصل الخامس

...

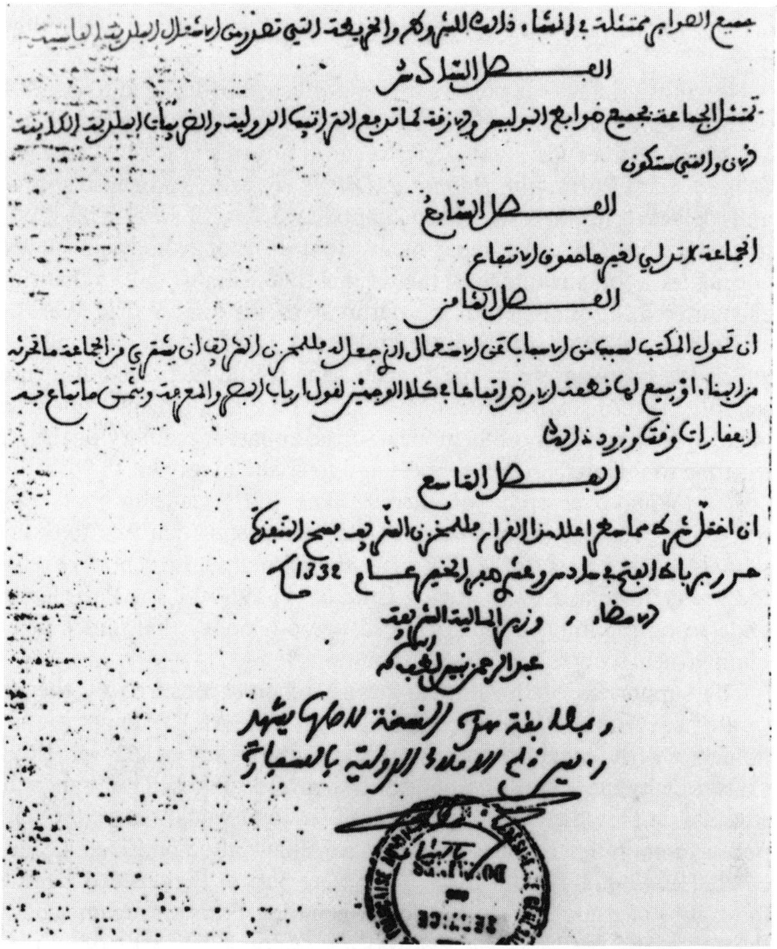

الفصل السادس

الفصل السابع

الفصل الثامن

الفصل التاسع

Figure 16. Sultanic *zahīr* dated 20 Rajab 1331 (June 25, 1913), granting the *Alliance* a parcel of land for the creation of schools in Fez

around the country where phrases such as *Vive la France* wee quite common.[19]

Notwithstanding, the politics of the protectorate deviated to a significant degree from French preprotectorate policies. A certain number of officials at the French educational department (known since 1920 as *Direction Générale de l'Instruction Publique*, DIP) were eager to neutralize the AIU and replace its network with French public schools for Jews. This group was led by Gaston Loth, the department's first director, who together with his colleagues, took advantage of the serious financial difficulties that the AIU encountered, beginning with the outbreak of the First World War.

Though in October 1915 Loth and the AIU signed an agreement under which the protectorate in the French zone would help subsidize the AIU schools, its terms, which included financial aid to augment student enrollment, were largely ignored. In view of the apparent inability of the AIU at the time to maintain all the schools and to create new ones, the protectorate began taking over some of them.[20] The Paris leadership of the AIU recognizing that its options were limited, was prepared at first to cede a few schools to the protectorate. But after the French set up schools exclusively for Jews known as *Ecoles Franco Israélites* in 1916–17, the Paris leadership understood the implications of the dangerous policy that aimed at undermining their schools' influence among the Jews.

The supporters of the Franco-Jewish school sponsored by the protectorate believed that they could dispense with the AIU. Though the services rendered by the organization for the communities since 1862 were doubtless praiseworthy the schools had outlived their usefullness. The Franco-Jewish schools, on the other hand, were tuition-free and would relieve the relatively poor communities of their burdensome financial commitments, and they offered good quality education. They were part of the protectorate's effort to establish an educational network, including Franco-Muslim schools for the Arabs and Berbers. The idea was to develop a hierarchy of educational institutions, controlled by the French; and in their view the AIU was in the way of extending their influence among the Jews. Therefore, despite pre-1912 considerations for close collaboration with the Paris organization, the AIU was given very strong hints to abandon its schools and make a graceful exit.

The reaction of the AIU to the challenge was inevitably a mixture of both anger and dismay. Already in July 1915 Narcisse Leven, AIU president, sensing that the Moroccan schools were in danger, wrote to Lyautey that by relinquishing its influence the AIU would be surrendering its moral credit in the communities; it would mean the halt to numerous projects started or envisaged since 1862.[21] He then outlined a plan whereby the AIU would direct its energies toward opposing child marriages and excessive promiscuity; alleviating unhealthy sanitary conditions; combatting poverty and caste distinctions; working to heal communal divisions; introducing order and regularity in the communities' organizational apparatus; establishing social and philanthropic institutions; intensifying vocational training, adult education; creating dispensaries, and other projects.[22]

Sémach was delegated by the AIU to meet with Loth and discuss the future of the schools in the zone. A meeting was arranged in December 1916. Sémach, using Tangier as his example, pointed out that of the estimated 2,500 Jewish youths of school age, 800 frequented the AIU, 200 an AIU-sponsored rabbinical school and another 200 frequented other schools which were community-sponsored; the rest, some 1,300, were working or roaming the streets; therefore, it was his opinion that the disturbing number of uneducated youths was intolerable, and if France would help the AIU financially, then the network could expand to accomodate all the youths; though acknowledging that the DIP would be entitled to exercise certain controlling measures over the schools, Sémach urged Loth to help the AIU expand in Tangier and French Morocco.[23]

How could this be achieved? The DIP would be granted a supervisory role over the schools' programs and would issue educational reforms relevant to French and secular education.[24] Most significantly, the administrative role and direction would remain in the hands of the Central Committee.[25] Yet at that stage, however, Sémach's strategy seemed like wishful thinking, for French officials at the DIP, Loth included, entertained different notions. Even Lyautey was critical. During his visit to various AIU schools in 1918, Lyautey, though impressed with the teachers' devotion to the communities, was nevertheless disappointed with the physical conditions of the school buildings and informed Loth that if the good name of the AIU was to remain, it would be necessary to find ways of improving the buildings' appearance.[26] Loth, in turn, sent a warning to Secretary Bigart, that a growing number of parents are sending their youths to the tuition-free Franco-Jewish schools.[27]

Although the Franco-Jewish schools appeared to pose a threat to the AIU, some of the organization's most devoted teachers did not hesitate to voice their criticism either. In 1919, Joseph Bensimhon, then director in Casablanca, complained about the relatively meager salaries granted by the Central Committee to its ENIO-trained personnel and compared the situation to the status of the Franco-Jewish personnel who were unionized public functionaries; the latter received 5,350 francs per month if they had a *brevet supérieur*; together with World War I indemnities, lodging expenses, and cost-of-living bonuses, these people received no less than 5,850 francs monthly; the AIU personnel, on the other hand, lacking these privileges, received a monthly salary of 3,300 francs.[28]

Despite complaints, Bensimhon affirmed that even if the budget did not allow the AIU to operate a large school network, the Central Committee had a moral obligation to Moroccan Jewry to keep the *oeuvre* viable.[29] How was the AIU supposed to maintain the network? Bensimhon insisted that the French government had to intervene on the AIU's behalf and accord its schools subsidies without too many strings attached, for the disappearance of the schools from the Jewish scene "would result in a serious setback for local Jewry, a burdensome responsibility which the Central Committee alone would have to bear."[30] He then offered a plan that actually laid the foundation for French policy vis-à-vis the AIU: he advised the AIU to take the position with the DIP that only it had the personnel best suited to become involved in Jewish affairs; a representative, appointed in Paris, would serve as delegate to maintain channels of communications between the Central Committee and the French authorities on the one hand, and the Jewish communities, on the other; it would be the delegate, empowered by the Central Committee, who would administer and direct the schools but would also inform the protectorate of all AIU plans.[31]

The AIU faced a dilemma: to continue the operation of the network despite existing French sentiments to the contrary could result in a clash with the protectorate. To relinquish the *oeuvre* long predating the protectorate, meant a surrender of a hard-fought campaign for institutional recognition and prestige among the Jews. The leaders of the AIU must have been completely baffled in 1920 when Sémach was inclined to support the educational authorities' position. He argued that times were changing and that the great exploits of the precolonial *temps héroïques* were rapidly approaching oblivion. The protectorate was developing its own educational systems for Muslims and Jews, and in comparison with the AIU, their financial resources were virtually inexhaustible. He wondered with candor whether the AIU in this day and age could respond to all the vital needs of the Moroccan communities who could not always in their economic situation respond favorably to the schools' financial needs.[32]

The AIU weighed other positions that challenged the purpose of the Franco-Jewish schools. Would they serve the communities better than the AIU? Would the teachers of the protectorate be as devoted to their tasks as their ENIO counterparts? Some reports received by the Central Committee clearly cautioned that the replacement of its schools by the Franco-Jewish ones would lead the Jews in the path of irresponsible assimilation and would confine the communities' youths to French Catholic teachers who have no notion of Jewish traditions whatsoever. Would the AIU tolerate seeing Jews being educated by institutions insensitive to their needs?[33] Under these circumstances it is true that the AIU could better listen to youth and parental complaints on a variety of communal problems, for its teachers had virtually round-the-clock contacts with the Jews. Besides, if the communities mistrusted the Alsace pioneers and did not always give an enthusiastic welcome to the ENIO teachers of Turkish or Greek background, all of whom were Jewish, what chance did French Catholics have in the long run?

Indeed, the lack of sensitivity on the part of the Franco-Jewish schoolteachers was acknowledged by Roger Gaudefroy-Demombynes, who related that the presence of the Franco-Jewish schools in the Jewish communities caused tension between the youths and the non-Jewish teachers; the latter were accused of not having the necessary tact in their dealings with the Jews.[34] The Franco-Jewish course program as outlined in Tables 15, 16, and 17 clearly points out that even if Hebrew was offered five hours weekly, there is no mention of biblical and postbiblical history. Further, whatever initial enthusiasm the communities showed toward these schools seems to have subsided. In Azemmour, the AIU school enrolled youths who defected from the Franco-Jewish counterpart as early as 1918, despite the fact that the AIU school charged tuition.[35] In Casablanca, notwithstanding the community council's financial difficulties, its leaders made important monetary contributions to keep the AIU schools in operation[36] even though there was a Franco-Jewish school in town.[37] Also, the Casablanca Franco-Jewish school was unsuccessful in attracting numerous Jewish youths, although the teachers were excellent and education was tuition-free.[38] This argument was echoed by Sémach in 1924, after he was suddenly convinced that the mission of the AIU in Morocco was perhaps not over after all.[39]

There was a small minority of Jewish intellectuals who by 1924 symbolized the graduate corps of the various French protectorate schools and who believed that the protectorate schools were the only institutions capable of preparing the Jews to become integrated into French civilization and culture. They felt that the AIU was an anachronism because its schools were

Table 15. The Franco-Jewish Schools: Curriculum for the First Year

Subjects	Number of Lessons	Duration	Weekly Total
Object and Language Lessons	2 daily lessons	1 hour	5 hours
French Reading	2 daily lessons	1 "	5 "
Arithmetic	1 daily lesson	1 "	5 "
Composition	1 daily lesson	1 "	5 "
Drawing	4 weekly meetings	30 minutes	4 "
Singing	2 weekly lessons	30 "	1 hour
Recreation	Morning & evening	30 "	4½ hours
Promenades	One afternoon weekly	1 hour	1 hour
Physical Education	1 daily lesson	30 minutes	2½ hours
Hebrew	1 daily lesson	1 hour	5 hours

SOURCE: Georges Hardy, "Plan d'études et programme de l'enseignement franco-israélite," *Bulletin de l'Enseignement Public du Maroc,* 7e année, no. 24, octobre 1920, pp. 420–438.

Table 16. The Franco-Jewish Schools: Curriculum for the Second and Third Year

Subjects	Number of Lessons	Duration	Weekly Total
Object Lessons	2 daily lessons	1 hour	5 hours
Reading in French	2 daily lessons	1 "	5 "
Composition	1 daily lesson	1 "	5 "
Arithmetic	1 daily lesson	1 "	5 "
Hebrew	1 daily lesson	1 "	5 "
Recitation	3 daily lessons	30 minutes	4½ hours
Singing	2 weekly lessons	1 hour	1 hour
Physical Education	1 daily session	30 minutes	2½ hours

SOURCE: Georges Hardy, "Plan d'études et programme de l'enseignement franco-israélite," *Bulletin de l'Enseignement Public du Maroc,* 7e année, no. 24, octobre 1920, pp. 420–438.

of Jewish character and not sufficiently advanced to prepare candidates to become assimilated in French mentality. Responding to their accusations, Gaudefroy-Demombynes, who was an astute expert on the French protectorate administration during the 1920s, defended the AIU saying that its teachers were better qualified intellectually than the Franco-Jewish ones to interact with Jewish children and thus maintain a greater level of influence over them.[40]

The Jewish opposition to the AIU was overcome by other elements, mostly the alumni of the AIU schools and by the community leaders who preferred the semisecular AIU schools to the almost purely secular institutions of the protectorate. In any case, the French authorities reversed the original plan envisaged for the AIU schools and offered a new policy. This came about in 1924, when the DIP and the AIU signed a new agreement in which the protectorate ceded control to the AIU over most of the Franco-Jewish schools and returned to the organization the schools that were taken over after 1915. The agreement stipulated that the protectorate would provide the AIU with annual subsidies depending on the number of youths enrolled in its schools and would assist in constructing or leasing school buildings upon the request of the Central Committee.[41]

The AIU made several concessions, too. The organization had to give preference to French citizens, including French naturalized Moroccan Jews in naming directors to its schools.[42] The AIU schools would be subjected to regular pedagogical and sanitary inspection by the DIP representatives who would recommend curricular reforms.[43] Finally, the AIU would create a delegation to represent it in contact with the Jewish communities, exercise the power of inspection over Judaic studies, and help supervise extraeducational activities such as patronage committees, alumni associations, and so on.[44]

The agreement spelled a victory to the AIU, for it legitimized its activities, formally and officially, with the French protectorate. The delegate

Table 17. The Franco-Jewish Schools: Curriculum for the Fourth, Fifth and Sixth Year

Subjects	Number of Lessons	Duration	Weekly Total
French Language	2 daily lessons	2 hours	10 hours
History	2 weekly lessons	30 minutes	1 hour
Geography	2 weekly lessons	30 minutes	1 "
Arithmetic	1 daily lesson	1 hour	5 hours
Bookkeeping	2 weekly lessons	1 "	2 "
Physical and Natural Sciences	1 daily lesson	1 "	5 "
Manual Training	1 daily lesson	1 "	5 "
Singing	2 weekly lessons	30 minutes	1 hour
Recreation	1 daily lesson	30 "	2½ hours
Physical Education	1 daily lesson	30 "	2½ hours
Hebrew	1 daily lesson	1 hour	5 hours

SOURCE: Georges Hardy, "Plan d'études et programme de l'enseignement franco-israélite," *Bulletin de l'Enseignement Public du Maroc*, 7e année, no. 24, octobre 1920, pp. 420–438.

appointed by the AIU was Sémach, who served in this capacity until his death in 1940. While the 1924 agreement did not apply to the Spanish and International zones where the AIU in conjunction with the communities continued to share much of the expenses for the schools,[45] the delegate's jurisdiction was extended to these areas and his authority was recognized. Four years later, in 1928, the agreement was reconfirmed by a new agreement. It also stipulated that the AIU would maintain control over the schools through directing and administering them; that the annual subsidies would continue to be granted according to the number of children; and that the convention would apply only to the French zone. The 1928 agreement was of major significance to the Jews in one respect: it relieved them of much of their financial commitments to the schools.

The agreement came to include in 1948 an understanding whereby the protectorate would aid the AIU in enrolling 2,000 new students yearly, thus increasing attendance from 22,000 in 1948 to over 33,000 (in eighty-three schools) on the eve of Moroccan independence. This benefit was achieved by Reuben Tajouri, delegate, and Jules Braunschvig, then vice-president of the AIU. But it was equally due to the friendly disposition of Roger Thabault, then DIP director whose devotion to the AIU was unsurpassed in the French administration. As a result of the new understanding the DIP leased the AIU buildings and increased the subsidies per number of youth to meet the educational needs of Jewish children in the post-1948 period.[46] Therefore, in 1954, for example, the budget of the AIU for French Morocco alone stood at one billion francs (over $3,000,000): 600 million francs were provided by the DIP and 400,000,000 francs by French and American Jewry, the latter through the American Jewish Joint Distribution Committee (JDC).[47] The aid offered by the JDC—an organization founded in the United States in 1914 to aid Jews in distress, and whose funds are largely derived from the United Jewish Appeal resources—also enabled the AIU to expand its educational activities into the small communities of southern Morocco. For its part, to meet the growing needs of the post-World II period, the AIU trained hundreds of teachers in Paris and Casablanca.[48]

The reaction among various protectorate officials to the French policy of aiding the AIU were not uniformally positive. As early as 1925 R. Lacoste, a protectorate educator, remarked that he could not see how Jewish youths would benefit from the Jewish schools of the AIU, being "outdated" as they were, unable "to combat superstitious beliefs among Jews."[49] He could not comprehend how the AIU schools were permitted to function in the colonial age, when the Jews had become westernized.[50] Lacoste, therefore, characterized the 1924 agreement giving new life to the AIU and dissolving most of the Franco-Jewish schools, as an anachronism, a violation of the principles of secular education.[51]

In conclusion, several factors explain the turnabout in French policy vis-à-vis the AIU:

1. The French government may have concluded that the education offered at the AIU by its zealous teachers was of high quality and should be retained.

2. The AIU refusal to surrender its influence over the communities, possibly included French Jewry's pressure on the French government to maintain the schools.

3. The AIU had become firmly institutionalized in the Jewish communities since 1862. Its activities required continuity, and education had to be provided by Jewish teachers, an advantage over the Franco-Jewish schools which were operated by French Catholics for the most part.

4. The French concluded that it would be better to allow the AIU to develop a monopoly over modern education among Jews: if the Jews were enrolled in Franco-Jewish and schools intended for the Europeans, then they would wish to become more closely integrated in French political life, a phenomenon that had occurred in Algeria and which had caused for the French administration there great turmoil.

Of these factors, the one indicating that Christian teachers were impeding Jewish educational development, as hinted by Gaudefroy-Demombynes, is least valid, for one might well ask if the French could not have dealt the AIU a death blow by recruiting Jewish teachers for the Franco-Jewish schools.[52] The institutionalization of the AIU in the major communities and its popularity can hardly be challenged. Nevertheless, the French in the final analysis rallied behind the AIU, not because of French Jewry's tenacious refusal to surrender the schools or because of the schools' popularity. The fourth factor was probably the major one during the 1920s. Despite Loth's desire to go ahead with developing the Franco-Jewish network, and despite reactions by Lacoste and others, supporting this development, the French government and the Residency in Rabat—Morocco's new capital—apparently concluded that preference ought to be given to the Jewish character of the AIU. It is likely that during the negotiations between the protectorate and the AIU, the French no doubt considered the long-range implications of neutralizing the AIU. And indeed, the few Jewish intellectuals who graduated from the primary and secondary schools set up by the protectorate for Europeans, schools that were part of the hierarchy of educational institutions for Muslims and Jews, wanted their children to enroll in the Franco-Jewish and European schools because their curriculum was more secularly oriented than the one at the AIU. The French at the time feared that Jewish blind imitation of French lifestyles, leading to "irresponsible" assimilation, such as occurred in Algeria, a phenomenon that could develop through the DIP schools, would lead to Jewish demands for a greater participatory role in the protectorate and, worse than that, French citizenship. Such a process could result in de-Judaization, Muslim hostility, and anti-Semitism among the Europeans, all of which could upset the hierarchy of the protectorate. Lyautey, at least, wanted to avert these problems. By allowing the AIU to function as a semi-private initiative, it would be responsible for offering the Jews a modern French education but not to the extent whereby they could become overly Europeanized through assimilation. Gaudefroy-Demombynes strongly hinted at this point.[53]

Consequently, surrendering the Franco-Jewish schools to the AIU, with a few exceptions, and permitting only a small minority of Jews to enroll at the schools built for the Europeans, was finally seen in protectorate political circles as the positive course. There were, however, subsequent deviations in the 1930s and 1940s in which the AIU was pressured to emphasize French education to a greater extent by the protectorate's educational inspectors.

The Controversy over French Naturalization: 1912–1936

Ironically, if the French entertained the possibility of avoiding problems in the Jewish communities through the AIU, the latter's representatives launched a campaign for French judicial reforms on the Jews' behalf to bring them closer to France. Yet they were disappointed from the start because the March 30, 1912, Fez Treaty did not make the slightest reference to Jewish rights; and the French protectorate did not intend to reverse the basic legal systems prevailing in Morocco. The French under Lyautey showed political prudence; they attempted to adjust their political interests to the customs, mores, and laws practiced through the centuries by the sultanate. The Jews had only one major judicial reform to their benefit: personal status matters—birth registration, divorce, inheritance laws—were regulated by the Mosaic Law and judged by the rabbinic tribunals which were established under the *ẓahīr* of May 22, 1918, as was a High Rabbinic Tribunal, a veritable court of appeals, with its seat in Rabat.

The AIU sought from Lyautey a concession whereby all Moroccans should benefit from French courts and the distinction between *protégés* and non-*protégés* should not be maintained by allowing only the former access to French courts.[54] But once the protectorate was established, the French, the Spanish, and the international zone's authorities abolished the capitulations. Only England waited until the 1930s to abolish capitulations in Tangier. The United States, which never recognized the French protectorate, did not abolish the capitulations in Morocco.

Despite their disappointment over French judicial reforms, AIU representatives sought the impossible. They tried to obtain French citizenship for the Jews in large numbers. Already in 1907 the French ambassador to Berlin—on the occasion of the anti-European riots in Casablanca that resulted in the flight of numerous Jews and triggered a movement among them to obtain foreign protection and citizenship—urged the *Quai d'Orsay* to act cautiously.[55] He warned that despite the massacres and pillage, it must not be forgotten that the Madrid Conference had placed certain restrictions over ways of obtaining foreign citizenship, and as Moroccan Jews were looking for European naturalization in large numbers rather than a slow progressive approach of individual selection, it constituted a dangerous challenge for France.[56] Doubtless, he was referring to the potentially volatile Muslim response to such a move, and proposed that if the French government had any ties with the AIU, it should collaborate with the latter in order to reassure Moroccan Jewry of French concern for their welfare and to elevate their confidence, without offering them anything concrete.[57]

However, neither educated Jews nor the AIU were willing to concede on the issue, and as early as September 1912, Albert Saguès of the Casablanca boys' school met with Lyautey to discuss it. During their deliberations, Lyautey tried to persuade Saguès that he was a loyal friend of the Jews, but he accused different Jewish factions in the French zone for catering to Spanish interests; he was particularly angry at efforts undertaken recently by Casablancan Jews to obtain Spanish citizenship, for he could not understand why any Jew would seek citizenship from a country that persecuted and expelled him; he was angry enough to ask if the Jews "wish to undermine French influence in Morocco."[58] Lyautey's message was loud and clear: he was vehement about pro-Madrid manifestations and warned that such behavior could result in the alienation of the Residency towards the Jews.[59]

Saguès assured Lyautey that the Jews preferred French citizenship but that France did not seem eager to comply and hence they were turning elsewhere for changes in their judicial status.[60] Lyautey, however, was un-committed on naturalization and asserted bluntly that he opposed the Crémieux decree granting Algerian Jewry French citizenship in large numbers; at the same time, however, he did not rule out the possibility of a careful selection process, whereby the protectorate would screen individual candidates for French citizenship once they proved to be thoroughly assimilated to French culture.[61]

The AIU did not relent. It was determined to pursue the matter and its representatives in Morocco and France applied various strategies toward their goal, among which the following are the most noteworthy:

1. They met with French officials to emphasize the need for large-scale naturalization for a people who were subjected to political and legal ine-qualities under the *makhzan's* jurisdication.

2. They pleaded this cause in AIU periodicals, notably the *Paix et Droit* which they knew was read in Morocco by AIU alumni, students, and by protectorate personnel, and in other journals and newspapers.

3. They entered their pleas in French Jewish journals such as the influen-tial *L'Univers Israélite* and the *Archives Israélites*, to enlighten French Jewry about the Jews of Morocco, and in order to win support *at home* for this policy.

4. They spoke in front of French and European audience as well as in in-tellectual circles throughout Morocco to stress the importance of the ser-vices that would be rendered to the protectorate by French-educated Jewish allies. Therefore, to reward them for their services, the protectorate had to consider granting French citizenship to as many educated French-speaking Jews as possible.

Of these strategies the second needs further elaboration. Its main proponent was Sémach. Even prior to his appointment as delegate, Sémach led the pro-naturalization school of thought in the French zone. During the early days of the protectorate (in 1913) he remarked that "surely the Jews . . . will not become French citizens overnight like their Algerian coreligionists. However, they will not remain in an inferior situation like their Tunisian coreligionists."[62] Although Sémach conceded that the aim of the AIU was to foster in the youths love for country, he contended that most of Morocco was now French: the new era promised prosperity and justice for all in-habitants, and for the Jews France had become the *patrie adoptée*,[63] a posi-tion shared by Sémach's colleagues.[64]

Pleading for naturalization in *Paix et Droit* (1927), however, Sémach was less patient than he was in 1913, for he sensed that no progress was made to implement French naturalization policies among the Jews since the creation of the protectorate. He gave a brief description of the condition of the 120,000 Jews who lived in the French zone then, and about the status of the 20,000 in the Spanish as well as the 10,000 in the International zones. He related the all-too-familiar story about the importance of the Jews as commercial intermediaries, and Jewish acceptance of French language and culture. When the French entered Casablanca in 1907 and laid the foundation for their protectorate, they found in the Jews reliable allies who aided them with great devotion, and when the military aspect of the occupation was over, the Jews were the first to assist in the promotion of modernization and economic development.[65] And thus in 1927, it was high time, in

Figure 17. Yomtov D. Sémach, *AIU* Delegate, 1924–1940

Sémach's opinion, to discuss naturalization seriously. With Théodore Steeg replacing Lyautey at the Residency, Sémach had hoped that a fresh initiative would be adopted. Though expressing vague optimism about Steeg's declaration at the French League for Human Rights meeting (1926), that the Jews were progressing more rapidly than the Muslims, and that educated Jews should become candidates for naturalization, Sémach wanted a clearer definition of naturalization with emphasis on large-scale naturalization.[66] He inisisted that during the Madrid Conference (1880) the Europeans wrested great concessions from the sultanate and could influence events in Morocco as they wished.[67]

What was Sémach implying? Was he prodding the French to convince Sultan Muḥammad V (1927–1961) that he consent to the naturalization of segments of his Jewish population, thus freeing them completely from the *makhzan*'s judicial jurisdiction? He must have been aware of the Madrid Convention's concession to Sultan Mawlāy al-Ḥasan, that any naturalization procedure required the consent of the sultan, for Muslims and Jews had to maintain perpetual allegiance to him. It is certain that Muḥammad V, who emerged as a forceful nationalist sympathizer and an advocate of Arab-Berber-Jewish solidarity, would have never gone along with such a scheme. But Sémach apparently thought that French pressure could outweigh previous decisions.

Not ignoring the possibility of Muslim hostility to pronaturalization pleas, Sémach presumed that they would eventually come around to accept French naturalized Jews.[68] And to defend his unrealistic position, he added that the Muslim states base their foundations on the principles of religious codes: they consider only believers in the *Qur'ān* as citizens; all others are considered foreigners, simply tolerated; the Jews felt today that by becoming French citizens, they would no longer be classified as second-rate inhabitants.[69]

But what exactly was Sémach's definition of large-scale naturalization? What was the process to follow? Sémach was not altogether clear on this point.[70] He stated in *Paix et Droit* (1928) that he "preferred collective naturalization of the Jews *by categories*," and dismissed the individual naturalization selection process as being "much too slow."[71] Yet he did not clarify what precisely the categories might be, and perhaps he chose to leave that decision open to the French. Although Sémach always emphasized knowledge of French as a criterion, there was more to the problem, and the fact that Moroccan Jews were loyal to France before and after 1912, was not sufficient for the protectorate to go along with the plan.

Sémach's efforts were supported by Alfred Berl, editor of *Paix et Droit*, an ardent advocate of large-scale naturalization. In 1928, for example, he openly accused the protectorate of indifference to the issue, arguing that the Jews were still enclosed in *mellāḥs* without being Moroccans or subjects of the sultan; though they were better off under the protectorate, they remained *heimatlos*.[72] Berl pointed to the Crémieux decree and asserted that Algerian Jews could serve in the French army and as important administrative functionaries.[73] Their Moroccan counterparts, he said, were not less advanced. He warned: "If Morocco's Jews are compelled to remain *sans patrie* the deceptions which they may encounter and become attracted to may be either Communism or Zionism."[74]

The feeling among the Jews in the French zone over naturalization was indeed in tune with the views of the AIU. In 1922, during a visit to Fez by the president of the French Republic, the community council demanded that Jews be permitted to move outside the *mellah* and purchase land in the Muslim quarter (just as Muslims purchased land in the Jewish quarter), that they be able to open retail stores in the Muslim quarter, and that Jewish testimony in judicial matters involving Muslim courts be received like a Muslim's testimony. It was further noted that those Jews who had fought during the First World War on the side of France and became French citizens were not denied equal rights anywhere.[75] The message was clear: Jews expressed the view that only by acquiring French citizenship would they be well treated.

Pronaturalization aspirations were supported by individual Europeans in the zone. In 1927, for example, Victor de Stahl wrote an editorial in *La Dépêche Marocaine*, saying:

Here is a race which was hermetically sealed in the *mellāhs* without daring to leave its gates, a race persecuted by the rest of the indigenous population, a race attached to its ancient traditions and customs. And here we see that same race today, perfectly assimilated, having been liberated recently after centuries of setbacks, in an advanced intellectual level, working and dressing in the same manner as we do . . . . There are those among them who qualify for becoming French citizens, based on their intellectual level. We can therefore say that *the hour has come to give Moroccan Jews the opportunity to become French*.[76]

But this approach was to benefit the "liberated," the most educated. De Stahl did not wish for the protectorate to make enemies among the Muslims, a position endorsed by Gaudefroy-Demombynes.[77]

Muslims, the early nationalist leaders included, did not welcome Jewish efforts to become French citizens at a time when they were seeking national unity. At the same time, however, nationalist leaders were sometimes inclined to understand Jewish motivations. One such figure, Muhammad al-Kholti,[78] wrote in *L'Action du Peuple* (1933) that Jews were officially harassed in the past and he deplored the pillaging of *mellāhs*. But he argued, the Jews were not worse off than their coreligionists in certain European countries; he remarked that amicable relations between Muslims and Jews went back to the distant past, and he appealed for a Judeo-Muslim entente, saying that this would be based on sincerity, on loyalty, and would constitute the starting point for the two people, leading to urgent reforms. In making an appeal to the Jews and by extending them a helping hand, al-Kholti believed it was necessary to reveal to them that today's educated Muslims, imbued with the sentiment of tolerance and love for humanity, would like to collaborate with their Jewish counterparts, but that harmony could not be durable unless there was complete equality between Jews and Muslims.[79]

The naturalization question requires analysis from several angles. First, what proportion of Jews were French educated or French speaking? Second, why were the French so apprehensive about a Crémieux-style decree? Third, how much of a factor was fear of adverse reactions from the Muslims?

It is unknown how many Jews in French Morocco were French educated or French speaking. This is unclear for 1912 when Saguès championed the naturalization cause, and it is unknown for the 1920s and early 1930s, when Sémach proposed the idea. It is believed, however, that in 1936, when the French conducted a census in their zone, at least 20,000 Jews out of 160,000 knew French.[80] Sémach challenged this figure and estimated that not less than 40,000 Jews in the zone knew French.[81] If the latter figure is at all accurate, then twenty-five percent of Moroccan Jews in the zone knew French. Although it is impossible to determine the level of language competency among the Jews, these figures represent those who could write and speak French. Doubtless, many Jews, small merchants and peddlers, had a lesser knowledge of French.[82] However, there were also AIU and *lycée* graduates who were capable of using French not merely for limited business use, but who spoke and wrote it with ease. Yet this was the case in 1936.

In 1912 or 1927–28, the latter period marking the "escalation" of the AIU's pronaturalization drive, it can be safely assumed that less than twenty-five percent of the Jewish population in the zone knew French. Nevertheless, during the 1920s there were probably several thousands of Jews who had various levels of competency in the language and might have been able to satisfy the protectorate that they were "citizenship material." Yet the potential for large-scale naturalization was unrealistic in view of the many Jews who had only minimal knowledge of French or had no contact with French education at all.

Concerning a Crémieux-style decree and its applicability to Morocco, its implementation was out of the question. Even if the French in Algeria granted most Jews citizenship regardless of their level of assimilation to French culture, they were unwilling to apply the same formula in Morocco having, as Lyautey would argue, paid the price of political animosity in Algeria for many years, as a result. Lyautey and his successors to the

Residency feared that once the Jews of Morocco, as did Algerian Jewry, obtain French citizenship, they would suddenly be on equal footing with the European settler community; the latter did not care much for the Jews and the Crémieux decree helped fuel the flames of discontent.[83] The French contended that Morocco, moreover, was not a colony like Algeria but a protectorate, and therefore they lacked authority in promoting large-scale naturalization policies. And they were doubtless reluctant to challenge the rabbinic courts over judicial matters. It was in Algeria, where French Jewry aided their Algerian counterpart in the 1840s to develop secularly oriented consistories, similar to those in existence in France since 1808, and this strategy led to community reforms and the enactment of the 1870 Crémieux decree. In Morocco, the French sought to accommodate the European community on the one hand and rabbis on the other. They were deterred to maintain political stability and to preserve the status-quo.

If the French were worried about these problems, they were equally apprehensive about adverse reactions from the *makhzan* and, since 1930, the nationalists. Any policy of *divide ut imperes* was challenged by these groups from the outset. Part of the opposition to judicial policies was attributed to French efforts in the post-Lyautey period (after 1925) to temporarily deviate from certain aspects of the status-quo and remove the Berbers from the influence of the *sharī'a* courts. In May 1930 a *zahīr* was published under French pressure, interpreting French policy for the placement of Berber tribes under French criminal law, and recognizing the judicial competence of the tribal *jema'a* or Berber customary court of appeal. This policy was clearly intended to reduce the influence of the *sharī'a* courts among the Berbers and thus, if implemented, would have created deep divisions between Arab and Berber communities. The *zahīr* was never implemented, for the opposition among the Muslims to this policy was overwhelming. The French were now more cautious than ever in granting legislative benefits to Moroccans.

The *makhzan* which sympathized with nationalist causes under Muhammad V's sultanate, would have certainly opposed large-scale naturalization and would have clashed with the Residency over the matter. Either way, the French after 1930, more than before, had their hands tied over the enactment of judicial reforms, and preferred to disappoint the AIU or any other force on the issue. They now appeared indifferent to selective naturalization candidacy as well. Conceding defeat in 1936, Sémach wrote to the AIU: "We have failed to score a success on the naturalization question; it is now impossible to obtain any concessions on this point."[84]

In the end, only a small minority of Jews obtained French citizenship, mainly those who settled in Algeria. Only Tunisia witnessed some movement in Jewish naturalization owing to a French law promulgated in 1923 under which Tunisian Jews would apply for French citizenship during the protectorate. Yet unlike the Algerian formula which rested on the Crémieux decree, the Jews in Tunisia could be naturalized on a much smaller scale.[85] Between 1923 and 1956, thousands of Tunisian Jews acquired French citizenship,[86] and this was attributable to the absence of agreements (like the Madrid Conference) in Tunisia between the Tunisian Bey and the powers, and due, in part, to greater Jewish assimilation in Tunisia to French culture as well as, most importantly, to less ethnic conflicts than in Morocco, and to a more liberal French administration. Perhaps had the AIU and French Jewry pushed for the selective formula instead of insisting on large scale concessions, more Jews in the French zone could have become French citizens before the uproar over the Berber ẓahīr took place.

The Situation in the Spanish and International Zones

The Spanish Protectorate: 1912–1940

The moment the Franco-Spanish accord of November 1912 was signed, giving Spain territorial jurisdiction over northern Morocco and the Rif mountains, the Spanish protectorate came into being. However, Spanish cultural and political activities, as we have seen, long predated the protectorate era. In 1911, Nissim Falcon, then director in the AIU at Tetuan, reported on the Spanish encroachment into Morocco. He related that the Spanish consul in Tetuan, Don Ferrer, assisted by several Muslim and Jewish notables, was zealously working to propagate the Spanish language and culture.[87] Tetuan was becoming a Spanish sphere of influence, and Ferrer had established a chamber of commerce with strong ties to Madrid and Barcelona.[88] Its purpose was to encourage Spanish businessmen and farmers to invest and even settle in Tetuan.[89] Also, the recent publication of *El Eco de Tétuan*, a Spanish-language newspaper, had further increased Spanish cultural presence; its editor, Y. Cazès was an AIU alumni.[90]

Falcon's initial reactions to Spanish penetration were pessimistic, for he did not think that the Spaniards were sufficiently liberal, and he feared that they would only intensify sectarian divisions in the north. Because of their fervent attachment to Catholicism, they would infringe on the traditions of Muslims and Jews alike; he also suspected that no major industrial projects would be pursued, as was the case in Ceuta and Melilla, which the Spaniards seized from Morocco several centuries earlier.[91]

Falcon's central concern, however, was the future status of the AIU once the Spanish protectorate would be established. Two rumors were circulating at the time: certain Jewish notables (Spanish *protégés*) were collaborating with Madrid and were advocating Spanish takeover of the AIU schools and their replacement with a Spanish network; there was an additional rumor that the Spaniards would pressure the AIU to eliminate French education in the schools.[92]

Falcon assured the Central Committee that the French consul in Tetuan, M. Lucciardi, wielded considerable influence among the Jews. Due to his continuous concern for their political welfare, Lucciardi had established pro-French feelings among them; but he cautioned that there was considerable opposition among Spaniards and eventually this could result in the neutralization of the AIU among the Jews. All that could be done for the time being is to maintain a low profile:

> The political activities of the Spaniards and their [indigenous] supporters in Tetuan, are largely intended to destroy French influence. It is around the *Alliance* schools that the French and Spanish consular agents have been quarreling. In this quarrel, we have to maintain absolute neutrality. For instance, Lucciardi is aware of an educational committee created by the *Alliance* in Tetuan. He would like to become its honorary president. Yet this move is unacceptable and Lucciardi is offended. This is the price which must be paid in order to maintain genuine neutrality. A certain Spanish protégé, M. Toledano, suggested that the *Alliance* make both Lucciardi and the Spanish consul [Don Ferrer] honorary presidents. This suggestion is unacceptable to Lucciardi who hinted to some Jewish notables that they lack gratitude and courage.[93]

About the time the Franco-Spanish accord of November 1912 was signed and the protectorate was established, the authorities seemed to go out of their way to win Jewish support for the new political system, mainly in Tetuan, Elksar, and Larache, the three most important Jewish population centers in the north.[94] To reassert Jewish-Spanish ties the authorities, in collaboration with pro-Spanish Jews, founded in Tetuan the *Asociación Hebreo-Español* with branches throughout the zone, in order to restore the historic bonds uniting Jews and Catholics, as they existing in pre-1492 Spain, and to defend Jewish rights.[95] M. Saavedra, secretary to the Resident General spoke to the Tetuan association on several occasions; and during a speech in 1914, he declared that the Sephardi Jews are Spaniards without a country. The loving mother country, Spain, and its noble King Alphonso XIII are thoroughly concerned with their problems, and the Jews will not find in Spain a mere friend, but more than that, a brother sharing the same history and destiny.[96]

This was obviously an attempt to appease the Jews to the point of encouraging them to accept Spain as their country of adoption, although no offers of naturalization were proposed. Saavedra went on to elaborate that Muslim rulers and institutions exposed the Jews to centuries of persecutions and neglect;[97] but he conveniently left out details in his speech of the horrible persecutions of the Jews in Spain during the Inquisition and of the expulsion policies.

The policy of the Spanish protectorate authorities toward the AIU was at first indifference. In extreme cases Spaniards did all they could to foment hostility to the AIU in the local press, and saw in its presence a symbol of French influence in their midst. Although Madrid granted the AIU schools of Tetuan a partial subsidy in the five years following the establishment of the protectorate, there was growing opposition. It appears that the early opposition to the schools was intended to minimize AIU influence in the Jewish community, then to replace it with Spanish schools and influence; and eliminate any vestiges of French political and cultural activities in the north. As the AIU had schools in Tetuan, Larache, and Elksar, the most important towns in the zone, the opposition grew stiff. Also, the efforts by the Central Committee to open AIU schools in Arzila, populated by several hundred Jews, never materialized: the protectorate authorities would not hear of this and instead a *Hebreo-Español* school was founded.

From the start, the AIU tried to maintain cordial relations with the Residency. In December 1913, Falcon met with the zone's representatives, who expressed admiration for the work of the AIU among the Jews of the north in previous decades.[98] However, M. Aguilar, the zone's director of the educational department expressed deep concern about the French character of the schools.[99]

On July 27, 1914, Saavedra visited the AIU schools in Tetuan. Although he confessed that from reports submitted to him about the schools, he had thought that they might be an instrument of French influence, he was now at ease.[100] He told Falcon that he was convinced that the schools were politically and culturally neutral.[101] Nevertheless, Saavedra insisted that the AIU intensify Spanish education, proposed that the teachers should prepare their students for the official primary school certificate (*Certificado de Primera Enseñanza*) and that the schools should become more Spanish oriented.[102] Saavedra's intentions were clear: while the AIU would be permitted to maintain aspects of the 1903 program prescribed in the *Instructions Générales*, the language of instruction, French, would be reduced in importance. Needless to say, while the AIU had to consent to increasing the number of hours devoted to Spanish language, history, and geography, and accepted the offer of the zone's official certification program, the language of instruction remained French.

The regular contacts between Falcon and Saavedra produced some favorable results for the AIU, and an annual subsidy of 2,000 pesetas was accorded to the schools of Tetuan by the Residency. The French, on the other hand, had misgivings about this policy, for they believed that this would give the Spaniards a controlling interest in the schools.[103] An exaggeration on the part of the French? No doubt. The subsidy was not significant and, in September 1917, this subsidy was cut off abruptly after the Resident General sent the AIU a perfunctory note attributing this measure to "budget difficulties stemming from the war."[104]

Perhaps budget difficulties stood behind the Residency's decision. But it is quite likely that the organization's refusal to tolerate *españolismo* in its schools was behind the measure. Meanwhile the press was mounting its attack on the AIU. In 1915, for example, a Franciscan Father, known by the pseudonym of Africano Fernandez, in the *Correo Español* (published in Tetuan) accused the AIU of suppressing from the curriculum and the minds of Jewish youths the history of Spain, of continuing to offer a strong French education program, and of planning to omit courses pertaining to the geography of Spain.[105] He further accused the AIU of serving both French and Jewish interests, and of anti-Catholic education; he claimed to have seen a history lesson notebook belonging to one of the children and discovered that though it discussed in great detail the history of France, its monarchs and wars, it neglected Spanish history and its glorious past.[106] Fernandez insisted that the AIU catered to Jews only, whereas since Spain granted the AIU subsidies, it should admit more Catholics to its schools and refrain from offering courses on Sunday.[107]

The campaign to discredit the AIU and win over Jewish support for the protectorate included the creation of *Hebreo-Español* schools.[108] In March 1917, when the protectorate's delegate for indigenous affairs visited the AIU schools, he contended that since the latter were performing up to expectation, there was no need for rival schools.[109] Nevertheless, from the time the war ended and well into the 1930s,[110] the protectorate established a small network of tuition-free schools for Spaniards and Europeans, Muslims and Jews. For the Jews, the protectorate opened several *Hebreo-Español* schools in Arzila, Larache, Elksar, and Tetuan. Despite these measures, the AIU schools continued to function regularly in Tetuan, Elksar, and Larache, though the pressure to adapt to official measures was constant. In the 1920s as before, the press continued to attack the policies of the AIU. One influential paper, *Heraldo de Marruecos*, charged that the AIU educated the Jews of the north, mostly of Spanish ancestry, in French traditions, thus alienating them from the Castilian heritage and suppressing from their hearts feelings of patriotism for Spain.[111] Educating Jewish youths at the AIU also meant the potential loss of these to employment in the French zone.[112]

The delegate of the AIU, however, contended that French education had to remain an integral part of the program alongside Jewish and Spanish education.[113] French was vital, he believed, because Spanish Morocco was contiguous to both the French zone and Algeria.[114] While Spanish had to be respectably represented in the AIU program which, in his opinion, was the case, the schools' graduates, equipped with a sound French education, could find work outside the Spanish zone if necessary; yet the delegate and teachers alike acknowledged that it would be advantageous for the authorities to recruit for the AIU Spanish language teachers who would be salaried by the protectorate.[115]

For a long time the authorities did not adopt such a policy, and instead chose to fortify the *Hebreo-Español* schools by offering mostly Spanish education with a touch of French, evidently to rival the AIU. But Spanish flexibility became a reality in the 1930s, when the protectorate appeared to show greater tolerance for the AIU. Already in 1932, there were reports from the AIU in Tetuan that the authorities no longer pressured the director to Hispanicize the program,[116] and late in 1935, when Sémach met with the Resident General, it was agreed that the protectorate would undertake the responsibility for offering Spanish education at the AIU through its own teachers.[117] The Spaniards no doubt realized that the attacks on the AIU schools and the pressure for adopting Spanish as language of instruction at the AIU could alienate the neighboring French protectorate and, if this was the case, then the AIU benefited from its "French connection."

The outbreak of the Spanish Civil War in July 1936, and the emergence of military rule in the Spanish zone as a result, did not cause major hostility toward the Jews or the AIU. In face of the conflicting loyalties that developed among Spanish residents and officials of the zone, the AIU chose the path of neutrality, even though its representatives expressed anxiety about pro-Franco and Fascist activities.[118] There were periodic harassments of Jews by Fascist youths in small towns, and various factions represented in the civil war pressured Jews to align themselves with different causes.[119] In Larache, the *junta* affirmed that it was not against Franco, yet it is feasible that this stance was adopted under pressure.[120] In Tangier, on the other hand, the Jews remained neutral and, given the international character of the zone, Spanish factions could not pressure anyone to adopt their political positions on matters not pertaining to communal affairs. In April 1939, one month after Franco's emergence to power, the boys' school director in Tetuan reported that the situation was stable and that relations of the Jews and the AIU with the authorities were quite cordial.[121] This was a calm before the storm: the outbreak of the Second World War and its consequences.

3. The International City of Tangier: 1923–1944

The Jewish community in Tangier had acquired a privileged status, and given local leadership support, the AIU schools developed rapidly and contributed to the emergence of a modernized elite in a far more comprehensive way than in other Moroccan communities.[122] The *junta* was well represented by Spanish Jewish descendants who were Spain's ex-*protégés* (the protections having been lifted after the creation of the zone) at a time when pro-French notables were not as well represented, a development which according to Sémach was advantageous to Spanish influence in the zone.[123]

Despite this phenomenon, the support for the AIU schools was overwhelming, particularly in the area of enrollment. Also, the school buildings were donated by the community.[124] Though the AIU received subsidies for its schools from the international administration (100,000 francs in 1932), in addition to its own contribution (120,000 francs that same year), the bulk of the money came from the community (330,000 francs).[125] The Board of Deputies continued its support for the teaching of English at the AIU.[126]

It was here that the AIU tried to maintain a delicate balance between the most important European languages; and if French remained the language of instruction, the teaching of Spanish and English was intensified after 1923 to accent the political neutrality of the schools in the presence of an apparatus where Spanish, English, and French enjoyed an official language status. To meet the demands of the community, Hebrew was also retained as part of the program, though Arabic was left out.

Politically, the Jews of Tangier during the protectorate enjoyed a measure of autonomy unheard of in the rest of Morocco. They possessed rights granted by the Tangier Legislative assembly and consented to by the *makhzan*. They had a council composed of fifteen members, which included the head of the rabbinic tribunal of Tangier who served as an advisor on matters relating to Jewish Law.[127] For the positon of community council president and members, as well as for candidates for the rabbinic tribunal (three candidates), it was the *mandūb* who gave his approval to the lists. Whereas the candidates for the rabbinic tribunals in French and Spanish Morocco had to undergo examinations before becoming eligible, the *mandūb* of Tangier simply approved the rabbinic lists.[128]

As for the community council, the duration of membership was usually three years. However, the same members were able to present their candidacy in subsequent appointments. Unlike the other Jewish community officers, the Tangier community president, the two vice-presidents, the secretary, and the treasurer were nonsalaried positions. In 1950–51, the *junta* had sixteen members, and of these only seven were Moroccan subjects, five were ex-*protégés* and four were naturalized citizens of various European powers.[129] The political and national heterogeneity of the *junta* and the multilingual program of the AIU schools reflected the Jewish contribution to the internationalization of the city of Tangier.

The whole administrative structure of the Jewish community as described was the outcome of the February 15, 1925 *zahīr* which legalized, within the zone, the presence of the community and the rabbinic tribunal.[130] It also stipulated that the community council was responsible for the administration of the Jewish schools, hospitals, asylums, maternity centers, charitable foundations, synagogues, cemeteries, and so on; this included the administration of taxes, gifts, and the supervision of the annual subsidies that the assembly allocated for the community.[131]

The Jews of Tangier, unlike any other Moroccan Jewish community, whether they were Moroccan subjects, naturalized citizens of other countries or ex-protégés, could serve in political and administrative posts of the assembly and the community council. According to the *zahīr* of February 16, 1924, the Legislative Assembly was to be composed of thirty indigenous and foreign nationals living in Tangier. In 1950, of the thirty members of that body four were Frenchmen, four were Spaniards, three were British, three were Americans, three were Soviets, one was Belgian, one was Italian, one was Dutch, and one was Portuguese; these members were chosen by their respective consulates, whereas six Muslims and three Jews were chosen from lists of candidates presented by their communities to the *mandūb* who approved them; the assembly was dominated by the British and Spaniards. Though presided by the *mandūb*, the assembly was composed of three vice-presidents: one French, one British and one Spanish; moreover, the *mandūb* had the right to participate in all sessions but could not vote.[132]

Jewish representation in the assembly actually equalled the Muslims. During the 1950 assembly, in addition to the three designated Jews, three other Jews were also represented. They were Moses Abensur, one of the three British delegates at the assembly; Haïm Bendelac, representing the single seat of Holland; and Jo Hassan, who, in addition to being the community president, was the Portuguese delegate to the assembly.[133]

The Jews received special privileges in the assembly's annual budget allocation, too. For example, during budget year 1950–51, out of the total allocation of 13,041,548.10 francs, 4,000,000 francs were allocated to the Jewish community, while 6,000,000 francs were allocated to the Muslims.[134] This was a sign of favoritism, and of powerful Jewish representation in the assembly that probably pushed for these allocations. At the time the allocation was made there were 12,000 Jews in Tangier as compared with well over 40,000 Muslims.

Of the political challenges confronting the Jews, the Spanish occupation of Tangier in 1940 is noteworthy. That year, Spain took advantage of the war to check the influence of the other countries represented in the assembly, countries which for the most part were in a difficult situation during the war. She occupied the zone, militarily, and only relinquished control after the war. During the period 1940–1945 two points were clear. First, the Spaniards dissolved the assembly, ordered the *mandūb* out of Tangier, and made the town a *de facto* Spanish colony. Second, the February 15, 1925, *ẓahīr* concerning the structural makeup of the Jewish community council and institutions was abrogated and all communal activities came under the supervision of the Spaniards. The administrative functionaries, most of whom were French, were replaced by Spanish functionaries who unsuccessfully attempted to threaten French educational institutions; parents preferred to send their children to French schools.[135]

The position of the Jews in Tangier under the new administration was precarious. Their economic enterprises were heavily taxed and new licenses were often refused by the authorities.[136] Further, Tangier Jewry had to play host, given the international character of their zone, to Jewish refugees. According to a Jewish Agency representative visiting Tangier in 1944, there were about 1,500 Jewish refugees there, most of whom arrived during the years 1938–39. A few came after the outbreak of the war; roughly half were Sephardim, the remainder, Central Europeans. The Sephardim originated from the Dodecanese Islands; a small section left Rhodes for Italy and France even before the introduction of anti-Jewish laws in 1938, and most of these families had three or more children. The men were craftsmen, shoemakers, drivers or small businessmen and spoke Italian, Spanish, Turkish, and French. The Central Europeans came mainly from Hungary and Poland via Italy, where a number of them lived for two years before 1938. As long as Tangier remained an international zone refugees were admitted without difficulty, and no regulations were in existence to prevent them from making their living. After the collapse of France in June 1940, however, when Spain occupied Tangier, these people were deprived of working facilities and their standard of living fell rapidly from that time onwards. The intervention of the World Jewish Congress, the JDC, and the AIU helped relieve them of some of their misery; between January and May 1941 JDC's relief committee expanded its support and, from April on, spent $12,000 monthly, apart from sums earmarked for school meals at the AIU.[137]

It is difficult to determine the status of the AIU schools in Tangier at the time, as no money could have come from Paris, where the Central Committee was dissolved in 1940. However, as there were no more than six schools in Tangier and Spanish Morocco combined, the communities and the AIU alumni association in Tangier may have salaried the teachers and participated in various other financial commitments; according to the Jewish Agency's representative, the AIU in Tangier continued to enjoy considerable prestige. While accusing Albert Saguès, the schools' director, of being "the prototype of that French-Jewish attitude which aspires to educate Jewish youths to be French and to spread French culture and customs," he conceded that Saguès "exercises a strong personal influence within the community; in particular some professional people and the rich families bow to his cultural outlook which they take to represent the circles that stand behind the *Alliance Israélite Universelle.*."[138]

4. Moments of Anxiety: The French Protectorate during Vichy Presence and Its Aftermath

If the degree of turbulence was pronounced in Tangier under Spanish control, the political situation in the French zone was more dangerous and chaotic, once Vichy influence became temporarily dominant. For the Jews and the AIU it marked a period of great anxiety.

The Second World War and the occupation of France by Hitler's armies inaugurated a new and uncertain era for Moroccan Jewry in the French zone. The AIU Central Committee was dissolved. At the same time, French colonies and protectorates came under the domination of Vichy-backed functionaries, particularly in Algeria where the Jews witnessed the temporary abrogation of the Crémieux decree and were compelled to carry identification cards providing information about their "native" and religious status. In Tunisia, they faced political and physical harassment at the hands of Vichyites, and the Germans, who controlled parts of Tunisia from the end of November 1942 until May 7, 1943; in Tunisia Jews were sent to labor camps, had to provide Germans with money and belongings, and, as was the case in the town of Sfax, were compelled to wear the yellow Star of David as were Jews in Nazi-occupied Europe. In Morocco the status of local Jews as well as Jewish refugees from Europe who entered the country prior to Vichy presence, to escape Hitler, was not quite as precarious. Nevertheless, they were targeted by the anti-Semites.

Already in 1939 Sémach was concerned about German Jewish refugees that were in Morocco and engaged in commerce. When the war broke out the authorities in the still pre-Vichy French protectorate, placed some of them in prison, for there were no concentration camps built in Morocco at the time. Sémach and Yahya Zagoury, a Jewish leader from Casablanca, met with French officials to have them released; having failed to do so, and having failed to convince the protectorate authorities to allow Moroccan Jewish volunteers to serve France in the war effort, Sémach turned to the AIU: "Can you not intervene in Paris in order to end this anomalous situation? Will [Moroccan] Jews have to constantly suffer from the error committed towards them since the establishment of the protectorate, in having them considered as natives?"[139] But the AIU could do nothing. And in 1940, whereas the rights of Moroccan Jews were further restricted under Vichy domination, Jewish refugees from Germany, Poland, and Austria, who came during the 1930s and early in 1940, were now placed in labor camps under the command of anti-

Semitic officers of the Foreign Legion. There were, for instance, refugee labor camps in Azemmour and one in the Sahara; of the refugees in Azemmour, four hundred were Jews. They remained there until the Americans liberated Morocco.[140]

The Moroccan Jews were also subjected the *numerus clausus*. According to a *ẓahīr* published in October 1940, and modified by another in June 1941, Legislation was set forth which led to the restriction of the number of Jews employed in various agencies.[141] For instance, Jews were limited to two percent of the total number of members in the law and medical professions,[142] a restriction which hurt mostly non-Moroccan Jews residing in the zone, for there were still relatively few Moroccan Jews involved in these professions. However, Moroccan Jews were restricted in other ways. In 1941 a decree forbid them to live in the European quarters.[143] As for those who already resided in these neighborhoods, it appears that they were probably chased out. Yet according to one source, the Jews of Fez lived in the European quarter or in the *mellāḥ*. In Salé, according to another source, Jews who resided among the Europeans during the pre-1940 period were permitted to stay.[144]

The 1940–41 restrictions stipulated that the Jews be barred from or restricted in working for newspapers, in banks, and in commerce; Jewish teachers who taught in protectorate schools, were subject to dismissal from their positions.[145] According to one source dealing with certain restrictions in Fez and Oujda, at least some Jews were dismissed from the following agencies: the protectorate's administration of records and registration; post office employment; collection agencies; public works; municipal services; hospitals; military administration; schools; the *Banque d'Etat* and *Banque Populaire*; and transportation.[146] In total, forty-five were expelled in fez and thirty-nine in Oujda; in Casablanca, on the other hand, Jewish students were expelled from the prestigious *Lycée Lyautey* before the end of 1941; and in vain did Jewish and other intellectuals plead before the authorities to reinstate them; they were told that the regulations were already in effect and could not be reversed.[147]

Jewish institutions were for the most part not harmed, ostensibly because the Vichyites did not have enough time between 1940 and the American landing in North Africa (November 1942), to carry out sanctions against them. In Casablanca, charitable societies of the AIU alumni continued to operate as did educational and agricultural committees founded by community intellectuals; the Māgēn Dāvīd Association, a Zionist-inspired group, remained unharmed; the same applied to scholarship foundations and to *'Olām Qaṭān* (Small World), a group that collected funds to help East European Jews; in Oujda the AIU alumni association, *Aide Scolaire* (another AIU-inspired welfare association), religious schools, and community-sponsored programs were untouched by the authorities; the same applied to Meknes, Safi, and Mazagan.[148] All in all, it appears that most communal projects and institutions survived the Vichy period, at least in the major towns.

The presence of a Vichy administration was a disappointment for many Jews, especially AIU graduates who over the years were taught to admire France. They most likely asked themselves and each other how Pétain, the hero of Verdun, on whose side their Algerian coreligionists fought during the First World War, could become suddenly the traitor at Vichy? How could the *patrie adoptée* carry out such measures against the Jews who had always admired her for the Revolution and for promoting human rights? Some of the most important aspects of the AIU's work were challenged by France: the abrogated Crémieux decree which their one-time president had fought so hard for;[149] and assimilation, dear to AIU leaders since 1860. Suddenly, things began to look different. In Morocco, the school directors and teachers who remained there throughout the war, must have questioned many of their cherished beliefs about *la famille française*. Sémach died at the age of seventy-one in 1940, just weeks before the German invasion of France and the emergence of Vichy rule. It would have been interesting to see his reaction had he lived longer. Sémach died at a time when he could still cherish the marvels of the French Revolution. It was his successor, the Libyan-born Reuben Tajouri, who had to face the challenge of maintaining the schools.

Indeed, during the Vichy period, 1940–1942, it is clear that the AIU schools continued to function. According to AIU statistics for 1940, there were 13,409 children in all its schools in Morocco; the following year, under Vichy rule, 13,462 children. In 1941, the number increased to 14,011 but declined to 13,876 the subsequent year. In 1943 there were 13,483 children in the schools of the three zones, and by the end of the war there were 15,140 in attendance.[150] The AIU schools, then, survived the war period without any direction from Paris and one wonders how the schools in the French zone, which were dependent on heavy financial subsidies from France, managed to survive under an anti-Semitic regime. In Spanish-occupied Tangier and in the Spanish zone, the AIU schools were fewer in number and received support from the communities. In the French zone, however, the forty-five schools could not subsist on small subsidies from communities too poor for the most part to finance them. We learn that Jewish intellectuals and AIU alumni raised funds to help pay the teachers' salaries and operated the schools' lunch stalls. However, that was all they could do. In the underground bulletin of AIU supporters in occupied France, an article appeared after the liberation of France in August 1944 which proclaimed:

It must be said that the [Jewish] communities, . . . sensing the danger in store for them if the schools would disappear, had given all their energy and made considerable financial sacrifices to the point of getting into debt, in order to maintain the schools . . . . The Joint Distribution Committee and the Jewish Colonization Association had collaborated closely with the school directors as well.[151]

Yet the JDC or other organizations which could have kept the AIU going during the war *from* November 1942, that is, since North Africa's liberation, could not have been active in French Morocco in the 1940–1942 period of Vichy domination. And the communities could help very little. How, then, did the network survive?

One plausible theory is tied to the support given by Roger Thabault, the director of primary education in French Morocco from 1929 to 1941. During his tenure Thabault established amicable ties with the AIU and admired its work in the modernization of the Jewish communities, for whom he had great sympathy. He inspected the AIU schools regularly and observed its teachers' zealous devotion to the communities, as well as how many AIU graduates were placed in administrative, industrial, and commercial posts, a fact which led to protests from Moroccan Muslims who had frequented the DIP schools and aspired, understandably, to obtain similar privileges.[152] According to Thabault, when Vichy authority extended to the French zone, there were pro-Vichy officials who sought to dismantle the schools or at least greatly reduce their subsidies; he protested to Resident General Noguès against these policies, and traveled to Vichy where he demanded the adoption of a protocol that would guarantee the normal functioning of the AIU schools.[153]

Be that as it may, even if Thabault obtained a protocol, it is difficult to judge the success of his mission for several reasons. First, he is vague on crucial issues concerning the concessions he might have wrested from Vichy officials. Second, he made enemies (for various reasons) in Morocco and France and in 1941 was relieved of his duties, only to return triumphantly in 1945 as the director of the DIP.

The question which remains unanswered is: did the Vichyites, notorious for their anti-Semitism, continue the subsidies for the AIU in the spirit of the 1928 agreement? Despite the authorities' stated position, it is clear that the subsidies continued under the Vichy regime.[154] According to a reliable source at the AIU who did not wish to be identified, the subsidies continued to arrive from France, though they were the same subsidies as for 1939, which meant that no new school buildings could be constructed and the teachers and directors lived on starvation salaries, for their status remained the same as before the outbreak of the war. This seems to be valid, as in

1939 the AIU had forty-five schools throughout Morocco and in 1942 as well as 1945 there were the same number of schools.

Why was Vichy willing to continue the subsidies? The answer is not completely clear. It is possible that to avoid Jewish or Muslim expression of opposition to Vichy presence, the authorities might have felt that it would be better not to upset established or indigenous institutions too much, and try first to stabilize their power. Another possibility is that while the Vichyites were reactionaries and old-style anti-Semites, they were not as virulent as the Nazis. Vichy may have liked the pro-French role of the AIU and felt that it would be better to let its schools survive.[155]

During these years of anxiety, it appears that unlike some of the Arab countries, such as Iraq, there was no evidence of organized pro-Fascist or pro-Axis violence on a large-scale in Morocco. Both Jews and Muslims appear to have detested Vichy rule and even the nationalist 'Alāl al-Fāsī who was exiled to Gabon in 1937 finally expressed his full support for Charles de Gaulle during the war.

The Vichy period and the abrogation by the Spaniards in Tangier of the February 15, 1925 ẓahīr granting the Jews political and administrative autonomy[156] meant that Europeans and not Muslims were emerging as villains. Writing in 1947, Roger Le Tourneau, who was intimately acquainted with Jewish intellectuals in Fez, where he directed the Collège Mawlāy Idrīs, worried that many Jewish youths might be turning their backs on France as a result of the Vichy experience and that they seemed to fraternize with the American liberators.[157]

5. Beyond 1942: Concluding Remarks on Politial Conditions

Did the Vichy period, as Le Tourneau suggested, alienate the Jews from France? Did they turn to the Americans? There are no ready answers. The refusal to grant Jews French citizenship, and the Vichy period, certainly may have alienated segments of Moroccan Jewry from French Morocco just as their Tunisian counterpart in certain segments became alienated from the French protectorate in Tunisia. The post-1942 period, however, in view of the rise of militant Moroccan nationalism on the one hand, and the creation of Israel on the other, encouraged educated and noneducated Jews to consider the Zionist idea and other alternative solutions for their redemption. Other Jews who were more deeply saturated with French culture through French schools and institutions of higher learning in France, did not allow the Vichy experience to deprive them of the opportunities to settle in France. They, similar to many of their Algerian counterparts of the post-

Vichy era, were inclined to let bygones be bygones. Some of them were too attached to France to turn their backs on her.

But there was yet the category of Jews who were determined to establish ties with Moroccan nationalists in order to share in the struggle for in-

Figure 18. Reuben Tajouri, *AIU* Delegate, 1940–1960

dependence. But this group, to be discussed in chapter IX, did not become at all active before the mid-1950s. Le Tourneau's observation, however, concerning the Jews' contacts with the Americans since the landing in North Africa, should not be taken lightly. Among the Americans who landed in Morocco, a not unimportant number of military personnel were Jews who developed amicable ties with their brethren. Moreover, this was the period when American and international Jewish organizations, among others the JDC, the World Jewish Congress, and the American Jewish Committee (AJC), the latter founded in 1906 to struggle for Jewish political rights internationally, focused attention on Morocco.

The JDC's presence was further prompted by Israel's existence. One of the main reasons for the increase of the JDC's program in Morocco after 1948 was because Moroccan Jews were streaming across the Mediterranean to JDC camps in Marseilles, unhealthy and unfit for emigration. In this process, the JDC obviously collaborated with the Jewish Agency. These activities could be undertaken because Muḥammad V had made an official pronouncement asserting that Jews who chose to go to Israel were free to leave; and of more practical significance, in the pre-1956 period, the French had been cooperative.[158]

The introduction of American and European organizations on behalf of Moroccan Jews is a complex subject, which requires some attention because of their close relations with the AIU. The direct role of the JDC, the OSE's (*Oeuvre de Secours aux Enfants*), medical clinics, and the indirect concern of the AJC came largely in the wake of post-1942 political changes in the country, notably in French Morocco. Similar to the JDC, the AJC after the massacre of six million European Jews turned increasingly toward the "other" Jewry of the Middle East and North Africa: the "forgotten million" who were suddenly discovered and who now became one of the last important segments of world Jewry. The ORT, too, which opened vocational schools in Morocco together with the AIU in 1946 was active in the prewar period on behalf of Eastern European Jews.

These organizations, like various Moroccan Jewish intellectuals, were generally in agreement that though the AIU since 1862 and the French protectorate since 1912, have prodigiously raised the level of education and standard of living among Jews, the French, at least, were probably not anxious to hasten Morocco to the point of "civilization" where Muslim nationalism and self-determination would be irresistible.[159] Consequently, such consideration would ultimately lead to a ceiling on the general social evolution of the area in which the Jews could be expected to share with the Muslims.

The JDC's collaboration with the Jewish Agency and other Zionist bodies suggested that its officials in Morocco did not consider that the Jews had any kind of future in the country and that emigration was a major objective of any long-term program. The AJC held the same position. Yet, until the realization of emigration, which would require a long process in view of the presence of close to a quarter of a million people, improvement would have to be made in existing conditions. The fight to ameliorate the social and political status of the Jews had to be waged in French Morocco, where the Jewish population was expanding through births and to where Jews from other parts of the country were emigrating, mostly to the developing metropolis of Casablanca.

In analyzing the political achievements of the AIU, the AJC, following a fact-finding mission in 1950 of Zachariah Shuster and Max Isenbergh, two of its representatives, to Morocco, found out that little was accomplished.

The AIU had failed in the past to obtain any sort of a breakthrough in legislation on behalf of the Jews. Although the AJC understood that Quranic law had to be maintained as the basis for decision in domestic and penal matters where Muslims were involved, it sought major concessions, such as French supervision of Muslim courts to see if legal decisions involving Jews were not discriminatory.[160]

The AJC representatives noted that there were some limited but favorable steps adopted during the protectorate era. Whereas in 1918 the Jewish communities were organized in accordance with a ẓahīr, limiting the community committee to the tasks of welfare, philanthropy, and religious affairs, the French (and the Spanish) authorities, after the Second World War, granted the communities wider powers. Among these: the communities themselves had to right to make decisions about and administer all matters pertaining to them; and whereas since 1918 the community committees were designated by the authorities rather than elected by the Jews, in 1945 a ẓahīr provided that the Jews could choose their own committees.[161] A further step was the creation in 1947 of the *Conseil des Communautés Israélites* (Council of the Moroccan Jewish Communities) which, for the first time, enabled the communities to coordinate their activities under an umbrella organization, a privilege enjoyed hitherto by the Algerian and Tunisian communities.[162]

Did this reorganization process increase possibilities that communities might be represented before the Moroccan government effectively? The AJC representatives pointed the success of the AIU before the French, of having obtained the appointment of six Jewish representatives of the council as members to the government's consultative council, a body authorized to advise the French administration on Moroccan affairs.[163]

But Shuster and Isenbergh concluded that the Jewish members of the council were ineffective because of their small numbers, and because of their subservience to the French administration, they could not bring about any greater changes in the basic position of the Jewish population.[164]

The representatives of the AJC indicated that though there was no disposition among most Jews to associate with Moroccan nationalists, Jewish emigration in highly significant numbers was not taking place; and it was observed that catastrophic developments that could produce a *Judenrein* in Morocco was not expected. Therefore, to improve the status of the Jews in Morocco the AJC was apparently seeking to develop political strength in the communities in collaboration with the AIU. The plan was to apply pressure on the French protectorate from Paris. According to Shuster's and Isenbergh's recommendations:

> While our representatives in Washington should be fully alerted to the situation, it must be remembered that the French government is extremely sensitive

toward any American activities regarding Morocco, being wrongly but understandably suspicious that these are a threat to French hegemony. As a consequence, direct political intervention by an organization like the AJC would seem to be imprudent, especially in view of our own government's desire not to worry the French.

The focal point for political intervention, probably, must be Paris. It is here that the major lines of the policy for the French protectorate of Morocco are drawn, despite the wide powers left to the sultan and the shadow areas of Moroccan sovereignty where it is not certain whether the French or the sultan make the effective decisions.

The *Alliance Israélite* is *persona grata* with the Ministry of Foreign Affairs. It is highly sophisticated and experienced in Moroccan problems. And it maintains continuous contact in the field. Therefore, our every effort regarding Morocco should be made in close cooperation with the *Alliance*. The AJC can contribute its international skill, and—in those situations where it is deemed necessary after due deliberations—its contacts with the U.S. authorities.

We believe it is advisable, therefore, that a committee on Moroccan affairs be formed in Paris, consisting of the *Alliance* and ourselves, to serve as a central planning and coordination board for political action. Such a committee could stimulate the *Alliance* in the field of social and political rights. We feel the *Alliance* sometimes has a tendency to exaggerate French sensitivity regarding Morocco and thus does not act as often as it should for fear of possible French government repercussions. Such a committee, moreover, should keep close contact with the efforts of the other Jewish agencies working in Morocco, like the JDC, because political, welfare and relief programs interplay so closely in dealing with Moroccan Jewish affairs.

There is also room for the AJC activity as regards the field of local Jewish community organization in Morocco. One reason why the community groups are not effective . . . is because the French limit their powers and activities very strictly and, we think, unnecessarily. To grant wider powers to the local Jewish groups would not involve the French in difficulties with the Arabs and might well help revitalize these groups. Here, too, close cooperation with the *Alliance* would be necessary to work on the French.[165]

It is not clear if the AJC forwarded these recommendations to the AIU in Paris. They probably did. Yet it is doubtful that any changes took place as a result. The AIU, with its many decades of experience in the field, knew that in the Moroccan political climate of the protectorate era such proposals and Jewish organizational interference were not prudent. It was particularly unwise in the volatile situation of the times, when the nationalists and the French were heading for violent confrontations, a situation that actually occurred between 1953-1955 but which was clearly predicted in 1950, when Shuster and Isenbergh were in Morocco. Besides, the failure of the AIU to obtain French citizenship for the Jews during the prewar period was a sufficient lesson. Furthermore, by 1950, other Jewish organizations (a subject to be discussed in chapter VII) to some extent encroached on the political influence of AIU, and the AJC was no exception. The AIU no doubt wished to protect its influence in the extraeducational sphere. It was also a matter of principle: the AIU would have never agreed that another Jewish organization was internationally more prestigious and sophisticated in the human rights field. If little was accomplished it is because every possible alternative was exhausted. After all, the AIU, it could be argued, championed Jewish rights nearly half a century before the AJC was created. And its president since 1943, René Cassin, was a promoter of human rights, a participant in the preparation of the 1948 draft of the United Nation's Human Rights Declaration. The AIU, therefore, was in no need of partners. Finally, AIU leaders and Tajouri preferred, after 1942, to resort to caution and diplomacy in view of the organization's financial dependence on the French. They avoided any action that might alienate the French and endanger AIU presence in Morocco.

Notes

1. For an analysis on Tangier, see Stuart Graham, *The International City of Tangier* (California: University of California Press, 1955).
2. On the role and political authority of the Resident-General, see John Waterbury, *The Commander of the Faithful: The Moroccan Political Elite* (New York: Columbia University Press, 1970).
3. The Resident-General was entrusted with the responsibilities of acting as the sultan's spokesman before foreign representatives and dignitaries; he was responsible for all affairs pertaining to foreign nationals residing in the French zone.
4. Waterbury, *The Commander of the Faithful*, pp. 34–35.
5. Ibid.
6. Ibid.
7. Rabbi David Ovadia, *The Community of Sefrou*, III: 177 (Jerusalem, Center for the Research on the Jewish Communities of Morocco, 1975).
8. Kenneth L. Brown, *People of Salé: Tradition and Change in a Moroccan City: 1830–1930* (Cambridge, Mass.: Harvard University Press, 1976), p. 197.
9. Yomtov Sémach was born in Yambol (Bulgaria) in 1869 and was educated at the AIU schools there as well as at the ENIO. He served subsequently as teacher and director of AIU schools in the Ottoman Empire, and went on frequent missions on behalf of the AIU to survey the conditions of Middle Eastern Jewry, particularly in the Yemen. He came to Morocco in 1913 and served as AIU school director in Tangier before being appointed delegate.
10. Y. D. Sémach, "Les israélites au Maroc," *La Revue Française de Tanger* ler année no. 4, 10 avril 1918, p. 15.
11. Ibid., p. 5.
12. Ibid., p. 12.
13. Ibid., p. 2.
14. Ibid.
15. Ibid.

16. Sémach to AIU, Tangier, May 26, 1925, Arch.AIU.LXII.E.946(3). There were as many as 400,000 Europeans dwelling in Morocco in the mid-1950s.

17. Raphaël Danon to AIU, Marrakesh, April 8, 1913, Arch.AIU.XXV. E.394(a).

18. Danon to AIU, Marrakesh, March 16, Arch.AIU.XXV.E.394(a).

19. See Danon to AIU, Mogador, September 12, 1912, Arch.AIU.II.B.14.

20. The schools of Safi, Rabat, Salé, Azemmour, and Sefrou were temporarily taken over by the protectorate after 1916. See Gaston Loth to AIU, Rabat, December 20, 1918, Arch.AIU.XLI.E.696.

21. Narcisse Leven to Lyautey, Paris, July 20, 1915, Arch.AIU.I.J.2.

22. Ibid.

23. Sémach to AIU, Tangier, December 4, 1916, Arch.AIU.LXI.E.946(b).

24. Ibid.

25. Ibid.

26. Gaston Loth to AIU, Rabat, December 20, 1918, Arch.AIU.XLI.E.696.

27. Ibid.

28. Joseph Bensimhon to AIU, Casablanca, June 17, 1919, Arch.AIU.IV.E.82.

29. Ibid.

30. Ibid.

31. Ibid.

32. Sémach to AIU, Tangier, March 31, 1920, Arch.AIU.LXI.E.946(c).

33. See Joseph Conquy to AIU, Rabat, October 29, 1919, Arch.AIU.XL.E. 685(e).

34. Roger Gaudefroy-Demombynes, L'oeuvre française en matière d'enseignement au Maroc (Paris: Librarie Orientaliste Paul Geuthner, 1928), p. 204.

35. Isaac Harroche to AIU, Azemmour, June 30, 1918, Arch.AIU.I.E.13.

36. Yahya Zagoury to AIU, Casablanca, April 15, 1916, Arch.AIU.I.B.2.

37. Bensimhon to AIU, Casablanca, March 15, 1918, Arch.AIU.IV.E.82.

38. Ibid.

39. Sémach to AIU, Tangier, October 21, 1924, Arch.AIU.V.B.24.

40. Gaudefroy-Demombynes, L'oeuvre française, p. 204.

41. Convention de 25 juin 1924, articles I et II, Arch.AIU.XLI.E.696.

42. Ibid., art. VIII.

43. Ibid., art. XI.

44. Ibid., art. XIII.

45. It is noteworthy that in Tangier, the Legislative Assembly accorded annual subsidies to Jewish institutions, including the AIU schools.

46. Interview with Jules Braunschvig, Jerusalem, February 8, 1976 (in English).

47. Pierre Flamand, Diaspora en terre d'Islam: Les Communautés israélites du sud marocain (Casablanca, Imprimeries réunies, 1959), p. 351; the figure cited by Flamand for the French subsidy is confirmed by Elias Harrus, delegate of the Ittiḥād (AIU) schools in present-day Morocco.

48. André Chouraqui, Cent ans d'histoire: L'alliance israélite universelle et la renaissance juive contemporaine (1860–1960) (Paris: Presses Universitaires de France, 1965), p. 499. In the early 1960s there were 434 trained teachers at the AIU schools.

49. R. Lacoste, "Une grave atteinte aux lois laïques," L'Ecole Emancipée 15 (1925), pp. 1–3.

50. Ibid., p. 3.

51. Ibid.

52. During the 1930s, the protectorate recruited Jewish teachers for the few remaining Franco-Jewish schools. Even these schools were required to adopt a greater Jewish character.

53. Gaudefroy-Demombynes, *L'oeuvre française*, p. 204.

54. Joan Gardner Roland, "The Alliance Israélite Universelle and French Policy in North Africa, 1860–1918," Ph.D diss., Columbia University, 1969, p. 211.

55. Cambon to Pichon, Berlin, August 12, 1907, A. E. Maroc. Série Administrative - C:142 dr2.

56. Ibid.

57. Ibid.

58. Albert Saguès to AIU, Casablanca, September 12, 1912, Arch.AIU.VIII. E.155.

59. Ibid.

60. Ibid.

61. Ibid.

62. Sémach to AIU, Tangier, June 16, 1913, Arch.AIU.LX.E.946(a). It is not clear if Sémach extended his views on naturalization outside the French zone into Tangier, which prior to 1923 remained neither a zone nor part of the French or Spanish protectorate.

63. Ibid.

64. See, for instance, Josué Cohen to AIU, Mazagan, April 22, 1915, Arch.AIU. XXIX.E.471.

65. Y. D. Sémach, "L'avenir des israélites marocains," *Paix et Droit* pt. I, 7e année, no. 6, mensuel (juin 1927), pp. 9–10.

66. Ibid., p. 10.

67. Sémach, *Paix et Droit*, pt. II, 8e année no. 6, mensuel, (juin 1928), p. 4.

68. Ibid., p. 5.

69. Ibid.

70. Ibid., p. 6.

71. Sémach's position on collective naturalization, as stated in 1927–1928, was thus: Nous preferions la naturalisation collective *par catégories*; naturalisation automatique, qui s'imposent comme un devoir général qu'on accepte parce qu'il n'y a pas moyen de s'y soustraire, l'Etat se réservant des garanties. La naturalisation individuelle est trop lente; elle exige de l'initiative, un effort moral, une energie qui ne sont pas à la portée des êtres simples, des hommes harcelés par la recherche du pain quotidien" (*Paix et Droit* pt. II, 8e no. 6, mensuel, juin 1928, pp. 4 and 6).

72. Alfred Berl, "Au Maroc, "*Paix et Droit*, 8e no. 4, mensuel (avril 1928), p. 2.

73. Ibid.

74. Ibid.

75. Letter of community council to the president of the French Republic, Fez, December 13, 1922, Arch.AIU.XVII.E.258.

76. Victor de Stahl, "La naturalisation des israélites marocains," *La Dépêche Marocaine*, 2 novembre 1927.

77. Gaudefroy-Demombynes, *L'oeuvre française*, p. 210.

78. For some background information on the early nationalists, see J. P. Halstead, *Rebirth of a Nation: The Origins and Rise of Moroccan Nationalism* (Cambridge, Mass.: Harvard University Press, 1967); R. Rézette, *Les partis politiques marocains* (Paris, Armand Colin, 1955); John Waterbury, *The Commander of the Faithful: The Moroccan Political Elite* (Columbia University Press: 1970).

79. Muḥammad al-Kholti, "Les israélites et nous," *L'Action du Peuple*, 18 août 1933.

80. Y. D. Sémach, "Le recensement de 1936 au Maroc," *Paix et Droit* 19, no. 6, mensuel (juin 1939), pp. 8–10. Knowledge of French was defined by the 1936 census and by Sémach as those "who could write or speak."

81. Ibid. Perhaps he was right as, according to interviews conducted by this researcher, French was rapidly becoming the dominant language among Jewish youths in the large communities during the late 1930s. Interview with Hanania Dahan, Bat-Yam, January 26, 1976; interview with Issachar Ben-Ami, Jerusalem, march 8, 1976 (in Hebrew).

82. Sémach argued: "Beaucoup de personnes se familiarisent avec le français par des moyens divers. Cette langue est celle des transactions commerciales et nos israélites qui en ont besoin, font des efforts pour en acquérir la connaissance . . . . Beaucoup d'autres la connaissant médiocrement, n'ont pas cru devoir le dire de peur qu'on ne se moquât d'eux . . . . Les colporteurs, les portefaix, les marchands d'habits s'adressent généralement en français à la clientèle d'occasion. Assurément leur langage est spécial, il n'est pas correct, il est mal prononcé, mais on le comprend cependant " Sémach, "Le recensement de 1936 au Maroc," *Paix et Droit*, pp. 9–10.

83. Michael Ansky, *The Jews of Algeria from the Crémieux Decree until Independence* (Kirjath Sepher, Jerusalem, 1963). In Hebrew, trans. from French by Abraham Elmaleh, p. xvi.

84. Sémach to AIU, Rabat, October 10, 1936, Arch.AIU.XLV.E.717(j).

85. André Chouraqui, *Between East and West: A History of the Jews in North Africa* (Philadelphia: The Jewish Publication Society: 1968), pp. 169–170.

86. Ibid., p. 170.

87. Nissim Falcon to AIU, Tetuan, November 27, 1911, Arch.AIU.LXVI.E.1010(a).

88. Ibid.

89. Ibid.

90. Ibid.

91. Ibid.

92. Ibid.

93. Falcon to AIU, Tetuan, March 20, 1911, Arch.AIU.LXVI.E.1010(a).

94. Falcon to AIU, Tetuan, November 18, 1912, Arch.AIU.LXVI.E.1010(b).

95. Speech delivered by Saavedra at the Hebreo-Español center in honor of King Alphonso XIII; Falcon to AIU, Tetuan, May 26, 1914, Arch.AIU.LXVI.E.1010(b).

96. Ibid.

97. Ibid.

98. Falcon to AIU, Tetuan, December 4, 1913, Arch.AIU.LXVI.E.1010(b).

99. Ibid.

100. Falcon to AIU, Tetuan, July 28, 1914, Arch.AIU.LXVI.E.1010(b).

101. Ibid.

102. Ibid.

103. Fernand Couget to *Quai d'Orsay*, Tangier, December 14, 1914, A. E. Maroc. II. 403.

104. Jordana to AIU, Tetuan, September 17, 1917, Arch.AIU.LXVII.E.1021 (in Spanish).

105. Léon Loubaton to AIU, Tetuan, December 24, 1915, Arch.AIU.LXIX.E.1034.

106. Ibid.

107. Ibid.

108. There is no evidence of the existence of these schools in the preprotectorate period.

109. Loubaton to AIU, Tetuan, March 12, 1917, Arch.AIU.LXIX.E.1034.

110. See a more elaborate analysis on the Spanish zone schools in chapter VIII.

111. Vial de Morla, "La Alianza en Marruecos," *Heraldo de Marruecos*, abril 4, 1926, p. 19.

112. Ibid.

113. Sémach to AIU, Tangier, April 9, 1926, Arch.AIU.LXII.E.946(e).

114. Ibid.

115. See, for instance, Isaac Haroche to AIU, Elksar, March 30, 1925, Arch.AIU.XI.E.188.

116. Moïse Lévy to AIU, Tetuan, January 5, 1932, Arch.AIU.LXVIII.E.1030(c).

117. Sémach to AIU, Rabat, December 20, 1935, Arch.AIU.XLIV.E.717(h).

118. Albert Saguès to AIU, Tangier, September 8, 1936, Arch.AIU.LX.E.943(e).

119. Ibid.

120. Ibid.

121. Moïse Lévy to AIU, Tetuan, April 3, 1939, Arch.AIU.LXXVII.E. no file number.

122. Sémach to AIU, Rabat, March 8, 1928, Arch.AIU.E. no file number.

123. Ibid.

124. Charles Hamet, *La communauté israélite de Tanger* (Tangier, 1951) (Ms. of C.H.E.A.M.), p. 74.

125. Saguès to AIU, Tangier, April 11, 1932, Arch.AIU.LIX.E.943(c).

126. "Ecoles de l'alliance israélite: Distribution solonelle des prix," *La Dépêche Marocaine*, juillet 13, 1933, p. 3.

127. Hamet, *La communauté israélite*, p. 9.

128. Ibid.

129. Ibid., pp. 111-12 (Jo Hassan, council president, was a Portuguese citizen; David Bergel, controller, American citizen; Messod Bengio, member, French citizen; Moses Abensur, member, British citizen).

130. Ibid., p. 13.

131. Ibid.

132. Ibid.

133. Ibid., pp. 25-27.

134. Ibid., p. 20. In 1950 there were in the city of Tangier 40,000 Muslims, 20,000 Spaniards, 12,000 Jews, 6,000 Frenchmen, and an additional number of other Europeans — a total of 83,000 city dwellers.

135. F. L. to Jewish Agency, Tangier, May 3-17, 1944 (Zionist Archives: S26/1397).

136. Ibid.

137. Ibid.

138. Ibid.

139. Sémach to AIU, Rabat, November 2, 1939, Arch.AIU.XLVII.E.717(q).

140. *Ha-Sofe* (February 7, 1944).

141. M.Y., R.S., R.B., *L'application du statut des juifs et des disposition raciales à la population juive au Maroc* (Février 1943). Ms. of the Ben-Zvi Institute in Jerusalem.

142. Doris Bensimon Donath, *Evolution du judaïsme marocain sous le protectorat français* (Paris, Mouton and Co., 1968), p. 109.

143. Ibid. This restriction was embodied in a *ẓahīr* published on August 19, 1941.

144. Interview with Mordehai Soussan, Jerusalem, March 1, 1976; interview with Hanania Dahan, Bat-Yam, January 26, 1976 (in Hebrew).

145. M.Y., R.S., R.B., *L'application du statut*; see also: Roger Thabault, "Le Maroc à l'heure du Vichysme," *Les Nouveaux Cahiers* 43 (Hiver, 1975–76), pp. 16–20. According to this source: Les enseignants israélites des établissement franco-européens devaient être demis de leurs fonctions." p. 18.

146. *L'application du statut.*

147. Ibid.

148. Ibid.

149. The Crémieux decree and French citizenship were restored toward the end of 1943.

150. "La rentrée scolaire au Maroc dans les écoles de l'Alliance," *Les Cahiers de l'Alliance Israélite Universelle* 11 (décembre 1946-janvier 1947), p. 6.

151. "Communications du comité central," *Bulletin Intérieur de l'Alliance Israélite Universelle* 2 (août 1944), p. 1.

152. Roger Thabault, "Le Maroc à l'heure du Vichysme," *Les Nouveaux Cahiers* 43 (hiver 1975–76), p. 17.

153. Ibid.

154. Interview with Haïm Zafrani, Paris, pt. ii, September 20, 1976 (in French).

155. Interview with Rabbi Albert Hazan, Jerusalem, February 8, 1976 (in Hebrew).

156. The February 1925 *ẓahīr* was reinstated in 1945.

157. Roger Le Tourneau, *Jeunesse européenne, juive, et musulmane en Afrique du Nord* (Fès 1947). Ms. of C.H.E.A.M.

158. Zachariah Shuster and Max Isenbergh to John Slawson, Paris, March 28, 1950. Report on Morocco-based visit, March 7-18, 1950 (JDC/ 10(b)), p. 12.

159. Ibid.

160. Ibid.

161. Jacques Dahan, "Les communautés israélites du Maroc," *Cahiers de l'Alliance Israélite Universelle* 91 (juin-juillet 1955), p. 9.

162. Ibid., pp. 9–10.

163. *Report of Morocco* (AJC), p. 15.

164. Ibid.

165. Ibid., p. 16.

CHAPTER VI

Zionism and Assimilation: The Emergence of Zionist Influence in Morocco and the Position of the *Alliance*

"No one can propagate new ideas without the consent and permission of the *Alliance* of Paris which dominates the Jewish public [in Morocco] like a tyrant with the effective aid of the French Residency" (Remarks by Anshel Perl, a Zionist activist, in Algeciras: May 1927).

"Le sionisme marocain n'a . . . aujourd'hui aucune importance, il ne pourrait devenir actif que s'il trouvait un propagateur capable de se mettre en rapport avec le sionisme européen" (Observation by Y.D. Sémach in Tangier: April 1919).

In Morocco as in numerous Jewish communities scattered throughout the diaspora, hope for a return to Zion, namely the land of Israel, has always existed. This hope rested on messianic and religious concepts rather than on a political program, and Moroccan Jewry always maintained links of communications with Palestine. There were rabbis who came from Jerusalem to visit and even live among the Jews of North Africa. Similarly, from time to time, Jewish families from Morocco and other parts of the Maghrib would visit or settle in Palestine. In Jerusalem Jewish families from the Maghrib were among the most active in cultural and religious affairs, long before any serious emigration, inspired by political Zionism, ever took place. Nevertheless, the emergence of political Zionism in the late nineteenth century was to gradually influence Morocco: the secular Zionist idea as espoused by Dr. Theodor Herzl was to enjoy a respectable status alongside traditional Zionism, based on messianic longing to Eretz-Yisrael.

1. The AIU and the Zionists: Jews in Conflict

From the inception of modern Zionism following the Basel Congress of 1897, a serious conflict had developed between the AIU and the Zionists.

The latter accused the AIU of sacrificing Jewish goals in favor of national interests (meaning France), because in order for the AIU to remain viable, it needed to obtain funds and political support for its educational and political activities. Therefore, the AIU, argued the Zionists, had to obtain the consent of the French government for its programs on behalf of the Jews. This, they felt, restricted the scope of AIU activities, for if certain actions did not please the French, then considerable Jewish sufferings would continue. Although, as noted earlier, the AIU did not hesitate to undertake activities contrary to French wishes on various occasions, the Zionists believed that the AIU and its sister organizations (for example, the Anglo-Jewish Association) were being used by their respective governments. As Richard Gottheil, a leader of early American Zionism contended:

> It was at one time hoped that the *Alliance Israélite Universelle* would serve as a unifying force, but the parallel societies founded in other countries rendered nugatory the hopes that had been set upon the larger program of the *Alliance*. The new societies are doomed to follow in the wake of the parent body. The very nature of their formation, the help which they are bound to demand from the governments under which they reckon for the furthering of their end, vitiate them at their source, as far as their general Jewish service is concerned.[1]

Some of the criticisms of the political role of the AIU were far more intransigent. Among its leading opponents was Theodor Herzl himself. In his *Zionist Writings*, Herzl contended in 1898 that those who refer to the AIU as a Jewish organization might as well describe the Freemasons as a Judaized association.[2] He regarded the AIU as a foolish institution which had done more harm than good: the "Universal Alliance" seemed to Herzl as neither universal nor an alliance, and with its pompous and hollow name it helped perpetuate the myth among anti-Semites that there existed a secret international brotherhood plotting to establish a Jewish world dominion.[3] Herzl, then, suggested that the sooner this "Alliance" disappeared from the face of the earth, the better, for Zionists most emphatically and most resolutely oppose any international association of Jews which, if it were effective, would constitute that "state within a state" which is justly taboo.[4]

The conflict was clear: the AIU aspired to transform and liberate the Jews in their respective countries and what it would do was to fight for legislative reforms, bringing the Jews closer to France. The Zionists, on the other hand, called for the solution to the "Jewish problem" not through assimilation but rather by physically uprooting the Jews from the diaspora and placing them in a homeland of their own. Such a solution was unacceptable to the AIU for quite some time.

Whereas Gottheil and Herzl attacked the political purpose of the AIU, others did not spare the organization criticism in the area of education. Nahum Sokolow, for example, was not at all happy with the educational program of the AIU for the Middle Eastern countries. Writing in 1909, he found it questionable whether the Jews ought to adopt French culture and not Turkish, Arabic, or what would be the most natural, their own culture. In his view, most AIU teachers represented French culture and promoted a sort of an arrogant and *parvenu* contempt for other people who did not *parler français* and had not the Paris chic. However, Sokolow distinguished between the educational activities of the AIU at the time of his writings and of previous years when the organization was young. He longed for a return to the policies of Adolphe Crémieux and Charles Netter, policies from which the AIU managed to deviate with the passing of each day.

What had to be done? The activities of the AIU had to be regenerated as in the days when Netter founded the Mikveh Israel agricultural college in Palestine. Instead of attempting to transplant a Parisian *boulevardier* or a Parisian student in the Mediterranean-basin communities, agricultural (and perhaps vocational) training, modelled on the Mikveh Israel example, would create a Jewish type of peasant who would be similar in many ways to a French small landholder.[5] Instead of striving toward assimilation to French culture, the AIU, through agricultural training, would help create the type of Jewish peasant who would resemble the French peasants of Bretagne, Normandy, and the isle of Oberon; they would become economically independent, producing their own fruit, milk, butter, cheese, and flour to make bread:

> Although many French peasant farmers are compelled to live extremely thrifty lives, barely making both ends meet, they are practically a prosperous people, and if they live simply and work hard, their lives are examples of contentment and happiness. It is they, and not the Paris snobs, who form the backbone of the nation.[6]

This, then, was the type of Jew that Sokolow wanted the AIU to form through its schools in the Middle East and North Africa.

The AIU leadership, however, though eager to launch diverse programs, agricultural training included, sensed that the Zionists intended to use the organization to render the Zionist cause more effective. The Central Committee did not wish to serve such causes; it opposed the Zionist intention to cluster the Jews of the diaspora in Palestine, and expressed its disapproval both verbally and in writing. In 1921, for example, an editorial appeared in *Paix et Droit* explaining the opposition to Zionist intentions for a national Jewish home in Palestine. The editorial depicted Theodor Herzl, Leon Pinsker, and Max Nordau as extremists, who, regardless of their earlier assimilationist tendencies, had turned to a form of destructive nationalism calling for a creation of a separate Jewish entity. The position of the AIU was that even if this sort of resurrection were unanimously desired by the

Jews, it would inevitably encounter obstacles that would render the dream of a national homeland in Palestine a nightmare.[7] According to the editorial, Palestine was neither vacant nor capable of absorbing the 11,000,000 Jews scattered throughout the world; the Zionists saw Palestine as a "no man's land." But aside from the 80,000 Christians who lived there, there are some 700,000 Arabs who have been living there for ages, and there could be no hope that these Arabs could somehow be persuaded to allow areas of land to be expropriated.[8] It was argued that perhaps the Zionists would succeed in gaining some influence among Eastern European Jews, but not in Western Europe and other parts of the diaspora.[9] In fact, however, the Zionists made significant inroads into the Jewish communities of Morocco.

2. Zionist Strategical Penetration in Morocco and the *Alliance*

The Pre-1939 Period

It is difficult to determine the exact date of modern Zionist penetration into the Moroccan communities. The earliest organized activity might have commenced after the first Zionist congress (1897), although one source estimated that activities began in 1900 when Dr. Y. Barliawsky, a Russian physician, settled in northern Morocco and established in Tetuan the *Shivat Sion* (Return to Zion) association; this association set up a Hebrew-language library to propagate the language and the Zionist idea among the Jews.[10] At the same time, a second association was founded in Mogador, known as the *Sha'arē-Sion* (Gates of Zion) association; it was probably the first group that popularized the *sheqel* in North Africa and had passed to the Zionist Federation in Cologne (Köln) over two hundred *sheqalim*, an amount that entitled the Mogador association to have two representatives elected to the Zionist congress, even if it did not take advantage of this opportunity.[11] A third association, *Ahavat Sion* (Love of Zion) was founded in the coastal town of Safi.[12]

The correspondent of the *Jewish Chronicle* to Mogador, reporting on November 8, 1897, at a time when the first Zionist congress was a controversial development in Western Europe, indicated that Moroccan Jews were aware of the event. The Jews of Morocco watched with interest Zionist progress in Europe:

Needless to say, here the Zionist idea finds a loud and sympathetic echo in the hearts of all coreligionists with almost no exceptions. It is quite interesting to note how enthusiastically the rabbis talk over the matter . . . . Perhaps this feeling of sympathy exists in the hearts of all Jews, only they do not care to expose their sentiments. All Jews may not be in agreement with items of the congress program, but it seems natural, from some Moroccan-Jewish points of view, that they should all sympathize with the spirit of the thing, without running the risk of feeling or showing any disloyalty for the native land in which they have been born and bred.[13]

As a matter of fact, Moroccan Jewry, like their Algerian and Tunisian counterparts were represented to European Zionism by Eugène Valensin, a young Algerian intellectual from the Jewish community of Constantine.[14]

After Herzl's death in 1904 Zionist activities in Morocco were temporarily halted, only to be revived in 1907 through the initiative of influential families in the interior (Fez, Meknes, Sefrou).[15] In 1908 the *Hibbat-Sion* (Admiration of Zion) society was founded in Fez; it sent letters to Cologne and began disseminating the *sheqel*, expanding activities to neighboring Sefrou and to Meknes.[16] And already then, though secularly educated Jews in the coastal towns and the interior were actively involved in Zionist activities, Moroccan rabbis such as the prominent Fez spiritual leaders — Raphaël Abensur, Mordehai Serero, Shlomo Aben-Danan and Vidal Ṣarfatī — were involved, too.[17] They joined forces for a common goal. As we shall see, similar associations sprang in Tangier, Casablanca, and in other key communities beginning in the post-1918 period.

In encountering early Zionist activities, representatives of the AIU were at first concerned with the interior. In March 1911 Amram Elmaleh, director of the AIU schools of Fez, reported that there existed a Zionist cell composed of thirty members who had financial and political links with Cologne. The society, founded in 1907 or 1908 in response to anti-European manifestations on the part of the Muslims which, in turn, resulted in an attack on the *mellāḥ* of Fez, encouraged similar developments of cells in Sefrou and Meknes; and by early 1911 pro-Zionist cells in these communities had a membership of approximately one hundred; they send annually sums of money to the Federation in Cologne.[18] Indeed, the Zionist archives do point to a series of correspondence since 1908 between *Hibbat Sion* and Cologne. One letter dated July 3, 1908, from David Wolffsohn to the association, expressed gratitude for the association's contribution of thirty-six shilings, the amount of which was obtained through the sale of *sheqalim* sent from Cologne; he encouraged its members to subscribe to *Die Welt*, but as he was aware that they were unfamiliar with German, Wolffsohn informed them that a Hebrew version of the paper, *Hā-ʻOlām*, was published in Vilna and could easily be obtained.[19]

Following *Hibbat Sion's* activities, Elamleh informed Paris that the cell's president had been Rahamim Benzimra who was also president of the Jewish community. The newly elected president, Haïm Cadosh Delmar, a

wealthy merchant, was a graduate of the AIU.[20] Though these were embryonic cells, they were beginning to play an active role in these communities and, furthermore, their main organizers included AIU graduates.
No doubt concerned with potential Zionist challenge to the AIU, Elmaleh
informed Paris that he had been lured by the idea of winning the support of
all AIU graduates to his side; that he has methodically and with utmost
discretion worked to remove these youths from Zionism by encouraging
them to form a social welfare organization that would operate under the
AIU's auspices; such an effort if at all successful in Fez, could extend to the
communities of Meknes and Sefrou, thus weakening Zionist cells and
transforming their character. In other words, neutralize the cells while they
are still small. Responding to Elmaleh, Secretary Bigart expressed astonishment and dissappointment at the news that Benzimra who had in the past
closely associated with the AIU, was prominent in such activities; he
favored the dissolution of the cells.[21]

Although the archives fail to mention Elmaleh's successes or failures in
his anti-Zionist missions, some evidence pointing to his or other people's
successes can be traced in Zionist sources. According to Joseph H. Lévy, a
Zionist leader in Fez, political pressure was applied on the association in
1912 to become integrated with the AIU and hence Zionist activities had
been temporarily halted.[22] Yet the Fez Zionists were not discouraged and on
the eve of the First World War they circulated political brochures and journals in the _mellāḥ_.[23]

Jewish intellectuals also created cells in Tangier and Casablanca. During
the early days of the protectorate the cells' activities were mainly confined to
the dissemination of literature and the _sheqel_. Since the early 1920s funds
were raised in the communities through envoys of the Zionist organization,
mainly envoys of the Jewish National Fund (KKL) and the Palestine Foundation Fund (KH).[24] The latter activity gained momentum after 1920 and was
tolerated by the authorities, who apparently failed to distinguish between
the collection of funds for Zionist causes and the money collected by the
rabbis for communal matters.[25]

The reaction of AIU representatives to the various Zionist developments
were mixed. In 1914, for example, Albert Moyal, director of the Meknes
schools, reported that the schools were challenged by various elements, and
he did not rule out Zionist opposition instigated by Wolf Hilperine, an East
European Jew who had anti-AIU inclinations.[26] Wolf Hilperine was probably Rabbi Ze'ev Hilperine, who came to Morocco during the first decade
of the protectorate and promoted rabbinic schools under the auspices of the
Em-Habanīm society (The Mother of the Sons).[27] These schools were
created mostly in the interior, and they competed with the AIU for influence in the communities.[28] But that was not all Hilperine promoted. The

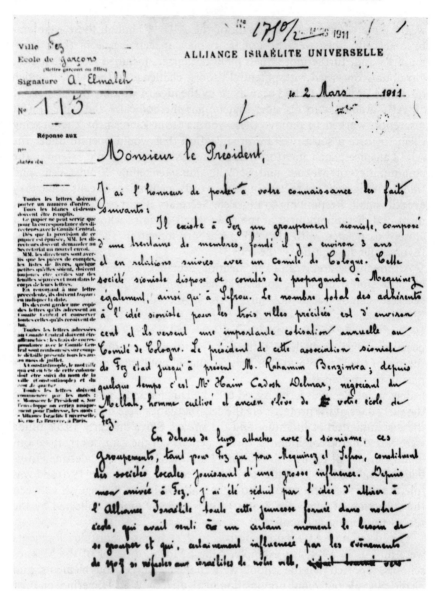

Figure 19. Reactions of Amram Elmaleh, Boys' School director in Fez, to early Zionist activities in Morocco, March, 1911

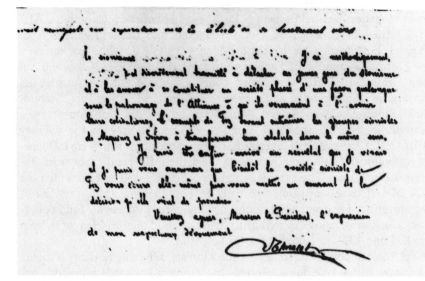

Figure 19. (continued)

rabbi attested in his correspondence with the Zionist Organization's central office in London that he also helped develop the *Bonē Yerūshālayīm* (Builder of Jerusalem) Zionist association in Larache.[29]

On the whole, AIU representatives were not genuinely alarmed by the Zionists before the early 1920s. Many made a mockery of the pioneer activists who collected funds for the *sheqalim* and founded small associations; and once again it was Sémach who occupied himself with the new trends. In 1919, as director of the Tangier schools, he considered Zionist activities as merely a joke and argued that though the AIU assisted in cultivating an educated elite, part of which could turn against French ideals, it was a disorganized elite and not very astute in political Zionism.[30] As for the dangers the rabbis could pose, Sémach categorized their Zionist inspirations as confined to a spiritual longing for Palestine and "they have not the faintest idea about the ideological basis of modern political Zionism as envisaged in Europe."[31] He conceded that in 1919 there were various Zionist committees in Tangier, and in Larache, where ocasional street processions were organized in favor of the movement. Yet he was convinced that Zionism had very little appeal in Morocco and was far from constituting a serious political current; and therefore, it could not become viable unless it found able propagandists capable of establishing bonds with European Zionists.[32]

Actually Sémach had failed to sense the attachment of the early political Zionists to their cause. First, a segment of them in the past were ranked as *"l'élite de l'Alliance"*: Delmar, Joseph H. Lévy from Fez; David Bohbot from Mogador; Samuel Daniel ("S.D.") Lévy, a former educator at the AIU who settled in Casablanca; Haïm Toledano and Moïse Azancot from Tangier, both former teachers and students at the AIU who were active in the Zionist Committee of Tangier of the post-1918 period. If they did not turn against the AIU they were nonetheless reluctant to support its ideological stance blindly, and they were disorganized only at first. Second, their Zionism always intact, Moroccan rabbis did not constitute a monolithic bloc of apolitical Zionists. During his stay in the country (1914–1922) Rabbi Ze'ev Hilperine had contacted rabbis who were influenced by political Zionist trends, among them the influencial rabbi from Tetuan, Léon Jalfon. The latter was active on behalf of KH and resented the lack of seriousness attributed to early Moroccan Zionism by the Zionist Organization. He urged the London headquarters to intensify fund collections for Zionist causes as well as to send dynamic *shelīhīm* (envoys) from the KH and KKL to complement his activities.[33]

Yet Sémach continued to belittle the Zionists, referring to them as *beaux phraseurs* and at one point asserted that Zionism has made numerous appeals to the youths, but how could it succeed? It was "a voice in the desert without an echo."[34] They were far too indifferent to such appeals and those who desired to become affiliated with its activities were uninformed about the movement, its ideals, its politics, and methods of action.[35] Despite Sémach's conclusions Zionist cells continued to spring up in different communities. Whereas, at first, they sprang up in the coastal or port towns of Tetuan, Mogador, and Safi, and emerged subsequently in the interior, they could later be found in the coastal towns of Tangier and Casablanca.

The French and Spanish protectorate authorities, like Sémach, seemed at first to have underrated the tenacity of the early Zionists. Henri Gaillard who before 1912 served as French consul in Fez and, through his negotiations with the *makhzan* was one of the architects of French colonial penetration, was less disposed to downplay the future role of the Zionists. He conceded in 1917 that Zionism had a limited following in North Africa. In Algeria where the Crémieux decree granted the Jews entrance into the *famille française* and in Tunisia and Morocco where AIU graduates were gradually adapting to French culture, there was no immediate danger.[36] But he did not discount the possibility that political Zionism and Muslim nationalism could eventually prove ruinous to French colonialism; he then urged the protectorate to prevent the rise of Jewish nationalism, pan-Islam, and pan-Arabism; the Jews had to be guided in the path of French civilization, a task in which the protectorate was ably assisted by the AIU.[37]

The Jews, meanwhile, warmly received the Balfour Declaration advocating the creation of a Jewish national home in Palestine (November 2, 1917), and with equal enthusiasm hailed the decision of the San Remo Conference (April 1920), granting Britain a mandate over Palestine as a first step toward the realization of Jewish aspirations.[38] There was even limited emigration to Palestine in 1920 — several dozen families from Morocco, but nothing of great significance.[39] More important, perhaps, was the arrival in the early 1920s of Nathan Halpern as *shaliaḥ* (envoy) of the KH and in the late 1920s, of his successor Dr. Ariel Bension, both of whom were mostly active in the Spanish zone and Tangier, but managed to extend their activities to French Morocco. In fact, the "outsiders" who before and after 1920 entered Morocco and propagated the Zionist idea represented two categories of activists: the political propagandists, including journalists of East European background, and the Zionist envoys of the KH and the KKL, who sought and obtained funds for Jewish colonization work in Palestine. They were assisted by local Zionists.

Who were some of these outsiders? What was the nature of their activities? Among the most outstanding ones were:

1. *Dr. Zeimig Spivacoff*[40] — a former president of the Zionist Committee of Tangier, founded in 1919, and active in Tangier on behalf of Zionist causes since his arrival there from Paris. Born in Odessa, he became a Zionist idealist and settled in Palestine in the 1880s among the early pioneers. In 1893 he settled in Tangier after completing his medical studies in Paris and being appointed chief physician at the *Hôpital Française* in that town. Though closely aligned with the AIU and its philanthropic activities, Spivacoff was among the earliest non-Moroccan Zionist activist along with Dr. Barliawsky in Tetuan.

2. *Jonathan Thursz*[41] — a Polish Jew who entered Morocco in the early 1920s when the country, as some Zionist representatives believed, was ripe for activities. Though he eventually settled in the United States, Thursz was an enthusiastic promoter of the *sheqel* in Casablanca, his headquarters, and the town which during the late 1920s emerged as the uncontested center of Zionist activities. He established important links with Moroccan Zionists, helped them reassert ties with European Zionism in general and the Zionist Organization in particular. Through his initiatives, the local Zionists became affiliated with the Zionist Federation of France in 1923. Thursz published between 1926 and 1940 the French-language and pro-Zionist journal *L'Avenir Illustré* in Casablanca, the most important organ of the Zionists in the country. The journal was challenged by *L'Union Marocaine* which represented the views of assimilation to French culture, and of the AIU. Its editor, Elie Nataf, was a Tunisian-born graduate of the AIU and former director of one of its schools in Casablanca.

3. *Augustine Anshel Perl*[42] — also known as Rabbi Asher. A militant Zionist active in Spanish Morocco, Tangier, and in Algeciras. Born in Poland, he once lived in Argentina. Having no formal ties with the Zionist

Organization like Thursz, he felt free to attack Jewish leaders, the AIU, and its alumni associations. He considered some of the most active Zionists, such as Moïse Azancot, as *"Alliancistes."* The AIU was apprehensive about his activities. Moïse Lévy, director of AIU activities in Tetuan claimed that Perl was employed by the Spanish-zone authorities as inspector of Jewish education and, upon his appointment, he plunged into Zionist activities.[43] He published the Spanish-language newspaper *Renacimiento de Israel* (*Israel's Renaissance*) in Algeciras but which was intended for Moroccan Jewry. In its pages he attacked local Zionist leaders for inaction; the AIU was also a constant target: he characterized the AIU representatives as the most implacable enemies of Zionism and its schools in Morocco as centers for the de-Judaization of the youths.[44] Perl accused the AIU and its alumni associations of plotting for the elimination of Zionist cells; he considered Tetuan's Rabbi Léon Jalfon as one of the few sincere and devoted Zionists in the whole country; he did not think highly of most Zionists in the country, insiders or outsiders. A complex man, Perl, who claimed to be a rabbi, was once converted to Catholicism before returning to Judaism. He was obsessed with the AIU and saw in all the evil that might have plagued Moroccan Jewry as a result of its schools. According to Perl, the infidel *"Alliancistes"* set up a forum for themselves and made France the new God of the Jews before whom they must bow in submission and in a lowly spirit.[45]

4. *Salomon Kagan*[46] – a Russian Jew active in Casalanca and for the Zionist Federation of France (Moroccan Section). He was a member of the Federation's branch executive committee and encouraged local Jewish intellectuals to express solidarity with East European Jewry; and he spread the word in the 1920s and 1930s about the deteriorating conditions of German Jewry; he was active in promoting the activities of fundraising for colonization in Palestine. Like most other outside Zionists, he spoke fluent French.

In addition to these, the *shelīḥīm*, of the KKL and the KH, whose activities increased since 1923, received a boost from the activities of Thursz's *Avenir Illustré*, which urged the Jews to make generous monetary contributions. The envoys of the above-mentioned organizations, as Abitbol observed, were often unfamilar with Moroccan Jewish customs, languages, and aspirations.[47] Nevertheless, they were devoted to Zionist causes and made some inroads within the communities by encouraging local Zionists to create new societies affiliated with the Zionist Organization. Further, it is noteworthy that these envoys succeeded together with local Zionist assistance, in tying activities to the French Zionist Federation and with the Zionist Organization office in London, ties which were extremely weak during the early days of the protectorate period. This development became so strong during the 1940s that mainstream Zionism prevented the effective penetration of Revisionist Zionism (the Jabotinsky camp) from becoming a serious movement in Morocco.[48]

Figure 20. Zeimig Spivacoff, physician and Zionist

Of the envoys, Halpern's activities are noteworthy. On one occasion in 1925, he spoke at the clubhouse of the AIU alumni association in Casablanca, a place that increasingly attracted sympathizers to the Zionist idea. He encouraged his audience to increase their vocational programs in the communities and to promote agricultural training; he cited the example of United States Jews who played an active role in major industries owing to their vocational skills; and though he did not praise the work of the AIU in

Palestine, Tunisia, and Algeria in the area of agricultural training, Halpern heaped praise on the Jewish Colonization Association (JCA) for its agricultural settlements in Argentina.[49]

Regarding Palestine, Halpern told the AIU graduates that the Jews there had made revolutionary progress in constructing a homeland, working with their hands, erecting buildings; in the area of manual education he praised the AIU *Ecole Professionnelle*, situated in Jerusalem for training skilled manual workers.[50]

For Morocco, Halpern suggested that the AIU alumni must do all they could to orient Jewish youths toward manual labor, for in the industrial age old-fashioned artisans had no role to play; and that the Moroccan Jewish communities must receive agricultural training in various farm and vocational centers.[51]

It is difficult to assess Halpern's motives in making such suggestions. However, by urging AIU alumni to support agricultural and vocational education rather than the type of learning that led to white collar and administrative employment, Halpern was encouraging the sort of education that would produce the very skilled workers needed in Palestine. As we shall see below, the Zionist envoys in Morocco appealed most particularly to the poor and tradition-bound for their emigration clientele. Yet for the purpose of collecting funds and enlisting leadership support, the Zionists relied heavily on the educated and the prosperous. Halpern probably knew that the AIU alumni wielded considerable influence in high AIU circles and that its members might be able to pressure the Central Committee to open vocational and agricultural schools in Morocco. These schools, in turn, would train skilled laborers for emigration to Palestine and hence the Zionists would be able to use the AIU for their own interests.

Informed by the Casablanca school's director about Halpern's meeting with AIU alumni, Bigart accused him of being a militant Zionist and suggested that his views on educational reform were not new. "Halpern," snapped Bigart, "did not discover America! We are all aware of the need for greater vocational education."[52] Bigart was worried about the damage which outside forces such as political Zionism might cause to the leading position the AIU enjoyed in Morocco. On the other hand, Halpern may have made some sense, for prior to 1936 the AIU had little progress in advanced vocational training.

Halpern's activities were not confined to Casablanca. He went from town to town where sizable Jewish communities existed. In 1926, for instance, he lectured in Rabat to Jewish youths explaining the raison d'être of the Zionist movement.[53] By that time, however, despite organizational problems encountered by Zionist leaders during the mid-1920s and subsequently, Sémach was now becoming concerned with Zionist activities, asking with some anxiety: *"Comment arrêter le courant?"* He noted:

The *Alliance* has accomplished its work calmly and with simplicity while the Zionists are making themselves felt through modern methods of publicity. Their functionaries are not concerned with scientific principles: they express with grandiloquence, a few ideas concerning justice, [Jewish] rights and equality with which few people can argue. This is how they triumph over their adversaries. The youths, having only superficial knowledge of political developments, accept their credo with enthusiasm. How can the [Zionist] current be stopped?[54]

Sémach was incensed by the activities of Halpern whom he considered a dangerous rabblerouser, who attracted the attention of the simple as well as the educated.[55] On one occasion Sémach actually confronted Halpern when the latter held a propaganda tour of Casablanca. During one speech Sémach interrupted Halpern and observed that political Zionism is dangerous and ought to be opposed; that the Jews of Morocco were well off under the French protectorate and their socioeconomic and political conditions were constantly improving.[56] Facing Halpern and his audience, Sémach argued that the Moroccan Jew made progress through French culture; to ask him to become a Zionist would constitute an obstacle to that progress.[57] He was equally incensed by Jonathan Thursz and *L'Avenir Illustré*. Although Thursz declared at the Sixteenth Zionist Congress in Zürich (1929) that the relations between the Zionists and the AIU were becoming "harmonious,"[58] the relations between the two were actually not so good from Sémach's point of view. In 1935 he insisted that since the founding of *L'Avenir Illustré*, Thursz had given the AIU nothing but trouble, and only now, after Thursz had realized that the AIU is extremely popular among the Jews, he wanted to work closer with it.[59] Sémach discouraged the AIU from assuming contacts with Thursz and affirmed that he, personally, would like to have nothing with the *Avenir Illustré*.[60]

The political and journalistic activities of the Zionists were confined to the very large urban centers. After 1930, however, their appeals for funds and other means of support extended to the smaller towns. In one southern coastal town, Safi, the boys' school director reported in 1934 that a KH representative, M. Turek, spoke to an audience and lectured them about the need for new orientations, patterned on the Halpern approach nearly a decade earlier; he said that the Jews were always lured by the free professions, commerce, and banking instead of turning to vocational and agricultural skills, and spoke about the deterioration of the status of German Jewry.[61]

On the question of Palestine, Turek described the transformation of a desert into an oasis: lawyers, doctors, and a variety of intellectuals were abandoning the diaspora and coming to Palestine to engage in physical work of nation building; it was in Palestine that the awakening of spoken, not merely biblical Hebrew, was a reality, and along with Arabic and English, it had become the official language of the British Mandate; the Jews of Rumania, Poland, Russia, and Germany had become zealous converts to Jewish nationalism and were emigrating to Palestine.[62]

The school director who witnessed the gathering reported his dissatisfaction with the affair, deploring what he called an increase in sympathy for Zionist concepts; there had been to his knowledge some defections from the AIU and these he interpreted as gestures of ingratitude to the very organization which had always stood by Moroccan Jews; he argued that the clustering of large Jewish emigrants in Palestine would not be productive: in the diaspora the Jews had been under constant pressure to produce; because by being Jewish they had to work extra hard and compete fiercely to succeed in the socioeconomic sphere. In Palestine, however, a Jewish entity would eliminate such pressure and competition. Given the so-called one happy family, Jewish productivity would inevitably face stagnation.[63] In response to the report, Bigart justified the AIU's indifference to the Zionist idea:

> Are we, who for many years have fought to attract people to the idea of emancipation of the Jews, able to support a movement which stands against our efforts? The process of emancipation, in our opinion, is the absolute adaptation of the Jew to his *patrie nouvelle*. Zionism with its dishonest characteristics condemns this adaptation.[64]

This policy laid down by the Paris AIU evoked sharp criticism not only among the Eastern European Zionists active in Morocco, but among the indigenous ones, including intellectuals who were AIU alumni who had turned Zionist. Among them was Joseph H. Lévy of the community of Fez. Joseph Lévy was particularly on the offensive, referring to the AIU as "the pretentious *Alliance Israélite*," a "pseudo Alliance" in whose schools Jewish education was receiving limited attention and where de-Judaization was very much part of the educational program.[65] Lévy directed his attacks at the closest ally of the AIU at the time, the Casablanca community president, Yahya Zagoury, who was also the protectorate's functionary as director and inspector of Jewish institutions. According to Lévy, Zagoury was influential among the Jews and in the protectorate's Residency, and being an *Allianciste* as well as a recipient of French medals,[66] he sought "to destroy our movement."[67] Further, Zagoury was attacked by the Hadida brothers, both influential Casablanca merchants who, as ardent Zionists, sought Zagoury's intercession before the Residency to allow Zionist activities to play a more intensive role in Casablanca of the early 1920s.[68] Based on their argument, Zagoury responded nastily, shouting "Non!!! Non!!! Non!!! The Resident General does not want any of this."[69] They added that thanks to Zagoury Zionist activities in Casablanca were restricted. Describing the situation in 1923, they said:

> The only single party responsible for the nonexistence of Zionism [in Casablanca] is Zagoury. Why is there Zionist activity in France? In Tunisia: a country under a French administration? Is our country not protected by the French? Then why are we restricted? It is because . . . we have a leader whose ideas represent the *Alliancistes.*[70]

Similarly, Abraham Laredo, a Zionist from Fez who during a 1936 conference of KKL and KH in Casablanca, praised the AIU for its social and philanthropic role in Morocco, argued nevertheless that it was insensitive to Jewish needs and considered any criticism directed at its activities as evidence of ingratitude.[71] Not so, claimed Laredo: the Zionists and other Jews critical of the AIU should not be viewed as that organization's enemies; and he was glad to notice that one young AIU leader, Jules Braunschvig, who often visited the Moroccan communities, understood Jewish needs and was pushing for educational reforms within the schools.[72]

As for protectorate policy vis-à-vis the Zionists, in 1923 despite opposition to their activities in different circles, French-zone Zionists could legally establish links with, and a branch of, the Zionist Federation of France and strengthen ties with the Zionist Organization, and expand the network of Zionist associations, especially in the 1930s. Spain too permitted the creation of a local federation.[73] The Tangier Zionists, on the other hand, living in a free and neutral zone, could maintain links with their mainstream Zionist counterparts in England and France. It is ironic that a Jewish organization such as the AIU turned out to be more hostile and indifferent to Zionism than the protectorates.

The center of Zionist activities shifted from the coastal towns of the north to the coastal and interior communities of the French zone in the late 1920s. Neither the French authorities nor the Moroccans were overly enthusiastic about Zionist activities. However the pre-1939 period did not witness considerable opposition to such activities. The Residency restricted certain activities that included the banning of the following Zionist cells and associations: Mount Zion Association in Mogador; a Zionist cell in Casablanca; a literary circle in Rabat; the Māgēn-Dāvīd (Shield of David) Society of Safi; and the Petah - Tikva (Opening of Hope) Society of Rabat—all in accordance with a *zahīr* published on May 24, 1914, that remained effective for many years.[74] On the other hand, societies flourished in Fez, Oujda, Sefrou, and Casablanca.[75]

When Zionist activities were in their early organizational stages, its representatives feared Lyautey, for he exercised practically dictatorial power in French Morocco, but argued that "as he is a very old man, a change will come, possibly in a person who will abolish the military character of the Residency and establish a civil administration."[76] Yet it was under Lyautey that the Moroccan branch of the Zionist Federation of France could be established.

Under Théodore Steeg's Residency, though the newspaper *Hā-'Olām*, Hebrew-language organ of the World Zionist Organization, was temporarily banned in the mid-1920s, the Resident General affirmed France's support for the national aspirations of Jews in the diaspora. In a letter to the Zionist organization (1926), Steeg pointed out that the Residency permitted (a) the maintenance of a linkage between Moroccan Zionists and the Zionist Federation of France, as well as local fundraising, the proceeds of which were sent to London and Paris; (b) the popularization of the *sheqel*, the creation of new associations, and the work of the Zionist Organization's envoys.[77]

Though France adhered to the Balfour Declaration and to the decisions adopted at the San Remo Conference, and under Steeg pro-Zionist newspapers were published, the Moroccan nationalists who emerged in the late 1920s and early 1930s in the urban areas were far from content. Yet even if the French-language organ of the early nationalists, *L'Action du Peuple*, warned the Jewish press to remain neutral over Palestine,[78] no violent anti-Jewish activities were reported in the French zone.

In assessing pre-1939 Zionist progress in Morocco it may be said that the activities of the Zionist envoys and of the local Zionists were to some degree important, for even if they were modest in scope, and local Zionism was plagued by divisions, the groundwork was laid for action and expansion after the war. No sufficient legislation, detaching the Jews completely from the *makhzan*'s jurisdication was enacted, and the Jews, mainly educated ones, disappointed with the reality, and seeking political involvement, looked for alternatives to Jewish emancipation *à la européenne*; and this was bound to gain the Zionists adherents. Political events in Palestine, signaling the development of the *yishūv*, and the increase of Jewish emigration to Palestine from various parts of the diaspora, encouraged segments of Moroccan Jewry to become more involved in the political activities of Zionism, especially after 1945. Poverty was still rampant in many communities where the AIU and the protectorates did not extend their influence or had done so only recently. Despite efforts by various Jewish organizations to help the large number of impoverished Jews in the heavily populated urban centers, poverty was a major problem. It became a precious instrument in the hands of Zionist organizational representatives in the 1950s. Whereas the French protectorate closed down certain Zionist clubs the Zionist representatives were allowed to enter the country, raise funds for Jewish settlements in Palestine, and advocate political Zionism.

It is difficult to estimate the extent of Jewish emigration from Morocco to Palestine in the pre-1948 period. One source, though not citing any statistical source, claimed that between 1920 and 1939 one thousand Jews left for Palestine.[79] Whatever the case may be, Zionist attention before 1939 was largely confined to the spread of the Zionist idea in the press and in encouraging Jewish participation in Zionist goals through fundraising. There were a few *'alīya* offices in Casablanca and Meknes which maintained ties with the emigration section of the Jewish Agency since the early or mid-1930s, in the attempt to obtain emigration certificates from the authorities of the Mandate in Palestine. But the number of emigrants was limited, partly due to the stiff restrictions imposed by the British over issuance of certificates, and partly due to the lack of regular communications between the Moroccan-based emigration offices and the Jewish Agency. Notwithstanding, the Zionists active in Morocco thus laid the foundations for more intensive activities in the future.

Although pre-1939 Jewish emigration seemed far from impressive, the AIU expressed both disapproval and alarm at any such developments. For example, in January 1923, *Paix et Droit* published a fiery editorial in reference to the departure at the time of Jewish families from Fez to Palestine. This event enraged the AIU, and its journal placed the blame squarely on Zionist propaganda, but also on the French protectorate for failure to improve conditions in the *mellāh* of Fez.[80] According to the journal, of the 9,000 Jewish inhabitants of Fez in 1922, 340 people (95 men, 125 women, and 120 children) had departed for Jerusalem.[81] The AIU seized the occasion to demand from the protectorate swift economic, legislative, and political reforms on behalf of the Jews. Pointing to specific issues, it brought to the attention of the protectorate two demands directly concerning Fez Jewry: that they be granted the right to buy land outside the *mellāh* and that they be granted permission to open retail stores in the Arab quarter.[82] Such reforms, it was argued, would improve the socioeconomic level of the Jews and would consequently halt the departure to Palestine.[83] The AIU, then, clearly feared that the Zionists, though appealing to some intellectual and prosperous elements of Moroccan Jewry for leadership and financial support, were acquiring support among the poor and tradition-bound.

The 1939–1956 Period

The period between 1939 and 1945 or even until 1956 was critical to the growth of Zionism and the establishment of ties among world Jewry. Some factors contributing to these developments were:

1. The landing of the Americans in Morocco in 1942 and the contacts established since then with American Jewry;

2. The Vichy experience and the Holocaust, and the identification of Moroccan Jewry with the sufferings of their European brethren;

3. The reorganization of Zionist activities, including the rejuvenation of Zionist associations, and the emergence of Hebrew cultural centers;

4. The penetration of the Jewish Agency representatives in 1944 into the Moroccan Jewish communities;

5. The radicalization of the Moroccan nationalist movement after the late 1930s.

Zionist strategies after 1939, especially in the immediate postwar period, were directed at encouraging massive emigration. The events since 1939 won the Zionists numerous adherents. A considerable number of AIU graduates and of *lycées* began to express different notions about emancipation. Many turned to the Zionists for political inspirations.

The intensification of Moroccan nationalist activities in the late 1930s was also a source of anxiety among Jews. Unlike its reformist brand of the early 1930s, Moroccan nationalism of subsequent years was less moderate. Its leaders' growing disenchantment with the protectorates on the eve of the Second World War, particularly in the French zone, resulted in the advocacy of a total break with the colonial system and the quest for independence. The radicalization of the nationalist stance did not seem a blessing to the Jews. The nationalists' growing identification with Arab political aspirations in Palestine did not comfort them either. Whereas the nationalists supported the Arab revolt of 1936–1939, pro-Zionist Moroccan Jews supported Jewish aspirations for a national home. In the Spanish zone there were continuous attacks in the nationalist press on the British Mandate in Palestine. The director of the AIU school in Larache expressed his anxiety concerning possible Arab reactions toward the Jews, and related that in July 1939 the Secretary of Hājj Amīn al-Husaīnī, the ex-*muftī* of Jerusalem, had arrived in the Spanish zone and managed to stir up support for the Arabs in Palestine. At the same time, the most influential Moroccan nationalist in the zone, 'Abd al-Khalīq Torrès, had given his full endorsement for the Arab revolt in Palestine during a series of conferences held in Elksar, Larache, and Tetuan.[84] There were even street processions calling for death to the Jews and British in Palestine.[85] However, there is no evidence in the archives that physical force was actually applied. Nevertheless, these activities greatly enhanced the position of the Zionists, for they could now play on the fears of the Jews, promising them a safe haven in Palestine.

During the 1930s the AIU was apprehensive about support for Jewish nationalist activities in Palestine. Its representatives, like the protectorate authorities and the Moroccan nationalists, warned the pro-Zionist adherents that their support for Jewish causes in Palestine would endanger their security. At the same time, however, an increasing number of AIU teachers were beginning to reconsider their own indifference to the Zionist idea. As the AIU served as one of the most important bulwarks against Zionist activities, the *réveil des consciences* of some of its members, might have facilitated the efforts of the Zionists, both Moroccans and the envoys from Palestine.

For example, in 1938 an AIU graduate who taught at the Safi boys' school, David Béhar, expressed enthusiasm about recent gains made by the Zionists in the diaspora. The teacher, a native of Turkey, related that he felt no allegiance to a country (Turkey) where he was only despised and degraded for being a Jew.[86] The emergence of Nazism was a bitter pill for him to swallow, demonstrating the shortcomings of assimilation.[87] Similarly, a directress in Casablanca was not less explicit and asserted that the Zionist idea could no longer be ignored by the AIU.[88] She expressed great anxiety about Hitler's Germany, arguing that "we must confront the most implacable enemy of the Jewish people," and that this was a time to reconsider past cherished ideas and a time for self-criticism. She called for the re-Judaization of the schools' program to reassert Jewish values over all others: The *Alliance*, which is in the forefront of Jewish activities, must take the lead in the new direction.[89]

Challenged from within, the AIU was reconsidering past ideas and the realities of the present. But it was too late. The outbreak of the war, the German occupation of France, and the rise of Vichy temporarily halted its activities. After 1945, the change finally came, The war had such a profound impact on the AIU that it could not remain indifferent to Zionism. The near collapse of the organization in France, and the destruction of European Jewry were rude shocks for its leaders, and under the presidency of René Cassin, a distinguished jurist and member of de Gaulle's government in exile, and the vice-presidency of Jules Braunschvig, a businessman and an indefatigable servant of the AIU, the organization took a new position. Though it never became a Zionist-oriented group, after the war the AIU spoke of the need for Jewish emigration to Palestine, particularly the settlement of the victims of Nazi Germany. Whereas in the 1920s and 1930s *Paix et Droit* expressed indifferent to Zionism, the editorials of the AIU bulletins in the post-1945 era were more sympathetic. In 1946, for example an AIU editorial indicated that the extermination of the Jews in Europe, the practical impossibility for the survivors of emigrating elsewhere, made Palestine a natural place for refuge. "The magnificent projects of industrialization in Palestine and the transformation of the country to a modern society, should enable many refugees to settle there," the editorial said, so that both Jews and Arabs could live together.[90]

This statement could well be interpreted as a plea for a binational approach to the problem, with Jews and Arabs cooperating and working toward a common goal, the development of Palestine. However, owing to developments in the two years that followed, the AIU recognized the new state of Israel.

It was about that time that the AIU made Morocco the testing ground for its Hebrew education program through the creation in 1946, with the Māgēn-Dāvīd Association, of the *Ecole Normale Hébraïque* in Casablanca.[91] The intention of the program, strongly advocated by Jules Braunschvig, was to teach the youths spoken Hebrew as it was utilized in Israel. However, even in the 1950s, when the AIU revealed greater sympathy toward Zionist efforts, it did not wish to openly admit it had contacts with the Jewish Agency and its envoys in Morocco, lest the Sherifian authorities become alienated.[92] Thus, a representative of the Jewish Agency active in southern Morocco complained in 1955 that the director of the Marakesh-based AIU agricultural school did not agree to make the school available for a meeting with Jews from neighboring towns and villages.[93] Instead, the meeting had to take place near the Marrakesh Jewish cemetery.[94]

By the early and the mid-1950s, the Jewish Agency was registering its clientele for emigration to Israel. In fact, there were two phases of emigration: the legal phase, where between 1948 and 1955 37,000 emigrated,[95] and the illegal emigration phase after Muḥammad V, who had been exiled by the French in 1953, returned to Morocco in November 1955, ordered a halt to these activities, and requested that all the envoys from Israel leave the country. In the early 1960s particularly after Muḥammad V's death (1961) and the ascendance to the throne of his son, Ḥasan II, legal emigration to Israel resumed.

The testimony of Yehuda Grinker, a farmer from Nahalal, an Israeli agricultural settlement, sent to Morocco in 1954 to organize emigration from the *bled*, and a report of the Twenty-Third Zionist Congress shed light on how the envoys of the Jewish Agency encouraged emigration to Israel, and to what socioeconomic sectors of the population they appealed.

As for Grinker's mission to the *bled*, mainly to the Atlas, the Zionists believed that the Jews of these agricultural communities were desirable emigrants to Israel. These Jews were mostly poor and usually enjoyed no more than the usufruct of the land produce; the land belonged to Muslim Berber chieftains. Given the Jews' poor social origin and their potential service for Israeli nation building, their presence constituted the best element for emigration. Grinker noted:

> The more I visited in these [Berber] villages and became acquainted with its Jewish inhabitants, the more I was convinced that these Jews constitute the best and most suitable human element for settlement in [Israel's] absorption centers. There were many positive aspects which I found among them: first and foremost, they all know [their agricultural] task and their transfer to

agricultural work in Israel will not involve physical and mental difficulties. They are satisfied with few [material needs] which will enable them to confront their early economic problems. It is possible to settle them in a mountainous region, in the Negev and elsewhere. There will be other problems, however: how to train them to utilize various modern tools which are so vital nowadays.[96]

Grinker found that educational institutions were lacking in many Atlas communities and that this was important in attracting emigrants to Israel, where they would acquire proper education.[97] Indeed, as we shall see, the AIU extended its school network to the Atlas mountains. But this penetration occurred only after the late 1920s, and when the protectorate period came to an end, numerous Atlas communities were still unaffected by the AIU or other school networks.

Grinker and his collaborators usually went to the most remote communities of the Atlas, gathered its inhabitants in meeting places and synagogues, preached to them about life in Israel, and encouraged them to register for emigration. However, Grinker did not always confine his activities to the Atlas. He was often in Marrakesh, Casablanca, and Salé, searching for emigration clientele in the most densely populated mellāhs.[98] The purpose was clear: Grinker entered the overpopulated communities where the inhabitants were seeking immediate relief from hunger, poverty, and overcrowded conditions, and disease. As neither the Moroccan government nor the protectorate authorities appeared able to ameliorate conditions, the Zionists seized the opportunity to offer the Jews a different alternative. These Jews who decided to emigrate were put on ships which made their way to Europe and then to Israel.[99] The creation of Israel and the defeat of the Arabs in the 1948 war increased the determination of Moroccan Jews who sought to emigrate. Moreover, the political tension and terrorist activities carried out by Moroccan nationalists against the French between 1954 and 1955, pressuring them to return Muhammad V to the throne and grant the country independence, won the Zionists adherents.

As for Grinker's own success in organizing Jewish emigration from the Atlas in 1954–1955, we find that he registered 2,491 families totaling 13,553 people.[100] Most of these were recruited from Ouled Zangia, Ait-Bougmaz, Amizmiz, Erfoud. Demnat, Talsint, Imintanout, Midelt, Sidi-Rahal, Kasr al-Suq, Risani, Rich, and Karrando. Of these, the communities of Ouled Zangia, Ait-Bougmaz, and Erfoud did not have AIU schools. All in all, Grinker's activities in the Atlas covered eighty-seven small communities.

As the Jews of the bled were physically fit for emigration and subsequent work in Israel, they were greatly sought by Grinker. Arab authors, when writing about the strategies used by the Zionists to organize emigration, contend that the sick and disabled were left behind; they were an obstacle for emigration, an economic burden for the state of Israel.[101] They also accuse these envoys of having made false promises to the Jews about the great opportunities awaiting them in Israel.[102] Grinker did not deny that he and his associates in Morocco sought able-bodied and younger people. The Jewish Agency preferred to leave behind the very sick, old and disabled, often splitting up families.[103] Only with the JDC's help did the Jewish Agency manage to remedy diseases of potential emigrants. Concerning the argument of false promises, Grinker denys this. He claims that Atlas Jewry were told exactly what was awaiting them in Israel: a young struggling nation with complex problems.[104]

Culturally, the Jewish Agency operated diverse social and educational networks in Morocco and other Muslim countries through the Department for Middle Eastern Jewry, created in September 1948 during the session of the Zionist General Council in Jerusalem. It was founded at a time when, according to the Israeli authorities, the Arab countries were already engaged in hostile activities directed against the state of Israel.[105] A report submitted at the Zionist Congress in 1951 stated that the Arab-Israeli war of 1948 served to aggravate the hatred of the Arabs toward the Jews in their midst. In view of the debacle of the Arab armies in Israel, a new wave of anti-Jewish oppression arose, so that the Zionist movement was faced with the urgent task of mobilizing all the resources at their disposal to save the Jewish communities of North Africa and other Muslim countries from demoralization, and in certain instances, also from destruction.[106]

During the first year of its existence, the department regarded its principal task as consisting in the establishment of organizational machinery, the promotion of contacts with the communities, and the training of a staff of emissaries to undertake activities in those regions. An office was opened in Paris which set itself the aim of establishing contacts with Tunisia, Algeria and Morocco, among other countries; the staff of emissaries was trained at a special seminar in Jerusalem.[107] Such activities were carried out with the full cooperation of other departments of the Jewish Agency. What were the department's activities? Its staff established district centers to act as bases for educational and social activities in the ghettos to help counteract unemployment. It attempted to cooperate, at times successfully, with the AIU, ORT, and the JDC. At the same time, the department dispatched a team of emissaries and teachers to teach Hebrew language and culture to the potential emigrants and their children.[108]

In Morocco, the department was extremely active after 1948, given Muhammad V's flexibility at the time toward activities by the Israeli envoys, and given the lack of opposition from protectorate authorities. The report emphasized that the AIU did not oppose the department's activities; the *Ecole Normale Hébraïque* of Casablanca actually facilitated the department's work in spreading spoken Hebrew, thus helping prepare emigrants for integration into Israeli society. The department in Morocco also concentrated on other activities. In 1950 a two-story building was rented in the *mellāh* of Casablanca and used to provide services to about four hundred young people. The center was visited by the youths' families, who were given information about emigration. Hebrew was taught only to those who were not absorbed by the AIU schools. The center had a sports section that catered to youths between the ages of fourteen and eighteen for social activities, games, and singing, and a similar center opened in Taroudant (in the Ante-Atlas).[109] These activities continued until 1955 and supplemented the activities of pro-Zionist scouting groups that emerged after the war.

In conclusion, then, the Zionists envoys appealed to the poor, to able-bodied youth, and to the wealthy and educated for financial backing and leadership. It appears that the Zionists were mainly successful among the poor and uneducated, and they received assistance from the JDC in preparing them for emigration.

3. Zionist Activities inside the Communities after the War

After 1945 some educated elite considered emigrating to France, while others, as will be seen, chose to remain in Morocco and work toward an entente with the Muslims. Nevertheless, local Zionist associations were founded in significant numbers and after the dormant war years Zionist reorganization was undertaken with much vigor. In fact, Zionists were especially active in Casablanca, and Casablancan Zionists dominating the now rejuvenated Moroccan Zionist branch of the *Fédération Sioniste de France* reported activities in favor of emigration to, and reconstruction of, Palestine, in Fez, Meknes, Marrakesh, Safi, and Rabat.[110] Hebrew cultural clubs, where only Hebrew was spoken and where information sessions were organized to report on political events in Palestine were founded.[111] Most activities were organized by the country's five chief Zionists of the postwar period: S. D. Lévy, Helène Cazès-Benatar, Paul Calamaro, J. R. Benazeraf, and Salomon Kagan.[112]

In 1945, Paul Calamaro, then secretary-general of the Moroccan branch of the *Fédération*, expressed hopes that the local movement would be able to cooperate with France of the post-Vichy period and stressed that many Zionist activities took place in close cooperation with the AIU alumni association in Casablanca, in whose headquarters reunions were organized every Sunday for the dissemination of information on the Jewish world.[113] Yet when writing to the Zionist Organization in 1946, Calamaro was more revealing:

Our diverse branches of education, of youth movements, of emigration to Palestine, our *Keren Kayemeth* and *Keren Hayesod* commissions, and our cultural commission are doing the utmost in order to obtain maximum ideological support . . . . The profit obtained through *Keren Kayemeth* funds since Rosh Hashana until now exceeds 1,200,000 francs, a figure never before reached anywhere in North Africa.[114]

But that was not all Calamaro was seeking. According to Jewish Agency sources in Morocco, Calamaro, a Jerusalem-born merchant, "asked us to organize defense. As we did not have the time [to do so], we enlisted two young men whom we trained in the use of a stick, knife . . . and in martial arts."[115]

In addition, Zionist-inspired groups working with the Jewish Agency, such as the *Jeunesse Liberale de Sion* (Free Youth of Zion) with two hundred and fifty members in Marrakesh and Safi, sprang up in 1950; *Drōr* (Freedom), also founded in 1950, branches in Morocco, and was possessed by the zeal of labor Zionism and the united kibbutz movement; the *Pō'ēl ha-Mizrahī* of religious labor Zionism had two hundred and fifty members in Marrakesh, Safi, and Mogador.[116] *Hashomer Hatzair* (the Socialist-Zionist kibbutz movement), *Gordonia* (a pioneer youth movement), and to a limited extent the Revisionist *Betar* youth movement became active after the war. On the cultural side, *Hōvēvē ha-Saffa* of Casablanca, a society for the popularization of spoken Hebrew, was legally recognized by the protectorate,[117] and collaborated with the Māgēn-Dāvīd Association and the Charles Netter Group. The latter published the *Nō'ār* (Youth) which for all intents and purposes, replaced *L'Avenir Illustré* — after Thursz's departure for the United States — as the most vital organ of Moroccan Zionism. Charles Netter and the *Eliezer Ben-Yehuda* movements promoted scouting and agricultural youth training on land outside Casablanca leased for the preparation of *'alīya* with an agricultural orientation.[118] *Hōvēvē ha-Saffa* and Māgēn-Dāvīd conducted cultural education which included singing Hebrew songs from Palestine to inspire national feelings; in 1944 Māgēn-Dāvīd created a Hebrew cultural center,[119] out of which was to emerge the AIU-sponsored *Ecole Normale Hébraïque*, which prepared teachers in modern Hebrew.

It has already been indicated that the AIU alumni association in Casablanca was gradually affected by Zionist ideology. Yet the same applied to other communities. In Salé, for example, Hanania Dahan, a former president of the local alumni association, conceded that his group had intimate ties with Zionist associations such as the *Eliezer Ben Yehuda* group for Hebrew cultural revival.[120] Indeed, it is no secret that there were Zionist activities among the rank and file of AIU graduates. Theoretically, French education was intended to gear the youths toward accepting the notions of emancipation through assimilation. Yet the institutions of the AIU, which also taught Jewish values, had wide-ranging effects on the youths, often in contrast with the schools' doctrinal motives. By imparting modern ideas and promoting Jewish solidarity, the AIU schools opened to their students and graduates new avenues of interpretation, and many began seeing Jewish emancipation in nationalistic terms. A classic example of a Zionized AIU graduate was Samuel Daniel Lévy.

Figure 21. Samuel D. Lévy, leader of Moroccan Zionism

Born in the *mellāh* of Tetuan sometimes in December 1874 to a deeply religious family, descendants of the *megōrāshīm* from Granada, he attended the AIU boys' school there. Exposed to general education, French, Spanish, and Hebrew, Lévy received a multicultured education. After graduation, he was chosen by Abraham Ribbi, his school director, to travel to Paris where he received pedagogical training at the ENIO. There, Lévy was exposed for the very first time to Parisian society and its intellectual fervor. When upon completion of training in 1891 he was sent to Tangier to work with Ribbi, his teacher in Tetuan during the 1880s, Lévy was embarking on an interesting career. From 1891 to 1893 he was assistant-director in Tangier; in 1893–1895 he directed the AIU school in Sousse (Tunisia); and from 1900 to 1902, the ones in Casablanca. In 1903 Lévy joined the Jewish Colonization Association and spent ten years as a teacher, manager, and social worker at the association's *Mauricio* agricultural colony near Buenos Aires, composed of East European refugees. When returning to Morocco in 1913 the country had already been under the protectorates of France and Spain. Lévy chose Casablanca as his new home.

It was in Casablanca that Lévy plunged into Jewish activities. Like other AIU graduates, Lévy was a product of French and Judeo-Spanish cultures. He surely welcomed the colonial era as an opportunity to bring relief to the Jews. Unlike most of his colleagues, however, he did not believe that France and Spain would lobby for judicial reforms to remove the Jews from their *dhimmī* status under Islamic jurisdiction, save perhaps a stratum of the French educated. He was doubtless skeptical about Spain, which expelled his ancestors and aggravated Jewish sufferings; and there is not a single trace of evidence that he favored a Judeo-Muslim entente. Lévy's sympathies at the time were with the leaders of the Zionist congresses in Europe and with the Jews who settled in Palestine and engaged in nation building.

Since 1913 Lévy became a member of the small Zionist groups that emerged in Morocco and was active in spreading the notion of Jewish superiority in all fields. This notion could be found in his early speeches given at the AIU alumni association in Tangier. In December 1896, for instance, only a year before the convening of the Zionist Congress in Basel, Lévy spoke of Jewish superiority and condemned anti-Semitism. Was he influenced by anti-Semitic trends in France at the time? It is not clear. Yet his views on Judaism and the Jewish people reflected an understanding that France, his *patrie intellectuelle*, was as susceptible to anti-Semitism as any other nation, regardless of human rights declarations and popular revolutions. While most other AIU members displayed respect for Jewish contributions to civilization, Lévy's outlook bordered on chauvinism. Speaking in 1896 he asserted bluntly that he thought Jews were always at the top of the intellectual ladder, a phenomenon revealing their superiority over Christians and Muslims. The latter, he believed, were jealous of this superiority and sought to reduce the Jews to the lowest level of society, stunting their progress, and placing them outside the law. But if the Christians and Muslims thought they could demoralize the Jews through depriving them of social and material privileges, as well as of religious freedom, they were mistaken, for the Jews during their exposure to discrimination and persecution, became ever more attached to their faith and to intellectual pursuits, as seen in Spain during the fifteenth century.[121]

In his 1896 speech and in subsequent speeches Lévy boasted of the great minds of Spain's and North African Jewry: Maimonides, Ibn Gabirol,

Alfassi, and Yehuda Halevi. After 1913 his activities in Jewish and Zionist circles included the presidency role of the KKL Morocco branch (since 1919), founding the Māgēn-Dāvīd Association of Casablanca for the spread of modern Hebrew, and after the 1930s, assuming the position as president of the Moroccan branch of the Zionist Federation of France. The latter position made Lévy the most influential Moroccan leader of mainstream Zionism.

As a member of the AIU Lévy understood well the raison d'être of the organization which he served for many years. Though he urged it to accelerate Jewish and Hebrew education, he brushed aside accusations that the secular character of the AIU was leading the youths in the path of de-Judaization. He defended the program of the schools, arguing that they had a special character all of their own, and he indicated that both secular and Jewish education were represented in the program.[122] Lévy defined spoken Hebrew as the national language of the Jews, representing the vital link binding together the people of Israel, scattered through the diaspora.[123] Therefore he believed that through the Māgēn-Dāvīd this dream could be achieved in Morocco for the realization of national revival.

Lévy also represented his communities in international and Zionist congresses. More than any Zionist leader Lévy established a direct link between Moroccan and world Jewry in the 1930s and 1940s, including U. S. Jews. He, for example, represented Moroccan Jewry at the World Jewish Congress meetings in Geneva (1933), and in Atlantic City (1944), where he was vocal in favoring intense Jewish colonization of Palestine.[124]

Lévy expressed the view that there were few friends for the Jews on earth, and among them one of his favorites was the already deceased Arthur James Balfour.[125] And though a leader of mainstream Zionism, his views after the war were hardly distinguishable from the Zionist-Revisionist position expounded by Ze'ev (Vladimir) Jabotinsky, particularly regarding the Arabs of Palestine. They would be well treated as a minority in *Eretz-Yisrael*, but they would have to accept the Jewish homeland in their midst, a homeland that Lévy believed would be born in the immediate future (*"Nous aurons Eretz-Israël, et nous l'aurons dans un avenir immédiat*[126]*"*). Yet he knew better. The Arabs would most likely not tolerate this development and consequently concluded that it would be necessary to use force (*"Nous ne gagnerons la Palestine qu'à la force de la poigne"*).[127]

His enthusiasm for a Jewish national home notwithstanding, Lévy, like many of his French-educated colleagues, never settled in Israel. Despite his advocacy for the spread of spoken Hebrew it is not clear if he knew more than the biblical language. One of his closest friends, whose identity must remain anonymous, maintained that when Israel was born, Lévy was seventy-four, much too old and useless for emigration. Further, his wife had been gravely ill, unable to travel. But this is unconvincing, for Lévy could have settled in pre-1948 Palestine. When in May 1970 he died at the age of ninety-five, the reasons which kept him in Casablanca until such a time, were probably buried with him.

Notes

1. Richard Gottheil, *Zionism* (Philadelphia, The Jewish Publication Society of America, 1914), p. 214.

2. Theodor Herzl, *Zionist Writings: Essays and Addresses*, vol. i:110, January 1896 to June 1898, trans. from the German by Harry Zohn (New York, Praeger, 1973).

3. Ibid., pp. 110–111.

4. Ibid., p. 111.

5. Nahum Sokolow, "French Models for the Jewish Revival in the East," *The Jewish Chronicle*, February 12, 1909, p. 20.

6. Ibid.

7. "Nationalisme ou assimilation," *Paix et Droit*, ler année, no. 4, mensuel (avril 1921), p. 1.

8. Ibid.

9. Ibid., p. 2.

10. Zvi Yehudah, "Zionist Activities in Morocco on the Eve of the Protectorate," (in Hebrew) in Abitbol's *Judaïsme d'Afrique du nord aux xixe-xxe siècles*, (Institut-Ben-Zvi, Jerusalem, 1980), p. 98; Zionist Archives: Z1/313).

11. Ibid., p. 102. A *sheqel* which in 1897 was the equivalent of one German mark, bought Zionist associations scattered in the diaspora electoral votes and representation in Zionist congresses.

12. Ibid., p. 102.

13. "Morocco," *The Jewish Chronicle*, November 26, 1897, p. 28.

14. Michael Abitbol, "Zionist Activities in North Africa Until the End of the Second World War," *Pe'amim* 2 (Summer 1979), p. 65 (in Hebrew).

15. Yehudah, "Zionist Activities," p. 102.

16. Elmaleh to AIU, Fez, March 11, 1911, Arch.AIU.XV.E.248(a).

17. Abitbol, "Zionist Activities in North Africa," p. 70.

18. Ibid.

19. Zionist Archives: Z2/309.

20. Elmaleh to AIU (above, note 16).

21. Ibid; and Bigart to Elmaleh, Paris, March 15, 1911, Arch. AIU.XV.E.248(a).

22. Doris Bensimon Donath, *Immigrants d'Afrique du Nord en Israël* (Paris: Editions Anthropos, 1970), pp. 52–53; letter of J. L. Lévy, Fez, July 22, 1927, to the Zionist Organization, London, Zionist Archives Z4/2669.

23. Donath, p. 53.

24. Jewish National Fund (*Keren Keyemeth le Yisael*) is a Zionist body which was responsible for fundraising for Jewish colonization in Palestine in favor of agricultural and other land development. Palestine Foundation Fund (*Keren Hayesod*) raised funds for similar goals since 1920.

25. Donath, p. 52.

26. Albert Moyal to AIU, Meknes, November 24, 1914, Arch.AIU.XXXII. E.549(a).

27. More is said about this society in chapter VII.

28. Ovadia, *The Jewish Community of Sefrou*, (Center for the Research on the Jewish Communities of Morocco 1975) iii:212–213.

29. Wolf Hilperine to Va'ad ha-Po'el of the Zionist Organization, Larache, January 3, 1921, Zionist Archives, Z4/2331 (in Hebrew).

30. Sémach to AIU, Tangier, April 4, 1919, Arch.AIU.V.B.24.

31. Ibid.

32. Ibid.

33. Léon Jalfon to Wolf Hilperine, Tetuan, December 15, 1921, Zionist Archives, Z4/2331 (in Hebrew).

34. Sémach to AIU, Tangier, October 19, 1919, Arch.AIU.LXI.E.946(c).

35. Ibid.

36. Henri Gaillard, "Le sionisme et la question juive dans l'Afrique du Nord," *Renseignement Coloniaux*, nos. 1,2,3, supplément à *l'Afrique Française*, janvier-février-mars, 1918, p. 4.

37. Ibid., p. 7.

38. See, for instance, letter of Larache *Bonē Yerūshālayīm* to the Zionist Organization, May 11, 1920, Zionist Archives, Z4/2331 (in Hebrew); Abitbol, "Zionist Activities in North Africa," pp. 76–77.

39. Abitbol, p. 77.

40. Jonathan Thursz to Zionist Organization in London, Casablanca, May 22, 1932, Zionist Archives, Z4/3245; see also "Zur Lage des Sionismus in Marokko," *Wiener Magen Zeitung*, November 1, 1925.

41. See especially Zionist Archives files: S5/491; Z4/2011; Z4/3245; Abitbol, pp. 82–83.

42. Moïse Lévy to AIU, Tetuan, January 9, 1925, Arch.AIU.LXVIII.E.1030(b).

43. Ibid.

44. See *Renacimiento de Israel*, July 15, 1927; and Dr. Ariel Bension to Zionist Organization (confidential), Tetuan, November 27, 1927, Zionist Archives, Z4/3245 (in English).

45. A. Perl to Zionist Organization, Algeciras, May 31, 1927, Zionist Archives, Z4/3245 (in Hebrew).

46. On Cagan, see "Les assises de la conférence des collaborateurs du Keren Kayemeth du Keren Hayesod et du chekel," *L'Avenir Illustré*, 27 février 1936, p. 9; Zionist Archives, S5/2214 (1936).

47. Abitbol, "Zionist Activities in North Africa," p. 82.

48. See, for instance, a memorandum prepared in London by the Zionist Organization: "Revisionist Propaganda in North Africa," Zionist Archives, Z4/3245, June 23, 1927.

49. Moïse Bibasse to AIU, Casablanca, February 16, 1925, Arch.AIU.IV.B.87.

50. Ibid.

51. Ibid.

52. Bigart to Bibasse, Paris, February 28, 1925, Arch.AIU.IV.E.87.

53. Sémach to AIU, Rabat, December 29, 1926, Arch.AIU.XLII.E.717(a).

54. Sémach to AIU, Rabat, March 21, 1927, Arch.AIU.XLII.E.717(a).

55. Ibid.

56. Ibid.

57. Ibid.

58. Protocols of the Sixteenth Zionist Congress held in Zürich, cited in Donath, *Immigrants d'Afrique du Nord en Israël*, p. 58.

59. Sémach to AIU, Rabat, March 4, 1935, Arch.AIU.XLIV.E.717(h).

60. Ibid.
61. Léon Pinhas to AIU, Safi, March 13, 1934, Arch.AIU.L.E.784.
62. Ibid.
63. Ibid.
64. Bigart to Pinhas, Paris, April 5, 1934, Arch.AIU.L.E.784.
65. Joseph H. Lévy to Dr. S. Bernstein of the Zionist Organization, Fez, March 4, 1921, Zionist Archives, Z4/2669.
66. Zagoury served as one of General Drude's and d'Amade's guides in conquering Casablanca and the Chaouia in 1907.
67. Ibid.
68. Hadida Frères to the Zionist Organization, Casablanca, January 21, 1923, Zionist Archives, Z4/2149.
69. Ibid.
70. Ibid.
71. Abraham Laredo, "La culture juive au Maroc," *L'Avenir Illustré*, 27 février 1936, no. 243, pp. 9–10.
72. Ibid.
73. Abitbol, "Zionist Activities in North Africa, p. 83.
74. Etienne Coidan, *Le Sionisme au Maroc: Contribution à l'étude du judaïsme au Maroc* (Rabat 1946). ms. of the Ben-Zvi Institute of Jerusalem, pp. 60–61.
75. Ibid., p. 61.
76. Memorandum of Zionist Organization to Dr. Chaim Weizmann, London, June 1924, Zionist Archives, Z4/2149.
77. T. Steeg to Zionist Organization, Rabat, June 16, 1926, Zionist Archives, Z4/2311.
78. Othman El-Fayache, "L'origine de la question de Palestine," *L'Action du Peuple*, 17 novembre 1933, p. 2, cited by Donath, *Immigrants d'Afrique du Nord en Israël*, p. 58.
79. Elias Sa'ad, *al-Hijra al-Yahūdīyya ilā Filasṭīn al-Muḥtalla* (Beirut, 1969), p. 157.
80. "L'exode des juifs de Fès vers la Palestine," *Paix et Droit* 3 no. 1, mensuel (janvier 1923), p. 7.
81. Ibid.
82. Ibid. This corresponds with the declaration made by the Fez community to the president of the French Republic during his visit to Morocco in 1922. See chapter V.
83. Ibid.
84. Arch.AIU. Larache, October 12, 1939, LXXIII.E., no file number.
85. Ibid.
86. David Béhar to AIU, Safi, December 12, 1938, Arch.AIU.LVIII.E.371.
87. Ibid.
88. Arch.AIU. Casablanca, December 9, 1939, V.E.106.
89. Ibid.
90. "La France et le sionisme," *Bulletin Intérieur de l'Alliance Israélite Universelle*, 2e année, no. 6 (mars 1946), pp. 4–5.
91. More shall be said on the *Ecole Normale Hébraïque* in chapter VII.
92. Interview with Rabbi Y. Rouche, Jerusalem, February 9, 1976 (in Hebrew).
93. Yehuda Grinker, *The Emigration of Atlas Jews to Israel* (Tele Aviv, The Association of Moroccan Immigrants in Israel, 1973), p. 74.
94. Ibid.
95. "Morocco," *Encyclopedia Judaica*, xii:344.
96. Grinker, p. 26.

97. Ibid., p. 28.

98. Ibid., p. 37.

99. Grinker related that often in the years 1947–1948 Oujda on the Algerian border served as a station from which Moroccan Jews were smuggled to Algeria and from there they traveled to Israel.

100. Grinker, pp. 97–99.

101. See, for instance, Elias Sa'ad, *al-Hijra al-Yahūdīyya ilā Filastīn al-Muhtalla*, pp. 160–161. He pointed out that the envoys sought mostly the physically able youths: *hijrat al-shabāb* and *siyāsat ikhtiyār al-muhājirīn*.

102. Ibid., p. 158.

103. Grinker, pp. 124–25.

104. Ibid., p. 149.

105. "The Department for Middle Eastern Jewry," *Report to the Twenty-Third Zionist Congress* (Jerusalem, 1951).

106. Ibid.

107. Ibid.

108. Ibid.

109. Ibid.

110. S. D. Lévy to Zionist Organization in Jerusalem, Casablanca, March 21, 1944, Zionist Archives Z4/10308.

111. Ibid.

112. Ibid.

113. Paul Calamaro to civil authorities of French protectorate, Casablanca, March 20, 1945, Zionist Archives, S5/794.

114. Calamaro to Zionist Organization, Casablanca, February 14, 1946, Zionist Archives, S5/794.

115. Memorandum sent to Zionist Organization, Casablanca, June 17, 1945, Zionist Archives, S5/794 (in Hebrew).

116. Pierre Flamand, *Diaspora en terre d'Islam: Les communautés israélites du sud marocain* (Casablanca Imprimeries réuies, 1959), p. 319.

117. Coidan, *Le sionisme au Maroc*, p. 61.

118. Memorandum to *alīya* section in Jerusalem, Casablanca, March 2, 1945, Zionist Archives, S6/1985I.

119. Ibid.

120. Interview with Hanania Dahan, January 26, 1976.

121. See, for instance, his speech before the Tangier alumni of December 27, 1896, Arch.AIU.LV.E.908.

122. S. D. Lévy, "Retour à nos traditions," *L'Union Marocaine*, no. 108 (30 septembre 1938), p. 1.

123. Ibid.

124. Elie Sikirdji, *S. D. Lévy: une belle figure du judaïsme marocain* (Casablanca, 1954), pp. 67–68.

125. Speech by Lévy on occasion of twenty-eighth anniversary of Balfour Declaration at headquarters of the French Zionist Federation—Moroccan branch, November 2, 1945, Zionist Archives, S5/794.

126. Ibid.

127. Ibid.

CHAPTER VII

The *Alliance* and the Social and Cultural Evolution of the Jews: 1912–1956

1. Educational and Sociocultural Factors

The AIU in Morocco intensified its social and cultural activities after 1912 and, after 1945, collaborated with a variety of international Jewish organizations. The political role of the school directors, on the other hand, diminished somewhat in the protectorate era, for the authorities in their colonial zones of influence eliminated the *jizya*, rural land purchase restrictions, and introduced sweeping reforms to implement pacification in the *bled*, the rural countryside. Nevertheless, the AIU continued to apply political pressures through its representatives, even if these proved ineffective.

The teachers launched intensive cultural and social programs in the major urban communities; they also succeeded in extending these programs to the more remote communities of the *bled*, particularly in the Atlas mountains. The food and clothing programs, which aided poor youths, doubtless were intended to popularize the AIU further and attract to its institutions students from the rabbinic schools or those who enjoyed no educational facilities whatsoever.[1] Given the growth of the Jewish population, (See table 18 for urban Jewish population) however, the AIU was unable to bear the financial brunt of complete subsidization of welfare programs alone, and after 1945 the JDC gradually assumed the role of financing social welfare programs at the AIU schools under the teachers' supervision. Further, the cooperation of the OSE (*Oeuvre de Secours aux Enfants*),[2] greatly facilitated the work of the AIU in the struggle for improved sanitary and health conditions among Jews.

The Work of the *Alliance* and Its Allies: JDC-OSE (1945–1956)

The JDC has many achievements to its credit since the end of the Second World War not only in augmenting the influence and scope of activity of the AIU, but in financially supporting a variety of American Jewish-

Table 18.
Jewish and General *Alliance* School Population in Moroccan Cities, 1936 and 1951[a]

Town	Jewish population: 1936[b]	AIU schools: boys and girls[c]	Jewish population: 1951[d]	AIU schools: boys and girls[e]
Agadir	503	61	1,500	202
Azemmour	459	99	300	89
Casablanca	38,806	3,853	75,000	7,683
Elksar	1,500	188	1,600	204
Fez	10,507	1,646	16,050	2,028
Larache	1,200	285	1,300	101
Marrakesh	25,646	1,107	18,500	2,569
Mazagan	3,525	696	3,800	670
Meknes	9,521	1,428	15,000	2,384
Mogador	6,151	888	6,500	906
Oujda	2,048	40	2,000	No data
Rabat	6,698	1,030	13,000	1,392
Safi	3,634	787	4,500	673
Salé	2,600	502	3,300	536
Sefrou	4,382	296	5,500	548
Tangier	10,000	1,072	10,000	1,088
Tetuan	6,000	488	6,000	419

[a]For statistical data on the *bled* communities, see Table 30 of this chapter.
[b]Based on the 1936 population census, analyzed by Y. D. Sémach, "Le recensement de 1936 au Maroc," *Paix et Droit*, 19e année, no. 6 (juin 1939), pp. 8–10.
[c]"Tableau des écoles de l'Alliance Israélite," *Paix et Droit*, 16e année, no. 4, mensuel (juin 1936), p. 16.
[d]"Etat comparatif des taux de scolarisation au Maroc: Années 1950–51", février-mars 1951, p. 8.
[e]Ibid. The population estimates for Tetuan, Elksar, and Larache (in 1936) are mine, based on archival information. This is also the case for Tangier (1936) and Oujda (1951). The Spanish zone did not have an official census until 1942. In Tangier, the International-zone authorities never conducted an official census.

sponsored religious schools, the OSE, clinics and health programs, technical schools, summer camps, community loan associations, food and clothing programs, and even in sending Moroccan would-be emigrants to Israel and France, or to rehabilitation camps in France. By 1948 the JDC had established offices in Morocco, directed by dynamic JDC officials, notably Samuel L. Haber, William Bein, and Louis Kirsch. The situation was quite bad after the war and the AIU found an important partner in combatting poverty. Conditions were particularly bad in the large urban centers (Casablanca, Marrakesh, Fez), but also in smaller communities such as Sefrou, where as late as 1956, of 750 families comprising some 3,850 people who inhabited the *mellāḥ*, almost seventy percent of the families—502 out of 750—comprising 2,200 persons, had only one room, or an average of at least four persons per room; of the 502 families, 210 had more than five persons in the family, some of them with as many as eleven persons occupying this one room.[3]

Samuel L. Haber maintained that disease control improved in Morocco after the end of the war:

> When we first began our work in Morocco . . . it literally appeared that we were faced with a bottomless pit of misery and in general an insoluble problem. But after a few years of work we can report that very substantial contributions have been made, particularly as far as the youth is concerned. When our work began we found appalling health conditions . . . . Our medical program, carried out through OSE, began a campaign against trachoma, a blinding disease of the eyes and against other dirtborne diseases, of ringworms, and others. In the *mellāh*s of the large cities a very high percentage were afflicted with trachoma. Many thousands have been treated and children who would surely have gone blind will now be able to see. . . .
>
> . . . A variety of medical services are provided in these clinics for the poorest of the poor children of Morocco. Children suffering from ringworm of the scalp are exposed to X-ray treatment, after which the diseased hair falls out. In the *Alliance*, in the religious schools, and on the streets, you can see these young children with egg-bald heads often wrapped in bandages and you can be sure that it is a Jewish child and that this disease born of filth is under treatment. The hair gradually returns and the possible disfigurement of a boy or girl has been arrested.[4]

The JDC food and clothing program was particularly extensive for the youth attending day-schools and their families. Given the poverty still prevalent in the Moroccan communities despite some progress the JDC offered considerable assistance. In 1956, for example, 6,200 adults received a monthly package consisting of supplies contributed by the United States Department of Agriculture (USDA) and distributed through the JDC, as well as clothing, and other items which were either imported or purchased locally; at the same time the JDC attempted to establish rehabilitation projects in two communities.[5]

Distribution of food extended to the summer camp and youth movement programs, too. The major Jewish youth organization in Morocco since the 1940s was the *Département Educatif de la Jeunesse Juive au Maroc* (DEJJ) and its leadership wished to cooperate with the Muslim youth movements. An example of such cooperation was a summer activity in Casablanca at one of the AIU schools, which consisted of about three hundred Jewish and an equal number of Muslim youth; this activity was carried on under the auspices of the youth ministry (of already independent Morocco), and the basic costs were covered by the ministry; the JDC furnished USDA and other supplies for the total group.[6] (Table 19 gives a clear picture of JDC financial support to organizations).

Table 19. Summary of Income of J.D.C. Subventioned Organizations 1953–1955 (in Francs)*

Receipts	1953	%	1954	%	1955	%
A.J.D.C.	242.114.709	50,5	266.786.947	48	294.976.221	49
Other Foreign Sources	91.014.310	19	96.930.956	17	103.375.088	17
Government	68.782.218	14	77.342.503	14	77.073.129	13
Local	75.019.850	16	110.187.701	20	123.616.938	20,4
Others	3.298.495	0,5	5.779.122	1	3.721.682	0,6
Total	480.229.582	100%	557.027.229	100%	602.763.058	100%
Alliance Schools	81.701.551		128.490.083		117.703.353	
Religious			22.854.805		21.042.525	
Ozar Hatorah	32.743.264		38.232.373		38.091.624	
Lubavitcher	28.322.290		43.459.663		54.359.410	
Hebrew Courses	9.866.310		7.345.983		7.641.100	
Various Child. Inst.	56.229.173		19.163.087		40.736.085	
Youth Organizations	21.358.486		22.714.412		22.042.405	
OSE Maroc	112.089.401		112.243.605		113.271.588	
Other Medical Organizations	12.446.582		14.608.802		12.078.775	
ORT Maroc	89.940.275		119.058.562		152.087.728	
Summer Camps	34.300.000		28.855.854		23.708.465	
Summer Feeding	1.232.250					
Total	480.229.582		557.027.229		602.763.058	

*Exclusive of Tangier and Spanish Zone.
SOURCE: JDC/330(a): October 1956.

Most, if not all, of the cafeterias belonging to the AIU were largely subsidized by the JDC. Since 1954 the JDC undertook a scientific study of nutrition in conjunction with the Nutrition Department of the *Institut National d'Hygiène* of France. A survey was carried out in five day school cafeterias in Casablanca, to establish criteria for improving the food programs. In two-thirds of the sample, family diets were found to be extremely deficient in animal protein—milk, milk-products, meat, fish, and eggs. These cafeterias were placed under strict nutritional and medical controls, and over a period of time, the height, weight and general health of the children was measured and evaluated. In three of the five cafeterias, diet was improved and changed, and in two the diet remained the same, in order to determine as scientifically as possible the real effects of improved diet. Two thousand, two hundred children were involved, ages 3–14. It has been reported that the girls age 3–6 and boys age 6–10 increased their weight in the pilot cafeterias. The growth increase was very evident for girls of 3–6: they grew one centimeter more in the pilot cafeterias than in the other cafeterias, and they showed no signs of vitamin deficiencies.[7]

In day-care centers and kindergartens that emerged after the war within the AIU and other day-schools, the AIU and the communities made effective use of JDC specialists in planning and constructing new kindergartens;

of the fifteen kindergartens to which JDC gave regular consultation there were twelve trained directresses in 1956, while the other three were too small to justify the employment of directresses; the day-care programs had been made possible only through the training of personnel by the JDC.[8] (Table 20 outlines support by JDC to kindergartens and nurseries).

The summer camp programs organized by the AIU and its allies (*Aide Scolaire* and DEJJ) were usually held in Mazagan, the Atlas mountains, Casablanca, Marrakesh, and Fez. The JDC subsidized these programs on a regular basis through funds, clothing, and food. It provided 6,630,000 francs in 1956 for these summer programs.[9]

Another kind of need which the AIU could not meet effectively was the adult welfare program. There was a kind of traditional welfare system, sometimes called the *hillūk*, which consisted of a form of weekly handouts

Table 20. J.D.C. Supported Kindergarten-Nursery Schools In Morocco
Comparative Table 1954–1956

| | | Number of Children | | |
		1954	1955	1956
Casablanca	OSE: S.D. Lévy	150	85	82
	Hermitage	250		
	Toledano (New Day Nursery)	200	300	310
	Maternelle	515	500	400
	Talmud Torah	360	420	403
	Camp Aliyah	50	-	-
		1.525	1.305	1.195
Agadir	Women's Committee	85	120	112
Fez	Jewish Community	-	180	150
Marrakesh	" " I.	450	450	425
"	" " II.	-	200	225
"	OSE Day Nursery	150	150	154
Mazagan	Jewish Community*	95	95	95
Meknes	Talmud Torah*	240	220	220
Mogador	Jewish Community	52	100	95
Rabat	" "	162	170	160
"	Women's Committee*	170	170	170
Safi	" "	150	150	129
Salé	OSE	92	115	110
Tiznit	Jewish Community	40	50	38
		3.211	3.475	3.278
Tangier	Jewish Community	197	200	200
		3.408	3.675	3.478

*Day nurseries not meeting all requirements and securing limited assistance only.
SOURCE: JDC/330(a): October 1956.

of a few francs; but so deep was the poverty that the JDC initiated and gradually expanded an assistance program to adults which by September 1956 embraced about 2,500 families, including 6,300 persons in twenty communities. The Casablanca community was added to the rolls early in October 1956, bringing total assistance to about 7,500 persons; and basic assistance consisted of USDA-contributed supplies, plus clothing distribution.[10]

The creation of CIRE (*Caisse Israélite de Relèvement Economique*, or *kassa*) in May 1953 is also attributed to the JDC; its funds were largely derived from the United Jewish Appeal drives. The CIRE was an economic rehabilitation program, mainly for artisans, worked out by the JDC with the Jewish Colonization Association. The JCA declared itself prepared to participate on a fifty-fifty basis, and the program's aims were to grant loans for raw materials and tools and to provide technical assistance to loan takers through practical advice in the handling of tools and machines to improve the quality of their production, and increase efficiency. As of June 30 1954, the loan *kassa* in Casablanca had granted 185 loans for a total amount of over 7,000,000 francs, of which 145 for raw materials and 40 for machines and tools.[11] By August 1956 the Casablanca loan *kassa* granted 738 loans since its inception in 1953 for a total of 30,879,847 francs.[12]

A loan *kassa* was opened in Fez (November 1955) and included support for nearby Meknes and Sefrou; between December 1955 and July 1956 the Fez loan *kassa* granted a total of 142 loans amounting to 6,365,000 francs.[13] Eventually *kassas* sprang up elsewhere after independence and continued to function. In fact, CIRE was found in Rabat and Marrakesh as well. As late as 1973 these *kassas* were functioning regularly under JDC supervision.[14]

The JDC program in the northern Spanish zone and in Tangier had its importance, too. New cafeterias were constructed in Larache; in El-Ksar and Arzila new rooms were rented for the cafeteria, and general improvements were introduced, through the installation of new cooking facilities and the purchase of refrigerators. In Tetuan, a new AIU school received financial support from the JDC, including dental facilities.[15]

In Tangier, a wide variety of services, supported by the JDC, were offered. Subventions were made to the AIU for their cafeterias, for two kindergartens, a milk distribution center and supplementary food to children of the poorest families, clothing distribution, and the continued assistance to the hard core of the refugees of the Nazi period who remained stranded in Tangier. Since the war a modern *yeshīva* for about eighty boys was constructed, largely through the generosity of a local religious leader and for which the JDC covered about fifty percent of the budget.[16]

Local Jewish efforts to supplement the social work of the AIU after the war was exemplified in Casablanca by the creation of the *mellāḥ* social center (*Centre Social du Mellah*), presided over by S. D. Lévy, which assisted youth ages 9–14, who, for numerous reasons, have not been integrated into regular day-schools. In 1953, 200 youths were attended to at the center where they were fed and educated — all of which was supported by the JDC.[17]

The JDC, which had become a dynamic force in the communities, a dynamo among Jewish organizations, local youth movements, and institutions, achieved considerable community influence in a relatively short time. One of the organizations it supported in addition to the AIU was OSE. OSE was founded for the purpose of helping destitute Jewish children and during the Second World War it came to their aid in Nazi-occupied Europe. OSE cooperated with the AIU in Tangier, where in 1949 it opened dispensaries and clinics, seventy to eighty percent of which was subsidized by the JDC. OSE had made trained physicians and nurses available to 31,851 children in 1950 and to 45,203 in 1952; to 4,214 adults in 1950 and to 6,565 in 1952.[18] Dental care in 1950 was provided for 1,892 children, advice on proper food and hygiene to 2,750 children, radiotheraphy and vaccination against tuberculosis to 26,996 people, and dermatology experts attended to skin problems among children and adults.[19] Medical services were extended into the AIU and traditional schools,[20] and infant mortality was greatly reduced.[21] Whether in the field of trachoma treatment, ringworm of the scalp, the widespread distribution of prepared-formula milk to thousands of sick children, prenatal, postnatal and well-baby clinic services, the activities of OSE resulted in better health and a better chance for survival for the thousands of beneficiaries. OSE operated clinics throughout the country. By far the largest program was in Casablanca where the impoverished masses of the *mellāh* had no personal resources to meet their health problems, nor means with which to fight off the scourges of the endemic diseases of trachoma, tinea, tuberculosis, and diarrheal diseases. The OSE Casablanca program comprised the following departments: general medicine, chest clinic, ophthalmology, ear, nose and throat, ringworm of the scalp (tinea), milk station (production and distribution), prenatal, postnatal and well-baby clinics, social service, kindergartens, school hygiene program, pharmaceutical department. The staff in Casablanca as of June 30, 1956, consisted of eighteen physicians, sixty-seven nurses and nurses' aides, ten social workers, fifteen kindergarten teachers and staff, ten laboratory assistants, ten administrative staff, and thirty miscellaneous.[22]

Yet despite these efforts, OSE faced problems. The paucity of trained personnel made it difficult to offer additional medical services.

As early as 1949 the AIU established special health centers annexed to the schools. In Casablanca and Marrakesh, schools to cure trachoma patients and a deaf-mute institution in Casablanca, were also created in 1949. That year seven hundred youths were divided into fourteen classes in the trachoma school of Casablanca, seven for boys and seven for girls, equipped with clinics.[23] This institution provided its pupils with general and Jewish education for twenty-five hours per week. Five hours weekly were devoted to medical care under a qualified physician and a trained staff; once cured, the children were placed in regular AIU schools.[24]

Furthermore, in the social sphere, institutional modernization was an ongoing task for the teachers. The battle against child marriages continued after 1912 and was intensified through the creation by the personnel of the schools of special commissions to investigate these practices. These commissions, as was the case in Meknes, were composed of influential rabbis, Albert Moyal (the school director in the early days of the protectorate), and community leaders; and sessions were held regularly to devise strategies to counter the positions of the practice's proponents.[25] The commission received considerable support from Joshué Verdugo, the chief rabbi of Meknes. Members demanded that the protectorate authorities enact a *zahīr* against the practice,[26] but to enact the decree, the protectorate needed ample proof

Figure 22. Teachers of the *Alliance*

of the extent of community support through a petition drive. This resulted in support of the practice and the failure of the AIU's initiative.[27] Nevertheless, Moyal pledged to continue his campaign.[28]

In Marrakesh, unlike Meknes, Raphaël Danon contended in 1913 that child marriages were declining among families of diverse economic strata.[29] Similarly, in Elksar the schools' director and his wife achieved success with various families in the drive against child marriages.[30] According to Albert Benaroya, "We persuaded the parents to keep their daughters in school longer instead of having them married young. Thus the girls are better educated and are more particular as with whom they ought to marry.[31] To enhance their role, his wife was determined not to be a mere teacher, "but a true and trustworthy friend, one whom the girls can come for advice in difficult times."[32]

In the cultural sphere and in other areas of social welfare, the work of the AIU in the post-1912 period became considerably wider. As educators in and out of the classroom, the teachers lectured at alumni association circles about a variety of topics ranging from fascism, nationalism, and hassidism as well as about contemporary figures dominating Jewish history. These activities included appeals for funds on behalf of Eastern European Jewry.[33]

In addition to these promotions, the AIU developed and supervised goodwill associations known as *Associations Aide Scolaire*. In 1935, for example, the directress of the Fez *mellāḥ* girls' school and her counterpart in the school situated in the European quarter, collaborated to create *L'Aide Scolaire*. This association, which by 1950 could be found in every important community as either AIU-affiliated or an independent body, distributed shoes, clothing, eyeglasses, and other necessities to poor youths and like the alumni associations had a central committee and dues-paying members. During Jewish holidays the two directresses in Fez would organize a door-to-door campaign to take collections from the wealthier members of the community, and encouraged them to give gifts for the children.[34] Between 1935 and 1937, some five hundred and fifty boys and girls benefited from the material aid of *L'Aide Scolaire* in Fez.[35]

Sports and gymnastics were important innovations introduced in the modern schools for both Jews and Muslims. The AIU also developed scouting and summer camping programs, phenomena popular in Morocco since 1930. These programs more than any others, provided important outlets from the *mellāḥ*.[36] Summer camp programs were especially well attended. Once again, *L'Aide Scolaire* constituted the apparatus responsible for this activity. Yet not all summer camping programs were the responsibility of *L'Aide Scolaire* and the AIU. Looking into data for 1946 we find that of the 4,129 French and Moroccan (Jews and Muslims) entering summer camps in French Morocco, 2,125 French youths were registered, as compared with 1,120 Muslims and 894 Jews; of the latter figure, 369 youths were sent by the AIU program.[37]

Finally, secondary education became no less important in the AIU program during the protectorate era. Perhaps the most notable reform was the institution of the *cours complémentaire* system. To meet new educational needs, and improve employment prospects for its graduates, the AIU, through Sémach's efforts created practical programs: bookkeeping, commercial correspondence, typing and stenography, and advanced French language training, all of which were integrated into the *cours complémentaires*. The *brevet elémentaire* issued after four years was meant to serve as a bridge for the *lycées*, leading to the *baccalauréat* or the *diplôme d'études commerciales*,[38] the latter intended for secretarial and commercial business.

The first *cours complémentaire* was created in Tangier (1925), and began as a two-year program.[39] In the 1930s the program in Tangier and other such AIU-sponsored schools was patterned after the four-year program. Some of these institutions included courses in commercial correspondence, drafting, and some vocational training. Secondary vocational schools were also created by the AIU as was a teachers' training school. But these reforms, largely undertaken during the last two decades of the protectorate era, require more detailed explanations (see below). Generally speaking, the AIU either expanded its projects from the preprotectorate period or became involved in new programs to meet Moroccan needs under the protectorates.

Jewish Educational Reforms: The Birth of the
Ecole Normale Hébraïque and other Jewish Developments.
The Importance of the Post-1945 Period Until Independence

The protectorate era witnessed important reforms in the area of Jewish education, mostly in the 1945–1960 period, reforms which after Moroccan independence were beneficial to the remaining Jewish communities. These reforms were in large part instituted by the AIU, though the efforts of the latter were complemented by special institutions set up and subsidized by American Jewry.

The reformist efforts of the Paris AIU in the post-Second World War period came about after many years of long and drawnout pressures on the AIU headquarters by community leaders, parents, Zionist activists, and even a growing segment of AIU school teachers and directors. These groups argued that if the AIU had failed to develop a comprehensive program during the organization's first fifty years of existence, it was high time to do so. Indeed there were frequent complaints to the AIU about the neglect of Jewish education. For example, in 1925 Haïm Abikssera, vice-president of the Meknes community, asked the AIU of Paris to allot at least two hours of Hebrew daily, lest parents refuse to enroll their children in the schools.[40] Abikssera noted, "Our community represents one of the most orthodox of Morocco's communities and we would like our youths to be as well educated in Hebrew as they are in French."[41] And, to display their respect for what the AIU had done for Moroccan Jewry but at the same time to protest the insufficient devotion to Hebrew in the program, many Jews sent their children to the AIU, but also they enrolled them in rabbinic schools at the same time. Consequently, we learn from Hanania Dahan of Salé that during the 1920s:

> There was an arrangement between the AIU and the Salé community in which we studied at both the AIU and the rabbinic schools. We went to the AIU from 8:00 to 11:30 a.m., ate lunch at the school cafeteria free of charge, came back to the same school at 1:30 and stayed there until 4:30 p.m. At 4:30 p.m. we went directly to the rabbinic school to learn Hebrew in addition to the Hebrew we picked up at the AIU, and stayed there until 8:00.[42]

However, this arrangement proved too demanding in the long run, as the youths often had to attend two schools in one day. Among the rabbinic schools frequented, the *Em-ha-Banīm* network is noteworthy. Its schools were created during the First World War, not so much to oppose the AIU as to organize Jewish education better. *Em ha-Banīm*, which in Hebrew means "the mother of the sons," was financially promoted and supported by the women in the communities, usually rabbis' wives. By 1930, these schools could be found throughout Morocco, mainly in the interior: Fez, Sefrou, Marrakesh.[43]

To facilitate the task of the youths who had to attend two schools, and also to attract other youths away from the rabbinic schools, several AIU teachers launched a strategy to tip the balance of enrollment in their favor.[44] This strategy entailed the promotion and sponsorship of modernized rabbinic schools that would offer both religious and secular education at the same time. In the early 1920s a modernized rabbinic school was created by the community and by Daniel Lerner, an outstanding teacher of the AIU and director of its operations in Meknes for several decades. The school acquired a virtual monopoly over education, that included religious studies, general education, and French. It developed rapidly and earned the AIU prestige in the community. In 1940, the community enthusiastically participated in the subsidization of the school and in fact agreed to pay the French language teachers' salaries.[45] In 1937, the school had twenty-three classes and an enrollment of 1,200, whereas the boys' and girls' schools of the AIU had altogether 900 students in seventeen classes.[46] The AIU teachers, it appears, had won a twofold victory: first, in perhaps the most orthodox community in Morocco it had won confidence in the schools and managed to encroach on the monopoly enjoyed by the old-type rabbinic schools in the area of Jewish education; second, as a result of the new addition all of Meknes' Jewish youths were enrolled in schools.[47]

In Tangier similar efforts to reform religious schools were made. Yet despite these two cases no progress was made in that direction prior to 1945. The lack of pedagogically qualified rabbi-teachers, and the absence of additional initiatives by the AIU in creating a network of modernized rabbinic schools — probably due to the Paris Central Committee's reluctance to alienate tradition-bound rabbis by encroaching deeply into their monopoly — hindered all possibilities for radical improvements in Jewish educational programs. There was a serious dichotomy that seemed to have emerged in the policy of the AIU during the protectorate era. One represented the position of the Central Committee in Paris which did not wish to alienate rabbis or the protectorates, notably the French, who since 1924 generously subsidized its schools. The other represented a growing segment of the teachers who, on the one hand realized the inevitability of Jewish educational reform, of offering a dual sacred-profane program in rabbinic schools (even if they were not unanimous on how much time should be devoted to Hebrew) and were, on the other hand, pressured, at least psychologically, since the 1920s by Zionists who goaded them and the communities to introduce modern and spoken Hebrew in the AIU program. And as no progress was achieved on a large scale, the AIU representatives frequently unsupported by the Paris headquarters, merely accused the rabbi-teachers of incompetence in Jewish education, of superficiality, and of limited knowledge of Hebrew.

The teachers of the AIU were discrediting the old rabbinic schools continuously since 1912, when they began to feel well entrenched in the communities, as part of a propaganda campaign to enhance their own influence in the Moroccan communities. They had applied similar tactics in other Mediterranean countries. On the other hand, the rabbinic schools could not meet the requirements of modern and colonial times. A consensus was developing among community leaders in Tangier that in the wake of the new realities, the rabbi-teachers had to become knowledgeable in general education, European languages, and modern pedagogy in addition to their sacred knowledge. But the initiative for a solution to the problem seemed to have been undertaken by the Tangier community alone. In 1924 the Tangier *junta* created a rabbinic seminary that intended to gear the future educators throughout Morocco toward Jewish studies, European languages, general education, and spoken Hebrew. This aspect of Hebrew was also neglected by the rabbi-teachers and could no longer remain that way. The duration of training at the seminary was five years, leading to the advanced *brevet*.

The initiative won the support of AIU representatives. Sémach, though of the opinion that the seminary might be Zionist inspired, believed that it would train qualified teachers for both rabbinic and spoken Hebrew. It also intended to train pedagogically qualified teachers for all Jewish schools, prepare rabbis, kosher meat slaughterers, and other members of the religious elite. And though Sémach was a devout anti-Zionist crusader he was of the opinion that the seminary's program, which included the propagation of spoken Hebrew, would eventually benefit the AIU for several reasons: first, the seminary's graduates would be able to replace the rabbi-teachers in the AIU; second, once the seminary students learned French and obtained a general education, they would be equipped intellectually and pedagogically to teach in modern schools, especially as they knew both Hebrew and French. Most teachers who taught at both the AIU and rabbinic schools did not know French; also, a teaching corps of well-educated rabbis would challenge the old *talmudē tōra* and *ṣlāa*. As a result, modernized rabbinic schools would come into being, offering both sacred and profane education, and thus facilitating the task of the AIU.[48]

Sémach's expectations, like those of well-meaning Tangier leaders, were not realized. The seminary which employed local influential rabbis who ran the program, never succeeded in developing a modern Hebrew program, and the teachers that emerged followed in the traditional methods of the rabbi-teachers, with the AIU continuing to recruit the same staff for religious education as it had since 1862. By 1950 the seminary had eighty students between the ages of 13–18, many of whom came from the Spanish zone; the institution's financial maintenance fell almost entirely on the Tangier *junta* alone.[49] General education, French, and Spanish were taught by AIU teachers, salaried by the International zone.[50] Charles Hamet in his study on the Tangier community argued in 1950 that "the low level of teaching in the seminary gave rise to wide-spread disenchantment and pressure on the part of young pro-Zionist intellectuals who wanted the school to teach modern Hebrew."[51]

Albert Saguès, who directed the AIU schools in Tangier, also attacked the seminary for its low educational standards, back in 1936. He suggested that the Central Committee consider one of three alternatives: first, recruit Hebrew teachers from Palestine; second, if that was not possible, the AIU could enlist Palestinian Jews who graduated from the ENIO and worked in Morocco; finally, it was feasible that the ENIO itself could guide an intensive Hebrew training program.[52] Saguès, like many other AIU teachers of the 1930s, despite their indifference to Zionism, argued that knowledge of spoken Hebrew would be useful for the Jews because a Hebrew renaissance was essential for re-judaization and not necessarily an instrument of political Zionism. In fact, the sacred Hebrew always taught in Moroccan schools was seen as a dead language like Latin and Greek, and though it was a valuable medium for rabbis and scholars, the *langue vivante* was the popular current. As Saguès explained eloquently to an AIU leadership worried about the rise of fascism in Europe:

> Hebrew in our times is a spoken and living language, used by thousands of people and the number of adherents to this renaissance is continuously rising. It is an undeniable fact which we must accept above all political considerations. While I do not subscribe to the political ideology of Zionism, and despite the tragic disillusionment to which our faith has been victim in the virtues of emancipation, I persist in clinging to emancipation as the political solution to the Jewish problem. However, this does not deter me from believing that the Jews must possess today knowledge of contemporary Hebrew language and culture rather than stick to the language for religious obligations. It is essential for Moroccan Jews to be able to read from the Hebrew press. It would be prudent for the *Alliance* to immediately introduce spoken Hebrew into the curriculum and thus we need the instruction manuals available in Palestine . . . . When I was teaching at the *Alliance* schools in Tunisia, I personally used the two volumes *Beth Sefer Ivri* (*The Modern Hebrew School*) by Grazovsky and the three volumes of *Haddibour ha-Ivri* (*Hebrew: The Spoken Language*) by Krinsky.[53]

The reply from the Paris AIU was quite adamant in rejecting Saguès's policy suggestion, a rejection that demonstrated the magnitude of the divisions that existed between the Paris Central Committee and a growing number of teachers of the AIU in Morocco. The secretary-general responded to Saguès:

> You would like to have Hebrew taught in such a way that our pupils will be able to speak the language. If our pupils, upon graduating, would be able to translate our prayers and the Bible fluently, this would already be a positive result. We do not think it is useful for the youths to speak Hebrew.[54]

Saguès's suggestion to recruit Palestinians was equally rebuffed, for employing teachers from Palestine would have been very costly; and Palestinians, even if they were good teachers, were not always recommended from the point of view of religion. And as the Moroccan communities were quite religious, such a policy could have become a sad experience for the AIU.[55] The AIU, then, was determined to turn down its teachers requests for serious Jewish and Hebrew studies reforms for obvious reasons. The Paris organization no doubt feared the possibility that hiring Hebrew teachers from Palestine could challenge the school's influence with Zionist ideas and transform the schools into pro-Zionist institutions. Further, as the French provided generous subsidies to the school network and given the Spanish zone subsidy for Spanish language and culture in the AIU program, the Paris leaders preferred not to risk confrontations in the protectorates' political arena.

Nevertheless, pressures on the AIU from a variety of forces — some of its own teachers, Zionists, community leaders, and parents — to reform the Jewish and Hebrew studies program and at the same time devote more hours to these courses, were mounting. One school director contended as early as 1931 that it was not sufficient to teach the youths about Jeanne d'Arc's heroism; it was equally essential to talk about Shim'ōn Bar Koḥva, who led a heroic rebellion in Palestine against the Roman Emperor Hadrian.[56] In Casablanca (1929) Reuben Tajouri, then director of an AIU school, expressed interest in recent pro-Zionist activities for organizing a conference to discuss the necessity of all Jewish schools to teach spoken Hebrew.[57] And though not unsympathetic to the idea of a Hebrew renaissance, Tajouri questioned the Zionists' wisdom in view of Moroccan Muslim support for the Arabs in Palestine at a time following the Arab riots in Hebron and Safed and the destruction of the Hebron Jewish community.[58]

When in the late 1930s pressures on the AIU headquarters intensified, owing to the relentless efforts of Saguès and others, who, in view of the growing signs of European anti-semitism, were eager to accentuate Jewish solidarity and education, the Paris leadership finally relented. It decided to dispatch to Morocco one of its most prominent members, Rabbi Maurice Liber, on a fact-finding mission to examine the state of Jewish education in its schools.

Liber carried out his investigation and in March 1939, in addition to his report, told a correspondent of *L'Union Marocaine* that[59] he had visited the AIU schools, the rabbinic schools, the Franco-Jewish schools controlled by the French protectorate, and various *yeshīvōt* in the interior and Tangier, and found that parents were generally more critical than the rabbis of the quality and quantity of Jewish education at the AIU schools. He acknowledged that disenchanted parents in several communities protested by sending their children to religious schools to supplement the secular education offered at the AIU. But this practice was inconvenient for the pupils and it would be desirable to offer a more balanced Jewish studies program.

The point was clear: a major figure of French Jewry and an ally of the AIU conceded that greater sacrifices were needed to meet the demands of the communities, which included instruction in spoken Hebrew. To achieve these reforms, the AIU had to open a teachers' training institute to prepare pedagogically qualified teachers who would also replace the rabbi-teachers. The outbreak of the Second World War and Vichy delayed this plan. But after 1945 the project was taken up again, and the developments that led to its implementation are noteworthy.

The Māgēn-Dāvīd Association of Casablanca under S. D. Lévy's leadership, which popularized spoken Hebrew and, in 1944, created a Hebrew language center, was mentioned above. When the AIU reorganized its activities in 1946 several of its leaders, notably Jules Braunschvig, showed great enthusiasm for the creation of a Hebrew training institution for teachers. Braunschvig, who read the Liber report after the war, was determined to introduce the necessary reforms. And since Morocco was the testing ground of the AIU for this reform, and as AIU leaders, particularly Braunschvig and Tajouri (the new delegate), were less assimilationist than Bigart and Sémach, the road to reform was cleared. Braunschvig, who was elected as the organization's vice-president, met with Tajouri and a distinguished Algerian rabbi from Oran, Ishāq Rouche in Paris. The three, after consultations with S. D. Lévy, agreed to take over the Māgēn-Dāvīd Hebrew center and transform it into a teachers' training college for Jewish studies and spoken Hebrew, under Rouche's direction.[60] His impeccable knowledge of both rabbinic and spoken Hebrew made him an ideal candidate for the task, and several of his students from Oran joined him to form the embryonic faculty of the training school.

From the outset, the AIU, through the new institution, *Ecole Normale Hébraïque* (ENH), began to replace the outmoded rabbi-teachers with qualified educators for ancient and modern Jewish language and culture. The school expanded after 1946 from the one class of the Māgēn-Dāvīd nucleus to four classes. The program led to the *brevet élémentaire* after four years of intensive Jewish and secular studies, plus a fifth year of teacher training. The elementary *brevet* was granted by the protectorate's DIP, even for ENH candidates from Tangier and the Spanish zone. Jewish studies and Hebrew examinations were conducted by the AIU through Rabbi Rouche and his disciples, Jo Medioni, Emile Sebban, and Albert Hazan.[61] As for subsidies, the school did not come under the jurisdiction of the 1928 agreement between the AIU and the French protectorate, most likely because the French did not want to support an institution that could serve, directly or indirectly, Zionist causes. The AIU alone maintained the school, and Braunschvig raised a large part of the funds to build and operate it, in Europe.[62]

The number of classes increased as did the students, most of them outstanding Hebrew students from the primary schools of the AIU.[63] By the time Morocco achieved its independence, the ENH had managed to replace many rabbi-teachers with its own graduates, leading to reforms in Jewish and Hebrew education in the primary and *cours complémentaire* schools of the AIU. The Franco-Jewish schools of the protectorate eventually recruited ENH graduates for its Jewish studies program, for they knew both Hebrew and French. Even in Israel, the Jewish Agency manifested considerable interest in the ENH, and through channels, the ENH instituted a special degree, administered from the Jewish Agency, the *Te'ūdā ha-Yerūshālmīt* (the "Jerusalem Certificate").[64]

Issachar Ben-Ami, now a noted Israeli scholar, a native of Casablanca, and a pioneer graduate of the ENH, explained that this certificate was granted to ENH students after the fourth or fifth year but also to non-ENH Hebrew specialists who showed excellence in their knowledge of spoken and written Hebrew.[65] Though certainly not a ticket of admission to an Israeli university, the certificate exam which tests the knowledge of the participants in the fundamentals of Hebrew language and culture, conferred upon the participants a privilege which was recognized by institutions of higher learning in Israel and exempted applicants to the Hebrew University from entrance examinations in Hebrew.[66] The certificate, then, was an effort to attract Moroccans to settle in Israel.

In April 1951, the ENH moved to the outskirts of Casablanca to the suburb of Oasis. The new school was impressive. It was a huge three-story building with cafeteria and dormitory facilities for students coming from different parts of the country—all tuition-free, providing that the students agreed to teach at the AIU schools for not less than a five-year period following graduation from the ENH.[67] In 1952 the ENH had not less than eighty trainees, exceeding the number of students at the ENIO in Paris, and community support for this initiative was forthcoming. In 1951, the pro-Zionist *Nō'ār* of the Charles Netter Association, praised the tuition-free program, the books, the clothing program, and the dormitory facilities; it also praised the contribution of Hebrew education at the AIU primary schools.[68]

After Moroccan independence the ENH offered a seven-year instead of a five-year program, equating it with the *lycée* system, leading to both the *baccalauréat* and the CAP (Certificate of Pedagogical Aptitude).[69]

According to Ben-Ami, though Rouche's disciples and teachers at the ENH were not always outstanding Hebraists, their spoken Hebrew was usually flawless, and they spent much time outside the classroom educating themselves in Hebrew literature and the Jewish tradition.[70] Prior to 1956, the program of the ENH was divided into two sections. The first section offered the same general and professional education available at the *cours complémentaires* of the AIU. The second section offered spoken Hebrew and traditional and modern Jewish history and literature. Finally, during the fifth year of study there was a course in psychology. The program of the ENH for the pre-1956 period is seen in Tables 21 and 22.

Table 21. Ecole Normale Hébraïque
(Hours per week)

Courses in the area of general education	CLASSES				
	First	Second	Third	Fourth	Pedagogical Year
French	6	6	5	6	2
Mathematics	5	5	5	5	-
Physical sciences	-	-	2	2	-
Natural sciences	1	1	1	2	-
History	2	2	2	2	-
Geography	1	1	1	1	-
Music	-	1	1	1	1
Design	1	-	-	-	-
Physical education	2	2	2	2	2
Classical Arabic	4	4	5	4	6
Moroccan Arabic	-	-	1	1	-

SOURCE: *Horaires Hebdomadaires des Matières Enseignées avant 1956: E.N.H.*. For providing me with the normal school's program, I would like to express my gratitude to the AIU delegate in Casablanca, Elias Harrus.

Table 22. Ecole Normale Hébraïque
(Hours per week)

Courses in the area of Jewish education	CLASSES				
	First	Second	Third	Fourth	Pedagogical Year
Talmud	3	3	3	3	12
The written Torah	5	4	4	2	4
The oral Torah	4	5	3	2	2
Jewish history	2	1	2	1	2
Jewish ethics	1	1	-	-	-
Hebrew composition	-	-	1	1	1
Liturgy	1	1	1	1	1
Hebrew penmanship and grammar	-	1	1	-	1
Psychology	-	-	-	-	2
Pedagogical theory	-	-	-	-	1
Probation (stage)	-	-	-	-	2-4

SOURCE: *Horaires Hebdomadaires des Matières Enseignées avant 1956: E.N.H.*

The offering of classical Arabic was an important addition to the program of the ENH, and eventually led to the emergence of specialized teachers in that language for the AIU and other Jewish schools. As for the Jewish studies program, Table 22 outlines the courses.

The history course dealt with the Jewish people from antiquity to modern times. Regarding the history of modern times, Rouche explained:

> We taught the future teachers of the AIU elementary schools the history of the Jewish people until 1860, with the great renaissance of the founding of the *Alliance Israélite Universelle*. From time to time we taught them about Jewish historical events since 1860, for so much has happened in the Jewish world already by the time World War I broke out. However, we deemphasized Zionist political history. The reasons were that the ENH was not an ideological center for Zionism, and we did not wish to alienate the French and Moroccan authorities.[71]

However, the names of Theodor Herzl, Max Nordau, and other prominent political Zionists often came up in class discussions. References to cultural Zionism were pronounced, for the philosophy and teachings of Ahad Ha'am, its leading proponent, became an integral part of the course.

The course pertaining to moral education (*mūsar*) was now based on moral lessons drawn from Jewish rather than French examples. The penmanship-grammar course pertained only to Hebrew. Finally, while no reference is made to spoken Hebrew and its contemporary literature, the two were taught intensively at the ENH, especially by Rouche, who undertook extensive teaching responsibilities. The latter recalled:

> We taught them about the Haskala movement led by Mendelssohn of which I personally took charge for teaching. It was I who taught them the Talmud, on the one hand, and the contemporary literature of Y. L. Gordon and Haïm Nahman Bialik, on the other. The opponents of the AIU were no longer justified in accusing us of de-Judaization. A complete education of both ancient and modern Jewish traditions and language was taking place in the school. The support for the ENH and the AIU schools in Morocco was greatly enhanced because of the teachers' training program. Children from the most remote corners of the Atlas communities enrolled at the ENH and, in fact, one of the most vociferously anti-*Alliance* rabbis, the great Baruch Toledano of Meknes, sent his children to study at the ENH.[72]

All in all, the program was intensive, lasting from 8:00 A.M. to 8:00 P.M. daily with small breaks and time off for sports and scouting activities. Recreational activities were supervised by Rouche's disciples. Students played basketball and participated in tournaments against other schools.[73] "We would be invited to the homes of our teachers," recalled Ben-Ami, "and spend much time with them. They were extremely encouraging and zealous. The work load for us was enormous because it was like attending two *cours complémentaires* at the same time: one sacred, one secular."[74] As for the impact of the ENH on the state of Hebrew education at the primary schools of the AIU, Ben-Ami related: "I was able, after my graduation from the ENH, to speak fluent Hebrew. You cannot imagine the joy and satisfaction we had when my pupils at the advanced elementary classes in Casablanca could after some time carry a conversation with me in spoken Hebrew."[75] (For Hebrew courses program throughout the country, see table 23).

When the question arose whether the AIU through the ENH, given the ties it had with the Jewish Agency, had an agreement with the Israelis to prepare emigrants for Israel in spoken Hebrew, Rouche avoided a direct answer, but said: "The aim of the ENH and the program was not to prepare emigrants for Israel. Rather, there was in Morocco already a desire to go to Israel long before the creation of the ENH. Moreover, the AIU always tried to meet the desires of the communities where the organization had schools. In Morocco the AIU was pressured to teach such courses and prepare teachers to achieve this aim. As was the case with other requests, the AIU fulfilled the wishes of the communities once again."[76]

When asked the same question, Ben-Ami said that while he did not know what was discussed behind closed doors at the Paris headquarters, he was quite certain that the AIU did not collaborate directly with the Israelis; the AIU, in his opinion, merely wanted to balance Hebrew (biblical and spoken) and Judaic studies with the general secular program in the primary and *cours complémentaire* schools.[77] Inevitably, educating the youths in spoken Hebrew and contemporary Jewish culture led the youths' knowing already in elementary school about Palestinian Jewry and the creation of Israel.[78] Even if the AIU tried to avoid teaching Zionism at the ENH lest it alienate the Moroccan authorities and nationalists, Stanley Abramovitch, a veteran JDC official, observed that all educational initiatives of the post-1945 period were meant to prepare Jews for emigration.[79]

In 1953, Abramovitch reported that the JDC served as a pressure group on the AIU to develop its Hebrew studies program because it was partly subsidizing its schools. He indicated that the AIU had now obtained the official sanction of the DIP to introduce seven and one half hours per week for boys in primary schools and five hours per week for girls in primary and secondary schools. He added that Braunschvig finally agreed with the JDC that the AIU should hire a first-class educator to supplement the work of Rouche and his staff; since it was impossible to find such a person outside Israel, the AIU would have to employ an Israeli.[80]

In 1955 there was no doubt about ties between Israelis and the ENH. Though members of the ENH staff, several Israelis were recruited through the religious department of the Jewish Agency. The matter became clear at

Table 23. Hebrew Courses Program (July 31, 1956)

Centers	Organizations	Summer Courses		Reg. Evening Courses	
		Number of classes	Number of pupils enrolled	Number of classes	Number of pupils enrolled
Casablanca	D.E.J.J.	-	-	14	486
"	Hoveve Hassafa	15	675	9	244
"	Magbit Jeunes	-	-	2	24
"	Centre Social	-	-	3	65
Rabat	Hoveve Hassafa	2	38	2	44
Salé	" "	6	240	3	90
Meknès	" "	-	-	10	283
"	Lycéens	-	-	2	35
"	Wizo	-	-	1	17
Marrakesh	Hoveve Hassafa	20	805	8	240
Mazagan	E.I.F.	-	-	2	34
Fez	Hoveve Hassafa	10	391	7	167
"	Wizo	-	-	4	80
Sefrou	Hoveve Hassafa	-	-	9	260
Oujda	Community	8	286	4	140
Beni Mellal	Hoveve Hassafa	2	90	8	240
Safi	" "	3	87	1	20
Goulimine	Community	-	-	1	20
Imintanout	"	1	80	-	-
Port Lyautey	"	3	118	-	-
		70	2.810	90	2.489

SOURCE: JDC/330(a)

the end of 1955, when Morocco was on the brink of independence, and local organizations were anxious to disassociate themselves in the public eye from the Israelis. Thus M. Akibi of the Jewish Agency had been informed that Tajouri had already complained to Rouche that the Israelis were giving too many lessons in that school and that he should find more Moroccan teachers to replace them.[81] And as Samuel L. Haber, JDC-Morocco director pointed out in 1956:

For many years the education department of the Jewish Agency in Jerusalem has conducted, during the summer months, a special seminar in Israel, for the graduates of the *Alliance* Normal school in Casablanca. This year, as a result of the political events, the *Alliance* decided to arrange for a similar seminar in the [ENIO] school (near Paris) instead of in Israel. This was done in collaboration with the education department of the Jewish Agency and the Jewish boy scout movement of France.[82]

Figure 23. The *Ecole Normale Hébraïque* in 1951

The JDC which collaborated with the Jewish Agency on Hebrew education was responsible for recruiting Israelis to teach at the ENH and for
strengthening the ties between the AIU and Jerusalem. According to
Abramovitch:

> We have found a way of utilizing the personnel of the education department
> of the Jewish Agency. They have helped us enormously in organizing short
> seminars for teachers, in assisting directors of religious schools to introduce
> improvements, in making teachers aware of their shortcomings . . . . In
> Morocco [we] have been able to benefit from the presence of Jewish Agency
> educators, especially of the religious education department, who have con-
> tributed much to the work in the . . . Hebrew teachers' seminar of the
> *Alliance.*[83]

The ENH, then, had ample contacts. And whereas Abramovitch argued
that the ENH had trained only twenty-six teachers by February 1954,[84]
Haber, who worked on the scene, indicated that since its inception, the
ENH produced yearly some twenty new Hebrew teachers.[85]

Enter *Oṣār ha-Tōra* and *Ohālē Yōsēf Isḥāq*

In 1948, an initiative by American Sephardi Jewry, subsidized by the JDC
and supported by the lobbying efforts of the AIU before the French protec-

torate authorities,[86] led to the penetration of religious schools known as *Osār ha-Tōra* (OH; The Wealth of the *Tōra*). These were reinforced in 1950 by the *Ohālē Yōsēf-Ishāq* institutions (AYI; The Tents of Joseph and Isaac) of the Lubavitch hassidic movement of New York. This, too, was the impact of American Jewish interests in their North African brethren after the 1942 Allied invasion. (For data on the OH and AYI, see Tables 24 and 25).

Figure 24. Rabbi Ishāq Rouche, director of the *Ecole Normale Hébraïque*

The OH, a New York-based Sephardi association founded by Isaac Shalom and devoted to the ideal of *Tōra 'im dērēh ereṣ* (comprehensive traditional education combined with general education), opened schools in some of the urban centers but also in the towns and hamlets of southern Morocco. The AYI of the Lubavitcher movement which originally was founded in Eastern Europe and eventually centered its activities in New

Table 24. Ozar Hatorah - French Morocco Schools subsidized by J.D.C. (Status July 1956)

		Number of Teachers	Number of Pupils
I.	Ozar Hatorah directly operated schools		
	Cities		
	1. Casablanca	14	628
	Small Villages		
	2. Ait Hakim	1	20
	3. Ait Yahia	1	30
	4. Amassine	1	18
	5. Amezrou	1	22
	6. Amizmiz	1	37
	7. Aoulouz	1	38
	8. Chichaoua	1	20
	9. Dechra	1	20
	10. Demnat	2	41
	11. Debdou	2	45
	12. Fedala	1	10
	13. Igui Nogo	2	89
	14. Imadiden	1	18
	15. Marrakesh	2	40
	16. Mazagan	2	80
	17. Mezzate	1	30
	18. Ouled Zangia	2	50
	19. Oumnas	1	14
	20. Ourika	1	35
	21. Tahnaout	1	22
	22. Tamaroft	1	14
	23. Tazenakht	1	30
	Sub total	42	1.351
II.	Ozar Hatorah partially supported and supervised Religious Institutions		
	24. EM HABANIM Casablanca	9	346
	25. TALMUD TORAH "	10	780
	26. " " Beni-Mellal	3	90
	27. EM HABANIM Fez	17	690
	28. TALMUD TORAH Mogador	5	156
	29. " " Meknes	22	998
	30. " " Ouezzan	3	70
	31. " " Rabat	4	137
	32. EM HABANIM Sefrou	9	360
	Sub total	82	3.627
	Grand total	124	4.978

SOURCE: JDC/330(a)

Table 25. Ohale Yosef Ytsak (Lubavitcher) Yeshivoth and small religious Schools subsidized by J.D.C. (Status June 30, 1956)

A. Institutions	Number of Teachers teachers	Number of Pupils pupils
1. Meknes Yeshiva	7	138
" Beth Rivka	4	100
" Evening Courses	2	60
2. Casablanca Yeshiva Guedola	9	190
" " Ketana	7	190
" Beth Rivka	9	224
3. Sefrou Yeshiva	3	75
" Beth Rivka	4	50
4. Midelt	6	200
5. Erfoud	7	320
6. Missour	2	60
7. Marrakesh	1	53
8. Agadir	3	82
" Evening Courses	2	140
	66	1.882
B. Small towns and villages		
1. Agoum	1	19
2. Ait Zagar	1	15
3. Ait Ouzin	1	15
4. Akhlout	-	13
5. Amkessoud	1	30
6. Aroumiyat Zagora	1	11
7. Aslim Agdz	1	15
8. Aslin	1	20
9. Asfalon	1	11
10. Berguent	-	25
11. El Aioun	-	30
12. Imini	-	22
13. Kasba Tadla	1	64
14. K.P.Jorf	1	12
15. Ksar Es Souk	3	150
16. L'Mahamid Tagounit	-	17
17. L'Kasba Tinzoulin	1	17
18. Oulad Yacoub Skoura	1	19
19. Oulad Bou Hamir	1	30
20. Rebat Tinzoulin	1	18
21. Rich	1	61
22. Rissani	1	65
23. Settat	3	100
24. Sidi Rahal	1	37
25. Sifa	1	17
26. Tabiya	1	30
27. Tamasint Oursazat	1	15
28. Talmasla	1	25
29. Tamnougalt	1	23
30. Targah	-	15
31. Teilit	1	35
32. Ticert	1	25
33. Tinerhir	1	38
34. Toundouf	-	15
	31	1.054
	66	1.882
	97	2.936

SOURCE: JDC/330(a) [French Morocco]

York, developed a twofold program: the boys received a full traditional education in *yeshīvōt* but practically no secular education; the girls received a primary and secondary education. By the early 1950s these American-based organizations, backed by the JDC, taught by qualified Moroccan teachers, had several thousand students aged 6-18. The OH offered some French education through AIU teachers, demonstrating that the AIU extended influence beyond its network of schools.[87] Interestingly, the AYI was opposed to heavy doses of the secular curriculum at the AIU. Abramovitch observed in 1955 that Rabbis Shlomo Matusof and M.Lipsker (AYI directors) were opposed to secular education in their schools.[88] But in 1956 Haber noted that some progress had been made by the JDC to persuade the AYI to introduce some kind of secular education for the boys, and more for the girls, who had already been receiving some secular education.[89]

Although the AYI representatives disapproved of the AIU, the vocal opposition generally emanated from the OH, which competed fiercely with the AIU. Joseph Shamah and Rabbi Z. Waltner, OH representatives, attacked AIU's policies in the context of Jewish education perhaps with the intention of discrediting its work and minimizing its influence in the communities. Regardless of differences on a variety of matters, ranging from occasional unhappiness over the quality of secular AIU teachers teaching at the OH, to conflicts — in the 1960s or even the 1970s — over combining AIU-OH schools in face of emigration and a dwindling population, seen by the OH as an effort by the AIU to "swallow up" its influence, a gradual but relatively effective coexistence developed between the two educational networks. There were always behind-the-scene quarrels, settled through the mediation of the JDC, but basically, for the sake of Jewish service, these organizations maintained their influence, together.

Originally, most attacks which the OH launched on the AIU were baseless. In 1948, upon entering the scene, the OH published the following statement:

> The activities of *Osạ̄r ha-Tōra* have not been limited to the founding of religious schools. Indeed, *Osạ̄r ha-Tōra* has been closely in touch with secular educational institutions such as the *Alliance Israélite* . . . . The numerous children who attend the *Alliance* schools are educated without any instructions in religious subjects. We have asked the *Alliance* headmasters to manage in the time table . . . two hours daily in the teaching of the *Tōra*. We hope that our intervention will turn out a success.[90]

Similarly, J. L. Soussan, vice-president of OH in Morocco, wrote to Isaac Shalom in 1950 that in view of the shortage of qualified teachers at the OH, and budgetary problems, the organization would need all the help it could get; otherwise the OH would remain a small and unimportant network and would disappear through absorption by the AIU. He remarked that the

ENH had now finished constructing its building on the outskirts of Casablanca; this school, entirely financed by the AIU, was winning support. When the AIU builds schools which might hold many pupils, OH pupils would certainly leave because they would find more possibilities and comfort at the AIU. If this situation should occur, it would be a shame, for the children of Morocco are the best for the study of the Torah; and the loss suffered would be most unfortunate for Jewry.[91]

The AIU had powerful allies in the Islamic diaspora and in Israel who discounted the logic behind the OH opposition at the time. Among them was Rabbi Moïse Ventura, a distinguished pedagogue from Izmir (Turkey), and spiritual leader of the Alexandria Jewish community (Egypt). Ventura had visited Jewish schools in the Middle East and North Africa; and in 1949 he recommended to the OH in New York that it collaborate with the AIU in developing Jewish education, a development that would yield long-range positive results.[92] Despite his religious training, Ventura sided with the AIU. He not only praised the AIU's efforts in Jewish education of the postwar era, but stressed that the ENIO, too, had undergone recent transformations in the training of secular teachers. Reporting on his visit to the ENIO after the war, Ventura commented:

> I spent a Sabbath-day in the *Alliance* teachers' school. . . , whose students come mostly from North Africa. I talked with the students and was present at their *Seudoth, Oneg Shabbat*, etc. I much enjoyed the sincere religious spirit that prevails in this institution, where the *Alliance* prepares her secular teachers. This happy orientation of the *Alliance* gives me the right to believe that she cannot help welcoming recommendations tending to a reasonable strengthening of religious spirit in here elementary schools.[93]

Finally, in the area of Jewish educational reforms, an important event occurred with the creation in Rabat (1950) of *L'Institut Marocain des Hautes Etudes Hébraïques*. This institution for religious and rabbinic studies served as a higher education center and was subsidized by contributions made by all the major communities. While the ENH served as an important institution in Casablanca for the training of Hebrew and Jewish studies teachers, the institute in Rabat sought to prepare qualified and dynamic rabbis who, by 1950, with the death of the most venerated rabbis (like Raphaël Encaoua, Mordehai Bengio, Yehuda Benchimol), were not as plentiful.

In the early 1950s, then, advanced level Jewish and Hebrew education was beginning to be offered mainly in the French zone. The AIU and the communities finally achieved success through close institutional collaboration. Moreover, Hebrew was taught in all AIU schools not less than five hours weekly.[94] The American initiative in Jewish education amplified the already significant achievements.

Arabic Education at the AIU until 1956

During the preprotectorate era, as already indicated, several AIU teachers taught the Arabic language in a few communities, Tangier, Fez, and Casablanca. This trend, however, did not continue after their retirement from service and, moreover, given the pressures of the French and Spanish authorities on the AIU to devote ample time to French and Spanish, respectively, classical Arabic was largely neglected. Yet this was not the only problem. Writing from Fez in 1913, Amram Elmaleh related that though he personally, in collaboration with a Muslim he recruited, taught Arabic at the AIU, it was becoming increasingly difficult to find Muslims who were willing to teach in Jewish schools.[95] He searched for Arabic scholars at the many Islamic teachers' seminaries of Fez and contacted elementary school Arabic instructors, yet the latter often revealed great repugnance to the idea of coming to teach in Jewish schools and hence have declined employment offers.[96]

On the other hand, there were serious obstacles originating in the Jewish communities themselves. Few among Morocco's Jews could read an Arabic text or manuscript. Elie Bercoff, a teacher of Palestinian origin at the Salé boys' school, outlined in 1917 several of the obstacles to Arabic education that were endemic to other Moroccan communities. He noted that religious and political animosities that exist between Jews and Muslims were major contributing factors, for neither Jews nor Muslims were eager to establish close ties and consequently neither group was interested in the language of the other.[97] Further, the absence of religious toleration had not helped the chances for a *rapprochement* in the past, and, in the case of Salé, Jewish parents were indifferent to the idea of teaching literary Arabic at the AIU: they simply preferred that their children concentrate on French instead, which they felt was more useful.[98] In Bercoff's opinion, the AIU had to pressure the communities to accept literary Arabic as an integral part of the educational program. He hoped that by learning written Arabic, the youths would establish closer relations with their Arab counterparts and at the same time obtain lucrative employment in the administrative machinery of the protectorate dealing with indigenous affairs.[99]

However, no serious efforts were undertaken to meet this challenge and, in the 1930s, there were a number of teachers urging this long overdue reform. They were of the opinion that Arabic was indispensable and reminded Paris that whereas its schools were in a country under a French protectorate, it was nevertheless Moroccan and Arab.[100]

Only in Tetuan was some headway reported. Arabic was introduced into the AIU program in 1937 because the relations between the Jews and Muslims there had improved noticeably in recent years and because Tetuan's Muslim leaders approached the boys' school director and asked that he introduce the literary language.[101] The director responded favorably: it would cultivate sentiments of fraternity between the two communities, it would be prudent for political reasons, and it would serve the interests of AIU graduates, for the latter would more easily procure administrative employment in the Spanish zone.[102]

A straightforward position on Arabic education was presented by M. Elbaz who taught in Marrakesh. A native of that community and an ENIO graduate, Elbaz wrote to the Paris leadership in 1939, arguing that literary Arabic education at the AIU would contribute to the much-needed Judeo-Muslim *rapprochement*.[103] And he did not hesitate to reproach the AIU, contending that Judeo-Muslim separation was aggravated by the emergence of the "modernized Jew". Everybody agreed that the *Alliance Israélite* had done a great deal for the Jews of Morocco; however, its schools appeared like a Jewish initiative in face of Islam, further aggravating the existing separation between the two elements of the population.[104] Was it too late to turn the tide? Elbaz did not think so. But he called on the AIU to offer intensive literary Arabic education parallel to Hebrew and general courses; with the emergence of a balanced education program he believed relations between Muslim and Jewish youths would improve dramatically.[105]

This stance, adopted by an idealistic and perhaps naïve teacher, appeared unattainable at the time. The interplay of different forces in both communities rendered the dream obsolete. The Muslims in 1939 were turning more toward a brand of nationalism calling for separation from France, whereas most Jews either preferred close association with France or turned increasingly toward Zionism. Yet the teaching of literary Arabic was essential. The outbreak of the war made it difficult for the AIU to implement such a reform, as was the case with Hebrew studies.

After the Second World War, young Jewish intellectuals, among them the very dynamic leader, Jacques Dahan, who experimented with Judeo-Muslim *rapprochement* made it plain to the AIU (during a meeting he had with the organization's leaders in 1955) that the twelfth hour for reform, in view of the imminence of Moroccan independence, had arrived.[106] His position was fully shared by Reuben Tajouri. Aware of the new realities in Morocco toward the end of 1955, and realizing that the end of the protectorate era was near, Tajouri called for immediate reforms. He outlined a new policy of the AIU and pointed that a nucleus of young men would be trained in Arabic within the framework of the ENH and would receive a teaching certificate in classical Arabic (*diplôme d'arabe classique*).[107] And although Tajouri insisted the reform indicated that the AIU was flexible and realistic in view of the situation in Morocco,[108] this effort coming only in 1955 required considerable work on the organization's part.

Vocational and Agricultural Training

Vocational Training

After 1912, the Central Committee, supported by the French protectorate and the International zone in Tangier, resumed the campaign to develop modern vocational education. The politics of pacification and the termination of the state of unrest through the Lyautey initiative, enabled the AIU to implement the reforms envisaged in the pre-1912 era. Of course, there were restrictions on Jewish employment options in the preprotectorate period, and Jews often engaged in professions which the Muslims were forbidden by religious practice. Moreover, Muslim guild masters rarely employed Jewish apprentices.

Among those advocating modern vocational training was Reuben Tajouri, who then taught in Salé. His first step, taken in 1922, was to assemble the Salé community council. He explained to them that the demand for modern trades in Morocco was great, especially in service of the French protectorate, that the CEPE degree was no longer sufficient as a passport to administrative employment, and that apprentice education programs founded by the AIU in Palestine, Algeria, and Tunisia had led to significant results and would do so in Morocco as well.[109] Tajouri was supported by the community's chief rabbi, Raphaël Encaoua, perhaps the most celebrated rabbi in Morocco at the time, who encouraged comprehensive modern vocational education, and together with the community council, decided to establish a special scholarship fund intended to place young apprentices in vocational centers in Salé.[110]

Community leaders, mostly dynamic graduates of the AIU, who under the protectorate were replacing the old-style leaders in the councils, also encouraged the Central Committee to intensify efforts in vocational training. Yahya Zagoury, president of the Casablanca community, wrote to the AIU in 1925, commending the organization for its work on behalf of the Jews for the past sixty-three years but contended that the mission of the AIU was still far from over. He indicated that Casablanca was attracting considerable numbers of Jews from the interior who were mostly from humble origins and, upon their arrival, the community had to procure employment for them, an impossibility at times. He then asserted that it was incumbent upon the AIU schools to commence manual education on a large scale to effectively combat unemployment.[111]

This position was seconded by Félix Guedj, a Western-educated Casablanca leader of Algerian background. He went as far as to alert Resident General Théodore Steeg to help the communities develop the modern vocations because:

the Jewish communities, especially in the major towns, are increasing in population and this leads the community leadership to ponder the emergence of a formidable danger. This danger can be summarized in one sentence: misery in the communities will lead to greater poverty, to the point of no return. Immediate steps must be initiated, especially the preparation of the youths for manual trades or agricultural occupations.[112]

The message rang loud and clear: since the late 1920s small AIU-sponsored workshops sprang up throughout Morocco, and the few remaining Franco-Jewish schools controlled by the French protectorate did not wish to be left behind in the drive for workshop formations, either. In addition, the independent activities of AIU teachers included seeking apprentice jobs for primary school graduates, a tactic resumed by the AIU from the preprotectorate era. Some of the Europeans living in Morocco agreed, due to the AIU's intervention, to recruit a considerable number of youths into their businesses, located in the newly built European quarters.[113] This was an important contribution, for it meant that Jewish youths could leave the *mellāh*s to work and even settle in the European quarters. In the case of Casablanca, French enterprises such as *Imprimerie Nouvelle*, the printing business which published the journal *Petit Marocain; Imprimerie Artistique*, which published countless books and pamphlets; and even the famous Remington corporation, which extended its work to Morocco, recruited Jewish youths.[114]

In their task of enlisting youths for vocational apprenticeship in European enterprises, the school directors found indispensable auxiliaries in the alumni associations.[115] Yet more was needed to supplement vocational training and to transform the occupational structure. The AIU mainly sought to reduce the number of Jewish moneylenders and peddlers, and its representatives contended that these *métiers* could no longer respond to their need for economic advancement.

In Tangier, where the AIU opposed moneylending and peddling and where it educated elites opposed to these professions, it also promoted the modern crafts. In 1925 Sémach bemoaned that the AIU had long enough cultivated an elite of commercial agents, and bank and administrative employees.[116] But he did not despair. The opening of a vocational high school by the French government in 1918 (*Ecole Professionnelle de Tanger*) marked an effort to complement French education at the *lycées* in the International zone, an opportunity not overlooked by the AIU.[117] Indeed, in 1925 Sémach placed fifty graduates of his school at the vocational school, forty of whom were placed in the woodwork section and ten in the metal shop.[118] It was a beginning.

The French did not neglect their own zone, either. They set up vocational centers as well as the reputable *Ecole Industrielle de Casablanca* to train highly skilled Europeans and Moroccans. In the Spanish zone, too, a network of vocational shools on the secondary school level was developed, but neither Jews nor Muslims appeared to have benefited from this.

To promote Jewish interests in the modern vocations, the AIU decided to adopt the initiative by creating, together with Guedj's help, secondary vocational schools—at least in the most important communities—similar to its programs in Jerusalem and Constantinople. The turning point came in 1927 when the *Ecole Profesionnelle de l'Alliance Israélite Universelle* was created in Casablanca. In 1936 a similar institution was founded in Fez and subsequently, in Rabat. At the Casablanca school there were at the end of 1927 fifty-five students enrolled; out of this number twenty-seven were graduates of the Casablanca Franco-Jewish school, while twenty-eight were graduates of the AIU.[119] Once recruited, they were divided into two sections: one for woodworking, the other for metalworking.[120]

The workshops of the Casablanca school were situated in a vast building leased from the protectorate, fully equipped with modern machinery and tools purchased by the AIU. The technical direction, however, was confined to a skilled Frenchman, and graduate of the *Ecole Industrielle* of Casablanca; general education and French were taught by AIU teachers.[121]

The vocational school developed gradually but with much promise; it increased its student population from 55 in 1927 to 70 in 1929,[122] to 76 in 1931.[123] It offered a three-year program in woodworking, metalworking and tailoring (for men) in the early 1930s, and introduced a drafting course. In 1936, an electricity section was added. By then the schools had multiple sections which included cabinetmaking, window-framing, plumbing, and European-style shoemaking. In fact, so great was progress that the wealthy elements among Casablanca's Jews were eager to send their sons to be trained there.[124] At the time, the program led to the *certificat d'apprentissage*, administered by the DIP. Yet, given the program's expansion after 1945, the school offered the *certificat d'aptitude professionnelle* which applied to highly skilled craftsmen.[125] In 1946, the school was attended by 156 students and in 1949, 360 were enrolled.[126]

The school in Fez was not less impressive. Similar to its counterpart in Casablanca, it was partly subsidized by the protectorate and the technical direction was confined to the DIP. When it opened its doors, the school had an enrollment of 31 students. Unlike the Casablanca school, it offered commercial correspondence, typing, and stenography (for women); technical educational included elementary notions of automobile mechanics, furniture-making, iron-smelting, and forging; technical education was offered 22 hours weekly whereas French and general education, 13 hours weekly.[127] For data on the AIU's vocational training program, see Table 26.

To introduce yet greater incentive, the AIU needed to expand its program, a most impossible task considering that training centers had to be equipped with the latest machinery, dormitory facilities for students coming from different parts of the country, and laboratories, all of which were expensive undertakings. Despite the effectiveness of its program and its success in promoting *the idea* of modern manual training, the AIU alone lacked the expertise essential to the realization of high-level goals.

Since the end of the Second World War, the AIU found a serious partner in the ORT. Although this organization today has an English title, Organization for Rehabilitation through Training, it was founded in Russia under the title, *Obshchestvo Rasprostraneniya Truda sredi Yevrevyev*.[128]

Table 26. Primary and Secondary AIU Vocational Training Institutions: 1947

Center	Type of Institution	Number of teachers General	Technical	Vocations taught	Attendance B	G
Casablanca	Ec. profes.	3	5	Woodwork	33	
				Metal	41	
				Tailoring	52	
				Shoemaking	30	
				Plumbing	8	
Casablanca	Workshop	1	1	Dressmaking		84
Rabat	Ec. Profes.	1	3	Woodwork	24	
				Metal	16	
				Leatherworks	22	
Salé	Manual section	-	1	Woodwork	18	
Mazagan	" "	-	1	Woodwork	12	
	" "	1	1	Dressmaking		16
Boujad[a]	" "	-	1	Bookbinding	10	
	" "	-	1	Dressmaking		15
Fez (boys')	Ec. profes.	1	2	Woodwork	12	
				Metal	18	
Fez (girls')	Workshop	1	1	Dressmaking		43
Midelt	Work section	-	1	Dressmaking		20
Marrakesh	Manual section	-	1	Woodwork	20	
	Workshop	-	1	Dressmaking		43
Mogador (boy's)	"	-	1	Bookbinding	7	
Mogador (girls')	"	-	1	Dressmaking		20
Tiznit	"	-	1	Upholstering		15
Demnat	"	-	1	Dressmaking		15
Tangier (girls')	"	-	1	Dressmaking		13
Tetuan (girls')	"	-	1	Dressmaking		14
Total		8	26		323	298

[a]Haïm Zafrani, who directed the Boujad coeducational school at the time, offered his pupils a course in notions of electricity and radio repairs.

SOURCE: "L'enseignement professionnel dans les écoles de *l'alliance israélite universelle* Les *Cahiers de l'Alliance Israélite Universelle* 20–21, février-mars 1948, p. 8.

The Russian title meant "Society for Manual [and Agricultural] Work To Spread [Artisan and Agricultural] Work [among Jews].[129] There were three important periods in ORT's history. In the first period, from its foundation in 1880 to 1920, the organization existed only in Russia. There is opened vocational schools for Jews and helped raise their standard of living. In the second period, 1920-1945, ORT moved its headquarters to Berlin and became an international organization under the title of ORT World Union. It opened schools in the Russian Empire (Poland, Lithuania, Latvia, Bassarbia) as well as in Germany, France, Bulgaria, Hungary, and Rumania. Until 1938, ORT functioned in the USSR, where it established factories, agricultural colonies, and cooperatives.[130] In the third period, 1945-1960, ORT entered Israel and the Third World. In the Middle East and North Africa, ORT created schools in Israel, Iran, Algeria, Tunisia, and Morocco. With its new headquarters in Geneva, and administrative branches in Europe and the United States, ORT became closely involved with the Jewish Colonization Association and the AIU.

There is no evidence of pre-1945 AIU-ORT collaboration for the spread of vocational education among Jews. However, after 1945, the vocational schools in the Mediterranean-basin communities were often administered jointly. In order to aid the AIU in Morocco, in 1946, ORT, through its Paris office, signed a joint accord with the AIU, stipulating such articles as: (1) the schools to be created by the two organizations would be referred to as *Alliance Israélite Universelle* and *Ecole Professionnelle ORT*; (2) vocational and theoretical education and training would be confined to ORT, while the AIU would be responsible for Jewish subjects and Hebrew, as well as French and general education, all through its own personnel, paid by the Central Committee; (3) the director of the ORT-AIU school(s) would be appointed by ORT's Central Committee in agreement with the AIU and its president, René Cassin; (4) the teachers for technical education would be appointed by the local ORT committee after conferring with the delegate of the AIU; (5) the nomination of directors of the schools' workshops would be subject to the consent of the DIP as well; (6) the duration of ORT-AIU agreement was to be five years, as of August 27, 1946.[131]

The first ORT-AIU school opened at the end of 1946 with a vocational center for boys on *Rue de Barsac* in Casablanca; at about the same time a girls' vocational school was opened on *Rue Malherbe*, also in Casablanca; the boys' institution taught mechanics, cabinetmaking, and blacksmithing; the one for girls offered dressmaking courses. Several months later, a new center was created some thirteen kilometers outside Casablanca, at *Aïn Sebaa*, where 40,000 square meters of land was put at ORT's disposal by a wealthy Jewish entrepreneur, Jules Senouf, then president of ORT Morocco.[132] The few small existing buildings were able to house sections of fitting, woodworking, and locksmithing.[133]

Beginning in 1949, a broad construction program was undertaken at the *Aïn Sebaa* site to build a central boy's school which would be able to serve a large number of students; the *Rue de Barsac* school, founded in 1946, was closed in 1950 and all the boys came to the *Aïn Sebaa center*.[134] The needs were such that this center grew rapidly in the next few years and by 1960, it had 780 boys and more than 600 boarding; the program was to prepare for the basic French vocational school diploma, the *Certificat d'Aptitude Professionnelle*.[135] After 1956, the certificate degree was administered by the Moroccan Department of National Education. The boys' school at *Aïn Sebaa* had an extremely varied curriculum: fitting, milling, automobile mechanics, automobile chassis, sheetmetal, welding, tinplating, plumbing, electricity, electromechanics, telephones and woodworking-cabinetmaking.[136]

In addition to *Aïn Sebaa*, Senouf contributed another plot of land, 4,000 square meters, in the *Val d'Anfa* residential section of Casablanca, for the construction of a girls' school. Here, too, work started in 1949 and the school on *Rue Malherbe* was able to be transferred completely by the end of 1950; the school expanded rapidly, increasing its enrollment steadily until 197 girl students were enrolled in 1961; in addition to the traditional needlework and domestic skills, the following new ones were offered: laboratory assistant course, industrial chemistry, cosmetic chemistry, hairdressing, window-dressing, secretary-stenographer, executive secretary. These were professions hardly learned by Muslim girls and thus it was relatively easier for the ORT-AIU representatives in Morocco to procure jobs for Jewish girls than for the boys who had to compete more intensely

Figure 25. The *ORT-AIU* Technical School of Aiñ Sebaa

with their Muslim counterparts for vocational employment. The girls, like the boys, were subject to an intense three-year program leading to the same certification. Hygiene and medical care in these schools was administered by the OSE.[137]

While the girls became well integrated into these schools, there were some problems at first. The *Val d'Anfa* school was intended for girls from Casablanca, since it was not thought that Jewish families would allow their daughters to study far from home. Due to the change in customs and the lack of many vocational job possibilities in the interior, girls coming from that part of the country put pressure on *ORT Morocco* to provide boarding facilities; beginning in 1955, work began on enlarging the *Anfa* school to add a boarding center; its capacity was increased in stages until 1960 and had room for 150 girls.[138]

Further, the combined efforts of the ORT and AIU resulted in the creation in 1953 of an apprentice service, which by 1960 successfully placed 1,030 boys and 502 girls in apprenticeships. In 1957, the ORT-AIU schools introduced manual training in a special school for the deaf which had been created by the AIU, ORT, and the JDC; this school eventually became mixed, attended by both Jews and Muslims.[139]

In 1956 the network extended to Marrakesh with an adult center, where training was provided in woodworking, electricity, and repair of farm machines. Since almost all of the 20,000 Jews in Marrakesh emigrated to Israel, this center was closed in October 1962; it gave training to 480 men and 90 women in its six years of existence. In Tetuan, a similar center was established in 1956, specializing in electromechanics, mechanics, and woodworking adult courses were given for mechanics, woodworking, and shirtmaking. The school closed in 1963 owing to Jewish emigration; but while it was open, it served 564 students; the *Val d'Anfa* schools in Casablanca continued to serve the remains of the Jewish community.[140]

The AIU had laid the groundwork long before ORT came to Morocco, through its own initiative and by promoting the *concept* of the modern vocations. However, it was ORT that generated the greatest impulse, and in a relatively short time, to vocational training.

Agricultural Training

The AIU turned to agricultural training in the mid-1930s after French pacification was implemented. Already in 1926, when Secretary Bigart visited Morocco, he met with Moïse Nahon who, following his retirement from service to the AIU, settled in Suq al-Arbaa of the Gharb region.[141] There Nahon helped set up agricultural programs with the help of European rural settlers and Muslims. He worked peacefully among the Muslims, encouraging the Jews to "return to the land," and acquired the reputation among Moroccans as the *colon du Gharb*. During their meeting Nahon in-

Table 27. ORT Student Body (1950–1960)

Jan. 1	Total enrollment			Vocational schools			Vocational courses			Pre-Apprenticeship			Apprentices			Institute for the deaf			Primary manual training		
	male	female	total	male	female	total	male	female	total	male	female	total	male	female	total	male	female	total	male	female	total
1950	503	400	903	484	400	884	19	-	19												
1951	562	455	1017	543	455	998	19	-	19												
1952	406	378	784	362	378	740	44	-	44												
1953	358	392	750	358	248	606	-	-	-		144	144									
1954	470	412	882	397	313	710	-	-	-		40	40	73	59	132						
1955	742	558	1300	477	404	881	-	24	24	45	-	45	265	154	419						
1956	968	807	1775	470	338	808	106	18	124	63	-	63	453	445	898						
1957	1166	826	1992	470	266	736	154	-	154	155	67	222	527	542	1069						
1958	1632	982	2614	605	307	912	151	-	151	152	62	214	634	590	1224	24	18	42	60	-	60
1959	1826	1052	2878	757	334	1091	-	-	-	116	-	116	667	631	1298	39	25	64	60	-	60
1960	1945	1111	3056	831	306	1137	140	220	360				755	561	1316	53	24	77	50	-	50

SOURCE: *ORT Union, Bureau Central*, Geneva. *Statistics on Morocco* (Courtesy of D. Alberstein).

dicated to Bigart that slowly but surely, the Jews were making a return to the land, as illustrated in the Suq al-Arbaa experiment. Already there were Jews who settled in the Gharb, among them Nahon's own sons who had enthusiastically accepted agricultural and rural existence; they had established irrigation works (under his initiatives), planted trees and vegetables, and were prepared to utilize the most advanced agricultural farm machinery.[142]

Nahon conveyed to Bigart that the Jews had to accept agricultural pursuits themselves by *imitating the French settlers* (my italics), an argument similar to Nahum Sokolow's plea to the AIU in 1909 (see above, chapter VI). Morever, he believed that the creation of training centers would encourage urban Jewish youths to turn to agriculture and farming in large numbers.[143]

An AIU agricultural center was founded in Marrakesh in 1936. It commenced its activities with twelve students who spent six hours daily in general, theoretical, and agricultural training. They were recruited among the most physically robust AIU primary school students in town.

After its creation, Sémach believed that the new school would yield positive results and would create Moroccan Jewish farmers who would cultivate the land like their Muslim counterparts; he shared Nahon's view that the concept of a Jewish farmer was not so remote once the proper initiatives were adopted by the AIU.[144] Unlike Nahon, who wanted to cultivate a Jewish farmer that would come in contact with his Muslim counterpart as well as the Europeans, Sémach envisaged in the Jewish farmer an ally of the Europeans only. Morocco, he argued, was the ideal place for agricultural work in the wake of pacification: the growing presence of the Europeans in the 1930s enabled Jews to find agricultural employment and, besides, Morocco was a country of vineyards and flowers. Some efforts toward the promotion of agricultural activities were attempted by affluent Jews after 1912, according to Sémach. In Meknes, Sefrou, and Midelt the number of Jewish gardeners rose; aside from emulating the example of the European settlers, wealthy Jewish merchants purchased rural land near Fez, Meknes, Rabat, Casablanca, and Marrakesh, where they developed vineyards.[145]

The French impulse, then, with the collaboration of affluent Jews, encouraged the AIU to open agricultural training centers. Exactly what was the purpose of the center in Marrakesh? Sémach contended that it was founded to train not agronomists but rather skilled laborers capable of living in a rural existence. In addition, if they wished, trainees did not necessarily have to be uprooted from the urban scene to find livelihood, for the recently created European quarters were dotted with villas having gardens that needed to be cultivated.[146]

The center's programs offered some attractive features in the area of modern agriculture. The two-year program was subsidized by the AIU and the French protectorate, under the direction of a Frenchman and graduate of the *Ecole Coloniale d'Agriculture* of Tunis.[147] The school was welcomed with enthusiasm by veteran AIU teachers such as Alfred Goldenberg, who remarked in 1937 that agricultural training, like vocational education, became essential in the 1930s. For many years the students who graduated from the AIU, obtained the CEPE and found lucrative administrative posts. However, Goldenberg believed that times were changing: AIU graduates were finding it increasingly difficult to find jobs in this sector in view of the global economic crisis; hence agricultural pursuits would be a viable alternative.[148] He realized, of course, that to develop agricultural projects in Morocco was a serious gamble, given the Jews' indifference to agricultural work, particularly the urban communities. But the early indications appeared to be encouraging: Marrakeshi youths were eager for this sort of training.[149]

The Marrakesh school developed rapidly, offering the two-year program that led to DIP accreditation known as the *diplôme de connaissance agricoles*.[150] As for the program, it was divided into the following categories:[151] (1) *theoretical courses*: offered two hours daily and included a general course on farming, grafting, tree nursing, fundamentals of viticulture, horticulture, arboriculture, botany, lessons in rural legislation and economics, and basics of the flour, wheat, and milk industries; (2) *applied courses:* which included workshops in carpentry and metalworking where the youths were trained in the applications of these skills to farming (in the metal shop, for instance, they were taught to repair farm machinery), and fieldwork: gardening, tree-planting, seeding, grafting and irrigation; (3) *general education:* taught by AIU teachers.

The school graduated a small number of highly skilled workers. It was a groundbreaking process which led to the creation of a small but selective agricultural elite. Its members were placed in farms in Suq al-*Arbaa* in the Gharb, in Marrakesh's agricultural areas, in Oued-Zem, Sidi Rahal, Taroudant (in the south), and in the Spanish zone. A very interesting development was the enrollment of trainees from other Jewish communities, Demnat in the south, Tetuan in the north, and from the coastal towns. At the end of 1938, there were twenty-six students at the Marrakesh school between the ages of 15 and 18. In March 1939, there were thirty-six students; that year alone eleven students graduated, all of whom were placed by the AIU in European farms especially in the Gharb where they were making good incomes while residing on the land.[152]

The outbreak of the war inaugurated an era of stagnation, even if training was not halted. Once the war ended, the AIU extended its energies in two directions. It reformed the Marrakesh program, and it created another center of the same caliber in Meknes. (See table 28 for the Marrakesh school). In Marrakesh, the reformed program stipulated that[153] (1) accep-

Table 28. The Weekly Program of the Marrakesh Agricultural School since 1945

	Course Description	First year	Second year	Third year
I.	*General Education*			
	French	4	4	4
	Mathematics	4	4	4
	Correspondence	-	1	1
	Fundamentals of Law	-	-	1
	Hebrew	4	4	4
II.	*Agricultural Education*			
1.	*Theoretical*			
	Botany	2	-	-
	Geology	2	-	-
	Study of Farm Animals	2	-	-
	Phyto-pathology	1	-	-
	Rural Economics	-	-	1
2.	*Applied*			
	Horticulture	-	2	2
	Arboriculture	-	2	2
	Forestry	-	2	2
	Farm Animal Rearing	-	2	2
	Poultry-Farming	-	1	1
III.	*Practical Work*			
	Carpentry	4	4	4
	Mechanics	-	2	2
	Field Work	17	12	10

SOURCE: *École Professionnelle Agricole de l'A.I.U.: Marrakesh.*

tance into the program was contingent upon completion of primary education, a requirement absent before 1945; (2) general education was approximately on the advanced level of a French *lycée*; (3) theoretical courses were the same as at the agricultural schools of the protectorate. With the support of the Jewish Colonization Association, which opened several cooperatives for Morocco's Jews after the war, the AIU introduced some advanced training in mechanics; (4) training was extended to three years, leading to the *diplôme d'apprentissage* (at both the Marrakesh and Meknes schools), the same diploma granted by the protectorate's agricultural colleges.

While no more than one hundred graduates left the two agricultural schools, the AIU made a significant change in this area of the occupational structure: it developed a small elite of farmers and attracted a growing number of urban Jews to engage in rural endeavors. Had it not been for the massive waves of emigration to Israel, France, and the Americas, it is likely that this evolution would have gained greater momentum.

Figure 26. AIU pupils in Marrakesh, 1936

Expansion into the *Bled*: The *Alliance* and the Communities

French pacification also enabled the AIU to extend its activities into the *bled*. Prior to French penetration into areas like Boujad (171 kilometers from Casablanca), the Atlas and Ante-Atlas mountains, the Jews were largely protected by local Berber leaders. Whereas in the *bled al-makhzan* of the pre-1912 period the Jews were required to pay the *jizya*, their counterparts of the Atlas were equally required to pay a protection tax. The Jews then received the protection they needed, which included escort protection from other local Berbers and neighboring hostile tribes. This form of protection became hereditary: the children of the protectors inherited the role of protecting the Jews' children.[154] These communities had managed to establish contact with the Jews of Marrakesh and other important urban areas through migrations, which brought them in touch with modernized society.

In what trades did Jews of the *bled* engage? We know about agricultural pursuits; however, these Jews were mostly artisans and shopkeepers. Except

Figure 27. The *AIU* Girls' School of Tangier during the 1920s

for manual laborers and blacksmiths, Atlas and other *bled* Jews were shopkeepers, wax and candle makers, goldsmiths, shoemakers and wine producers. They also manufactured weapons for the Muslims.[155]

In the Atlas area, the relations between the Jews and Muslim Berbers were cordial during the protectorate period. Some communities did not even have a *mellāh*. The anti-Jewish Vichy legislation of the early 1940s did not upset the relationship.

In the Atlas communities, there were no rabbinic tribunals and some communities had not organized councils. Owing to some AIU lobbying efforts, *zahīrs* were published by the Sherifian government that facilitated the creation of such councils. In 1927, the AIU decided to extend its educational network to the *bled*. This began with Ouezzan in the interior and extended into other forgotten communities of Beni-Mellal on the fringes of the Atlas, as well as Ber-Rechid, Boujad, and Settat, small towns not far from Casablanca. From there, the network extended to Midelt (in the Middle-Atlas, 180 kilometers from Meknes), Ben-Ahmed (near Casablanca), Demnat (in the High-Atlas and the vicinity of Marrakesh),

Kasba-Tadla (near Boujad on the fringes of the Middle-Atlas), and Tiznit (of the Ante-Atlas).[156]

By 1934, the AIU had extended its educational activities to the *bled* communities situated on the periphery and within the Atlas mountain chains. The sort of activity undertaken there enabled the teachers to exercise a role reminiscent of the one played by the pioneer AIU teachers during the 1860s. It was like starting all over again. The teachers who came to the *bled* complained about the surroundings: "The *mellāḥ* is sordid and is cramped with people who live in small homes. People and animals occupy the same habitat in rooms no larger than four square meters.[157] This was the initial reaction of the director of the Kasba-Tadla community upon his arrival there in 1933. In Beni-Mellal, the director of the new school reported that some signs of the *bled al-sība* had not disappeared altogether as late as 1927. from 7:00 A.M. to 8:00 P.M. people could leave town but had to take great precautions. Prior to 7:00 A.M. the French military authorities prohibited any outward movement as neighboring tribes could attack Beni-Mellal's inhabitants wandering outside their domain. After 11:00 P.M., no one was permitted to roam the streets of Beni-Mellal itself under any circumstances; for the AIU school director, there was little excitement, and aside from teaching and social work, staying at home was the only form of entertainment.[158]

The teacher in the *bled* nevertheless enjoyed great prestige among the

Figure 28. The William Oualid *AIU*-Community School, 1952

Jews, who over the years heard of the services rendered by the AIU to the larger communities. In the 1920s and 1930s, given the institutional standing of the AIU in Morocco, its representatives in the *bled* were not subjected to the sort of opposition manifested against their predecessors in years past. However, the lack of strong opposition was partly due to the absence of local tribunals and councils.

The feeling of enthusiasm on the part of the teachers grew once they became an integral part of the *bled* communities. The director of the school in Ber-Rechid reported in 1929 that he maintained excellent rapport with all the inhabitants; there existed there a special bond between the educator and the parents which facilitated his task and fortified his influence.[159] The school in Ber-Rechid served as an important center for Jewish activity especially for the celebration of Jewish holidays.[160]

On the other hand, the penetration of the AIU into the south in particular was of prime importance to both the protectorate and the Jews. The French supported the AIU in the hope that spreading knowledge of French would enhance their position in pacified areas. The AIU wanted to educate Jews, many of whom continued migrating into the large towns, in French and general education to prepare them for the bustling life of Marrakesh, Mogador, Agadir, and Casablanca. There, knowledge of French enabled the migrants to advance economically. Finally, the teachers were eager to educate Jews who chose to remain in the *bled* and advocated extraeducational activities leading to reforms.

What werre some of these reforms? Why were these teachers so adamant in their quest for change? Among the reforms pursued, the following are noteworthy: (1) combatting child marriages; (2) creating community councils; (3) spreading knowledge of French; (4) changes in attire and gallicization of names; and (5) coeducational education.

Combatting child marriages was not more difficult in Demnat, Midelt, or Tafilalt than in Fez or Marrakesh. In challenging this practice, the AIU needed the endorsement of local rabbis and sought the support of the *Bureau des-Affaires Indigènes* which administered the pacified *bled* for the French protectorate. The *bureau* support was not easily obtainable, for their personnel, in the spirit of preserving traditional hierarchies, had to confirm that AIU representatives were supported by local rabbis before they themselves could go along with the plan. Once the AIU, the *bureau*, and rabbis collaborated, effective results usually followed. As Alfred Goldenberg, director in Demnat (1937) reported: "I complained to the head of the office for indigenous affairs concerning [child marriages] and my efforts were successful. At this time only four families still cling to this practice."[161] Similarly in Midelt, the AIU school director reported in 1937 that he succeeded in obtaining a *ẓahīr* opposing child marriages.[162] He enlisted the support of the rabbis and the *bureau* and together they registered all the girls.[163] Though he claimed success, the director failed to mention the minimum marriage age stipulated by the *ẓahīr*.

Rabbinic support for the abolition of child marriages was at times difficult to obtain, particularly when powerful rabbis were determined to duck the issue out of fear that their status within the communities would be impaired. Such appears to have been the case in the communities adjacent to the province of Tafilalt in the south. There, the girls were married in their early teens as late as 1950; and after representatives of the AIU penetrated the region, they mounted a fierce campaign to restrict these marriages and, to facilitate their task, requested Chief Rabbi Yisrā'ēl Abūhṣīra's intercession before the parents. However, the AIU accused the rabbi of closing his eyes to the issue and claimed that he was apprehensive about supporting their policy, for his immense prestige among the Jews would decline. Therefore, it was necessary to go over his head to Rabat to seek the support of the council of chief rabbis.[164] This may be explained by the fact that the rabbinic council meeting, held in 1948, stipulated that the earliest allowable marriage age for girls was fifteen.[165]

Creating community councils in the *bled* is attributed in part to the AIU. The first elected council created through the AIU's initiative was in Midelt. Its founder, the school director, also instituted reforms in the community's financial administration, introduced a tax on kosher meat, and organized charity drives on behalf of the indigent.[166] Whereas similar welfare programs existed in the larger urban communities of Fez, Marrakesh, or Meknes, this was not the case in much of the *bled* prior to 1930.

As for the teaching of French, this was a slow process. To intensify French education, the AIU, in addition to educating the youth in day schools, created adult courses. The communities in the *bled* that benefited the most from these policies were contiguous to Casablanca: Beni-Mellal, Boujad, Ben-Ahmed, and Ber-Rechid, to name only a few. The reasons were as follows. Casablanca was a major metropolis where daily contacts between Jews and Europeans were quite regular. The latter extended their economic activities to the small communities and many of them settled there as farmers; consequently, knowledge of French enabled a significant portion of the Jews to utilize and advance their spoken knowledge of the language. Moreover, the AIU sent primary school graduates from these communities to Casablanca to pursue secondary education at the spacious *cours complémentaires*[167] and at the ENH where they were trained to become teachers in Jewish and general education. Finally, unlike the *bled* communities near Casablanca, AIU schools in the southern *mellāhs* of Rissani, Imintanout, Tiznit, El-Kelaa, Inezgane, Amizmiz, Sidi-Rahal, and Illigh were created only after 1945 and therefore, French education was not so deeply rooted there. Exceptions could be found in Midelt, Demnat, and

Taroudant, where the AIU was active since the late 1920s and 1930s. It is doubtful, however, that many AIU graduates from the south pursued secondary education in Marrakesh, which, like Casablanca, was a major center for the communities of the *bled*. This is because Marrakesh did not have as diverse a network of secondary schools as Casablanca did.[168] Only migration to developing towns offered a solution to this problem.

Spreading knowledge of the French language was closely related to Europeanization of attire and gallicization of names. Once again, these were most prevalent in the *bled* communities adjacent to Casablanca, and in Demnat, which was in the forefront of modernization in the south.[169] One of the clearest indications of the spread of French in Demnat was the gallicization of names. When the AIU school opened its doors for the first time in 1932, these names were all Jewish. The enrollment list in October 1950, however, showed twenty-one French names and forty-four Jewish names. The French names were mostly adopted by the girls, the most common being Rosette, Jacqueline, Alice, Ninette, Jeanette, Denise. Among the boys there were several Charleses and Victors.[170] But this phenomenon extended to less "Western-oriented" *bled* communities after 1950. David Corcos, a member of a well-known southern Moroccan family and a perceptive scholar of Maghribi Jewry, observed with some astonishment not completely devoid of criticism:

> French influence penetrated even into the small cities of the interior; into the Jewish villages of mountains and the Saharan regions. . . . Since the 1940s in Sefrou, Debdou, in the Sous Valley, and in the Atlas, mothers . . . sometimes called their daughters Marcelle, Angèle, Alice, Colette, Denise, Josiane, Gisèle, Jaqueline, Nicole . . . and even Clotide! What the *megōrāshīm* and their descendants did not succeed in carrying out during four and a half centuries, the *Alliance Israélite* and . . . the women and girls of the French officers for indigenous affairs managed to achieve, unconsciously, in only several years.[171]

And this phenomenon was closely connected with the Europeanization of attire, once again largely noticeable in the *bled* adjacent to Casablanca, and in Demnat. Speaking about Demnat for the 1930s, Goldenberg recalled: "Little girls had [once] worn handkerchiefs or headbands on their heads; now their hair was arranged in the European fashion. The boys, at first, wore black smocks over their jallabas, but soon they abandoned their native costumes."[172]

Finally, in view of financial difficulties and the relatively small size of the communities, the creation of coeducational schools was an inescapable alternative. However, instituting a coeducational system in these com-

Figure 29. Milk distribution at the Gourrama *AIU* School

munities where girls never attended schools before the arrival of the AIU, and where boys and girls attended classes under the same roof, receiving the same educational benefits and enjoying the same facilities, was a major transformation.

The devotion of the teachers to these communities was well known. In the *bled* the teachers' roles were both educational and extraeducational. Reflecting on the community of Boujad, Haïm Zafrani, the director, recalled:

> It was not the policies of the AIU in Paris which mattered in the *bled*. It was the policies of the school director who aided the communities in every way possible. His influence resulted in enhancing the prestige of the AIU. He did everything: he taught courses, fed the children, at times he even taught them a trade.

> When I directed the AIU school in Boujad, I taught three classes, prepared the youth for the CEPE examinations, and at the same time, taught them "radio-electricity," a trade which I myself acquired while studying at the *Ecole Industrielle* of Casablanca. I also offered some agricultural training. We used a small parcel of land belonging to the school to encourage the children to develop agricultural skills. We planted potatoes and flowers, and spent considerable time in the task of cultivation.[173]

This devotion included the constant campaigns on the part of teachers to enroll as many children in the schools as possible, in order to combat illiteracy. Table 29, for the year 1951, reveals that large numbers of youths attended during the final decade of the protectorate. While it is doubtful

Table 29. AIU Student Enrollment in the Bled (1951)

Town	Total Population	Boys in AIU	Girls in AIU	Talmud Torah[a]	Public Schools	Total	Şlā or Heder	No Education	Total	%
Berrechid	350	34	52	-	1	87	-	-	-	100
Kasba-Tadla	750	76	72	-	1	149	25	12	37	80
Oued-Zem	400	48	34	-	9	91	-	-	-	100
Ben-Ahmad	475	69	57	-	-	126	-	10	10	92.6
Boujad	800	94	100	-	-	194	-	-	-	100
Tounza	317	25	15	-	-	40	-	40	40	50
Ouezzanne	2350	148	218	-	3	369	99	-	99	78.8
Midelt	1700	128	118	-	-	246	30	100	130	65.4
Rich	578	74	27	-	-	101	-	20	20	83.4
Khenitra	171	21	20	-	1	42	-	-	-	100
Kasr al-Suq	1100	50	4	-	-	54	-	15	15	78.2
Rissani	500	32	19	-	-	51	-	30	30	69.9
Gourrama	450	36	17	-	-	53	-	38	38	58.2
Talsint	270	35	27	-	-	62	-	8	8	88.5
Kerrando	200	30	14	-	-	44	-	10	10	81.4
Taroudant	950	80	53	-	-	133	-	65	65	63.4
Inezgane	450	18	25	-	7	50	-	40	40	55.5
Tiznit	450	36	65	20	-	121	-	-	-	100
Demnat	1800	85	70	50	-	205	100	75	175	53.9
Imintanout	360	37	38	-	-	75	-	-	-	100
Sidi-Rahal	600	29	21	-	-	50	-	60	60	45.4
Amizmiz	593	28	29	-	-	57	48	45	93	38
El-Kelaa	620	34	36	-	-	70	12	19	31	69.3
Tinehrir	600	39	22	-	-	61	-	60	60	50.4
Taourirt	450	60	44	-	-	104	-	-	-	100
Taza	520	25	31	-	33	89	-	15	15	85.6

aIt is not clear if the Talmud Torah refers to Otzar ha Torah schools as well as the traditional and/or renovated rabbinical schools.

SOURCE: "Etat comparatif des taux de scolarisation au Maroc," *Les Cahiers de l'Alliance Israélite Universelle.* nos. 50–51 (février-mars 1951), p. 8.

that the religous schools shown in Table 29 refer to the OH and Lubavitch schools active in Morocco after 1947, it is certain that the AIU attracted the largest number of youths of school age,[174] thus playing the greatest role in the reduction of illiteracy. In the south, for example, according to the data for 1951, over half the children of school age were enrolled in Midelt, Rich, Kasr al-Suq, Gourrama, Rissani, Talsint, Taroudant, Demnat, Inezgane, El-Kelaa, and Tinehrir.[175] In Tiznit, Imintanout, and Taourirt, there was one hundred percent school attendance.[176] Yet, while the AIU extended its network in 1954 to Gouilimine (thirty-five students), Ifran (thirty students), Illigh (forty-two students) and Oulad Berhyl (fifty-two students),[177] there were still communities as Oulad Zangia, Ait-Bougmaz, and Erfoud that were not affected by the network.

Supplementing the activities of the AIU were OH and AYI. Similar to the AIU, these schools did not promote secondary education in the *bled*. According to Hirschberg, who visited Morocco in 1955, the AYI could be found in M'Hamid, Erfoud Zagora, and Agoine,[178] all situated in the south. Schools competed for spheres of influence in the south and, prior to Moroccan independence, made some headway by encroaching on the educational monopoly of the AIU in combatting illiteracy.

As for medical attention, whereas the AIU and OSE shifted greater attention to the promotion of dispensaries and clinics in the large towns, mostly in Marrakesh and Casablanca, and in the *bled*, the Jews of the south required less assistance. In the first place, the large communities, due to massive migrations from remote corners of the French and Spanish zone,

Figure 30. Jewish children at Tazenakht

absorbed a substantial number of Jews, an influx that caused overcrowded conditions. Consequently, diseases plagued towns like Casablanca to a greater extent than the sparsely populated *mellāhs* of the *bled*. Secondly, the Jews in the *bled*, men and women, despite hunger and disease, were relatively healthier and more robust than their counterparts in the urban centers: they engaged in more physical activity.[179]

Midelt, in the Middle-Atlas, was a strategic town for the French protectorate, linked to the south militarily and economically. Among the first towns in the Atlas to be penetrated by the French, Midelt was placed under a large French administration. In 1928, when Vitalis Eskenazi created the AIU school, it was still impossible to leave town after 6:00 P.M. People were murdered in broad daylight, and Eskenazi carried a firearm to protect the children and his family.[180]

In 1928, the indigenous population was 16,000 (14,000 Muslims and 1,200 Jews) whereas the French population was made up of military and administrative personnel.[181] Unlike most southern communities, the *mellāh* in Midelt was inhabited by a relatively heterogeneous population: Sephardi Jews from the interior mainly from Fez, Meknes, and Sefrou, Saharan Jews, and Jews who had lived in Midelt for many centuries.[182] As for those who came from the interior, they entered Midelt in order to open, among other things, grocery stores. Eskenazi remarked that the Jews from the interior speak French and own stores. They have all been students of the AIU schools and they cherish their former teachers. [Joseph] Conquy, [Amram] Elmaleh, [Israël] Benaroya and [Haïm] Djivré were teachers whose names they pronounced with respect and recognition.[183]

Indeed, the presence of French-speaking AIU graduates was felt, for it was this very element that helped popularize the language among the Jews.[184] One may wonder why Jews from the interior or other major towns settled in the *bled* at a time when a reverse process of migration to the urban centers was the dominant trend. It appears that during the 1920s there were many French troops stationed in and around Midelt, the latter serving as the administrative center for the south. Through this facility, the protectorate monitored instability and maintained a vital channel of communications with diverse towns in the Atlas.[185] Jews from the interior, who were merchants and businessmen, were determined to benefit from French presence in Midelt by selling products to soldiers and functionaries. In later years Midelt became an important tourist attraction which no doubt attracted Jews to that area.

In the late 1920s, however, Eskenazi was not entirely optimistic about Midelt's importance in the future as the administrative and commercial center of the south. Already in 1929 he predicted that Midelt would gradually be stripped of its importance because certain regions in the south, undergoing pacification, would replace it as vital communication centers. Would these trends lead to massive migrations to the large towns? Eskenazi believed that most Jews would remain behind regardless of future trends:

> The administrative transformation will not change the lives of most Jews who work with the Muslims and who will not follow the French troops to the deep south in order to engage with them in commercial transactions. If in the near future Midelt is stripped of its importance in relations to other southern regions, the Jewish population — composed of artisans, agricultural laborers, and indigenous textile merchants — will remain in Midelt as they did in the past.[186]

Was this a sound position? In the first place, there is no available evidence to indicate that Midelt's strategic vitality declined. Second, the Jewish population, as envisaged by Eskenazi, did remain stable. During his visit to Morocco in 1955, Hirschberg discovered that a new Midelt was built during the 1930s and the old *mellāh* situated in the suburb of Uthman Musa was deserted, its synagogues and homes sold to Muslims. The new Midelt had no *mellāh*, suggesting perhaps that Jews and Muslims enjoyed an important degree of coexistence. There were 1,450 Jews — as compared with 1,200 in 1928 — and they had an AIU school and synagogues in the vicinity of a large mosque.[187] The emergence of Midelt as a tourist attraction contradicted Eskenazi's prediction of economic decline. As many Jews by 1955 had graduated from the AIU, it is likely that their education enabled them to enter this lucrative sector of the local economy.

Although we shall discuss the elite that emerged out of the AIU schools in Morocco in greater depth later in this chapter, the modernized elite of the *bled* requires a separate comment. The elite that paralleled the traditional elements was a tiny stratum. In contrast to the urban centers, where educated Jews were represented in the protectorate's administration, in large-scale commerce, and in the free and modern vocational professions, their counterparts in the *bled* were underrepresented. What were the characteristics of the modernized elite? Two components were important. There were, first of all, French-speaking teachers, merchants, community leaders, and businessmen, mainly AIU graduates from Mogador, Marrakesh, Meknes, Fez, and Sefrou. This component, then, may be divided into a locally cultivated elite and an "imported" elite. Second, there were OH and AYI alumni (mostly teachers) who were Moroccans that pursued secondary education at these organizations' *yeshīvōt* in Casablanca and Tangier. The dual program of religious and secular education received at OH *yeshīvōt*, as opposed to the pedagogically outmoded rabbinic institutions, placed these graduates among the modernized elite. Once again, this group was composed of both *bled* elements and alumni of the schools in the large towns, recruited to teach in the *bled*. The OH and AYI teachers, however, emerged late as vital forces, as these American-inspired organizations entered Morocco after the war. Nevertheless, several Moroccan teachers at the OH may have pursued elementary religious education in other schools but attended the OH and teacher-training schools in England, France, and Morocco already in the late 1940s. The one noticeable absence in the *bled* elite were the AIU alumni associations, the latter usually existing only in the urban communities.

Notwithstanding, relocation appeared in several communities as the best alternative to escape poverty in the pre-1945 period. Subsequently, during the 1950s, the urban centers were often too crowded to accomodate an onslaught of migrants knocking on their gates, and the AIU and JDC, as well as OSE, had their hands full combatting poverty and disease. Therefore, Jews in the *bled* who could not settle in the urban areas turned increasingly to the representatives of the Jewish Agency.

Contrary to their prewar policies, the AIU and the JDC, looked with approval on the Jewish Agency's activities in the *bled*, even if the AIU did not always wish to collaborate with the representatives directly. In fact, other organizations, notably the OH and its representatives, though eventually employing Israeli teachers of the Jewish Agency, were warned not to support all the Zionist envoys, particularly the left-wing envoys. In a memorandum from 1949, Ventura suggested that instead of OH representatives accusing AIU teachers of being irreligious ("he who regardeth his soul should keep far from them"), emphasis had to shift to OH-AIU collaboration. Otherwise: if the OH would yield to an illusive quarrel of principle with the AIU instead of combining forces with it to educate as many more children as possible, a countless number of youths would be placed in the hands of "irreligious" members of the Socialist MAPAM movement.[188]

However, the position of the Jews became more difficult during the 1950s to the point where they could not shun the Zionist envoys any longer. As shown by a report prepared by community leaders at Amizmiz in November 1955, the eve of independence, their problems were both economic and political. It was noted that Muslims in parts of the *bled* were pressured to boycott Jewish business. The Arabs would come to the *bled* to talk to their Muslim compatriots and tell them they must give no money to the Jews, even money they owed them because that money would go to Israel and serve for purchasing arms which could be turned against Nāsir's Egypt. If the Jews turned to the local *qā'id* for protection, the man would tell them that there was nothing he could do, that it was none of his business. The Jews of Amizmiz were worried about the political climate and the fact that the *qā'id*, who was rather friendly, could do nothing, Most of the Jewish merchants of Amizmiz had their business in association with Muslims as was the case in other parts of the *bled*, and there was little hope for them to recover anything from their associates.[189]

The MAPAM members, then, had their work cut out for them. The roads leading to the *bled* that brought the pioneers of the AIU, and later the OH and AYI, to better the lives of the Jews, were the same roads used by Grinker, Hirschberg, and other devoted zionists to redeem them through emigration to Israel. The longing for Zion, the modern Zionist idea, the creation of Israel, and Moroccan nationalist ferment were a combination of factors that led to the dismantling of the Jewish *bled*. (For statistical data on the *bled*, see Table 30.)

Impact of Education

Evolution of Ideas, Institutions, and the Rise in Literacy

Among the ideas that were disseminated, particularly in the south and the interior, was belief in the need to break with *mellāh* culture, to move out of the insulated ghetto. While this was hardly feasible before 1912, it gradually became so afterwards. During the First World War, when the AIU continued to urge its students to abandon the *mellāh*, at least temporarily, the French and Spanish protectorates were erecting European residential quarters. In the French zone *villes européennes* were established since 1916. All the major towns—Casablanca, Mazagan, Marrakesh, Fez, Meknes, Mogador—had such quarters added, and advocacy of collaborating with the Europeans at the AIU schools could now be considered on certain levels. Also the developing opportunities during the protectorate era enabled AIU graduates to abandon their traditional neighborhoods and move into these new quarters. The best AIU graduates adamantly opposed the idea of confinement to a ghetto and believed that modern education and the emergence of the protectorate period would strengthen their ties with the Europeans through integration into their communities. In Fez, for example, where Jewish traditionalism was deeply felt, a significant exodus of Jews to the European quarter took place between 1936 and 1960, as Table 31 shows. In fact, of 635 lots placed for sale in the European quarter, 155 were allotted for Moroccans: 57 for Muslims, 97 for Jews.[190] Similarly in other traditional communities, young people and intellectuals especially moved from the *mellāh* to the European quarter, a step that helped change ideas, styles, and fashions. In Fez, European furniture generally replaced the traditional low tables.[191]

Table 30. Comparative Statistics on the *Bled* Communities where the *Alliance* Opened Schools after 1927 (Data for 1936 and 1951).

Town	Jewish Population: 1936[a]	AIU School: boys and girls[b]	Jewish Population 1951[c]	AIU School: boys and girls[d]
Amizmiz	601	-	593	57
Ben-Ahmed	201	69	475	126
Beni-Mellal	1914	31	-	-
Ber-Rechid	171	43	350	86
Boujad	753	131	800	194
Demnat	1691	99	1800	155
El-Kelaa	380	-	620	70
Gourrama	410	-	450	53
Imintanout	256	-	360	75
Inezgane	?	-	450	43
Kasba-Tadla	541	93	750	148
Khenitra	?	6	171	41
Kasr al-Suq	832	-	1100	54
Kerrando	?	-	200	44
Midelt	1200	91	1700	246
Oued-Zem	200	-	400	82
Ouezzane	1668	208	2350	366
Rich	405	-	578	101
Rissani	?	-	500	51
Sidi Rahal	721	-	600	50
Talsint	269	-	270	62
Taourirt	550	45	450	104
Taroudant	926	162	950	133
Taza	194	-	520	56
Tinehrir	?	-	600	61
Tiznit	357	76	450	101
Tounza	624	-	317	40

[a]Y.D. Sémach, "Le recensement de 1936 au Maroc," *Paix et Droit*, 19e année, no. 6, mensuel, juin 1939, pp. 8–10.

[b]"Tableau des écoles de l'Alliance Israélite," *Paix et Droit*, 16e année, no. 4, juin 1936, p. 16.

[c]"Etat comparatif des taux de scholarisation au Maroc: années 1950–1951," *Les Cahiers de l'Alliance Israélite Universelle*, nos. 50–51, février-mars 1951, p. 8.

[d]Ibid., p. 8. Note that these were only *bled* communities where the *Alliance* maintained schools. There are numerous towns and hamlets with extremely small communities still not affected by the AIU but rather by the Otzar ha-Torah network.

Changes in ideas and customs were not less evident in the traditional communities than in the more modern ones. In 1955, Hirschberg found that the wealthier stratum in the Meknes community had become modernized, and aside from the 2,600 youths attending AIU schools, several families sent their children to schools in France.[192] These changes in Morocco were ac-

Table 31. Jewish Population in Fez

Year	Mellāh Population	European Quarter Jewish Settlers
1936	10,219	756
1952	11,540	1,554
1960	4,846	3,843

SOURCE: Donath, *Evolution du judaïsme marocain sous le protectorat Français*, 1912–1956 (Paris: Mouton and Co., 1968), p. 51.

companied by other aspects of westernization, some of which were perhaps superficial and symbolic, like gallicization of names and westernization of attire. This, as we have seen, was found in every community where AIU (and protectorate) schools existed, the remote *bled* included. French, too, became the dominant spoken language among the Jews of the major towns. While certainly the case for French Morocco, the spread of French was also evident in the Spanish and International zones, too. By 1939, French was spoken by youths of these communities. Judeo-Arabic, Judeo-Spanish, and Spanish had gradually receded in favor of that language in French Morocco, even though most Jews continued to utilize them at home and in family and social circles. Regarding the Spanish zone, there occurred an important linguistic evolution. Spanish continued to play an integral part in the school program, but French was the language of instruction. AIU graduates were therefore bilingual or multilingual, and this helped them get good jobs in Tangier, the French zone, Algeria, and in Latin America. In Tangier, according to Hirschberg's findings, a segment of young educated Jews were multilingual: they spoke French, Spanish, and English,[193] all of which were taught at the AIU.

Institutional changes resulting from modernization can be analyzed in accordance with the following: (a) the status of women; and (b) the challenge to the rabbinic schools.

The presence of the AIU and protectorate schools fostered and encouraged the education of women; and indeed, moving to the European quarter, abandoning the traditional dress in favor of the Paris fashions, working as secretaries, laboratory assistants, in department stores, and studying at AIU *cours complémentaires* or French *lycées*, created new concerns and priorities for some Jewish women.

However, by persistently opposing child marriages not only before parents and ordinary rabbis, but before the highest rabbinic authorities of the land, the AIU pressed the communities to undertake vital reforms on behalf of women, and finally succeeded. During the 1934 council session of Moroccan chief rabbis it was agreed upon that no girls ought to be married before the age of twelve; during their session in 1948, however, the chief rabbis agreed unanimously that girls should not be married before the age of fifteen.[194] Finally, in 1952, the rabbinate in Rabat issued another reform, stipulating that "a woman has the right to refuse to live or continue to live with her parents-in-law."[195]

Reforming the rabbinic schools, like the challenge to child marriages, was a major preoccupation of the teachers of the AIU who were behind this idea; and by promoting the creation of modernized religious schools over a long period of time, they attracted wide support for reform in the post-1945 period. They in fact helped reform the rabbinic school programs by taking charge of general education alongside the traditional curriculum, especially in the interior.

Of these schools, the AIU was particularly interested in the *Em-Habānīm* network, essentially in Sefrou. The community's most influential rabbi, David Ovadia, believed that by offering general education and French, he could eventually attract more youths from the Sefrou boys' school to the local *Em-Habānīm* counterpart, which was his pride and joy.[196] Even a kindergarten was established to attract young children to the school from the start, so as to keep them from turning to the AIU boys' school.[197] While Ovadia was an opponent of the AIU's secular orientations, he nonetheless respected the organization's contributions and achievements on behalf of the Jews, and considered the idea of renovating and modernizing religious schools as a prudent one. Recalling the situation in Sefrou, Ovadia defended his decision to introduce curricular reforms, saying that one of the major obstacles to Torah studies was involved with the fact that the graduates of the *Em-Habānīm* were unable to find employment in the protectorate's administration or in banking; this was all at the time when the graduates of the AIU found such employment. The personnel and directors of *Em-Habānīm* in Sefrou therefore decided to institute reforms, with AIU teachers recruited to teach French in the program.[198]

What is more, the local religious schools were usually reserved for boys, and *Em Ha-Bānīm* was no exception. In Sefrou, the leadership was well aware that the presence of the AIU schools meant that the girls were getting both a secular and religious education for the first time. Here, too, the AIU served as an effective agent for modernization and as a pressure group. Ovadia, for example, noted that before the arrival of the AIU in his community, there was no attention given to girls' education; once the protectorate was established, and with it, the AIU schools of Sefrou, reforms were considered.[199] To emulate the AIU, religious schooling for girls began, and though this reform was introduced only after 1945, it must be understood that the process of modernization, especially in the interior, was a slow one. The effort began with the creation of the *Beit Rivka* schools which introduced religious, secular, and vocational education.[200]

In its reforming tasks, the AIU and dynamic community leaders like Rabbi David Ovadia of Sefrou, were aided by the JDC and OH. The OH and the AIU worked closely with Ovadia to reform outmoded rabbinic schools in other interior communities where this illustrious rabbi had managed to extend his spiritual influence. These reforms had to be revised continuously. From AIU literature for 1950–1953, we can discern attendance in outmoded schools. Table 32 shows the dwindling strength of the old schools since 1950, a phenomenon that gained momentum because of rabbinic legislation, too. During the fifth rabbinic council session, a pedagogical commission was created, charged with inspecting the religious schools in Morocco; the rabbis who were put in charge intended to abolish the old schools (*hadārīm* and *ṣlās*) in favor of building modern ones;[201] and by 1960, most of the old schools had disappeared.

Despite reforms, important traditions were adhered to, perhaps more so in Morocco than in other Jewish communities of the Islamic diaspora. Thus the Sabbath and Jewish holidays were scrupulously observed for the most part, and most youths who left their families and lived in the European quarters continued to show traditional attitudes of respect toward their parents and grandparents. Students attending French and Spanish *lycées* observed the Sabbath regardless of the policies of these schools to remain open on Saturdays. Religious attachments remained intact. And when AIU teachers at times chose to deviate from certain traditions, communal reactions were rather bitter. Such a situation occurred in Salé, where despite the trends toward modernization, the traditional authorities did not tolerate *hilūl* Shabbat (desecration of the Jewish Sabbath). That community's inhabitants used to tell a story about an incident that took place in 1919 when a teacher at the AIU girls' school of Moroccan origin died. Her body was not buried in the customary place, because she had acquired the reputation of not observing the Jewish Sabbath. Instead, she was buried in a section of the cemetery reserved for prostitutes, and only later, after the intervention

Table 32. Hadarim Attendance

Year	Received no Education	Studied in *Hadarim*	Total
February 1950	7,368	5,692	13,060
June-July 1950	5,261	3,794	9,055
May 1953	4,761	3,204	7,965

Source: *Les Cahiers de l'Alliance Israélite Universelle*, issues of March, June-July 1950, and of May 1953. The figures apply to all three zones. There is no sex breakdown in statistics for those who did not attend schools.

of the Jewish community of Rabat, was her body exhumed and properly buried in the section of the cemetery reserved for the blessed.[202]

As a way of fighting illiteracy, the AIU worked to increase its enrollments, and with considerable success. Based on its data for May 1939, there were 18,612 students attending AIU and other modern schools throughout Morocco.[203] At the same time, approximately 35,000 Jewish children were of school age. This means that in 1939 between fifty-three and fifty-four percent of the youths were attending modern schools and the rest, forty-six to forty-seven percent fell in the categories of those attending rabbinic schools and those not attending schools at all.

The most reliable data on this subject, however, are found in the census findings for 1951-1952, and for 1960. The 1960 census covers both Jewish and Muslim groups in a unified and independent Morocco, including the three former zones. Based on the 1951-1952 census, covering the French zone only, 62.9 percent of the boys and 56.25 percent of the girls (10-14) were in school; at the time only between 10-15 percent of Muslim youths of the same age category were in school.[204] In Casablanca alone, 60.36 percent of the boys and 54.91 percent of the girls (ages 10-14) were in school.[205] Comparing the AIU data (May 1939) with the 1951-1952 census, we are unable to arrive at any concrete evaluations because these figures do not include the traditional schools whereas the 1951-1952 census does; these figures do not deal specifically with any one age group or category as does the census; and, most important, these figures apply to the three former zones whereas the 1951-1952 census applies to French Morocco only.

The 1960 census, on the other hand, helps clarify the ambiguities to a considerable extent. The census taken by the Moroccan government gives data on the levels of Muslim and Jewish literacy (reading knowledge of Arabic, French; for those who knew only Hebrew letters werer counted as illiterate) and was based on a sample of 2 percent of the overall Jewish population aged 5 and over. There was no breakdown for sexes or geographical regions (table 33). Early in 1960 some 30,000 children were enrolled at the AIU (ORT-AIU included), namely the majority of children of school age (6-19) while the rest attended the various European schools, locally sponsored religious schools, the OH and AYI. That means the AIU made the most significant contribution to the eradication of illiteracy. Table 33 points to some startling developments. While the children in the age category 5-9 were less than 50 percent literate, this was not necessarily as some argue,[206] the fault of the AIU and protectorate schools, but perhaps due to the fact that many children in the age category 5-6 were not yet in school and hence were too young to be considered literate.

The percentage data of 81.9 percent literacy for the 10-14 age category, on the other hand, shows that notable progress was made by the modern

Table 33. Literacy Levels for Jews in 1960

Age Category	Illiterate: Reading and Writing %	Literate: Reading and Writing %
5–9	50.3	49.7
10–14	18.1	81.9
15–19	24.9	75.1
20–29	37.4	62.6
30–39	45.6	54.4
40–49	59.3	40.7
50–59	55.2	44.8
60 +	76.3	23.7
Total Average:	43.2	56.8

Source: *Royaume du Maroc. Service Central des Statistiques*. Resultats preliminaires du recensement de 1960. Sondage au 1/50. Avril 1963, pp. 31–32; Donath, *Immigrants d'Afrique du Nord en Israël*, Editions Anthropos, 1970, p. 34; *Donath, Evolution du judaïsme marocain sous le protectorat*, Paris: Mouton and Co., 1968, p. 29; Robert Attal, "The Population Census in Morocco," *Be Tefusōt ha-Gōla* (Spring, 1964), p. 43 (in Hebrew).

school in the battle against illiteracy. Among Muslim youths of the same age category only 29.8 percent were literate, roughly matching the literacy level of old Moroccan Jews of the 60 and over age category (23.7 percent). The 75.1 percent literacy rate for 15–19 age category is equally impressive, showing that significant progress was made on the postprimary educational level. As for higher education, there were then only 239 Jewish university students, of whom 151 studied abroad: all in all, 56.8 percent of the Jewish population — based on the census sample — were literate.[207] Among the Muslims, only 13.5 percent were considered literate.[208] For the Jews, a near 60 percent literacy rate was important. Though it may be argued that the significant Jewish emigration between 1951 and 1956, including uneducated Jews from the Atlas mountains, improved the literacy level among remaining Jews, most of whom dwelt in large towns in 1960, there is little doubt that, had the uneducated remained in Morocco, they would have been eventually integrated into the AIU, ORT, OH, AYI and other schools sponsored by the JDC and the ministry of national education.

The Modernized Elite and the Evolution of the Occupational Structure

The following groups strongly supported the AIU: the Moroccan-born ENIO graduates, the commercial entrepreneurs who served as the indispensable intermediaries between Moroccans and Europeans, and consular and administrative employees of various ranks. In the area of the modern vocations, the preprotectorate era offered few opportunities for the Jews. The same applied to agriculture. Yet during the protectorate period the Jewish elite grew in importance and diversity while school graduates began to assume greater community leadership responsibilities. In examining the elite and its components we shall concentrate on several categories: (a) commerce; (b) administrative and white-collar, including law, medicine, journalism, and teaching; (c) the modern manual vocations.

Regarding commerce, Moroccan Jews were exposed to certain changes not always to their likings. The preprotectorate Jewish monopoly over much of the large-scale commercial transactions, and their role as intermediaries suffered a relative decline. The influx of Europeans, mainly Frenchmen and Spaniards since the early 1930s broke the Jewish commercial monopoly. No longer were the Jewish commercial houses in the coastal towns so crucial and no longer were the Jews the only element fluent, or at least familiar with European languages. European talent and capital infiltrating Morocco constituted a serious challenge to their dominance and ended it. Nevertheless, there were some significant exceptions, notably in Tangier. Despite the large number of French, British, and Spanish inhabitants in the International zone, the Jewish community still dominated the commercial arena in different sectors as late as 1940. Blandin, who studied the population of Tangier in 1940, noted that the Jew remained the indispensable agent of all affairs, big and small. From the sale of Spanish and French lottery tickets to the enormous real estate deals, the Jew served as the intermediary; in the wholesale leather goods business, the Jew controlled exports to England and the United States, and it was he who exported all indispensable products to the Spanish protectorate: textiles, automobiles, furniture, flour, spices, both wholesale and retail.[209]

Examining the administrative and while-collar professions we find that Jews were employed by governmental (mostly in the French and International zones) and private agencies and banks. Beginning with banking, they easily found work in Tangier at *Banque Hasan, Banque Pariente*, and at the *Crédit Foncier*. In Mazagan, they were employed at the *Crédit Foncier* and at the *Taxe Urbaine*.[210] In Fez, they were recruited at the local branch of *Banque Algéro-Tunisienne*, at a local British bank, and at the *Comptoire Maroc*.[211] In industry, moreover, educated Jews were employed as administrators and clerks at such enterprises as the *Compagnie des Transports des Camions* in Mazagan;[212] in Fez they could be found at Vacuum Oil.[213] This trend to recruit Jews into administrative and white-collar professions slowed down considerably after 1930. While many Jews were still represented in these categories, the favorable trends of the pre-1930 period toward large-scale recruitment were reversed. Many of the administrators, clerks, white-collar employees were working for the protectorates, save the Spanish zone where Jews and Muslims were scarcely recruited. But the Jews were given less priority for administrative recruitment after 1930 for the following reasons. First, the large influx of Europeans into Morocco after pacification and the final surrender of 'Abd al-Krīm and his rebels in 1926.[214] Second, the emergence of the early nationalist movement which, among other reforms, demanded greater participation by Muslims in the colonial administration. Third, the global economic crisis of the 1930s which made it hard for the protectorates, particularly in the French zone, to meet the demands of all segments of the population.

From the beginning of the protectorate era and until 1930, the Jews had employment priorities in administration and white-collar professions because, in the absence of large European colonies and their administrators, the Jews represented the only educated indigenous element capable of fulfilling colonial needs. Whereas before 1930 only high-level posts were given to Europeans while middle- and lower-level positions were granted to Jews, the latter, after 1930, were restricted in these categories, too. The same applied for Tangier where after 1923, the most privileged professions and administrative posts were monopolized by Europeans, mainly the French. The Spanish element was almost seven times larger than the French, but they were mostly wage laborers, construction workers, and taxi drivers; their women worked as domestic help and some one hundred and fifty Spaniards worked in agriculture; but rare were Spaniards who became administrative functionaries and white-collar executives.[215] Next to the French, the Jews were relatively well represented, though their position after 1923 was not as strong in view of French administrative and economic dominance. In Spanish Morocco, on the other hand, the administration was much too small, and as tables 34 and 35 clearly indicate for several categories, the administrative apparatus was understaffed: few Spaniards, Muslims or Jews were represented in the system.

The nationalist movement that emerged after 1930 soon become vocal on the issue of greater Muslim participation in administrative agencies, especially in French Morocco;[216] they resented the fact that Muslims were, as Waterbury put it, "marginal participants"[217] in the administration. And as the French were not so dependent on educated Jews after the influx of their own people from France to Morocco,[218] and as they had to accommodate the nationalists after the Berber ẓahīr fiasco, fewer Jews were recruited.

Finally, the world economic crisis of the 1930s had a harmful effect on French recruitment of AIU and other French school Jewish graduates into the protectorate administration. To minimize expenditures, the French decided to be more selective, with Europeans receiving first priority in rank and number and the Muslims given consideration as well. Thus the Jews, though still sought out after 1930, gradually became less important in administrative roles.

Table 34. Spanish Administration, 1942

Town	Technicians	High and Middle Ranks	Subaltern	Police	Fireman
Tetuan	3	44	131	112	19
Larache	4	16	23	38	7
Elksar	4	15	36	50	1
Arzila	2	3	27	11	-
Xauen	2	4	37	15	-
Villa Sanjurjo	1	11	23	13	-
Ríncon de Medik	1	-	1	2	-
Villa Nador	5	8	12	23	-
Castillejos	-	1	1	1	-
Puerto Capaz	-	2	1	-	-
Targuist	1	2	9	4	-
Monte Arruit	1	-	-	2	-
Zaio	-	-	-	2	-
Zeluán	1	1	1	2	-
Karia de Arkeman	-	1	1	3	-
Segangan	3	2	1	3	-

SOURCE: *Ministerio de Trabajo: Dirección General de Estadistica.* III: *Administración Local Zona de Protectorado y de Los Territorios de Soberanía de España* (Madrid, 1943), p. 351.

Nevertheless, though more Muslims entered the French protectorate and private administrative agencies, Jewish administrators on all levels and white-collar professionals, were still better represented in their employed population than the Muslims were in theirs. In the 1951–1952 census (see Table 36), which discusses the employed population,[219] we can analyze the extent of Jewish representation in various posts, mainly in the French protectorate's administration. Once again, it should be remembered that the 1951–1952 census applies to French Morocco only; and it includes both protectorate employment and employment in private enterprises. Yet many administrative and white-collar positions were handed out by the protectorate's machinery. The census deals with two categories that relate to our analysis: first, the clerks, office employees, bookkeepers, accountants, and minor officials, classified as *emplois de bureau*; second, upper-level ranks: the more important administrative functionaries and other professionals classified as *emplois administratifs-professions intellectuelles*.

Examining the first category, we find that out of a total employed *urban* Jewish population (44,219) 2,537 Jews were employed.[220] This figure comprised 1,772 men, or 5.25 percent of the total employed male Jewish population, and 765 women, or 7.27 percent of the total employed female Jewish population.[221] Among the employed Muslim population represented in the first category, we find that out of a total employed *urban* Muslim population (460,465) 6,325 Muslims were employed.[222] This figure comprised

Table 35. Spanish Administration, 1948–1949

Town	Technicians		High and Middle Ranks		Subaltern		Police		Firemen	
	1948	1949	1948	1949	1948	1949	1948	1949	1948	1949
Tetuan	6	7	57	64	85	114	103	112	32	22
Río Martin	2	2	5	3	11	11	4	4	-	-
Larache	3	5	25	26	42	33	41	42	10	10
Elksar	4	4	16	18	24	29	53	52	-	-
Arzila	2	2	8	7	23	11	9	9	-	-
Xauen	1	1	8	7	3	3	12	12	-	-
Villa Sanjurjo	2	2	11	11	16	20	19	19	-	-
Villa Nador	4	4	17	11	11	24	24	24	-	8
Ríncon de Medik	1	2	4	3	4	4	-	3	-	-
Castellejos	1	3	3	1	3	3	4	4	-	-
Puerto Capaz	-	-	1	1	1	1	-	1	1	-
Targuist	1	2	5	4	10	9	5	5	-	-
Monte Arruit	-	1	2	1	-	-	1	2	-	-
Zaio	-	-	2	1	4	4	3	3	-	-
Zeluán	1	-	3	1	-	-	2	2	-	-
Karia de Arkeman	-	-	1	1	1	2	1	2	-	-
Segangan	1	1	3	2	3	2	3	2	2	2

SOURCE: *Presidencia del Gobierno: Instituto Nacional de Estadistica.* III: *Administración Local*, p. 463. *Zona de Protectorado y de Los Territorios de Soberanía de España* (Madrid, 1949–1950).

6,220 men, or 1.67 percent of the total employed male Muslim population, and 105 women, or 0.11 percent of the total employed female Muslim population.[223]

In the second category, *emplois administratifs-professions intellectuelles*, there were out of a total employed *urban* Jewish population (44,219) 1,117 employed Jews.[224] This figure comprised 946 men, or 2.80 percent of the total employed male population, and 171 women, or 1.62 percent of the total employed female Jewish population.[225] Among the employed Muslims in the second category, out of a total of 460,465 employed in the *urban* areas, 11,675 were employed.[226] This group comprised 11,490 men, or 3.09 percent of the total employed male Muslim population, and 185 women, or 0.20 percent of the total employed female Muslim population. In examining the total Moroccan Jewish population covering both *urban* and *rural* areas, we find that out of a total employed population of 53,685, 4,143 Jews were employed in *both* categories.[227]

From the data in table 36 (urban Morocco, French zone) we can deduce the following conclusions for 1951. First, Jewish women were better represented in the category *emplois de bureau* in proportion to their total employed female population than Jewish men were in proportion to theirs. Second, both Jewish male and female *employés de bureau* were considerably better represented in proportion to their total population than were their Muslim counterparts. Finally, Muslim women were especially underrepresented in this category of urban employment. Concerning the *emplois administratifs-professions intellectuelles* category, we can deduce several interesting conclusions there as well. Jewish men were better represented in proportion to their total employed population than Jewish women were in proportion to theirs. Muslim men, on the other hand, were better represented than Jewish men in their respective categories (3.09 percent Muslims, 2.80 percent Jews). However, even in this category of employment, considering that Jewish women were better represented than Muslim women, the *total* representation of Jewish employees (male and female) was almost identical: 2.52 percent for the Jews and 2.53 percent for the Muslims. Combining *both* of the above categories relevant to Jews and Muslims, we find that in the *urban* areas, 8.25 percent of Jews (male and female, 5.73 percent of the first category and 2.52 percent of the second) and 3.90 percent of Muslims (male and female, 1.37 percent of the first catgory and 2.53 percent of the second) were employed. On the whole, then, it is evident that despite greater Muslim participation in the above professions after 1930, the Jews were still proportionally better represented in this area as late as 1951 than the Muslims.

Finally, it is noteworthy that the category of *emplois administratifs-Professions intellectuelles* of 1,117 *urban* Jews included physicians (15 men, no women), dentists (37 men, 11 women), and pharmacists (337 men, 13 women)[228] There is no mention of journalists. However, we already know that AIU graduates pioneered in journalism and that of the newspapers and journals published during the protectorate era (for example, *L'Union Marocaine, L'Avenir Illustré, Nō'ār, La Voix des Communautés*), all employed educated Jews.

As for teachers, the 1951-1952 census indicates that in 1951 there were 17 Jewish professors (men only), 21 school directors (19 men and 3 women), and 340 teachers of elementary and secondary schools (169 men, 171 women).[229] However, several points must be clarified. First, one cannot be certain whether the census referred to "Jewish teachers" as a general category, or "Moroccan Jewish teachers," as there were still non-Moroccan Jews from the Middle East and Balkan countries teaching at the AIU schools. Second, there is no indication whether the census included teachers and directors of *all* types of schools, namely, AIU, Franco-Jewish, ORT, OH, AYI, and the various outmoded and renovated schools. If this were the case, then the figures are far too low. Third, the figure of only three directresses is surely inaccurate, considering that in 1951 the AIU had fifty schools in the French zone. If we combine the "Jewish teachers" and

Table 36. The Employed Urban Jewish and Muslim Population:
1951–1952 (French Morocco)

	Jews						Muslims					
Profession	Both sexes	%	Men	%	Women	%	Both sexes	%	Men	%	Women	%
Fishing and navigation	99	0.22	99	0.29	-	-	4,525	0.98	4,525	1.21	-	-
Forestry	6	0.01	6	0.01	-	-	300	0.06	275	0.07	25	0.02
Agriculture	169	0.38	164	0.48	5	0.04	16,155	3.50	14,500	3.90	1,655	1.86
Mining	29	0.06	29	0.08	-	-	965	0.20	965	0.25	-	-
Metallurgy	1,822	4.12	1,803	5.34	19	0.18	12,330	2.67	12,300	3.30	30	0.03
Electrical and radio trade	316	0.71	311	0.92	5	0.04	2,420	0.52	2,420	0.65	-	-
Glassmaking	161	0.36	161	0.47	-	-	45	0.01	45	0.01	-	-
Production of construction material	34	0.07	34	0.10	-	-	3,510	0.76	3,485	0.93	25	0.02
Public works and ship-building	1,556	3.51	1,552	4.60	4	0.03	56,405	2.24	53,710	14.45	2,695	3.03
Chemicals industry	267	0.60	200	0.59	67	0.63	2,535	0.55	2,435	0.65	100	0.11
Food industry	1,158	2.61	1,000	2.96	158	1.50	24,760	5.37	17,155	4.65	7,605	8.56
Textiles	276	0.62	104	0.30	172	1.63	24,510	5.32	6,955	1.87	17,555	19.76
Clothing and dressmaking	8,470	19.15	3.930	11.74	4,540	43.20	24,760	5.37	9,790	2.63	14,970	16.85

"Moroccan Jewish teachers" together, there is no doubt that more than three women directed schools. Yet if we concentrate on "Moroccan Jewish teachers" only, there were still more than three directresses employed by the AIU.

Finally, we see that the westernized component of teachers, mostly ENIO graduates of Moroccan background, continued to grow, overshadowing in importance the non-Moroccans (Turks, Greeks, Balkan states elements). Further, the creation of the ENH in Casablanca gave additional impetus to the broadening of the teacher elite corps. In the case of the ENIO, since the early 1950s, the number of AIU primary school graduates in Morocco had begun to increase dramatically and the number of the candidates for the ENIO in Paris grew significantly. In addition, the Turkish Jews who attended the ENIO served in the past as source of teachers in Morocco and the former Ottoman Empire. However, Kemal Atatürk's turkification program, which resulted in the nationalization of many AIU schools, and the surrender of the rest of the schools to the local communities during the 1930s, reduced, if it did not eliminate, Turkish-Jewish representation in

Table 36. The Employed Urban Jewish and Muslim Population:
1951–1952 (French Morocco) (*continued*)

	Jews						Muslims					
Profession	Both sexes	%	Men	%	Women	%	Both sexes	%	Men	%	Women	%
Leather trade	4,132	9.34	3,702	10.98	430	4.09	14,080	3.07	13,755	3.70	325	0.36
Woodwork	1,315	2.97	1,301	3.85	14	0.13	10,635	2.30	10,580	2.84	55	0.06
Paper and bookbinding	829	1.87	783	2.32	46	0.43	955	0.20	905	0.24	50	0.05
Jewelry and goldsmithy	709	1.60	700	2.07	9	0.08	325	0.07	325	0.08	-	-
Transport	1,015	2.29	1,011	3.00	4	0.03	16,130	3.50	16,130	4.34	-	-
Shopkeepers	1,145	2.58	1,081	3.20	64	0.60	99,000	21.50	91,125	24.52	7,875	8.86
Commerce	8,975	20.29	3,354	24.78	621	5.90	53,185	11.55	52,415	14.10	770	0.86
Domestic Service, Health attendants	4,288	9.69	1,638	4.85	2,650	25.21	45,840	9.95	14,490	3.89	31,350	35.29
Office work	2,537	5.73	1,772	5.25	765	7.27	6,325	1.37	6,220	1.67	105	0.11
Administrative, professional, intellectual employment	1,117	2.52	946	2.80	171	1.62	11,675	2.53	11,490	3.09	185	0.20
Entertainment	149	0.33	123	0.36	26	0.24	1,555	0.33	1,270	0.34	285	0.32
Army and Defense	51	0.11	48	0.14	3	0.02	15,390	3.34	15,285	4.11	105	0.11
Unspecified trades	3,594	8.12	2,858	8.47	736	7.00	12,150	2.63	9,085	2.44	3,065	3.45
TOTAL:	44,219	100%	33,710	100%	10,509	100%	460, 465	100%	371,635	100%	88,830	100%

SOURCE: *Gouvernement cherifien. Service central des statistiques Recensement genéral de la population en 1951/1952*, Vol. IV, p. 80 and Vol. III, p. 34; Doris Bensimon Donath, *Evolution du judaïsme marocain*, p. 139.

enrollment at the Paris normal school. At the same time, the Moroccan elementary schools and *cours complémentaire* network became the bastion of the AIU and naturally, the number of Moroccan students sent to Paris for pedagogical training was higher than those from the rest of the countries where the AIU had schools. This meant that Moroccans from the ENIO were sent to teach in Morocco in greater numbers as well as in other countries. The data in table 37, confirm this argument.

From table 37 we learn that out of a total ENIO student body of 49 in 1948, 28 were Moroccans; out of 68 in 1951, 59 were Moroccans. Added to the ENIO group was the element that attended the ENH. In 1951 there were 75 students in attendance; they were AIU elementary school graduates recruited for training from around the country. Therefore, it appears that in 1951 alone, 134 potential educators were undergoing training.

Skilled vocational and agricultural workers were also members of the elite. The ORT schools as well as the AIU vocational centers of Casablanca, Fez, and Rabat, carried further the early activities in this domain, began by the AIU. Despite the presence of the Meknes and Marrakesh schools, the number of youths who turned to agriculture was not great. Yet, most of them found lucrative employment on European farms. In contrast to agricultural activities among *bled* Jews, the graduates of the AIU agricultural schools engaged in modern agriculture and were also skilled in the modern manual crafts, the latter trades having been taught as part of these schools' program.

As to the vocations and related artisan-type employment, the 1951–1952 census with data (vol. IV, pages 66–73) for both *urban* and *rural* French Morocco, is most useful. It is noteworthy that reference is once again made to the employed Jewish population, males and females. Of the *total figure* of 25,693 employed Jews in the category of vocations and artisan activities,[230] the following are the most important:[231] (1) *blacksmithing and locksmithing*—235, or 0.91 percent of the total figure; (2) *sheet-metal production*—702, or 2.73 percent of the total figure; (3) *mechanics*—1,014, or 3.94 percent of the total figure; (4) *electricity and radio repairs*—335, or 1.30 percent of the total figure; (5) *construction and public works—193, or 0.75 percent of the total figure; (6) plumbing*—258, or 1 percent of the total figure; (7) *house painting and decorating*—1,185, or 4.61 percent of the total figure; (8) *butchering*—717, or 2.79 percent of the total figure; (9) *baking*—457, or 1.77 percent of the total figure; (10) *textiles*—457, or 1.77 percent of the total figure; (11) *clothing industry* (dressmaking and tailoring)—8,058, or 31.36 percent of the total figure; (12) *sack, net, and tent production*—443, or 1.72 percent of the total figure; (13) *house furnishing*—1,036, or

Table 37. ENIO Attendance for 1948 and 1951

Country	Boys 1948	Girls 1948	Boys 1951	Girls 1951	1948	Total 1951
Algeria	-	-	1	-	-	1
Egypt	-	2	-	-	2	-
France	2	1	-	-	3	-
Greece	-	-	-	1	-	1
Iraq	-	3	-	-	3	-
Iran	-	3	-	-	3	-
Israel	2	4	1	-	6	1
Lebanon	1	-	1	1	1	2
Morocco	22	6	27	32	28	59
Syria	-	-	-	-	-	-
Tunisia	1	2	3	1	3	4

SOURCE: Tabulations are based on data found in the *Alliance* bulletin. For 1948: "L'école normale israélite orientale," *Les Cahiers de l'Alliance Israélite Universelle* 27 (novembre 1948), pp. 4–5; for 1951; 57–58 (novembre-décembre 1951), p. 7.

4.03 percent of the total figure; (14) *leather, saddle, and harness manufacture* — 736, or 2.86 percent of the total figure; (15) *shoemaking* — 5,374, or 2.09 percent of the total figure; (16) *carpentry and cabinetmaking* — 1,484, or 5.77 percent of the total figure; (17) *typesetting and printing* — 610, or 2.37 percent of the total figure; and (18) *jewelry* — 974, or 3.79 percent of the total figure.

From the data it is evident that a small but growing elite of the manual professions was employed in important nontraditional (for Jews) areas such as sheet-metal, mechanics, electricity, plumbing, cabinetmaking, and in typesetting-printing. A few other nontraditional professions were not well represented. The rest continued in the traditional artisan-type activities. It is clear, however, that an important elite of nontraditional or even modernized employees and employers was emerging as the protectorate era was drawing to an end.

To define and classify the elite components that developed between 1912 and 1956, especially in the French and International zones, we have: first, important lower-middle and middle strata of administrators of diverse ranks and white-collar professionals. This was largely due to the educational efforts of the AIU, but credit is also due to the protectorate's Franco-Jewish schools (in the French zone and Tangier), to the *lycées*, and to other institutions. This group included journalists, teachers, pharmacists, lawyers, and physicians (who acquired higher and more specialized education). Regarding teachers, 70 percent of the AIU's personnel in the immediate post-1956 period were Moroccan Jews. The number of women in the category of administrative-white collar-profession, and office work, was important. In 1960, the *employés de bureau* constituted the most important segment of this class: 13.2 percent of the employed male population and 23.8 percent of the employed female population.[232] Are the 1960 figures an indication that the Moroccan government in the postindependence era employed more educated Jews in the administration to keep them from emigrating to Israel? Was it due to the massive departure of French and other colonial personnel and the need, by the government, to employ all available qualified and educated people? It would require a separate investigation to determine the reasons.

Second, the commercial elite class, which suffered a decline during the protectorate era. The decline was attributed to the reduction in the Jews' role as large-scale merchants and intermediaries. Even though the Jews continued to play a prominent role in Tangier and, as table 36 for the French zone shows, commercial activities of different levels ranked high in the employed Jewish population, the Jews lost their monopoly as the most important intermediaries in most of the vital towns. The emigration of Jews, especially from Spanish Morocco to Latin America, lost the Jews of the north a considerable number of would-be merchants.[233]

Third, a rapidly developing elite class of modern manual craftsmen, and, to a lesser extent, agricultural workers and farmers. The extraordinary representation of women in the dressmaking profession, windowdressing, and laboratory work is largely attributed to the AIU, ORT, and the programs promoted by the alumni associations of the AIU.

Women, social workers, and community leaders were important members of the elite. Regarding women, by 1947 more than twice the number of Jewish women were working in the French zone than had been in 1936. They comprised 15 percent of all Jewish women. This was even higher than the proportion among European women (12.5 percent) and more than twice as high as that for Muslim women (6.4 percent).[234] The reason for this disparity among the communities was that the Muslim woman was the least emancipated; she worked when family conditions were extremely poor and stopped working as soon as a slightly better status had been achieved.[235] Owing to her education at the AIU and other European schools, the Jewish woman, who did not have the same cultural prejudices against outside employment, continued working to help her family pursue the path of social and economic advancement. She was equally active in elite organizations like the AIU alumni associations and *L'Aide Scolaire*.

The expansion of the social workers category, either AIU alumni activists, or the increase in the number of Western-educated elected community leaders, resulted in the introduction of community reforms. There efforts enhanced the work begun by the AIU, and that of the ORT, OSE, and the JDC.

Notes

1. N. Attié to AIU, Safi, March 8, 1918, Arch.AIU.XLVIII.E.729.
2. OSE was originally founded in the ghettos of Russia toward the end of the nineteenth century; subsequently its headquarters moved to Berlin and, in Hitler's time, to Paris.
3. JDC Eleventh Annual Country Directors Conference, report by Samuel L. Haber on Morocco, Paris, October 1956 (JDC/330(a)).
4. Ibid.
5. Ibid.
6. Ibid.
7. Ibid.
8. Ibid.
9. Ibid.
10. Ibid.
11. Stanley Abramovitch: JDC Country Directors Conference, Paris, 1954 (JDC/9(c) 10(a)).
12. Haber, Eleventh Annual Country Directors Conference (above, note 3).
13. Ibid.
14. JDC Memorandum: 1973: (JDC/233(b)).
15. Haber (above, note 3).

16. Ibid.
17. "Le centre social du mellah," *Le Petit Marocain*, 12 août 1953.
18. Rapport OSE-Maroc 1952, Sess. Plén. d'OSE, 15 juillet 1952 (JDC/263(b)).
19. Charles Hamet, La communauté israélite de Tanger (Tanger 1951). Ms. of CHEAM, pp. 62–64.
20. Ibid.
21. Doris Bensimon Donath, *L'evolution de la femme israélite à Fès* (Aix-en-Provence, Faculté des Lettres, no. 25, 1962), pp. 151–152.
22. Haber (above, note 3).
23. "L'école des trachomateux de Casablanca," *Nō'ār*, 3e année, no. 2 (novembre 1, 1949), p. 2.
24. Ibid.
25. Albert Moyal to AIU, Meknes, January 30, 1913, Arch.AIU.XXXII.E.549(a).
26. Moyal to AIU, Meknes, January 24, 1916, Arch.AIU.XXXII.E.549(a).
27. Ibid., January 7, 1918.
28. Ibid.
29. Raphaël Danon to AIU, Marrakesh, January 24, 1913, Arch.AIU.VII.B. no File Number.
30. Albert Benaroya to AIU, Elksar, July 9, 1914, Arch.AIU.XI.E.181.
31. Ibid.
32. Madame A. Benaroya to AIU, Fez, December 19, 1919, Arch.AIU.XII.E.210.
33. Ibid.
34. Stella Toledano to AIU, Fez, March 23, 1937, Arch.AIU.I.B.5.
35. Ibid.
36. Moïse Bibasse to AIU, Marrakesh, December 27, 1939, Arch.AIU.XXIII.E.381.
37. M. Nouvel, "Les camps et colonies de vacanes au Maroc," *Bulletin Economique et Social du Maroc* 8-9, nos. 31–32 (octobre 1946 - janvier 1947), pp. 474–479.
38. Y. D. Sémach to Henri Bertin (French Legation), Tangier, July 26, 1914, A. E. Maroc. II.403.
39. Sémach to AIU, Tangier, April 19, 1925, Arch.AIU.LXII.E.946(e). At the time, English, typing, shorthand and bookkeeping were taught on the coeducational level in the age category of 15 and up. English was subsidized by the Board of Deputies.
40. Haïm Abikssera to AIU, Meknes, January 28, 1925, Arch.AIU.II.B.12.
41. Ibid.
42. Interview with Hanania Dahan, January 26, 1976.
43. In Sefrou alone, out of a Jewish population of 5,000 (approximately 40 percent of Sefrou's Moroccan population in 1934), 500 children frequented the *Em-Habānīm* school while no more than 310 frequented the AIU school (Arch.AIU.LXXVI.E. no File Number, October 29, 1934).
44. Reuben Tajouri to AIU, Meknes, January 9, 1918, Arch.AIU.XXXII.E.559.
45. Daniel Lerner to AIU, Meknes, January 4, 1940, Arch.AIU.XXXII.E.543(b).
46. Ibid., April 21, 1937.
47. Ibid.
48. Sémach to AIU, Tangier, November 12, 1924, Arch.AIU.V.B.24.
49. Hamet, *La communauté israélite de Tanger*, p. 76.
50. Ibid.

51. Ibid., p. 77. The program was divided thus: (1) general education — eighteen hours weekly; (2) Hebrew — six hours weekly; (3) religious instructions — twelve hours weekly.

52. Albert Saguès to AIU, Tangier, April 20, 1936, Arch.AIU.LX.E.943(e).

53. Ibid.

54. *Alliance* to Saguès, April 28, 1936, Arch.AIU.LX.E.943(e).

55. Ibid.

56. Daniel Lerner to AIU, Meknes, December 20, 1931, Arch.AIU.II.B.12.

57. Reuben Tajouri to AIU, Casablanca, November 15, 1929, Arch.AIU.IX.E.172(b).

58. Ibid.

59. 'M. Le Grand Rabbin Liber retour du Maroc," *L'Union Marocaine*, 8e année, no. 114 (mars 31, 1939), p. 1.

60. Interview with Rabbi Ishāq Rouche, Jerusalem, February 9, 1976 (in Hebrew). Rabbi Rouche served as the chief chaplain of Jewish North African volunteers in the war against Germany. He retired as school director after 1956 to be replaced by Emile Sebban.

61. Interview with Rabbi Rouche.

62. Ibid.

63. Ibid. In the beginning when the ENH was in its embryonic stages, and subsidies were still scarce, it was Braunschvig who paid the salaries of the teachers at the ENH out of his own pocket.

64. Rouche, ibid.

65. Interview with Issachar Ben-Ami, Jerusalem, March 8, 1976 (in Hebrew).

66. Ibid.

67. Ibid.

68. "L'école normale hébraïque de l'Oasis," *Nō'ār* 34 (avril 19, 1951), p. 2.

69. Interview with Rabbi Rouche.

70. Interview with Ben-Ami.

71. Rouche, ibid.

72. Ibid.

73. Ben-Ami, ibid.

74. Ibid.

75. Ibid.

76. Rouche, ibid.

77. Ben-Ami, ibid.

78. Ibid.

79. Stanley Abramovitch, "Jewish Education in Morocco," *Jewish Education* vol. 43 no. 1 (Fall 1973), p. 25.

80. Memorandum by Stanley Abramovitch: December 1953 (JDC/9(c)10(a)).

81. Henry Selver to M. Beckelman, December 1, 1955 (JDC/9(c)10(a)).

82. Haber, Eleventh Country Directors Conference, 1956 (JDC/330(a)).

83. Abramovitch: Country Directors Conference, Paris, 1954 (JDC/9(c)10(a)).

84. Abramovitch: February 1954 (JDC/9(c)10(a)).

85. Haber (above, note 82).

86. Interview with Jules Braunschvig, Jerusalem, February 8, 1976 (in English).

87. "Osār ha-Tōra et l'éducation réligieuse de la jeunesse juive marocaine," *Nō'ār*, 3e année, no. 5 (décembre 16–31, 1949), p. 3.

88. Abramovitch, Report on Educational Activities in Morocco, Visit of November 14–December 11, 1952 (JDC/10(b)).

89. Haber (above, note 82).

90. *Beit ha-Osār* (1947/48), p. 2. Published in Morocco. Collection of the Central Archives for the History of the Jewish People, Jerusalem (bilingual, English-French bulletin).

91. J. L. Bensoussan to Isaac Shalom 1950, n.d. (JDC/9(c)10(a)).

92. Moïse Ventura, *For the Establishment of Hebrew Religious Schools and the Improvement of its Existing Institutions* (New York, 1949), p. 6.

93. Ibid.

94. Reuben Tajouri, "L'enseignement de l'hébreu dans les écoles de l'alliance israélite universelle au Maroc," *Cahiers de l'Alliance Israélite Universelle* 18-19 (décembre 1947 - janvier 1948), pp. 7-8.

95. Amram Elmaleh to AIU, Fez, June 26, 1913, Arch.AIU.XII.E.195.

96. Ibid.

97. Elie Bercoff to AIU, Salé, March 31, 1917, Arch.AIU.LXXV.E. no File Number.

98. Ibid.

99. Ibid.

100. Arch.AIU.XXIV.E.392. Marrakesh, December 17, 1936.

101. Moïse Lévy to AIU, Tetuan, February 5, 1937, Arch.AIU.VII.B. no File Number.

102. Ibid.

103. M. Elbaz to AIU, Marrakesh, December 28, 1939, Arch.AIU.XXV.E.396.

104. Ibid.

105. Ibid.

106. Jacques Dahan, "Les communautés israélites du Maroc, " *CAIU* 91 (juin-juillet 1955), p. 11.

107. Reuben Tajouri, "L'année scolaire 1955-1956, dans les écoles de l'AIU au Maroc," *CAIU* 95 (février 1956), pp. 24-25.

108. Ibid., p. 25.

109. Tajouri to AIU, Salé, June 22, 1922, Arch.AIU.LXXV.E. no file number.

110. Ibid.

111. Yahya Zagoury to AIU, Casablanca, June 20, 1925, Arch.AIU.VII.B. no file number. It is noteworthy that in the mid-1920s, Casablanca was gradually replacing Tangier and Mogador as the most important urban, commercial, and economic center. From the Jewish point of view, Casablanca became the most populated community, surpassing Marrakesh. Whereas in 1890 there were no more than 3,000 Jews in Casablanca, there were 85,000 in 1955. This is partly attributed to Jewish migration from the interior, the north, and the south.

112. Félix Guedj, "L'enseignement professionnelle à Casablanca," *L'Avenir Illustré*, numéro spécial (décembre 1928), p. 12.

113. Moïse Bibasse to AIU, Casablanca, June 2, 1925, Arch.AIU.IV.E.87; for Tunisia, where AIU teachers engaged in similar activities, see Jacques Taieb, "Regards sur le Tunis juif de la 'belle epoque' (1895-1913)," *Les Nouveaux Cahiers* 60 (printemps 1980), pp. 41-53.

114. Bibasse, ibid.

115. The alumni associations broadened their field of activities after 1912 by helping the schools establish manual education workshops. They raised funds to subsidize the costs of keeping young men and women in vocational enterprises in the European quarters. In Tangier much of the association's budget, a remarkable amount of 2,250,000 francs (in 1950), was used for that purpose (see, Hamet, *La communauté israélite de Tanger*, pp. 65-66); in Casablanca the alumni during the 1920s placed numerous apprentices in European firms. For example, in 1926 the

alumni in town placed 5 electricians, 19 blacksmiths, 21 printers, 5 carpenters, 11 dressmakers, 2 plumbers, 2 mechanics, 4 typists, and 5 upholsterers (see Arch.AIU., Casablanca, February 22, 1927, IX.E.172(a)); in 1927, the Casablanca alumni placed 110 AIU graduates as apprentices in European factories and provided them with food and a monthly allowance while undergoing training (see Arch.AIU., Casablanca, November 27, 1927, III.E.52); in 1938 the Casablanca alumni placed apprentices among AIU graduates in various enterprises: 6 upholsterers, 4 typographers, 4 bookbinders, 3 electricians, 2 mechanics, 3 carpenters, 1 automobile mechanic (see Arch.AIU., Casablanca, January 12, 1938, X.E.172(g)). While the Tangier alumni operated their program with little outside assistance, the ones situated in French Morocco were, in addition to fundraising, supported by European banks, the AIU, the municipalities, the DIP, and the Jewish communities.

116. Sémach to AIU, Tangier, May 26, 1925, Arch.AIU.LXII.E.946(e).

117. Ibid.

118. Ibid.

119. Reuben Tajouri to AIU, Casablanca, November 24, 1927, Arch.AIU.IX. E.172(a).

120. Ibid.

121. Ibid.

122. Sémach to AIU, Rabat, October 18, 1929, Arch.AIU.XLII.E.717(b).

123. Tajouri to AIU, Casablanca, May 29, 1931, Arch.AIU.IX.E.172(c).

124. Tajouri to AIU, Casablanca, December 9, 1936, Arch.AIU.VII.B. no file number.

125. "Ecole professionnelle israélite de Casablanca," *Bulletin d'Information du Maroc*, (avril 15, 1949), p. 40.

126. Ibid.

127. Albert Gomel, "L'école professionnelle israélite de Fez," *Paix et Droit*, 18e année, no. 6, mensuel (juin 1937), pp. 7–9.

128. "ORT," *Encyclopedia Judaica*, vol. 12, p. 1482.

129. Ibid.

130. Ibid. A substantial portion of the money to fund ORT's activities came from wealthy German-Jewish entrepreneurs. This was in addition to funds raised by the organization through its own initiatives. Since 1945, ORT, like the AIU, has received a large portion of its money for Morocco from the JDC.

131. In 1944, some 500 graduates from these AIU vocational schools, including the Marrakesh agricultural college, were working. Of these 125 obtained diplomas after 2–3 years of training. These gains covered the period 1935–1944. While this was a modest gain, it was important nonetheless (Prosper Cohen, "Rapport sur la situation du judaïsme marocaine presenté au congrès juif mondial," *Conference extraordinaire de guerre*. (Novembre 1944), p. 152; cited from Donath, *Evolution de judaïsme marocain sous le protectorat français*, pp. 27–28.). The convention signed by the AIU and *ORT France* has been renewed and is still in effect.

132. D. Alberstein, *The Activities of ORT in Morocco*. ORT Union, Central Bureau (Geneva, 1969). Ms. of ORT, a valuable primary source.

133. Ibid.

134. Ibid.

135. Ibid; see also "Les activités de l'ORT au Maroc," *La Voix des Communautés* (octobre 1955), p. 3.

136. Alberstein (above, note 132).

137. Ibid.

138. Ibid.

139. Ibid.

140. Ibid. According to ORT data, from June 1947 to Decembe 31, 1968, 20,443 students attended all ORT schools in Morocco; of this number, 10,245 completed their studies successfully through diplomas and 1,484 completed normal training.

141. The Gharb is a fertile rural region within the confines of the former French zone, bordering on the former Spanish zone near Elksar.

142. Sémach to AIU, Tangier, April 26, 1926, Arch.AIU.LXII.E.946(e).

143. Ibid.

144. Sémach to AIU, Rabat, August 15, 1936, Arch.AIU.XLV.E.717(j).

145. Ibid.

146. Ibid.

147. Alfred Goldenberg to AIU, Marrakesh, December 10, 1936, Arch.AIU. XXIV.E.407. The vast school building was leased by the AIU from the protectorate, as was a sizable plot of land on the town's outskirts (with an olive grove) for field work. The land of Marrakesh was particularly fertile, and the settling of French farmers in this region enabled the school's graduates to find employment as cultivators, farmers, and managers.

148. Alfred Goldenberg, "La vie dans les écoles de l'alliance israélite: comment fonctionne l'école horticole de Marrakesh, "*Paix et Droit*, 17e année, no. 1, mensuel (janvier 1937), p. 9.

149. Ibid.

150. Goldenberg to AIU, Marrakesh, March 26, 1939, Arch.AIU.XXIV.E.407.

151. Ibid.

152. Ibid. In 1950, no fewer than fifty students attended the school.

153. *Ecole professionnelle agricole de l'AIU. Marrakesh: programmes et horaires des divers enseignements et travaux aprés 1945.* Data prepared for this study by the AIU (*Itthād*) delegation in Morocco.

154. Pierre Flamand, *Les communautés israélites du sud marocain* (Imprimeries réunis Rabat, 1959), p. 50.)

155. Bashan, *Jewish Craftsmen*, p. 14.

156. "Les écoles de l'alliance israélite: les écoles du *bled* au Maroc," *Paix et Droit*, 15e année, no. 8, mensuel (octobre 1935), p. 10.

157. Ibid.

158. Ibid.

159. Arch.AIU., Ber-Rechid, April 3, 1929, II.E.29.

160. Ibid., January 3, 1929.

161. Alfred Goldenberg to AIU, Demnat, February 15, 1937, Arch.AIU.II.E.40.

162. "A propos les marriages précoces," *Paix et Droit*, 17e année, no. 4, mensuel (avril 1937), p. 10.

163. Ibid.

164. "Enquête dans la région sud de Marrakesh: tournée du Tafilalt," *CAIU*, nos. 40–41 (février-mars 1950), p. 8.

165. *IIIe concile des grands rabbins du Maroc: recommendations* (Rabat 1948), p. 29, cited from Donath, *Evolution du judaïsme marocain*, p. 76.

166. "Ecoles de *l'alliance israélite*: les écoles du *bled* au Maroc," *Paix et Droit*, 15e année, no. 8, mensuel (octobre 1935), p. 10.

167. See, for instance, Arch.AIU., Boujad, May 7, 1932, II.E.40.

168. In Casablanca before 1945, there were *cours complémentaires* and vocational school of the AIU.

169. See Alfred Goldenberg, "A Teacher in the *Bled*," *Alliance Review* 46 (fall 1975), p. 32.

170. Pierre Flamand, *Un mellah en pays Berbère: Demnate* (Paris, 1952), p. 25.

171. David Corcos, "Les prénoms des Juifs du Maroc," *Studies in the History of the Jews of Morocco* (Rubin Mass: Jerusalem, 1976), p. 180-181.

172. Goldenberg above note 169), p. 33.

173. Interview with Haïm Zafrani, Paris, May 17, 1976, pt. i, (in French.)

174. Table 29 excludes towns and hamlets in the *bled* not affected by the AIU but rather by the OH and AYI schools.

175. Table 29.

176. Ibid.

177. *Etat des effectifs des écoles de l'AIU au Maroc: Statistiques du 10 novembre 1954.* Unpublished data.

178. H. Z. Hirschberg, *Me-Eres Mēvō ha-Shēmēsh* (Jerusalem: Goldberg Press, 1957), pp. 101-102, 108, 119.

179. See, for instance, "Extension des services de l'OSE au Maroc," *Nō'ar*, 4e année, no. 12 (Avril 16, 1949), p. 1. As for *bled* women, Grinker noted that during his visits to the Atlas communities, he found the women to be of vital importance: "They are active in agriculture, particularly in harvesting. This is in addition to their role in the household: cooking, baking, washing and so on." Yehuda Grinker, The Emigration of Atlas Jewry to Israel (Tel-Aviv: Association of Moroccan Immigrants in Israel, 1973), p. 30.

180. Vitalis Eskenazi to AIU, Midelt, October 5, 1928, Arch.AIU.XXXIII.E.564.

181. Ibid.

182. Ibid.

183. Eskenazi to AIU, Midelt, March 29, 1929, Arch.AIU.XXXIII.E.564.

184. Ibid.

185. Ibid.

186. Ibid.

187. Hirschberg, *Me-Eres Mēvō ha-Shēmēsh*, p. 135.

188. Moïse Ventura, *For the Establishment of Hebrew Religious Schools and the Improvement of its Existing Educational Institutions* (New York, 1949), p. 6.

189. M. Lugassy: Report, Amizmiz, November 29, 1955 (JDC/9(c)10(a).

190. Donath, *L'evolution de la femme israélite à Fès*, p. 116.

191. Donath, *Evolution du judaïsme marocain sous le protectorat*, p. 76.

192. Hirschberg, *Me-Eres Mēvō ha-Shēmēsh*, p. 192.

193. Ibid.

194. *Ille concile des grands rabbins du Maroc: Recommendations*, 1948. p. 29, cited from Donath, *Evolution du judaïsme marocain sous le protectorat* p. 76.

195. *IVe concile des grands rabbins du Maroc*, 10-11 juin 1952, *Recommendations*, p. 14, cited from Donath, *evolution du judaïsme*, p. 79.

196. Interview with Rabbi David Ovadia, Jerusalem, February 16, 1976 (in Hebrew). According to Ovadia, this reform took place after 1945.

197. Ibid.

198. Rabbi David Ovadia, *The Jewish Community of Sefrou*, III, p. 219 (in Hebrew).

199. Ibid., p. 91.

200. Ibid.

201. *Ve concile des rabbins: recommendations* (Rabat 1953), p. 16, cited from donath, *Evolution du judaïsme*, p. 27.

202. J. C. Goulven, *Les mellahs de Rabat-Salé.* (Paris, 1927), p. 111.

203. Albert Saguès to AIU, Tangier, May 7, 1939, Arch.AIU.IV.E.24.

204. *Gouvernement Chérifien, Service Central des Statistiques, Recensement Général de la Population en 1951–1952*, Vol. IV, pp. 21, 110–111.

205. Ibid. See, for instance, Attal's comprehensive study "Population Census in Morocco," *Be Tefūsōt ha-Gōla* (Spring 1964), p. 43 (in Hebrew).

206. Attal, ibid.

207. Between 1951 and 1960, not less than 90,000 Jews left the country, mainly for Israel and France. It would be difficult to deduce the rate of literacy for emigrants as compared to those who remained, based on the comparative data of the 1951 and 1960 census. This is because the 1951 data applied to the French zone only whereas the 1960 data covered the whole country.

208. Comparing Jews and Muslims in their *literacy rates* in the age range of 10–29 (from children to young adults) we find (Royaume du Maroc [1960 census statistics], pp. 31–32): (1) *age category 10–14*, 81.9 percent for Jews, 29.8 percent for Muslims; (2) *age category 15–19*, 75.1 percent for Jews, 19.9 percent for Muslims; (3) *age category 20–29*, 62.6 percent for Jews, 11.3 percent for Muslims.

209. Blandin, "La population de Tanger en 1940," *Revue Africaine* 88 (1944), p. 97. Blandin related that in 1940 there were in Tangier 10,000 Jews, 37,000 Muslims, 14,000 Spaniards, 2,500 Frenchmen, 1,200 Italians, 800 Englishmen, 350 Portuguese, and other diverse elements (mostly consular personnel) which amounted to an additional 300. The coming of Jewish refugees from Eastern and Central Europe to Tangier in the late 1930s, strengthened the Jewish community with an additional 2,000 people. See also p. 115.

210. Iaraël Benaroya to AIU, Mazagan, July 23, 1914, Arch.AIU.XXVIII.E.461.

211. Ibid.

212. Ibid.

213. Ibid.

214. 'Abd al-Krīm was a Berber rebel in the Rif mountains of the north; he sought to eliminate the colonial presence and expansion of Spain (and France) in Morocco. It took the combined military efforts of the Spaniards and the French to contain and defeat this rebel, during the years 1921–1926.

215. Blandin, "La population de Tanger en 1940," p. 104.

216. Donath, *Evolution du judaïsme marocain sous le protectorat*, p. 41.

217. Waterbury, *The Commander of the Faithful* (New York, Columbia University Press, 1970), p. 33.

218. Abdelkader Benabdallah, "La politique française a l'égard des juifs marocains," *L'Opinion*, août 29, 1976, pt. I.

219. The table of the 1951 census deals with the occupational structure in the *urban* areas (see table 36); in French the census refers to the occupational structure as *Population active urbaine israélite et musulmane—26 groups*, namely, it refers to *employment* only. Furthermore, the age groups used to determine percentages of the employed population are usually 15–65. In this census, the French formulation used reads thus: *Moins de 15 ans* and ends with. *70 ans et plus*.

220. *Gouvernement Cherifien, service central des statistiques, recensement général de la population en 1951–1951*, Vol. IV, p. 80. See table 36.

221. Ibid.

222. Ibid., Vol. III, p. 34; see table 36.

223. Ibid.

224. Ibid., Vol. IV, p. 80; see table 36.

225. Ibid.

226. Ibid., Vol. III, p. 34; see table 36.

227. Ibid.

228. Ibid., Vol. IV, pp. 68–76.

229. Ibid., pp. 74–76.

230. Ibid. Employed population in this category refers to three elements of the employed: the "patrons," the salaried, and the apprentices. Of the 25,693 total employed Jewish artisans and craftsmen in the French zone, 6,300 were women. The overwhelming majority of the latter were in clothing (dressmaking and tailoring).

231. *Gouvernement Cherifien, service central des statistiques,* pp. 66–73.

232. Donath, *Evolution du judaïsme marocain sous le protectorat,* pp. 47–48.

233. In Spanish Morocco it is evident, despite incomplete census statistics on the occupational structure, that many AIU graduates, including those who continued their secondary French education in Tangier, Algeria or France, usually migrated to the French zone and Tangier. However, the bulk of them, as was the case during the nineteenth century, made their way to Latin America. Most Jewish inhabitants of the Spanish zone continued to exercise the old professions, mostly as small merchants and artisans. The activities of ORT in Tetuan (1956–1963) cultivated a small manual crafts elite of several hundred people. For the most part, however, the pre-1956 period did not reveal progress in this area because Jewish attendance in the protectorate vocational schools was minimal.

234. Chouraqui, *Between East and West: A History of the Jews in North Africa* (Philadelphia: The Jewish Publication Society of America, 1968), p. 225.

235. Ibid.

CHAPTER VIII

The Jews and the Muslims: Comparative Aspects of Education and Problems of Social Conflict

Education

Jewish and Muslim traditional education was similar: the Jews attended the *talmūdē tōra* and *ṣlā*s, while the Muslims attended Quranic schools. Both were taught by indigenous teachers: rabbi-teachers in the Jewish schools and *fqih*s in their Muslim counterparts. The educational approach of both was basically the same, recitation and repetition of biblical passages for the Jews, and Quranic verses for the Muslims. One taught Hebrew and the other Arabic, following basically similar pedagogical approaches. Like the Jewish schools, the *msid*s were largely attended by poorer children, whereas Muslim leaders, like their Jewish counterparts, often hired private tutors for religious and traditional studies. Moreover, like the rabbis in the Jewish schools, the *fqih*s were often pedagogically outmoded but well informed about the religious traditions and language. Similar to the rabbi-teachers, the *fqih*s were socially inferior in their communities. Roger Gaudefroy-Demombynes argued that although the *msid* teacher was vital to the community, he was not sufficiently paid by the youths' parents, and often, like his Jewish counterpart, had to supplement his earnings by becoming a small merchant or a craftsman.[1]

Both types of traditional schools were community sponsored for the most part. Some Jewish schools received the benefits of the religious endowments known as *heqdēsh*, while the *msid*s were subsidized from the benefits of the Islamic endowment known in Moroccco as *hubus* and in the Middle East as *waqf*. Once primary education was completed the youths coming from rabbinic and other influential families were usually admitted to *yeshīvōt*. The youths belonging to prominent Muslim families and the religious scholarly elite (the *'ulamā'*) would proceed to the reputable *madrasas* of Fez and Marrakesh, and some would continue their higher education at the *Qarawīyīn* in Fez, the most noted high Islamic studies university in the Maghrib. The youths of the masses in both communities would usually follow their fathers' footsteps in traditional jobs.

An evolution of hereditary social, economic, cultural, and intellectual hierarchies occurred first among the Jews. The penetration of the AIU to Morocco beginning in 1862 opened new horizons for Jews of all classes. The Muslims did not fare as well as the Jews, partly because they did not have the advantage of modern schools in their communities fifty years before the coming of the protectorates. After 1912 when the protectorates set up modern schools for Muslims in all three zones, many Muslims were at first suspicious of European intentions, particularly of French policies. Their suspicions, though diminishing somewhat in the 1920s and 1930s, were attributed in part to great misgivings about sending their youths to modern schools whose teachers — until the 1930s — were mostly French, with the exception of the personnel responsible for Arabic and Islamic studies. For the Jews, however, the AIU, both through the schools and through political efforts on their behalf, became a guide for positive changes and contacts with the West. Its teachers, moreover, were Jewish. And whereas the French, especially during the 1920s, did not wish to see the Jews advance too far along the path of French civilization, the Jews felt encouraged to adapt to European education in order to better their social and economic conditions. The Muslims, on the other hand, were considered more dangerous by the Europeans in general and the French in particular. They were not particularly encouraged to attend modern schools in considerable numbers and consequently, with traditional opposition to secular schools emanating from indigenous circles, and the French policy of maintaining the status quo, Muslims lagged considerably behind the Jews in European acculturation. Despite French advocacy in its colonies and protectorates of the *mission civilisatrice* and the *conquête morale*, French eduation and its benefits influenced a small elite among the Muslims.

In fact, the French policy toward Muslims was contrary to what the AIU was permitted to accomplish among the Jews. The French, due to Lyautey's and Gaston Loth's planning, set up franco-Muslim schools on the elementary level for the youths of prominent families, known as *écoles des fils de notables; écoles urbaines* for the youths of Muslim artisans; and *écoles rurales* for Arab and Berber youths coming from the rural and agricultural sectors. Lyautey's idea was to maintain a *belle hierarchie*, a system of preserving the social and political status quo of Moroccan Muslim society and therefore, he and Loth envisaged the creation of an educational system that would correspond to the existing hierarchy of the society. Consequently, the graduates of these French protectorate schools went different ways afterwards: the urban schools' graduates entered the family trade or a vocational high school; the rural schools' graduates went into their parents' profession of agriculture and farming, whereas the youths of prominent families

enrolled in the *collèges musulmanes*, high schools established by the protectorate in Fez, Casablanca, Rabat, and even in Azrou of the *bled*, exclusively
for Muslims. The components of the Muslim intellectual elite were eventually recruited from the *collèges* for bureaucratic employment, mostly in
the *makhzan*'s institutional hierarchies but also to an extent in the protectorate's administrative apparatus.[2] In other words, an artisan remained an
artisan, a peasant remained a peasant, and the middle classes, the
distinguished, and the wealthy retained their status also. The European colonies in Morocco, on the other hand, sent their children to the *écoles
européennes*, with Jews and Muslim being accepted into these primary and
secondary schools on a more selective basis (See Tables 38 and 39).

The AIU, however, by integrating Jews of different socioeconomic
backgrounds in its classrooms before and after 1912, and by not placing
them in hierarchical educational formations as was the case with the
Franco-Muslim schools, enabled its graduates of even humble origins to
become part of a Western-educated elite, an elite which was composed of
legendary school directors, community activists, and civic leaders. Even
though the Franco-Jewish schools (*écoles franco-israélites*) — established
during the First World War to compete with, and neutralize, the
AIU — were part of the *belle hierarchie* model developed by Lyautey, they,
too, were not as divided as the Franco-Muslim schools, for Jewish children
of various backgrounds were integrated into them regardless of social class.
Interestingly, though Muslim leaders of the nationalist movement (since
1930) who graduated from the *collèges* or French *lycées* were usually from
relatively affluent families (for example, Aḥmad Balafrej, Muhammad al-
Kholti, and Muḥammad al-Wazani), AIU elementary, *cours complémentaire*, and ENIO graduates (for example, S. D. Lévy, Moïse Nahon, Amram
Elmaleḥ) originated from middle and lower-middle classes; but owing to the
policy pursued by the AIU in the pre-1912 period and during the protectorate era after 1912, graduates of its schools were able to improve their lot
in spite of different social and economic backgrounds.

The French insistence on preserving the traditional hierarchies and

Table 38. Comparative Muslim-Jewish-European Enrollment in
Primary French Schools Intended for Europeans

Group	1945	1946	1947	1948	1949	1950
Muslims	849	1171	816	1114	1528	1867
Jews	1132	1230	1342	1479	1833	1939
Europeans	32346	33568	36568	39704	43238	46805

SOURCE: *Direction de l'Instruction Publique au Maroc: Bilan 1945-1950*. Ecole du Livre
(Rabat, 1950), pp. 146-158.

Table 39. Breakdown of Muslim and Jewish Attendance (French Zone)
(Lycées for Europeans)

Group	1938	1939	1940	1941	1942	1943	1944	1945	1946	1947	1948
Muslims	366	343	350	283	307	241	273	393	477	649	738
Jews	823	831	759	435	512	515	610	619	754	884	928

SOURCE: André Chouraqui, *La condition juridique de l'israélite marocain* (Paris: Presses du Livre Français, 1950), p. 241.

their refusal to allot more time for Arabic in the Moroccan school systems in the pre-1945 period, was a contradiction which dated from the early days of the Lyautey administration. Further, Lyautey's policies of maintaining the status quo in Moroccan society were bound to alienate segments of the indigenous population. Moroccan Muslims who were taught French at the rural and urban schools, for instance, would be told they could not enroll in a *collège* but only in a secondary vocational or agricultural school. Muslim alienation from the protectorate because of educational policies was also evident among the French educated, due to the failure to integrate—at least during the pre-1945 period—the Muslims from various socioeconomic backgrounds, in the elementary and secondary (*lycées*) schools intended for Europeans. In *Majallat al-Maghrib*, an Arabic-language journal, several articles appeared during the 1930s calling for reform in the Franco-Muslim school system. One individual wrote in 1933 that the French protectorate ought to promote free access for Muslims to the French *lycées* and not confine them to the prescribed *collèges musulmanes*.[3] He also advocated that more emphasis be given in the Franco-Muslim schools to Arabic education, to reflect Morocco's Islamic past.[4] Though not expressing the desire voiced by later nationalists, for separation from France, but rather requesting reforms (like other nationalists of the pre-1935 period), he had hoped to see greater balance between Islamo-Arabic and secular education at the *collèges musulmanes* themselves, observing:

I say this and I do not wish that what I say is misunderstood: [as if] I am against French education and the French language. Indeed, it is necessary for us and our country; and the French language is dear to us. But [Arabic] . . . is dearer, because it is the language of the Maghrib and . . . of its religion . . . .[5]

This call for Arabic education and the plea for greater Muslim attendance of the schools intended for the European populations was in some ways similar to the pleas of Moroccan Zionists like S. D. Lévy to the AIU to attach great significance to contemporary Jewish culture and spoken

Hebrew. However, whereas the Muslims insisted that Arabic be the language of instruction in all schools, the Māgēn-Dāvīd and Charles Netter associations accepted and respected the fact that French remained the language of instructions at the AIU. The position of the Muslim nationalists over Arabic was most obvious, as that language had always been spoken by the Arabs.

When the French protectorate did not heed Muslim demands, a segment of the nationalists represented by charismatic figures such as 'Alāl al-Fāsī known for his deep devotion to Islam, reacted by supporting the "Free Schools." The Free School movement gained momentum during the 1930s and 1940s and was supported by Sultan Muḥammad V, French- and Spanish-educated intellectuals, and Muslim reformists (salafists) who wanted to cleanse Islam of its impurities. Once this was achieved, they argued, Islam could select ideas and techniques from the West without risking irresponsible secularization. The founders of these schools devised a curriculum based on Islamic studies and French, and in 1952 successfully enrolled 20,000 youths.[6] Yet even if they disliked the policies of the Franco-Muslim schools, they were equally disenchanted with the outmoded msids. They won support among Muslims with secular tendencies who lost patience with the French protectorate's educational and political policies. Like Muslim traditional and modern intellectuals, the Jewish leaders of Māgēn-Dāvīd and Charles Netter resented the pedagogical policies of the old-fashioned rabbinic schools, and together with the AIU, as we have seen, they pressured the old schools to become modernized. Like the Muslims, Jewish intellectuals could be found who were inclined to criticize the Lyautey belle hierarchie for Morocco which deprived Jews of privileges that their Algerian counterparts had obtained. At the same time, however, despite Jewish and Muslim intellectuals who voiced their desires to benefit from Western culture, most of these were unwilling to emulate the West blindly. Finally, both Muslim nationalists and Zionists transformed their French schools' alumni associations into centers for political activities. Consequently the Association des Anciens Elèves de Collège d'Azrou and its counterparts in Fez, Meknes, and elsewhere organized discussions and nationalist activities whereas the AIU alumni associations in Casablanca, Tangier, and Fez were transformed into centers for the dissemination of Zionist ideas.

Enrollment in the AIU schools rose from 160 to 1862 to over 33,000 in 1955, due to their popularity and as a result of French and JDC support. Muslim enrollment in the protectorates' schools remained low, especially in the French zone, in proportion to the youth population of school age. Despite the different types of protectorate schools, there were only 42,000 Muslim youths in the French zone in 1945, 114,000 in 1950, and 187,000 in 1955, when there were 1,360,000 such children of elementary school age in the zone, meaning that only 14 percent of them were enrolled.[7]

The low enrollment levels of Muslims in French-type schools was criticized by both Muslim intellectuals and by those French-educated Jews who sought to arrive at a Judeo-Muslim *rapprochement*. One such Jew was Jacques Dahan, a dynamic leader of Casablancan Jewry and, at least during the 1950s, a firm advocate of Moroccan national independence. At an AIU gathering in Paris (1955) he sharply criticized Lyautey's social hierarchies as sharpenings divisions in Moroccan society:

> Lyautey had very particular ideas and I had the occasion to say once that he had engaged in what may be referred to as "political romanticism." He had a hierarchical conception of the society . . . . [He believed] in separate elements, and within each element [he believed in] subelements; and therefore, instead of [achieving] a progressive fusion of all the elements of the society, there remained the status quo as well as a juxtaposition of the elements of the population, [instead of] coexistence, and that has been very unfortunate, I must say, for our community.[8]

Finally, in the French zone, educating girls and higher education were topics of interest to some educated people. Neither Jews before the arrival of the AIU in 1862, nor the Muslims until 1912, were eager to see their daughters obtain formal education. The religious Jewish schools, like their Quranic counterparts, usually admitted only boys, with the girls receiving the rudiments of traditional education from the women at home. In modern times, however, both Jews and educated Muslims would point out their respective religions did not interfere with or prohibit girls from receiving schooling. Moroccan Jews, for instance, pointed out that the daughters of influential rabbis did receive traditional education long before 1862, though they were few in number; Muslims advanced similar arguments. For example, one writer remarked in 1935 that there was nothing in any Islamic doctrine opposing education of girls.[9] Another wrote that the Prophet Muḥammad himself was a staunch supporter of educating girls and believed that all women, his wives included, should be well versed in the *Qur'ān*; he noted that in the ninth century, Fez was an important center for educated women, who studied Islamic literature.[10] Just as influential Moroccan rabbis insisted that secular and profane education for girls was essential to meet the demands of post-1912 Morocco, the Muslim author of the above-mentioned argument believed that female illiteracy was now anachronistic.[11] (For data on comparative Jewish-Muslim Girls' Attendance in the French *lycée* of Fez, see Table 40).

Though there are hardly any data on higher education, aside from some information about a few institutions created in the protectorate period, modern higher education in Morocco was underdeveloped, with the exception of specialized institutes in Rabat or the Spanish zone. Selected in-

Table 40. Comparative Jewish-Muslim Girls' Attendance in French Lycées: Fez (1957–1960)

Year	Jewish Girls	Muslim Girls
1957	143	91
1958	168	105
1959	160	106
1960	180	90

SOURCE: Doris Bensimon Donath, *L'evolution de la femme israélite à Fès* (Aix-en-Provence: Faculté des Lettres, no. 25, 1962), p. 141.

dividuals among Jews and Muslims went to French and Spanish universities. One source indicated that in 1954 there were only 350 lawyers in the French zone: 302 Europeans, 27 Muslims, and 21 Jews.[12] Whereas it is doubtful that many Jews and Muslims had obtained the *baccalauréat* or its equivalent in the French, Spanish, and International zones, there can be no doubt that the number of Jews attending AIU-sponsored *cours complémentaires*, *lycées*, and the general education section of ORT-AIU was comparatively higher than the number of the Muslims, who were poorly represented in all secondary-type schools.

The International and Spanish zones were similar to the French zone. Beginning with Tangier, most of the schools attended by Muslim, Jews, and Europeans were French-sponsored and in part subsidized by the zone's authorities. Aside from French schools, including the AIU, there were the Spanish schools, both elementary and secondary. The data in Table 41 furnished by M. de la Girardière in 1947, gives an idea on enrollment which clarifies that the Jewish population in the zone was proportionally better represented in French-sponsored schools (elementary and secondary) than the Muslims. Whereas the Muslim population of the town (1947) stood at 40,000, only 1,355 of their youths attended modern French schools.[13] Jewish school enrollment stood at 1,325 out of a total Jewish population of 12,000. Others attended traditional schools, though no data are available. Table 42, on the other hand, shows that in 1947 there were no Jews attending the Spanish schools. And though occasionally Jews attended *Lycée Alphonzo XIII*, they were few in number. This indicates that Jews (like Muslims) preferred the French schools. There were English and Italian schools not mentioned by de la Girardière. However, it is not clear if more than a handful of Jews or Muslims attended them. The Jews, at least, were hardly in need for an English school because the language was offered at the AIU. In the Hispano-Muslim schools in Tangier, which were modelled slightly on the hierarchical model of Lyautey, the language of instruction was Arabic, and Spanish and French were secondary in importance.

Table 41. Jewish-Muslim Enrollment in French Schools: Tangier (1947)

Types of Schools	Number of pupils	Muslims	Jews	Observations
Franco-Muslim (Primary)	1153	1153	-	Seven schools
French schools (Primary)	128	28	100	
French schools (Secondary)	465	154	311	Lycées Regnault and Saint-Aulaire École Professionnelle
AIU	914	-	914	Two primary schools and a *cours complémentaire*
Total:	2660	1335	1325	

SOURCE: M.de la Girardière, *Rapport sur les institutions sociales et d'enseignement mises à la disposition de la population marocaine* (Tanger, 1947), p. 15 (MS of CHEAM).

The French-sponsored vocational high school in Tangier offered a sound manual education for both Jews and Muslims in carpentry, mechanics, electricity, and drafting in a three-year program leading to the *diplôme d'apprentissage*.[14] At *Lycée Regnault*, both Jews and Muslims could prepare for the *brevet commercial* in bookkeeping, office work, typing, and stenography instead of pursuing the *baccalauréat*.[15] At the *lycée* in 1947 there were 156 Jews and 74 Muslims taking courses in office work, bookkeeping, English, Spanish, economics, geography, and arithmetic.[16]

As for the Spanish zone, from the census taken in 1949–50 there were 1,294 Jewish youths enrolled at the AIU and the *Hebreo-Español* schools of Tetuan, Larache, Elksar, and Arzila — or 89.2 percent of Jewish youths of elementary school age.[17] In secondary education, Jews who graduated from the AIU often moved to Tangier, the French zone, or to Algeria to continue their education. The only important secondary school for Jews in the Spanish zone was the rabbinic *Instituto Maimonides* at Tetuan, created in 1947. In 1948–49 only eighteen students were trained at the institute where they enrolled in advanced courses pertaining to Jewish law, Hebrew, Arabic, Spanish, and French.[18]

For the Muslims, there were the Free Schools, the *msids*, and the *madrasas*. In 1949 there were 502 students attending the *madrasas*.[19] At the Madrid-sponsored Hispano-Muslim schools, there were 4,836 youths attending primary schools in the major towns: 2,531 boys and 2,305 girls; for the rural schools in the countryside, 1,567 boys and 63 girls attended Hispano-

Table 42. Jewish-Muslim Enrollment in Spanish Schools: Tangier (1947)

Types of Schools	Number of pupils	Muslims	Jews	Observations
Hispano-Muslim (Primary)	268	268	-	Girls' school
Hispano-Muslim (Primary)	197	197	-	Boys' school
Spanish schools	127	127	-	Primary and secondary schools, including Lycée Alphonso XIII
Spanish schools (Private)	68	68	-	
Total	660	660	0	

SOURCE: M.de la Girardière, *Rapport sur les institutions sociales et d'enseignement mises à la disposition de la population marocaine* (Tanger, 1947), p. 15 (MS of CHEAM).

Muslim schools in fourteen locales.[20] The 63 girls were enrolled at Farhana and Tamasint.[21] We do not have complete data to determine what percentage of Muslims of school age were enrolled in these schools. However, it is obvious that in rural locales, the girls were noticeably underrepresented. Although data are not abundant, there is enough information to assess Jewish-Muslim enrollment in Spanish-zone high schools, shown in Table 43 for the years 1940–1949.

Finally, although the Muslims were not always well represented in the Spanish schools as they should have been, it appears that the Spaniards showed greater respect for Islamic traditions and culture than the French.

Table 43. Secondary Education in the Spanish Zone: Jews, Muslims and Spaniards: 1940–1949

Year	Spaniards	Muslims	Jews
1940–41	773	27	108
1941–42	1178	40	46
1942–43	1253	17	46
1943–44	1287	17	53
1944–45	1176	21	40
1945–46	1125	23	80
1946–47	1037	9	48
1947–48	1114	9	88
1948–49[a]	679	13	33

SOURCE: *Presidencia del Gobierno Instituto Nacional de Estadistica. Zona de Protectorado, 1949/50*, p. 388.
[a]Figures for Tetuan only.

Unlike the French zone schools the Hispano-Muslim schools of the protectorate were often directed by Muslims.[22] The language of instruction of all courses—with the exception of home economics, music, and physical education—was Arabic.[23] The Spanish authorities, however, had a different policy vis-à-vis the Jews. Jews attending the primary *Hebreo-Español* schools had Spanish as language of instruction. Protectorate officials considered this policy to be justifiable, for many of the Jews in their zone of influence were of Spanish ancestry. Thus Hebrew and Arabic were not taught extensively (if at all) in the Spanish schools designed for Jews. The teaching of Hebrew and French at the AIU schools was not especially welcomed by the Spanish authorities: they tried unsuccessfully to deter the AIU from teaching in any other language but Spanish.

In conclusion, while the colonial authorities, mainly in French Morocco, did not go out of their way to encourage Muslims to attend protectorate schools and certainly not the ones intended for the European population, the Muslims, apart from the educated elite, were far from unanimously favoring sending their youths to these schools.

The Problem of Social Conflict

The educational progress of the Jews before and after 1912, the social consequences of the cultural and educational diversity among Muslims and Jews, the policies of the colonial systems, and the activities of the AIU in all aspects of communal and educational activities deepened the already existing divisions between these two peoples.

Muslim intellectual reaction to the colonial system in the late 1930s leaned toward separation from France and Spain, especially France, once it was evident that the colonial authorities did not welcome the idea of having the Muslims benefit from diverse aspects of modernization. Thus, articles expressing political and social reconciliation that appeared in the early nationalist journals such as *L'Action du Peuple*, were replaced after the late 1930s by political slogans far less well disposed to the brand of nationalism that once advocated cooperation with and integration into, the protectorate apparatus; they called for increasing separation from the colonial presence. Even the old nationalist movement of the early 1930s, the *Comité d'Action Marocaine*, aiming at bringing about, by legal methods, autonomy for Morocco within the famework of the protectorate system, was dwarfed after 1937 by more revolutionary parties. French determination to exile radical leaders and, in 1953, Sultan Muhammad V as well, because of the latter's sympathies for the nationalists' activities, did not preserve the political status quo. The French had to release all exiles and eventually, together with Spain and other powers, had to succumb to the nationalist desire for independence.

On the eve of Moroccan independence, most Jews felt uneasy in the wake of nationalist victories over colonialism, for they feared negative Muslim reactions toward themselves. Their fears were clearly justified because the Muslim intellectual and nationalist elite, composed on the one hand of *lycée* and *collège* graduates and of former students of the *Qarawīīn* in Fez, on the other, were not merely angry over divide-and-rule policies manifested in the Berber *ẓahīr* of 1930 and other French decisions such as the imposition of surveillance, arrests, and exiles. They resented the determination and zeal of indigenous elements, notably the Jews, who sometimes went out of their way to identify and collaborate with the colonial authorities. The Jews' growing contacts with Zionist ideas and activities aggravated Judeo-Muslim relations further. These developments placed the Jews between two forces that were partners and adversaries, the colonialists and the colonized. The Jews were then accused of organizing into a separate group and, to make the situation worse, were asked by the nationalists to choose sides. As will be seen in chapter IX, in the post-1956 period a minority of Jews opted for a Judeo-Muslim entente (*wifāq*) whereas most Jews chose the French and the Zionist idea over the Muslims. Most of the pressure on the Jews derived from the radical wing of the *Istiqlāl* (Independence) Party, founded in 1944 and destined to become in the 1950s Morocco main advocate of independence.

Though certain forces within the *Istiqlāl*, including political radicals such as Mahdi ben Barka, refrained from pushing the Jews into a corner, the majority of members did not hesitate to accentuate the "negative" role played by the Jews in aiding French colonial and Zionist interests, sometimes even suggesting that Jews were *both* French and Zionist agents. And in the "plots" planned against the Moroccan people, according to *Istiqlāl* spokesmen, the AIU emerged as a most prominent villain.

Aware of the activities of the AIU the *Istiqlālists* resented the AIU's presence in the *mellāḥs*, its past political lobbyings, and its close ties with France. They attacked the organization in their press and some went so far as to suggest that thanks to the AIU, Judeo-Muslim ties were irreparably damaged, and that the Jews were brainwashed and acculturated by the AIU to despise everything that was Moroccan, traditional, and Islamic.

A classic example of this resentment could be found in two articles of Abdelkader Benabdallah, an *Istiqlālist* and editorialist for the party's newspaper, *L'Opinion*. Though written in 1976, twenty years after independence, Benabdallah echoed the positions of *Istiqlālists* of the past. The articles reveal a two-pronged attack on the AIU: one intending to depict the organization's members as agents of French colonial penetration before 1912; and one accusing these agents of aiding French and Zionist interests and consequently, *creating* a Judeo-Muslim separation. On the role of the AIU members he observed:

It would be quite erroneous to downplay the contribution of the *Alliance* to the advancement of French colonialism in Morocco. Encouraged by the French government, the *Alliance* became a powerful force in Morocco, capable of obtaining the necessary information the French needed to penetrate country, long before the creation of the protectorate. We know that until 1912 it was virtually impossible for the Europeans to wander inside Morocco, particularly in the unsafe interior. Those who did were generally spotted and wound up being driven out. In other words, the services rendered by the *Alliance* school directors long before the protectorate, became a precious instrument for the colonialists in Paris. Owing to the presence of the *Alliance* schools in nearly all the major towns, France had in her service, a network of loyal informers and spies across the land. The information forwarded by these *Alliance* agents enabled the French to properly plan the opportune time for the penetration of the country.[24]

Benabdallah's argument was farfetched. Although the AIU envisaged many opportunities under French or another colonial presence in Morocco, including a protectorate system, and in fact welcomed these developments, there is no evidence that school directors served the powers with "information" to penetrate Morocco. The relations between the representatives of the powers and the AIU were most cordial. These, however, were confined to the issue of insuring political security for Jews in distress.

In his second attack, Benabdallah portrayed the AIU as an instrument of both colonialism and Zionism, despite the ideological conflicts between the two phenomena:

Numerous are the Jews who were victims of the operations of this organization and have consequently felt like foreigners rather than Moroccans. Having lost all contact with their Muslim compatriots, these westernized Jews were in fact overwhelmed by a genuine persecution complex, seeing in the Moroccan Muslim a potential enemy. By cultivating this feeling of insecurity among the Jews, the *Alliance Israélite* paved the way for the exodus of these Jews to Israel . . . . The departure of . . . Jews to Israel was planned by the Zionists since the end of the nineteenth century, the epoch when the schools of the *Alliance israélite* began to spread their influence across Morocco.[25]

These accusations are in part justified but for the most part inaccurate, and at times, insensitive. Even if one accepts the premise that the Jews became victims of the AIU, one must look closely at the Jews' quest for outside help. Feelings of insecurity and persecution complexes were neither figments of Jewish imagination nor were these implanted in Jewish minds by the AIU. Was Benabdallah unaware of the discriminatory practices of *makhzan* officials? It would be difficult, however, to deny that the AIU guided Jews in the path of French culture during the protectorate era and, after 1945, in the direction of contemporary Jewish and Hebrew culture, hence aggravating the already *existing* Judeo-Muslim separation, cultivating a French-educated elite, and facilitating Jewish emigration to Israel, France, and the Americas. The AIU, then, sharpened divisions culturally, but was not at the root of the conflict, for the Jews *were* separated from the Muslims in *mellāḥs* long before 1862 and in accordance with legislation.

What the AIU should have done was to propagate literary Arabic education and to accentuate local Islamic culture in its schools after 1862 in accordance with several of its teachers urgings. By doing so it would have, in addition to French education, trained several generations of Jews astute about their Muslim neighbors' milieu. And instead of aggravating divisions the AIU could have played a constructive role of trying to promote an entente between the two groups. AIU leaders had been warned that emphasis on French education would lead to counterproductive results.

On the other hand, it was natural for the Jews to choose collaboration with the AIU: they realized that its schools would open for them new opportunities even if, as we have seen, not all the opportunities were realized under the protectorate system, if only because of colonial political considerations. It was equally if not more natural for the Jews to identify with political and cultural Zionism in subsequent years. The potential effects of AIU education and Zionist affiliation were regarded as escape mechanisms from political and other restrictions. To offer a rosy portrayal of pre-1862 Judeo-Muslim unity, as Benabdallah and the nationalists before him attempted to do, is misleading.

The educational, cultural, and social situations studied in this and the preceding chapters require additional analysis in view of two crucial developments: Moroccan independence and Jewish interests in emigration to Israel, France, and the Americas, the subjects of the final chapter. (For data on Jewish emigration to Israel between 1951 and 1956, see Table 44).

Notes

1. R. Gaudefroy-Demombynes, *L'oeuvre française en matière d'enseignement*, p. 20. (Paris: Paul Geuthner, 1928).

2. See John Damis, *The Free School Movement in Morocco: 1919–1970*, Unpublished Doctoral Dissertation, Fletcher school of Diplomacy, Tufts University, 1970, pp. 29–32.

3. Maghribi, "Mushkilat al-Ta'līm," *Majallat al-Maghrib* (October 1933), p. 11. The reason for the plea for Moroccan entrance into the French *lycées* is that the *collèges musulmans* led only to the first part of the *baccalauréat*, whereas the European *lycées* led to the second part as well, paving the road to higher education. The French and also the Spaniards, of course, wanted to avoid or delay such pleas.

4. Ibid., pp. 11–12.

5. Ibid., p. 12.

Table 44. Emigration to Israel

	Year					
	1951	1952	1953	1954	1955	1956
January	182	158	311	153	1.462	2.548
February	505	219	343	0	1.913	3.338
March	372	37	442	132	2.326	2.896
April	434	370	189	74	1.090	4.021
May	256	424	3	149	1.030	3.810
June	585	720	304	144	2.444	1.560
July	826	999	292	475	1.594	1.000*
August	943	520	158	1.190	2.525	2.880
September	1.544	288	0	2.050	2.847	3.500
October	297	286	202	1.276	4.104	1.000*
November	226	450	0	2.423	3.158	1.000*
December	270	212	179	2.195	2.368	1.000*
	6.440	4.683	2.423	10.261	26.861	28.553

Total 6 years: 79.221.

*Estimated.
SOURCE: Arch.JDC/330(a) (Eleventh Annual Country Directors Conference, Paris, October 1956)

6. Damis, *Free School Movement*, p. 153. These schools did not issue certificate degrees, nor were they geared for preparing candidates for specific careers. In the 1940s the *'ulamā'* issued certificates for a five-year program on the elementary level and in 1955, it expanded its secondary-level educational program (p. 179).

7. Ibid., p. 196.

8. Jacques Dahan, "Les communautés israélites du Maroc," *CAIU*, no. 91 (juin-juillet 1955), p. 9.

9. "Al-Mar'a al-Maghribīya wa ta'līm al-Banāt," *Majallat al-Maghrib* (August-September 1935), p. 1.

10. Muhammad al Hajawi, "Ta'lim al-Banāt," *Majallat al-Maghrib* (August-September 1935), p. 2.

11. Ibid.

12. Anonymous, "Les lignes de force du Maroc moderne," *Politique Etrangère*, no. 4 août-septembre 1955), p. 408.

13. M. de la Girardière, *Rapport sur les institutions sociales et d'enseignement mises à la disposition de la population marocaine* (Tanger, 1947), p. 15. An additional 440 attended the Free Schools, *msid*, and *madrasas*.

14. Ibid., p. 20.

15. Ibid., p. 25.

16. Ibid.

17. *Presidencia del Gobierno: Instituto Nacional de Estadistica, Zona de Protectorado, 1949/50*, p. 395.

18. Ibid.

19. Ibid., pp. 385–387, 394.

20. Ibid., p. 382.

21. Ibid.

22. *Oeuvre de l'Espagne dans sa zone marocaine*: Fernando Martinez, *Organisation Culturelle dans le Protectorat* (Madrid, 1952), p. 13.

23. Ibid.

24. Abdelkader Benabdallah, "La politique coloniale française à l'égard des juifs marocains," *L'Opinion* (août 15, 1976).

25. Abdelkader Benabdallah, "La politique française à l'égard des juifs marocains," *L'Opinion* (août 29, 1976).

SECTION III

THE JEWISH COMMUNITIES AND THE *ALLIANCE ISRAÉLITE UNIVERSELLE* BETWEEN 1956 AND 1962

CHAPTER IX

The *Alliance* and the Jewish Communities in Independent Morocco: 1956–1962

Dans le Maroc indépendant les juifs ne seront victimes d'aucune discrimination. Aḥmad Balafrej, *Istiqlal* Party Secretary in 1955.

1. Educational and Social Activities: The Impact

The massive departure of Jews to Israel, France, and the Americas from both urban centers and from the Atlas mountains after the protectorates were dismantled and Morocco was unified, did not signify a complete dissolution of their communities. Whereas 240,000 Jews lived in Morocco in 1952, the communities remained sizable: 160,000 in 1960, with continued emigration since the early 1960s. As late as 1966 thre were 60,000 Jews in the country, and only after the Arab-Israeli War of June 1967 did the size of the community decrease significantly once again. Yet in 1962 the communities were still of great numerical significance despite the departures. Whereas in the late 1950s and early 1960s Algerian Jewry on the eve of the country's independence were hurriedly leaving for France, and where a similar trend was already in motion in Tunisia, the Moroccan Jewish communities moved more slowly. As seen in chapter VII, 13.2 percent of the employed male and 23.8 percent of the same category of employed female Jewish population were employed in the administrative sector of independent Morocco (1960). Further, the educational and extraeducational activities of the AIU, the OH, the Lubavitchers, ORT, and OSE eventually continued to function unhampered, even if, as we shall see, they were confronted with difficulties. These organizations now faced reduced problems. And as impoverished Jews from the Atlas and other regions departed for Israel and overcrowded conditions in the *mellāh* of Casablanca to which Jews migrated in the 1940s and 1950s was reduced through emigration, these organizations could better concentrate on the urban population.

Educationally, the AIU led the way with more than eighty schools and 33,000 students in 1956. The AIU supported the arabization policies and, at the same time, continued to develop Jewish education together with the OH. It also collaborated with ORT, the JDC, and other organizations.

The problem of arabization was foreseen by Reuben Tajouri in the pre-1956 period. Until his death in November 1960 and his replacement as AIU delegate by Elias Harrus, and unlike Sémach, his less compromising francophile predecessor, Tajouri had faced reality: Arabic had to be taught at all grade levels at the AIU, in order to win sympathy for the network from a future independent Moroccan government on the one hand, and to prepare Jewish youths, culturally, for the new Morocco. But Tajouri's tactic of training Arabic teachers at the ENH and thus solving two problems at once, preparing both Arabic and Hebrew teachers, was perhaps relevant for young emerging teachers. Yet what was supposed to be done with teachers already employed at the AIU schools who had known French and Hebrew, but no literary Arabic? After all, both the Moroccan-born teachers, now a majority of the network's personnel (70 percent), and their non-Moroccan counterparts were not prepared to meet this new challenge.

Tajouri, however, found a devoted partner in Haïm Zafrani, one of the few AIU teachers from the ENIO who had learned literary Arabic at his native community of Mogador and later at several French institutes for Arabic language education in Rabat and Casablanca. He was destined, after 1956, to become both an AIU functionary and an inspector in the new Ministry of National Education, for Arabic studies in Jewish schools.[1] As the AIU was in a hurry to expose its personnel to Arabic education, Zafrani, together with his wife, prepared special Arabic instruction manuals for the teachers in the early part of 1956 and organized "crash" courses in Arabic during evenings, weekends, and vacations; the AIU did not wish to be left behind as Morocco moved toward independence and, at the same time, wanted to avoid alienating the nationalists, most of whom considered the AIU an anachronism and did not acknowledge the AIU position that without its presence Jewish education in the communities would be endangered. The AIU, then, was arabizing as rapidly as possible for the privilege of preserving its immense influence in Morocco.

Zafrani's efforts brought concrete results. And the dual effort of the ENH and Zafrani led o the emergence in the late 1950s and early 1960s of a group of qualified teachers, mostly Moroccans. During the celebration in Paris (June 1960) of the AIU's centenary, Zafrani reported that the Arabic language programs prepared by the educational commission in 1956 (*Commission Royale de la Réforme d'Enseignement*), of which Zafrani was a member, were attempting to reconcile the differences in the curricula of the Muslim and Jewish schools. In October 1957, Zafrani, as well as the new minister of National Education, and Tajouri undertook the first crucial step toward arabization, by introducing six hours of Arabic per week in the first elementary school year. In 1958 this program extended to the second school year, and by October 1959 to the fourth elementary school year; they hoped to extend the program to the fifth and sixth (final) elementary year, with ten weekly hours devoted to Arabic.[2]

The progress in Arabic achieved by the AIU in the period right after 1956 was acknowledged by the Moroccan authorities. In 1957 when Muḥammad al-Fāsī, minister of National Education, visited AIU schools in Meknes and Casablanca he expressed his satisfaction with these efforts and the results; the *Istiqlāl* party's Arabic organ, *Al-'Alam*, in a rare compliment to the AIU, emphasized "the extraordinary success achieved by the Jewish teachers in charge of Arabic education in the area of language, reading, writing, and speaking."[3] Zafrani himself boasted in 1960 that "we may claim that our Arabic education program is more effective than the program offered in a good many purely Muslim schools."[4]

The massive "reconversion" of the AIU personnel benefited other Jewish schools, who relied on the organization's teachers to supply them with Arabic teachers. Therefore, the Zafrani and ENH efforts had positive long-range results for the arabization process in most Jewish day-schools. The efforts of the ENH, however, had wide-ranging implications in othe areas. Indeed, the Casablanca training school emerged after 1956 as a multipurpose institution. It trained Jewish and Hebrew studies teachers for the AIU schools; secular teachers for the AIU and OH schools; served as a *lycée*; and graduated dynamic people who entered social work and became community leaders.

The training process of Jewish and Hebrew teachers at the AIU was essential in the early 1960s and after due to the size of the communities, despite emigration. And as shall be seen, the AIU managed to obtain a concession from the Moroccan government to recognize both written and spoken Hebrew as a legal language in the communities and, together with the OH, engaged in intensive training of teachers capable of offering a sound Jewish education confronting the challenge. Further, the educational program of the ENH, which since 1956 was directed by Emile Sebban, one of Rouche's disciples from Oran, has undergone vital transformations. Whereas until 1956 trainees had to receive their education in a four-year program leading to the elementary *brevet*, plus a fifth year of teacher training, the post-1956 program offered—in a seven-year program—the Certificate of Pedagogical Aptitude, or CAP, transforming the ENH into an advanced normal school.

Most significant perhaps was the impact of the ENH outside Morocco. During a 1955 meeting of the AIU in Paris, the organization's secretary-general, Eugène Weill, put forward a constructive suggestion that tended to become a policy in subsequent years. He argued convincingly that though Morocco had to remain the AIU's major preoccupation given the fact that Morocco had the largest school network, the role of the ENH should not be confined to the local communities; instead, it would be beneficial to bring to Morocco graduates of the elementary and secondary institutions of the AIU in the Mediterranean-basin area (Syria, Lebanon, Tunisia, and Algeria) to undergo training at the ENH. Jewish education would be improved in these countries once the trainees returned.[5]

Actually, already by 1962 many teachers had graduated from the ENH since its inception in 1946;[6] but given the Moroccan government's disinclination to allow foreigners to either teach or receive training on its soil, except for the teachers of the French Cultural Mission, the Weill proposal could not be fully implemented. Nevertheless, the idea of the ENH extending its role beyond Morocco was translated into action, despite the fact that numerous ENH graduates did not obtain employment outside Morocco in their area of specialization, and took other available jobs. Others who during the 1950s and 1960s emigrated) to Israel, France, Belgium, Venezuela, Argentina, Spain, and Canada procured employment successfully as community schools' Hebrew and Judaic studies teachers as well as directors. They were much needed in these communities, for unlike Israel or the United States, these communities where the Moroccan teachers of the ENH settled, suffered from chronic shortages of qualified teachers. Some of these communities are today made up largely of North African emigrants, notably Montreal, Brussels, Madrid, Barcelona, and Paris. The AIU, to maintain cultural and historical continuity with the North African communities, either opened schools for them (e.g., the *Ecole Secondaire* in the Paris suburb of *Pavillion-sous-Bois*) or helped finance community schools with which it became affiliated (e.g., one school in Brussels, two schools in Montreal, and one school each in Madrid and Barcelona).[7] Yet in addition to offering financial aid, the AIU provided these community schools with principals and Jewish studies teachers who, included ENH graduates from the 1950s and 1960s. All these developments are noteworthy particularly in view of the local communities' concern over their children abandoning Jewish traditions.

Training secular teachers for the AIU and other Moroccan-based private and community schools became an obvious burden for the ENH after 1956. The Moroccan Ministry of National Education did not look favorably upon the presence of foreign teachers at the AIU. Nor was the ministry pleased to see Moroccans receiving teacher training from private Jewish institutions overseas. Therefore, the traditional (since 1867) role of the Paris-based ENIO in training Moroccans and non-Moroccans in secular education had to end so as not to alienate the educational authorities in Rabat. In addition to the CAP for Jewish studies teachers, after 1957 the ENH conferred the degree upon its candidates for teaching secular subjects.[8] Had it not been for the existence of the ENH, or had the educational authorities refused the AIU permission to open another training school in its place, it is doubtful if the network which in 1962 celebrated its one hundredth anniversary in

Morocco, would have survived much longer. The ENH, moreover, served as the main source for French and general education teachers for the OH schools.

After independence the ENH was the most important *lycée* of the AIU in Morocco and perhaps the most impressive secondary-level Jewish institution in Casablanca. Already in the late 1950s the ENH graduated students who had successfully passed the official examinations for the *Baccalauréat de l'Enseignement Secondaire*.[9] For the first time girls were admitted to the institution which, before 1956, admitted boys only.

Finally, it is clear that the ENH made important contributions to leadership roles. Generally speaking, however, the Casablanca school as a Jewish and secular training college, an Arabic language training school, and as a *lycée*, from 1956–1962 and later graduated young men and women who filled vital leadership gaps created by the departure of numerous community rabbinic and lay leaders for Europe, Israel, and the Americas. But ENH graduates who themselves emigrated and who obtained higher education abroad filled essential leadership roles in their new communities. They became university professors and high school teachers in Israel, France, and the Americas. They became scout and youth movement leaders in Morocco and Israel since the early 1950s. They even emerged as community leaders and organizers in countries where large North African population concentrations developed after 1956.[10]

Turning to the relations between the AIU and the OH, in addition to the AIU-ENH policy of replacing the outmoded rabbi-teachers and reforming the Jewish educational structure in its schools, the AIU-OH coexistence since 1956 requires several observations. First, the coexistence that had developed became all the more vital after 1956 when the AIU and OH had to fulfill wide-ranging tasks in a milieu which did not wish to abandon its ancient traditions. Though the AIU and OH now worked more closely together, their systems varied. The AIU through the ENH and its primary schools concentrated on language and selections of text from Torah, Mishnah, and the Rambam. The aim of OH (and Lubavitcher) was to bring the student to the study of the Talmud by leading him as quickly as possible through mechanical reading, Torah and Rashi, the early prophets, and the study of Mishnah; all schools taught *dīnīm*.[11]

It appears that the Moroccan government of the post-1956 period allowed the AIU and OH to develop Jewish studies programs. The Central Committee of the AIU and the leaders of the OH in New York sent curricula to their schools which had to be followed scrupulously. Supervisors and teacher-guides visited the schools to ascertain that the programs were carried out.[12] But despite curriculum variations, diverse educational approaches, and other areas of disagreement the two organizations coexisted and seem to have been largely responsible for the preservation of Jewish education by supplying religious literature at a time when there was chronic shortage of this material. Stanley Abramovitch of the JDC with thirty years of experience in the educational field of the North African, Western European, and Middle Eastern scene, observed about Morocco:

> Books were imported from Israel and the [United] States as long as the French were in charge. The situation changed drastically with Moroccan independence. No book printed in Israel could be imported. It became difficult to import any Hebrew texts. It was necessary, therefore, to print books in Morocco.
>
> Plates were made of a *Siddūr,*[13] *Hūmash*[14] with Rashi, and four Hebrew language texts. These books were printed and reprinted in many tens of thousands of copies. The standard prayer book used until this day in synagogues of Morocco and the *Hūmash* used in all schools and most synagogues comes from the stock of books printed locally.
>
> The AIU and OH created a host of teachers' aids. Model lessons, teacher-guides, pupil workbooks, booklets for all festivals, Hebrew conversation manuals, poems and excerpts from modern Hebrew literature were prepared on stencils and sent to all schools. At one point, the book of Joshua was no longer available in Morocco. The whole book was therefore typed on stencils, run off and distributed. The same is being done with parts of the other books of the Bible which cannot be imported.[15]

Who were the main personalities in charge of the AIU-OH Jewish studies programs? Since 1956 the ENH program was developed and supervised by Emile Sebban and Joseph "Jo" Medioni, both from Algeria. Jo Medioni was the real driving force behing the ENH and the Jewish studies programs at the AIU. It is due to his efforts that a spoken Hebrew program could be developed even after 1956. Medioni's zeal resembled that of the European pioneers in Tetuan, Tangier, and Mogador one hundred years earlier. He taught himself and spent his vacations in Israel; he built up a curriculum which became an integral part of the AIU schools; he fought for years, often alone, against challenges from all sides to change the image of the Hebrew teacher and Hebrew studies at the AIU.[16]

Medioni's work was reciprocated by Rabbi Z. Waltner of the OH in Tangier and after 1960, by Rabbi Aron Monsonego as well. The latter, a native of Fez, who as late as 1980 directed the OH program in Morocco, was a scion of an old rabbinic family in Spain. He had received his training in Aix-les-Bains at a *yeshīva,* and there became fired by the aim of *zikkui harabīm*: to work for the good of the many, to set up schools and build up an orthodox education system.[17] He had started during the 1950s as an OH teacher and emerged to the position of the program's director during the 1960s. Monsonego's duties varied and certainly have multiplied as Jewish emigration out of Morocco gained momentum. Monsonego settled local disputes or intervened before a district governor for the good of the Jews; he advised communities how to handle property; he checked plans for taking care of the poor; he collected money to arrange respectable marriages for needy couples; and he visited lonely old couples in Jewish homes for the aged.[18] Monsonego's role, then, complemented the activities undertaken on a large scale by the AIU.

The role of the Lubavitcher was also impressive. Their Morocco representatives, Ashkenazim for the most part, traveled from village to village in the name of the Lubavitcher-Rebbe of New York. They took into

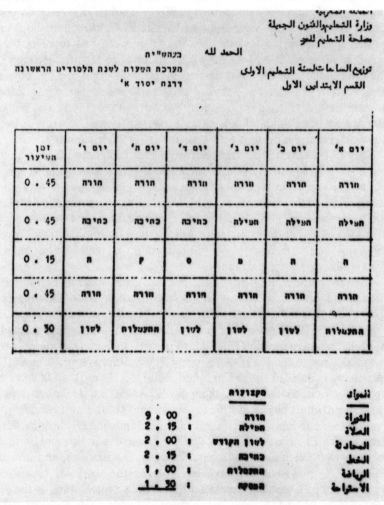

Figure 31. A sample of the Jewish program for the *talmūd tōra* schools based on the decisions of the educational reform commission

their schools the poorest girls and boys of the distant communities, and whereas before independence, the AYI school system expanded in the south the program of the post-1956 period became diversified, to include the expansion of girls' education on the secondary-school level. Their *yeshīvōt* included special workshops to train *shōhatīm* and scribes of *mezūzōt* and *tefillīn*.[19] It appears that despite their modest salaries[20] the Lubavitcher did not complain and always carried out their activities with great zeal.[21]

AIU cooperated with ORT as well as with OH. It has already been seen that the impact of the ORT-AIU effort on promoting modern vocational training was quite important. In 1960–1962 the ORT-AIU schools of Casablanca developed steadily along two lines. On the one hand, the network regularly added new courses whose purpose was to offer the best possible educational and training opportunities to talented teenagers. On the other hand, the network, despite emigration, expanded its courses for basic vocational training, its adult programs, and its apprenticeship programs; these were programs for men, women, and teenagers who could not attend vocational high schools either because they had to work or because their elementary education was insufficient for high school.[22]

The ORT-AIU expanded the secretarial education field for girls. Both the Val d'Anfa girls' school in Casablanca and the Marrakesh counterpart gave three-year courses in typing, bookkeeping and stenography.[23] And whereas the purpose of the network was to shift girls away from the needle trades to the secretarial and administrative fields, successful efforts were made at the ORT-AIU boys' centers to shift away from traditional trades over to mechanics, automechanics, radio-television, aviation, and television sales—all to meet the demands of the 1960s.[24]

The ORT-AIU schools which in 1962 had 2,996 students enrolled,[25] still maintained centers in Tetuan and Sefrou in addition to Casablanca and Marrakesh. During the early 1960s Women's American ORT, an important branch of the ORT movement, provided aid to these programs through the M.O.T. (Maintenance ORT Training) projects, which gave support to the schools; through the E.P.I.C. (Earning Power Improvement Courses) project aid was provided to ORT apprenticeship, accelerated, adult and similar nonhigh school courses; through the Social Assistance (Guardianship) Project (SAP), which provided stipends and money for the construction of dormitories, dining halls, and cultural facilities; and finally, through the Student Health Projects which provided for preventive health and basic treatment services, such as periodic examinations, inoculations, and first aid.[26]

The JDC played a preponderant role in the work of these Jewish organizations. It not only replaced the French protectorate as the AIU's main source of financial support but it took upon itself much of the subsidization of *all* Jewish organizational activities. Although the JDC was active in other countries, Morocco of the late 1950s and early 1960s was the

Table 45. The OH Schools in 1960

Town or Village	Number and Types of Schools	Number of Students
Amizmiz	1 Elementary	70
Casablanca	4 Elementary	1,935
	1 Boarding	67
	1 Vocational (Girls)	77
Debdou	1 Elementary	66
Fez	3 Elementary	700
	1 Evening Program	300
In Five Unspec- ified Villages in the Atlas	5 Elementary	313
Marrakesh	2 Elementary	350
	1 Boarding	30
Meknes	1 Elementary	1,032
	1 Boarding High School	42
Mogador	1 Elementary	208
	1 Evening Program	169
Ouazzan	1 Elementary	60
Rabat	1 Elementary	370
Sefrou	1 Elementary	330
	1 Teacher Training	85
Tangier	1 Elementary	200
	1 Teacher Training (Boys)	60
	1 Teacher Training (Girls)	90
	1 Rabbinic Seminary	10
Total	32 Schools	6,564

SOURCE: OH New York.

JDC's largest operation in the Muslim world. Of a Jewish population of 170,000 in 1959, approximately 60,000 had received JDC aid.[27]

After Moroccan independence, Jews from outlying districts began to move to the larger cities, increasing the demand for JDC services. While children and young people were the major beneficiaries of JDC, the general Jewish population benefited, too. Looking into the data for 1959 we find that the JDC's efforts to establish and maintain acceptable standards of nutrition and hygiene benefited 28,000 Moroccan Jewish youths in school cafeterias whereas 12,000 adults regularly received food parcels; that 1,500 other persons received free meals in soup kitchens and anti-TB centers throughout the country; that of key importance to these food programs were the farm surpluses freely donated by the U.S. Department of Agriculture, of which the JDC imported and distributed about 4,000,000 pounds that year; that the JDC distributed clothes valued at $250,000 to the neediest youths at the ORT-AIU schools; that the battle against such common diseases as tuberculosis, trachoma, tinea, and others was carried on through JDC support for the OSE budget, which then operated twenty-six clinics and dispensaries with a monthly patient load of nearly 8,000; that JDC funds have also made possible the establishment and functioning of infant child, and maternity centers; and that in the field of economic rehabilitation, the JDC in cooperation with the Jewish Colonization Association, expanded the CIRE. Between January and June 1958, 467 loans were granted to artisans and small businessmen whose livelihood had been seriously treatened by the then general economic decline in Morocco.[28]

It is obvious that the Moroccan authorities eventually pursued the liberal policies of the French protectorate to allow private and semiprivate Jewish organizations to function among the Jews. But the 1956–1962 period, at least, witnessed fluctuations in governmental policy, and serious opposition to these organizations, from local Muslim nationalists and their Jewish sympathizers. The Moroccan authorities themselves were pressured by nationalists to impose sanctions on these organizations. To alleviate pressures the authorities had to make concessions.

2. The Political Status of the AIU

In 1955, just months away from Moroccan independence, the leaders of the AIU were extremely concerned about the future of their most important network of the Mediterranean-basin countries. They had had enough experience with the demise of their important networks in Turkey, Greece, and Iraq, and they were well aware that their Egyptian schools, few as they were, survived on borrowed time in Jamāl 'Abd al-Nāṣir's Egypt. They knew that their influence in Algeria was dwindling, and in the wake of the Algerian Revolution this influence could end following a massive departure of Jews for France. Despite substantial enrollment in Tunisia, that nation was about to obtain independence, too. With only six schools in Lebanon, one school in France, and one school apiece in Libya and Syria, as well as a dozen schools in Israel, there was just one network, in Iran, composed of thirty-four schools, that was of some significance. That network, too, might have been threatened had Muhammad Mossadeq – an antimonarchist nationalist – succeeded in his 1953 plan to remove Muhammad Reza Pahlavi from his throne. The loss of Morocco, the bastion of the AIU at the time, would have weakened the AIU tremendously.

In the immediate postindependence period, AIU leaders had good reasons to worry. When in November 1955 Muhammad V had returned from exile, which had been imposed on him in 1953 by the French owing to his support for radical nationalist causes, AIU president René Cassin and Secretary-General Eugène Weill, met with him (now king) to discuss the future of the AIU.[29] They were received warmly by the monarch who promised to permit the AIU to continue its work.[30] Yet these promises apparently did not take into account an array of political views espoused by various nationalist forces, particularly within the *Istiqlāl*, views which Muḥammad V would have to consider in face of accusations directed against the organization, such as collaboration with the colonialists, and serving the educational interests of the new Zionist state. Would Muḥammad V adhere to his promise of November 1955, or would he succumb to nationalist pressures?

After March 1956, the month in which Morocco gained independence, the king appeared at first to be adhering closely to his 1955 promises. Pressure was mounting on him from both sides: from the AIU, which had to adjust to the new realities in a Morocco *sans France,* and from regular political attacks against the schools by various forces including the nationalists. The king and minister of National Education were contacted by Cassin on several occasions. His influence as a human rights advocate and as an important public figure in France, was utilized by the AIU. Cassin did not hesitate to write about or to make public declarations on the subject, either. Since 1956 he repeatedly suggested to the Moroccan government that they must understand the feelings of their Jewish population: the more they threaten them and prevent their free movements, the more they will encourage them to emigrate. If, on the other hand, the authorities preserve their institutions, such as those operated by the AIU, and if they offer them security, the Jews' choice would be free: those who would like to leave could do so, but those who wished to stay on native soil, should be given an honorable chance to do so, too.[31]

On the surface the position of the AIU was to express concern for the safety of the Jews. But in reality it was a tactic to discourage the Moroccans from imposing restrictions on their schools. In other words, by hinting that if the AIU and other institutions would be restricted or nationalized, the Jews would feel threatened and consequently they would not feel safe in Morocco.

The nationalists, communists, and labor unionists with left-wing inclinations pressured the Palace over this issue. Both conservative Istiqlālists like 'Alāl al-Fāsī and the left wing of the party represented by a former prime-minister, Abdallah Ibrahīm, wanted to minimize the influence of the AIU through nationalization.[32] The UMT (*Union Marocaine de Travail*) left-wing labor organ, *L'Avant-Garde,* on several occasions advocated that the AIU, which before and during the protectorate era gave to "our Jewish youths essentially a foreign education," contributed to their "maladjustment"; and through is "famous delegation" in Casablanca continued since 1956 to control Jewish minds and thus the artificial separation between Jew and Muslim was becoming permanent.[33]

The mounting attacks on the AIU raised protests in the Jewish world, including in the United States, where American Jewry and its United Jewish

Appeal (UJA) program were increasingly subsidizing the AIU networks through the JDC. Yet concern in American or other Jewish circles also put pressure on the AIU, since Jewish concern in its undertakings did not necessarily mean blind endorsement of the schools in the new Morocco. Thus, already in 1956, when Vice-President Braunschvig of the AIU argued at a JDC meeting in Paris that "we are a really disinterested educational organization; we are not in favor of any imperialism; our educational system, though Jewish, is liberal, and we are open to any kind of agreement . . . with local governments," Rabbi Herbert A. Friedman, executive vice-president of the UJA, argued:

> We were told that in the *Alliance* schools it will be necessary to teach Arabic, or more Arabic culture. Whatever that means for the future we are not sure and, conversely, it means that there might be less Jewish orientation in the course of studies. If that is the case, then it raises the question about the role and the function of Jewish organizations in Morocco, who, because they might have to integrate [Muslim pupils], might have to work against the question of whether we must continue to concentrate on the question of emigration, because perhaps emigration is the only way to save Jews in spirit as well as in body.[34]

There was actually an alarm in November 1957. Rabbi Z. Waltner of the OH had met with Tajouri, who had informed him of a decree in the making calling for the government takeover of all AIU secular teachers previously under AIU control. Tajouri, according to Waltner, suggested that the OH join forces with the AIU: the AIU would strive to develop the elementary Hebrew curriculum while the OH would concentrate on religious education.[35] But nothing came of the takeover. True, there were French citizens among the non-Moroccan personnel of the AIU who left Morocco during the middle and late 1950s and who were integrated into the French Ministry of National Education, once they emigrated to France. Yet the teacher corps of the AIU, almost overwhelmingly composed of Moroccan ENIO-ENH graduates, remained AIU functionaries. As late as 1959 Morocco JDC director, Louis Kirsch, observed that in view of the prevalent atmosphere of uneasiness about governmental designs, it should be particularly noted that governmental contributions to the AIU — in the spirit of the 1928 agreement — and ORT were generally maintained with respect to participation in teachers salaries, and in the case of the AIU with respect to cafeteria costs also.[36]

In October 1960, however, when the AIU still operated seventy-seven schools and 28,684 students were enrolled in the former three colonial zones, the first critical challenge was under way. To avoid a complete takeover of the schools the authorities could no longer resist nationalist and other pressure groups for altering the system of the AIU from its preindependence status. The authorities requested that the AIU cede one-third of its schools to the Ministry of National Education, including the students in these schools, while the rest, two-thirds, would remain in the hands of the AIU. The authorities promised AIU officials that Hebrew would be kept in the curricula of the nationalized schools, although Jewish observers claimed that the teaching of Hebrew in the nationalized schools had been so readjusted as to be limited to the reading of the Bible, rather than conveying a knowledge of the living language. As a result of the move the program in the nationalized schools was de-Judaized.[37]

The decision to nationalize one-third of the AIU schools was made official on March 3, 1961, through *ẓahīr* 1-61-006, which led to the following developments: (a) the AIU was now left with 20,000 students and sixty-four schools; and (b) the 1928 agreement signed between the AIU and the French protectorate was annuled. The move in itself was alarming to the AIU which probably feared that the authorities were implementing a step-by-step nationalization policy. This was a difficult turning point for the AIU in its long history in Morocco, a time when one setback followed another. First the Moroccan decision to nationalize, and then, the sudden death of delegate Tajouri, a dynamic figure in the Jewish communities. His position was filled through the creation of a duumvirate of Elias Harrus and Haïm Zafrani. The latter retired from the AIU in 1962 and settled in France, where he entered into an academic career. Harrus was still delegate in 1982. But after 1960 he did not wield the kind of influence as did his illustrious predecessors and meanwhile, the attacks on the AIU continued. In addition to the *Istiqlāl* and the UMT, the communists through their organ, *Al-Mukāfiḥ*, accused the AIU in 1962 of Zionist activities and opposed future government financial aid to its schools. The decision to allow the AIU to function with 20,000 students, the paper said, was a dreadful mistake: there will emerge a "new scandal" added to the old one when emigration to Israel was permitted by the authorities.[38]

Concerned with developments and seeking to hold on to its sixty-four schools, which still gave them the leading educational position in the communities, the leaders of the AIU in 1961–1962 were willing to consider various sacrifices. On July 19, 1962, an additional measure was adopted by the authorities: a *ẓahīr* (1-62-058) that was subsequently modified by *ẓahīr* 1-63-079 on April 16, 1963, envisaging the integration of the teachers of the AIU (Moroccan nationals) into the ranks of the Moroccan Ministry of National Education.[39]

The Paris AIU would have somehow coped with the implementation of this measure and would have probably accepted a reduced role by raising funds to maintain the schools as long as these preserved their Jewish character, and as long as the AIU would enjoy some authority over them.

Searching for a solution in 1962, the AIU asked one of its leaders, Marcel Franco, to contact the Moroccan authorities in order to negotiate a compromise with them. A former graduate of the AIU in Greece, an industrialist who since 1939 had lived in the United States and Mexico, and vice-president of the AIU, Franco had intimate ties with Moroccan officials, given his role as an American businessman helping to extend American business into independent Morocco.[40]

It is unclear what exactly Franco achieved during his contacts with the Moroccans regarding the schools and the teachers. It is, evident, however, that the policy to integrate the teachers into the public sector was received with mixed reactions by the teachers. There was a group of teachers who considered integration and nationalization of the schools, yet many considered this move imprudent[41] and preferred to remain within the framework of the AIU. Their conditions over the years had improved. Since the early 1950s their pay was on par with the salaries of the protectorates' functionaries, at least in the French zone.[42] Furthermore, since 1956, all AIU teachers were unionized for the first time. Despite the contradiction of the term "unionized missionaries" most teachers, if not possessed by the zeal of their illustrious predecessors, and attracted by the good life, were nonetheless devoted. The AIU, with the help of the JDC and other sources, met unionist demands for their teachers.[43] And therefore, when the 1962 and 1963 decrees were published the overwhelming majority of the teachers *refused* to become state functionaries, considering, moreover, that they were paid better by the AIU than they would have been paid by the Ministry of National Education.[44]

One more measure was imposed on the AIU in 1961–1962: it had to adopt the name *Ittihād-Maroc*, the arabized version of its name. This arrangement was still valid in 1982 and Harrus, in collaboration with several Jewish colleagues, administered this education branch of the AIU through the *Ittihād* Committee composed of Jews only. The AIU, which in addition to being a recipient of JDC funds for its work in Morocco, has since the 1960s received subsidies from the Moroccan government in spite of ongoing opposition from radicals.

Finally, it should be noted that spoken Hebrew had been taught five hours weekly since 1957. Zafrani, who was a member of the royal commission for educational reform, negotiated for this concession. Whereas several of the commission's members objected to his plea on the grounds that this would mean that the AIU propagated the language of the Zionists, two other influential members of the commission, Mehdi ben Barka and Muhammad al-Fāsī (minister of Education) argued that Hebrew, the language of the Jews, had to be respected just as Arabic had to be promoted among Muslims. And the measure passed thanks to their intercession.[45]

3. Political Jews: Moroccan Independence and the Controversy over Judeo-Muslim Entente

The coming of independence meant that Jews themselves had to confront complex issues, particularly Judeo-Muslim relations and emigration. AIU alumni, constituting the bulk of Morocco's Jewish intellectuals, were in the forefront, voicing their opinions, demands, and anxieties. Among the elite of the new era was Charles Bensimhon, one of the outstanding teachers of the AIU, whose family had produced a long line of ENIO-trained teachers and directors. Born in Marrakesh, educated in Morocco and France, and familiar with the new realities in the country, Bensimhon, at a speech to an AIU audience in Paris (1957) described the AIU pioneers who came to Morocco from Europe and the Mediterranean world: they came to a Morocco devoid of political security, a Morocco where disease and misery was the order of the day.[46] The mission of the AIU teacher of 1957 appeared to Bensimhon to considerably easier than of his predecessor who, under impossible conditions, had brought about the evolution of the communities. "Today," he said, "the work has been cut out for the personnel, as the teacher finds a blossoming school, vast classrooms with the sun penetrating . . . . He comes to a town where pleasures are by no means lacking and where material conditions are often enviable."[47]

Yet were the new conditions so mush less challenging in 1957 than in the days of the European teachers? The Moroccan-born teacher of the AIU was caught in a complex web of conflicting interests. First, there was Mococco, his *patrie*. Second, there was the newly established state of Israel, the *cradle of his religion*. Finally there was *France*, the source of his culture and emancipation. Regarding the *patrie*, he said:

> Settled in our country for more than 2,000 years, we have witnessed great historical transformations, as did our fathers and ancestors. The Jews, be they of Berber origin or those who came [to Morocco] in search of refuge, all consider this country as theirs. There are several strong bonds which attach us to this land: the mother country, the fertile soil, our families and friends, the climate and the familiar horizons.[48]

Bensimhon was convinced that the relations between Jews and Muslims were bound to improve in the new Morocco where the lines of *rapprochement* would be laid on foundations of democracy and freedom. And he placed great confidence for the realization of this dream in Muhammad V, saying:

> More than the native soil . . . one single sentiment which we cherish in our hearts is the deep love for Muhammad V. The Jews of Morocco are eternally

grateful for what their monarch had done for them. Since his ascendance to the Throne [1927], His Majesty has not for one moment ceased to reveal his paternal sympathy for us as well as his vigilant protection. At the darkest hours of the Jewish people when Europe was occupied by the Nazis and France issued its racial laws at Vichy, it was he and he alone who came to our defense and bravely resisted the anti-Jewish manifestations in Morocco. Since his return from exile, Muḥammad V had proclaimed total equality between Moroccans, promising the Jews full liberation from humiliation.[49]

Concerning Israel, he affirmed:

Even if we are strongly attached to *notre patrie*, it is impossible to ignore Israel, the cradle of our religion. Neither the Catholics of France, nor the Muslims of Morocco, nor the Jews of England can remain indifferent in the face of the three great spiritual centers of the world: the Vatican, Mecca, and Jerusalem.[50]

In other words, while the Jews had to express loyalty to their native soil, they nevertheless were entitled to a Jewish vatican, a spiritual center, a philosophy that had to be inculcated in the minds of the students:

An intransigent patriotism and a full loyalty toward Morocco does not exclude faithfulness toward the Holy Land. If we are separated from Israel by citizenship, Moroccan Jewry is united with world Jewry by a common religious doctrine. Yes, we are Moroccans, but we are also Jewish. This is something our Muslim compatriots understand full well. When we speak of integration, this word is à la mode. . . . In the Larousse dictionary the word *intégrer* signifies to enter into a whole. If one defines the word as integrating the Jews into a nation, have them participate actively in all aspects of national life, and respecting their spiritual values, then we are wholeheartedly for such an integration. On the other hand, if one defines integration as the disaggregation of our communities, the scuttling of our cultural and social institutions, the abandonment of our identity and traditions, then the answer is no. No one can ask us to relinquish our identity. We believe in assimilation into the new Morocco but an assimilation with dignity and honor.[51]

Bensimḥon, then, was representing the new thinking of the AIU elite. If the Muslim nationalists expected straight answers from the Jews concerning loyalty and patriotism, the Jews, too, needed assurances. The above statement contained an implicit warning: the Muslims would have to tolerate Jewish sympathies toward Israel, and Jewish institutions must not be tampered with as part of the price for the Judeo-Muslim entente. This attitude was reflected clearly in René Cassin's remarks concerning the possible consequences if the AIU would suddenly disappear from Morocco. As to France, Bensimḥon asserted:

From the age of six we escape the *mellāh* in order to enter the enchanted garden of French culture. It is with joy that we breathe, on the benches of the *Alliance* schools, the air of a rational civilization. We are subjected to Western discipline . . . and we become liberated of our prejudice and superstitions until we receive our primary school certificate. It is a painful road for some who aim at the *brevet supérieur* [at the ENIO]! After having stuttered the fables of La Fontaine at the primary school, vibrated with Corneille, laughted with Molière, and cried with Racine in the *cours complémentaires*, we are finally ready to enter the normal school with enthusiasm; and there we are exposed to deep philosophy, complex mathematics, and literary finesse.[52]

So despite loyalty to Morocco and spiritual attachment to Israel, French culture was still an integral part of life. As Bensimhon said of one old directress of Moroccan nationality: *"Elle se sentait Gauloise jusqu'au bout des ongles."*[53]

The ideological conflict of the elite was extended into the schools. In independent Morocco love for the *patrie*, solidarity with Israel and with French culture required intellectual integration. Would the youths succeed in assimilating the distinct vocabularies of Arabic, Hebrew, and French? Said Bensimhon:

A heavy responsibility rests on the [*Alliance*] educator of Moroccan origin in independent and democratic Morocco. Would the education be uniquely devoted to French culture? Would it be strictly a Jewish education? Or would it succumb to total Arabization? Educate young people open to French culture, cultivate good Jews devoted to their ancient traditions, prepare loyal Moroccan citizens. This is the solution to the educational problem of our pupils — a solution which will once again demonstrate the universality of the *Alliance* and the perennity of its activities.[54]

It is noteworthy that Bensimhon was active in the proentente movement since 1956, which also included Jews with strong leftist views, less moderate than his own views. It was through intellectuals like Moïse Nahon that Judeo-Muslim *rapprochement* efforts were made long before independence. Jewish views, however, leaned increasingly toward greater identification with France on the one hand or toward the Zionist movement, on the other. Yet the proentente group cannot be completely ignored, either. This is because relatively speaking Jewish efforts to identify with nationalist forces were perhaps more intense in Morocco than in any Muslim country. In all trends or outlooks — toward France, toward Jewish nationalism, toward patriotism — AIU graduates played a crucial role.

Proentente Jewish intellectuals had pinned great hopes on Muhammad V's liberalism and tolerance. They sought accomodation with *Istiqlā lists* and other nationalists, too. A Judeo-Muslim entente became embodied in an *Istiqlālist* movement known as *Al-Wifāq* (Entente), which included Jews and Muslims. The movement, founded in January 1956, included intellectuals such as Joe Ohana (a merchant who had contributed to *Istiqlāl* treasury), and Marc Sabah. Together with their Muslim counterparts they sought to reconstruct the new Morocco where both elements would enjoy equal rights. The Palace encouraged their activities, and during one conference attended by the then Prince Hasan II, the latter asserted: "The sympathies of some of you are with Cairo, others with Jerusalem. I understand your positions. However, your feet are touching on Moroccan soil."[55] Though he seemed to be hinting that he would not favor pro-Nāsir or pro-Zionist activities, Hasan II encouraged dialogue and national unity.

To accomodate the Jews, the authorities appointed Dr. Léon Benzaquen, a Jewish physician and member of *Al-Wifāq* as minister of the Post Office, Telegraph, and Telephone for the first Moroccan government under the moderate leadership of the PDI (The Progressive Democratic Party of Indepedence); he held the position until May 1958, when a virtually all *Istiqlāl* cabinet — under Ahmad Balafrej — with no Jewish members at all, came to power.[56] At the time of Benzaquen's appointment another Jew was appointed as a judge, several others were appointed to diplomatic posts, and in an outstanding effort toward assimilation, Jews were able to participate in municipal elections.[57]

An Egyptian writer observed that the efforts to establish a Muslim-Jewish entente through *Al-Wifāq* could have been far more successful than in the Arab East, partly because the Arab-Israeli conflict did not have such a profound impact among Arab nationalists of the Maghrib as it had in the Mashriq.[58] Furthermore, unlike the other Arab countries from which the Jews emigrated in the 1940s and early 1950s, most of Morocco's Jews remained behind until the early 1960s.[59] John Waterbury, however, observed that the entente experiment was essentially over before the 1960s; and commenting about the Jewish members of *Al-Wifāq*, Waterbury noted: "These young Jews were especially close to Mehdi ben Barka, who was sympathetic to their projects, and today feel more at ease with members of the UNFP [National Union of Popular Forces] than with these of any other party."[60] On the whole, however, the society of the entente turned out to be an ill-fated mission, and Waterbury blamed both Jews and Muslims: "The indifference and lack of urgency on the part of the Muslim elite members and the hesitation and fear on the part of the bulk of the Jewish community brought these plans to nothing."[61]

What were the Jewish fears that contributed to the failure of the entente? On the surface, the efforts of the Moroccan government and the Palace on behalf of the Jews in the 1956–1958 period, were sincere. However, these efforts, which included political security for the Jews, political representation, and communal autonomy were perhaps too little in scope and certainly too late. Many of the Jews feared that despite Muḥammad V's benevolence and the *Wifāq*, the end of the protectorate era would ultimately mean a regression to the *dhimmī* status. These fears intensified when Muḥammad V tried to stop Jewish emigration and showed an inclination to sympathize with Arab states opposed to Israel. His links with the Arab League were strengthened and Moroccan regional policies became increasingly anti-Israel. Legal Jewish emigration came to a halt and any further emigration was achieved through illegal channels. The collapse of the moderate PDI government in May 1958 and the dismissal of Benzaquen from the cabinet, aggravated Jewish feelings of uncertainty. And when in December 1958 'Abd Allāh Ibrāhīm came to power, representing the left wing of the *Istiqlāl*, he sowed panic among the Jews.[62]

Ibrāhīm sought to reduce tensions in his meetings with Jews in Morocco and abroad during his administration (December 1958-May 1960). While in New York he met with local Jews and in an interview issued information. Here are some important statements he made:

> I really do not like to speak in terms of Jews or Muslims . . . since we have really only Moroccans . . . . After we achieved independence we had to reorganize and modernize our administration, and replace many civil servents with Moroccans. However, access to administrative positions is open under equalitarian competition, without mention of religion. Our identity card does not mention whether we are Jews or Muslims. Today there are few Muslims in our telecommunications systems, the majority in that service are Jews. When I was minister of Labor my chief of Cabinet was a Jew. Now an attaché in my cabinet is a woman who is a Jewess. The economic counselor until recently was a Jew. That is why I refuse to speak of Muslims or Jews—I speak only of patriots. The law is the same for everybody . . . .
>
> As to postal relations [with Israel that were severed], we are members of the Arab League and have ratified the Arab League convention affecting international relations. That is why we must observe our obligations as a state. It is in some way a result of the poisoned situation in the Middle East. The good will of the entire [area] would benefit by the settlement of this [Arab-Israeli] problem.
>
> I regret that some [Jewish] organizations create propaganda and make difficulties. Morocco will never allow radicalism which would be a denial of its historic traditions.[63]

Yet difficulties were mounting. Jews were attacked in various parts of the country, an AIU school was burned to the ground in Mazagan, and Jewish organizations, including welfare and cultural groups, and even burial societies were suspected of Zionism. The director-general of ORT-AIU was deported by the police without warning, without notice, and without even the fiction of legal proceedings, despite the fact that he represented an international organization.[64] A series of articles depicting "the many headed Zionist hydra," which were published in a leading daily newspaper, caused further tension.[65]

Dr. Benzaquen who in 1956 declared that the future of the Jews "will be as the Moroccan Jews want it to be," that "they must set to work without delay, they must preserve and maintain their faith, their culture and their ethics," and that "there is no incompatibility between this and Moroccan citizenship,"[66] was finding himself in 1962 protesting against 'Alāl al-Fāsī of the *Istiqlāl* for announcing that the Jews were not to be regarded as Moroccans but as residents enjoying Moroccan protection.[67] Indeed, the political climate in the late 1950s since 'Abd Allāh Ibrāhīm assumed power and until the early 1960s, differed from the more promising trends of 1956–1958.

The Jews, encouraged by Zionist pleas and by the leaders of the *Kadīma* (Forward) movement for emigration (now banned), continued to try to flee the country by clandestine means. The saddest and most dramatic episode in this period took place in January 1961, when a fishing boat, the "Pisces," filled with Jewish refugees foundered between Tangier and Gibraltar and forty lives were lost. Muhammad V died the following month. His son and successor, Ḥasan II, who had acquired Western education and ideals, took the direction of his country's affairs. The basic right of the Jews to emigrate to Israel was resumed in the early days of his reign.

The Jews who chose to remain in Morocco after 1961–1962 were at first confronted with confusion and dilemmas: loyalty to Morocco, solidarity with Israel, and identification with France. These who went to France, Spain, and the Americas identified with their surroundings and with Israel, although they preferred to speak French for the most part. Those who emigrated to Israel fulfilled the ancient prophecy of the return to Zion. This was basically the shaping of events in 1962: one hundred years since the arrival of the AIU in Morocco.

Epilogue: Until 1980

Since the early 1960s the Jews of Morocco have lived in tranquility under the protection of the Palace. The outbreak of the 1967 Arab-Israeli war placed the 60,000 remaining Jews on the verge of panic even though there was no major threat to them. Political forces on the right and left sought to use the fact that the king had protected the Jews to discredit him. There were rumors of synagogues being burned and Jewish shops being looted; but this was not on a large scale and the culprits were arrested. The AIU and other organizations continued to function normally, and the relations between the Jews and the Muslims remained reasonably cordial despite the

Table 46. Student Enrollment at the AIU — 10 November 1964 and 10 November 1969

	1964		1969		Increase or Decrease: 1969 over 1964	
Item	Number of Classes	Number of Pupils	Number of Classes	Number of Pupils	Number of Classes	Number of Pupils
Elementary	256	8,876	118	3,711	(138)	(5,165)
Secondary (*lycée*)	9	211	9	173	-	(38)
Secondary (Cours Comp.)	53	1,349	43	1,366	(10)	(17)
Commercial and Technical (Advanced classes)	6	91	11	164	(5)	(73)
Commercial and Technical (Beginning training)	48	973	33	612	(15)	(361)
Total	372	11,500	214	6,026	(158)	(5,474)

*While elementary classes account for 77 percent of total school population of 11,500 in 1964, by 1969 they constituted only 62 percent with advanced grades taking on greater importance. The decrease in Jewish population between 1964 and 1969 was from 80,000 to 40,000 (50 percent). AIU population decreased from 11,500 to 6,026 (48 percent); estimated annual disbursements of JDC to AIU (1964–1969: decrease from $1,700,000 to $914,000, or 54 percent).

SOURCE: Jules Breen to L. D. Horwitz, January 9, 1969: JDC/402(b).

defeat of Arab armies at the hands of the Israelis. There were extremists who tried to heighten tensions, as the following quotation from the newspaper *Al-Masā'* shows:

There are no Zionists, only Jews, no more, no less . . . . We do not wish the authorities to harm the Jews. They are on the same footing with the Muslims by the terms of the constitution. But we want the heads of the Jews if they betray the Muslims . . . . We do not want the authorities to carry on a war destroying everything as did Hitler, for the Islamic religion forbids this; but in the name of this religion we demand that they punish severely those who betray this religion that protects them, this country that gives them abode, food and drink, and shelters them from all fear . . . . We only want to say this common truth that all men in Morocco know. The feelings of the Jews do not change. They are upholding the little state [of Israel] with money and none of them fail in this. We defy anybody among them to prove the contrary. The emigration campaigns from Morocco is very clear and evident to all. We demand of the authorities that, on this occasion, they protect their citizens from the provocation and defiance of the Jews, and that they should not guard the

Jews when the latter organize receptions and festivals to express their joy [with Israel's victory in the 1967 Arab-Israeli War] under the guard of the police protecting them.[68]

These were harsh words expressing deep frustration in face of Arab defeat. But they were not necessarily shared by the common people who continued to coexist with the Jews. Whereas in past years attacks were focused against the AIU, other organizations were targeted during the middle and late 1960s for their efforts to intensify emigration, particularly the HIAS (Hebrew Immigrant Aid Society, founded in 1898 to encourage and finance Jewish emigration to Israel and the United States). The latter organization operated in Morocco since the mid-1950s and ceased activity in the aftermath of the June 1967 war.

During the 1970s, with the exception of two attempted *coups d'état* against the monarchy (summers 1971 and 1972), the Jews felt secure for the most part. But Moroccan Jewry was moving slowly but definitely toward its liquidation. The school population was perhaps the best yardstick to gauge the situation. There was a decrease of about 15 percent in enrollment of Jewish day-schools between October 1972 and October 1973; there had been a further decrease of about 5 percent since October 1973.[69]

Several communities delayed complete departure partly because they owned large pieces of property worth many millions of dollars. These properties were registered with the Ministry of Interior and could not be sold without the ministry's permission and the proceeds of the sales had to be either kept in cash in a bank or reinvested in other property.[70] On the other hand, the Palace, since 1975, when 22,000 Jews had still remained in the country, considered policies that would lead to the repatriation of Jewish emigrants settled on the outside. Moroccan officials claimed that some 145-175,000 Jews went to Israel, 50,000 to France, and 25,000 to North America; unlike other Arab countries Morocco now allowed Moroccan-born Jews to come back to visit, even with Israeli official stamps in their passports.[71]

Only a few returned. Upon their arrival they were given board and lodging at government expense and were helped to find jobs; several were enrolled in a hotel school to provide future executives in the growing tourist industry.[72] Haïm Shiran, who left Morocco in 1959 for France and later for Israel, visited in July 1978. He entered the *mellāḥ* of his home town, Meknes, and noticed that Jews and Muslims were now integrated into what was once a Jewish quarter; that Jewish quarter streets continued to bear such names as Berdugo, Toledano, Jerusalem and Zion.[73] He noted:

My biggest moment was when I encountered at the *Alliance* school a history teacher who was with me at the school thirty years ago. This was an emotional meeting, though after nineteen years away from Morocco, I felt that the links between us were not the same. There was a certain distance, a certain rupture. He stayed in Meknes, preserved his roots but did not really develop. We had conflicting aspirations and ambitions, and time and distance surely contributed to this situation.[74]

He further noted that the *Ittiḥād* schools placed great emphasis on Arabic, yet, curiously French was well represented in the educational program.[75]

Other Jews who returned to Morocco to visit or settle usually had positive impressions of their ancient homeland. Robert Asseraf and his family left in 1967 to settle in Paris but in 1979 the Assarafs returned to live in Casablanca where Robert entered into business partnership with a Muslim and said relations were "very good at every level."[76] However, Jewish sources in Morocco emphasized that a basic reason for the improvement in the atmosphere was the decrease in the number of Jewish inhabitants. When Morocco won independence many Frenchmen left and French-educated Jews who graduated from the AIU tended to take their place in business, trade, and administration, which caused resentment. "Now the areas of competition and possible conflict have been reduced," Assaraf said.[77] As the country arabized the administration, Jews and Europeans found it increasingly difficult to compete, except in private business.[78] The big problem for the Jews who stayed were the children. Parents were sending them abroad in their mid-teens to assure them of more options in the future.[79]

On the whole, however, the Jews were content. As late as May 1980 when Tamar Golan, an Israeli journalist, visited Morocco, she could claim that in Casablanca where most Moroccan Jews lived, 2,000 youths were enrolled in Jewish schools and that their spoken Hebrew was better than of their counterparts in other areas of the diaspora.[80] She quoted David Amar, president of the Casablanca Jewish community and head of the Council of Communal Presidents saying:

> In the midst of anarchy that prevails in our world today, given the destructive danger that threatens mankind, there exist to our good fortune, those who struggle for human solidarity. Among them are King Ḥasan II. No attack from the outside, no irrational fanaticism will make the king deviate from his policy.[81]

Indeed, the king's policy enabled Shiran and others to search for their roots even if most visitors do not choose to resettle. Despite Ḥasan II's admirable policy to bridge the gap between Jews and Muslims and between Arabs and Israelis, his representatives at home and abroad often spoke strongly for Jewish repatriation. For example, in November 1976 at the United Nations, 'Alī Benjelloun, Morocco's representative affirmed:

We see today signs of disenchantment among the Jewish populations of Israel who are victims of the politics of population uprooting. The statistics of departure from Israel and [the small Jewish] emigration [to Israel] speak for themselves. I take this opportunity to recall the decision of His Majesty King Hasan II concerning the right to return to the country which is reserved to all Moroccan citizens of the Jewish faith who, due to a systematic propaganda campaign, have emigrated to Israel. The necessary instructions [to achieve the aim of repatriation] have been given to all our diplomatic representatives and consulates. I note with pleasure that certain Jewish elements have welcomed the royal appeal for repatriation with profound enthusiasm.[82]

As for the Jews who remain in Morocco, they are well treated, even if their exact political status has been debated and remains to be studied.[83] The work of Jewish organizations in the area of education remains intact. Although in 1980 there were about 2,100 students enrolled at the *Ittiḥād-Maroc*, which continued to maintain the enrollment lead, it is not clear how much longer the communities will survive. It has been suggested that it is "in the interest of the Jewish people to make sure that this school system is not dismantled as long as Jews live in Morocco."[84] This will depend on Morocco's continued political stability.

Notes

1. Interview with Haïm Zafrani (May 17, 1976), pt. i.
2. *Les Droits de l'Homme et l'Éducation: Actes du Congrès Centenaire de l'Alliance Israélite Universelle* (Paris, 1961), p. 91.
3. Charles Bensimhon, "La mission de l'instituteur marocain de l'alliance," *CAIU* 111 (septembre-octobre 1957), p. 63.
4. *Les droits de l'homme*, p. 92.
5. Emile Sebban, "L'éducation juive dans les écoles de l'A.I.U. au Maroc," *CAIU* 91 (juin-juillet 1955), pp. 23–32.
6. Interview with Jules Braunschvig (Jerusalem, February 8, 1976).
7. See Eugène Weill, "Rapport moral: acivité scolaire," *CAIU* 199 (novembre 1978), pp. 25–30.
8. Interview with Isḥāq Rouche (February 9, 1976).
9. See, for instance, list of degree examination to which AIU candidates could apply: Eugène Weill, "Rapport moral," *CAIU* 193 (octobre 1975), pp. 35–37.
10. Interview with Ben-Ami (March 9, 1976).
11. Judgment on Jewish laws. See Stanley Abramovitch, "Jewish Education in Morocco," *Jewish Eduation* vol. 43. 1 (Fall 1973), p. 25.
12. Ibid.
13. There are two sorts of prayer books that came into use. One contains only the original prayers; it is intended for private use and therefore sometimes is provided with a translation; this prayer book goes under the name of *Siddūr*. The other is a more comprehensive collection of the original prayers and is known as *Mahzor*.
14. Pertaining to the books of Jewish law. Tradition identifies the Torah of Moses with five books — Genesis, Exodus, Leviticus, Numbers, and Deuteronomy,

generally known as the *Hūmash,* a short term for the five-fifths or five folds of the law.

15. Abramovitch, "Jewish Education," p. 25.
16. Ibid., p. 26.
17. Ibid.
18. Ibid., p. 27.
19. *Mezūzōt* (sing. Mezīzā): tiny scroll of Torah on doorpost of Jewish homes; *Tefillīn*: phylacteries used in Jewish prayer by the more observing Jews.
20. Abramovitch, "Jewish Education," p. 27.
21. Ibid.
22. *Women's American ORT News* 3 (January-February 1962), p. 1.
23. Ibid., p. 3.
24. Ibid.
25. *ORT Union. Bureau Central. Geneva. Statistics on Morocco* (Data by David Alberstein).
26. *Women's American ORT News*, p. 3.
27. *JDC: The Healing of the Wound* (1959 Statistics: JDC Budget, New York), p. 9.
28. Ibid., pp. 9–10.
29. Chouraqui, *L'alliance israélite universelle et la renaissance juive contemporaine* (Presses Universitaires de France, 1965), p. 337.
30. Ibid.
31. *CAIU* 100 (juillet 1956), p. 5; Chouraqui, p. 338.
32. See, for example, *L'Avant-Garde* (1 mars 1959).
33. Ibid.
34. JDC: Eleventh Annual Country Directors Conference, Paris, October 1956 (JDC/330(a)).
35. Z. Waltner to Isaac Shalom, Tangier, November 13, 1957, (JDC/9(c)10(a)).
36. Fourteenth Country Annual Meeting, Paris, 1959 (JDC/9(c)10(a)).
37. Joseph Schechtman, *On Wings of Eagles* (New York, 1961), p. 303.
38. *Al-Mukāfih* (August 27, 1962).
39. Eugène Weill (secretary-general of the AIU) to Michael M. Laskier, Paris, November 13, 1978 (E/1987).
40. See speech delivered by Elias Harrus in 1980: *CAIU*, no. 202 (octobre 1980), pp. 54–55.
41. Interview with Zafrani (September 20, 1976), pt. ii.
42. Ibid.
43. Ibid.
44. Weill to Laskier (above, note 39).
45. Zafrani, interview, pt. i.
46. Bensimhon, "La mission de l'instituteur marocain de l'Alliance," *CAIU* 111 (septembre-octobre 1957), pp. 58–59.
47. Ibid., p. 59.
48. Ibid., pp. 59–60.
49. Ibid., p. 60.
50. Ibid., p. 61.
51. Ibid.
52. Ibid.
53. Ibid., p. 60.
54. Ibid.
55. Ibid., p. 63.
56. Schechtman, *On Wings of Eagles*, p. 287.

57. Salāḥ al-'Aqqād, "al-Yahūd fī al-Maghrib al-'Arabī," *Ma'had al-Buḥūth wa al-Dirāsāt al-'Arabīyya* 3 (March 1972), p. 54.

58. Ibid.

59. Ibid.

60. Waterbury, *The Commander of the Faithful*, p. 127.

61. Ibid.

62. Chouraqui, *Between East and West*, p. 269.

63. *Jewish Telegraphic Agency* (October 27, 1959).

64. Chouraqui (above, note 62), p. 270.

65. Ibid.

66. *Jewish Telegraphic Agency* (October 7, 1956).

67. *Jewish Telegraphic Agency* (September 4, 1962).

68. *Al-Masā'* (June 22, 1967).

69. Stanley Abramovitch, visit to Morocco, March 18–25, 1974 (JDC/247(b)).

70. Ibid.

71. *The Washington Post*, (November 25, 1976).

72. Ibid.

73. *Yēdī'ōt aḥarōnōt Weekly Magazine* no. 762 (September 29, 1978).

74. Ibid.

75. Ibid.

76. *New York Times* (April 18, 1979).

77. Ibid.

78. Ibid.

79. Ibid.

80. *Ma'ariv*, (May 9, 1980).

81. Ibid.

82. "Le Maroc réitère son appel pour le retour des juifs marocains," *L'Opinion*, (novembre 24, 1976).

83. Donath pointed out in 1968 that le Maroc indépendent gardait ses structures féodoles at théocratiques. En définitive, malgré certaines réformes et certaines velleités de modernisation, le juif resta le *dhimmī*. Paradoxalement, c'est ce statut même qui assure aujourd'hui aux juifs marocains leur tranquillité: l'allégeance perpétuelle les lie au Sultan qui lui-même est lié par elle à ses sujets." Donath, *Evolution du judaïsme marocain sous le protectorat*, p. 119.

84. Abramovitch "Jewish Education," p. 28.

Conclusion

The history of Jewish education in Morocco deserves to be recorded in great detail. It is a glorious chapter, a real success story in recent times. When the Jewish world faces such an enormous crisis of Jewish education in the West, Morocco can serve as an example of concrete and impressive achievements in spite of difficult conditions . . . . The [reason] lies in the calibre of the people who directed the program.

Stanley Abramovitch, 1973.

In the period ranging from the early 1860s until 1962, the AIU maintained the lead in educating several important components of the modernized elite. The expansion of the schools into the *cours complémentaire* system and the contribution of the protectorates' schools, *lycées* in particular, enhanced the process of modernization. In assessing how the AIU contributed to change in these communities during this one hundred year period, we shall consider the following:

1. The significance of AIU education and activities during the protectorate era.

2. The shortcomings of AIU activities since 1912.

3. The activities of the AIU in Morocco as compared with its activities in other parts of the Muslim and Mediterranean world.

1. Significance of AIU Activities

1. There is no doubt that prior to 1912 the activities of the AIU in Morocco were significant, for its schools were the most effective causes for reform. They were perhaps the first serious French-type schools in the Sherifian Empire and they attracted Jews and non-Jews. Though it is true that since 1912 AIU activities were supplemented by protectorate schools and, since 1945, by other organizations, the AIU was still in the forefront of reforms, in the struggle against illiteracy, and in Jewish educational development. Moreover, there

347

were important distinctions between AIU teachers and those employed by the protectorates. The personnel of the AIU were a devoted force throughout this period despite their desire after 1956 to become unionized. Well-informed educational representatives in Morocco concluded that the AIU teachers were not merely models of first-rate educators but that they surpassed the zeal of the public schools' teachers.

It certainly appears that the teachers were most adequately prepared to meet the challenges presented by community problems. Besides carrying on works begun in 1862, they were gradually entrusted with teaching responsibilities in community-sponsored schools, at the OH and ORT institutions. Furthermore, they worked overtime to improve their own credentials and often received secondary technical and vocational training in order to promote the modern vocations among their students.[1] Indeed, unlike their protectorate school counterparts, the AIU teachers were social workers, family counselors, reformists, and educators of the community. And if the ENIO was a secular training school, the two AIU normal schools (ENIO and ENH) strongly enforced the idea of Jewish solidarity among the future teachers, and that "all of Israel is responsible for each other." The colonial authorities did not recruit or train teachers in this spirit. One would not have expected them to do so in light of political considerations.

2. The significance of the AIU was also reflected through the ENH in Casablanca. Although the OH schools emphasized Hebrew and Jewish studies, their program rested more on religious education and rabbinic Hebrew whereas the ENH concentrated mainly on spoken Hebrew, an area of study which served a practical purpose since 1948.

3. The significance of the AIU schools in the Spanish zone and Tangier reflected the distinction between these schools and other institutions. In Spanish Morocco the AIU schools were among the very few educational institutions representing French culture. And although the Spaniards set up schools for Jews and in fact taught some French, the AIU counterparts were more popular and offered a solid program in French and Spanish. In Tangier, on the other hand, European schools sponsored by the various powers offered mostly their national languages and cultures, the only exception being *Lycée Regnault*, which offered, alongside French, English, Spanish, and Arabic. Yet the AIU schools were the only primary-level institutions that offered a multilingual program.

4. The AIU's major contributions were to expand secondary and vocational training. This is seen in the creation of *cours complémentaires* in the major towns and in the collaboration with ORT. Not only were several thousand youths attending the secondary and semisecondary schools of the AIU, but there were as many as 3,000 attending the ORT-AIU in 1960, where AIU teachers were responsible for secondary-level French, Jewish, and general education.

5. The AIU not only created community leaders, but also effectively combatted illiteracy in the major towns, mainly through the teaching of French. In addition to AIU schools, there were community-sponsored schools, ORT, OH, the Lubavitcher, and several Jewish institutes for rabbinic training. Most youths were enrolled in schools on the eve of Moroccan independence and the AIU led the way with perhaps 60 to 70 percent of these youths enrolled in its schools.

6. The elite that emerged out of the AIU usually belonged to three schools of thought: (a) those who were attached to French and European culture and underwent the process of secularization, yet without becoming totally divorced from Jewish traditions. These were assimilationists but were not de-Judaized as a result, for they chose not to emulate the West or French culture blindly. Only those who attended protectorate schools (mainly in the French zone), and they were a small group, were deeply influenced by secular culture, given the total absence of Jewish education in the *lycées*. Members of this group held diverse positions, as some were firm advocates of Jewish solidarity at home and with international Jewry, or, like Moïse Nahon, of Judeo-Muslim solidarity. The Zionist idea did not appeal to them for the most part; (b) those who despite French educational influence chose to find the solution to Jewish emancipation in the modern and secular Zionist idea. In fact, most modern Zionists who maintained contacts with the outside world and gradually cultivated a small and dynamic movement alongside ancient Zionism, which was buried deeply in the hearts of many Jews, were products of the AIU; (c) during the early and middle 1950s those who chose to collaborate with Muslim nationalists in actively seeking and later preserving Moroccan independence as well as national unity. And although this group was relatively limited in influence, it was the most active intellectual group seeking national unity in comparison to such Jewish groups in other parts of the Islamic diaspora at the time. Of these schools of thought the first two eventually contributed to the direction which the communities chose to take.

Ironically, although the authorities ascribed to the AIU in the 1920s the role of providing a solid French education to the Jews, and at the same time kept them away from protectorate schools to avoid their exposure to "over-Europeanization," the graduates of the AIU in the major towns gradually moved to the European quarters. A substantial portion of this group eventually settled in France. The French succeeded in blocking the entrance of numerous AIU graduates to the world of privileges enjoyed by European residents of Morocco by placing restrictions on Jewish employment in governmental agencies and on the process of obtaining French citizenship. But they could not stop all the Jews from financial and social success, as reflected in Jewish settlement in European quarters and the emigration of 50,000 or more Jews to France since the late 1950s.

2. Shortcomings of AIU Activities Since 1912

In this category there are several factors that warrant analysis.

1. Some people mistakenly believe that the AIU contributed to the process of de-Judaization through (a) providing an assimilationist educational philosophy indifferent to the traditions of the Torah; (b) contributing to the loss of Jewish spiritual identity; (c) gallicizing the youths' names; and (d) teaching the youths about Christian holidays, notably Christmas. Most of Morocco's Jews remained attached to their traditions despite exposure to secular education. Undeniably, the AIU should have tried harder and *earlier* to emphasize Jewish and Hebrew education. But when it did not do so, many youths were placed by their parents—outside AIU school hours—in the rabbinic schools, to assure that their religious education would not be neglected. Despite their respect for secular education, these parents believed that religious traditions were equally important, so they enrolled their children in both types of schools.

It would seem that if any accusation ought to be directed against the AIU, it is that of not devoting sufficient time to Jewish subjects and Hebrew before 1945. Yet many children attended the rabbinic as well as the AIU schools and thus enjoyed both worlds: profane education with some Jewish and Hebrew instructions; and sacred education of the *talmūd* tōra and *slā*. Was there indeed a danger of de-Judaization? Or was it simply that sacred education offered at the AIU was not sufficiently emphasized and not of the best quality? The latter seemed to have been the case. The term 'de-Judaization' was often misused when the quality of Jewish eduation and the time allotted for this education was the crux of the problem. The AIU was doubtless responsible for allotting insufficient time for this education after 1912, but responsibility for the poor quality of Jewish instructions had to be shared with the rabbi-teachers who taught for many years at both the AIU and the rabbinic schools.

Teaching about Christmas or changing the names of the students *à la européenne* did not signify a process of de-Judaization. In the first place, the texts of the *métropole* included information about this holiday, and it could not hurt Jewish youths to know about Christian traditions especially in light of the fact that a sizable Christian community resided in Morocco since 1912. In the second case, the changing of names certainly signified a trend toward westernization, but not the kind accompanied with total secularization. Some could argue that this was a superficial form of westernization, for it even influenced the *bled* where European ideas penetrated very slowly. Though not completely accurate, the following statement by an anonymous observer on Moroccan Jewry has its merits: "[La communauté israélite] est . . . une communauté très vivante, occidentalisée dans sa vie sociale, sans renier ni sa foi religieuse, ni ses attaches sentimentales avec l'Etat d'Israël."[2] The Moroccan Jews remained more attached to Jewish traditions than any other Jewry in the Islamic diaspora.

2. As for serious shortcomings, the AIU did not provide permanent Arabic language education prior to 1955. It should have been integrated effectively and systematically into the program at the expense of another language. The *makhzan*, too, was at fault as far back as the 1860's for not encouraging the AIU to teach the language.

3. Another area where the AIU was criticized concerned dependence on the French government. This is a classic argument cherished by the Zionists who argued that the help the AIU demanded from France, a country upon which the organization depended, would discourage it from carrying out vital activities on the Jews' behalf. It is inaccurate to suggest that the AIU neglected vital Jewish goals, as we have seen. Nevertheless, before 1945, Jewish education should have been emphasized, and here the Zionist argument is valid. From this study it is clear that the AIU, at least until 1945, was largely dependent on French subsidies for its schools after the First World War, a situation that was gradually altered when the JDC began to cover its expenses. Regardless of supervision over the AIU curriculum exercised by the French, the teachers had considerable flexibility and freedom in the communities in so far as reforms and educational policies were concerned. Nevertheless, it is likely that the insufficiency of formal Hebrew and Jewish studies before 1945 was due to French pressure and financial support, or to the AIU leaderships' fear of alienating the French.

It is this author's estimation that there were three main periods in the activities of the AIU: (1) the years 1862–1915 when the *oeuvre* was almost completely independent, having no dependence on governmental subsidies but only on fundraising and communal support; (b) the years 1913–1945, mostly the interwar period, when the AIU was dependent on financial assistance from the French protectorate and when the time allotted to Jewish education was particularly insufficient; and (c) the period since 1945, when the AIU realized that Jewish educational goals deserved priority over and beyond other educational commitments. Although during the post-1945 period the AIU received generous French governmental subsidies to enlarge the network, the JDC was forthcoming with substantial financial assistance, and one should not rule out possible JDC pressure on the AIU to strengthen Jewish education in return for that support.

4. Another shortcoming was the inability of the AIU along with the protectorates, ORT, OSE and organizations like WIZO[3] – to attend to all problems of poverty, partly resulting from a rapidly growing population during the 1940s and 1950s. Moreover, whereas the AIU created an elite class and therefore helped modernize the occupational structure, a large segment of the Jews continued to belong to the traditional occupations, their economic conditions did not improve, and they continued to dwell in the *mellāhs*.

This applied to the poor urban population and to the communities of the *bled*. And it is among these elements that the representatives of the Jewish Agency and Zionist youth movements (that sprang since 1947)[4] attracted emigrants to Israel.

3. Comparative AIU Activities: Morocco and Other Muslim Countries

The Moroccan AIU school network was in some ways similar to its counterparts in other countries. The AIU was a pioneer in educating girls in most countries, save Algeria, where the Jews enrolled in public schools, and in Egypt and Iraq, where the communities were exposed to Western education long before 1862. The AIU also offered secondary education, encouraged a dual program of sacred and secular education, and promoted goodwill societies and alumni associations. Morocco was no exception. Further, the AIU enrolled Jews and non-Jews in its Middle Eastern and North African networks, thus partially extending its cultural influence beyond the Jewish communities. Once again, the Moroccan case was no exception.

In the precolonial period the AIU spread European-style education to other places besides Morocco. Although the AIU established schools in Egypt after the British occupation of 1882, and in Tunisia at roughly the time when the French protectorate was created, its schools in Iraq, Palestine, Syria and Lebanon predated the British and French mandates by over forty years. Notwithstanding, the AIU activities in Morocco fifty years before the protectorate era were far more significant than in these countries.

Finally, it is known that in the Muslim world the AIU served as a bulwark against the missionary schools by recruiting Jewish youths for its classrooms and thus neutralizing the dangers of conversion. While this problem did not concern the AIU in Morocco, it does not mean that Morocco was unique in this sense. It is noteworthy that Christian missionary activities in the Maghrib as opposed to the Mashriq (Middle East) were not as intense. Moreover, in Morocco and Tunisia numerous Jews were too firmly attached to their traditions and few among them considered sending their youths to missionary schools.

Thus far we have seen the most pronounced comparative features of AIU activities in the Muslim world. We shall now concentrate on the distinguishing features which should confirm the supreme importance of the Moroccan network. In the first place, the AIU network in Morocco reflected its superiority over other networks in both the number of schools and student clientele: eighty-three schools and over 33,000 youths enrolled in 1956. This educational network at the time was larger than all the other AIU networks combined (see Table 47).

Table 47. AIU Schools in 1956

Country	Number of Schools	Number of Pupils
Morocco	83	33,100
Tunisia	5	3,607
Libya	1	98
Israel	12	4,223
Syria	1	422
Lebanon	6	1,510
Iran	34	7,955
France (ENIO)	1	62
Total:	143	50,977

SOURCE: Georges Ollivier, *L'Alliance Israélite Universelle: 1860–1960.* Documents et Témoignages, 1959, p. 212.

Secondly, the Moroccan network enjoyed over the years greater political and financial support from the colonial powers than did the AIU schools in other countries. In no other country were there three zones of colonial influence to contend with. Also, more than in any other Muslim country, the big powers who vied for political and cultural influence looked to the AIU for assistance to help them spread their educational philosophies and languages. Aware of the unanimity among the representatives of the powers over the importance of the AIU schools for their political and cultural interests, the school directors seized the opportunity to wrest from these representatives political concessions on behalf of the Jews.

Thirdly, the AIU in Morocco had to contend with educational adaptations and reforms unheard of in its other networks. It instituted a Hebrew and Jewish studies normal school whose intellectual standards were praised by both Moroccan rabbis and educational authorities in Israel. It had to devise educational programs before 1912 to meet the needs of Jews from diverse backgrounds (Judeo-Spaniards, Judeo-Arabs, Judeo-Berbers), arising from internal migrations and communal integration; to unite them under one roof, and to attempt to dispel their mutual distrust and discrimination. After 1912 the AIU was compelled to prepare educational programs for three different zones of influence without relinquishing its French character. This phenomenon hardly existed in other Muslim countries. Also, the AIU after 1927 extended its influence into new areas such as the *bled* and confronted new problems in regions where educational institutions were virtually nonexistent. It was like starting all over again. In other countries the AIU usually created schools in urban centers and confined its activities to these locales only.

Fourthly, the AIU in Morocco was catering to the largest Jewish communities of the Muslim world. More than other communities, excepting Iran, the Jews of Morocco drew their modern educational, social, and political inspiration from the AIU. The Moroccan communities were not financially affluent or socially organized, as, say, their counterparts in Algeria, Syria, Egypt, and Iraq were. The latter managed to establish excellent schools already in the nineteenth century on their own initiative which paralleled the work of the AIU. The penetration of American educational organizations further revealed the extent to which Moroccan Jewry continued to rely on external assistance.

Finally, the variety of AIU schools in Morocco in all areas of education, and on the primary and secondary levels, greatly surpassed the organization's efforts elsewhere in the Muslim world.

All of these achievements in Morocco are praiseworthy, most particularly during the pre-1912 period. At that time, which was the *belle époque* and *temps héroïques* of the AIU, and unlike other networks, the directors and teachers had to work under the constant threats of *bled al-sība*: the territory not under *makhzan* jurisdiction. Despite these obvious intrusions and the risks involved, the schools continued to function and produced positive results.

Unlike other European institutions of the precolonial and colonial periods in the Third World, which folded on the occasion of independence, the AIU continued to function strongly in several developing countries, particularly in Morocco. In the latter case, the authorities learned to tolerate its presence and in many situations appreciated the role it was playing in the Jewish community. The ability and willingness of the AIU throughout its long history in Morocco to adapt to new realities enhanced its chances for survival and for the continuation of activities, through the *Ittihād*-Maroc, the educational arm of the AIU in independent Morocco.

Notes

1. Interview with Haïm Zafrani, May 17, 1976, pt. i.
2. Anon. "Les lignes de force du Maroc moderne," *Politique Etrangère* 4 (août-septembre 1955), p. 408.
3. Women's International Zionist Organization. Active mainly in Casablanca since 1950 in social work.
4. The activities of youth movements like *Drōr* and *Habōnīm* are beyond the scope of this study.

Selected Bibliography

Archival Sources - A

I. Archives of the Alliance Israélite Universelle. Part I: Communities (Each number represents a file of letters)

I.B.1-8   Casablanca 1877-1940; Demnat 1935-1939; Elksar 1878 and 1901; Fez 1876-1928; Kenitra 1917; Larache 1872

II.B.9-13   Marrakesh 1900-1935; Mazagan 1874-1939; Martinprey 1912; Meknes 1897-1939

III.B.14-22   Mogador 1864-1935; Ouezzan 1909: Oujda 1911-1915; Rabat 1902-1937; Safi 1864-1936; Sefrou 1935; Settat 1912-1913

IV.B.23-24   Taourirt 1936; Tangier (a) 1865-1891, (b) 1864-1939

VI.B.15-27   Tetuan 1862-1926; Tafilalt 1918-1919

VII.B. No file number   Miscellaneous local communities

II. Archives of the Alliance Israélite Universelle. Part II: Schools (Each number represents a file of letters)

I.E.1-16   Azemmour 1911-1939
I.E.17-19   Ben-Ahmed 1928-1932
II.E.20-25   Beni-Mellal No years listed
II.E.27-32   Berrechid   ″   ″   ″
II.E.33-41   Boujad   ″   ″   ″
II.E.43-48   Demnat   ″   ″   ″
III.E.49-81   Casablanca 1880-1940
IV.E.82-94   Casablanca 1900-1938
V.E.92-121   Casablanca 1901-1940
VI.E.122-136   Casablanca 1897-1940
VII.E.137-153   Casablanca 1896-1940
VIII.E.154-158   Casablanca 1908-1909
IX.E.159-172   Casablanca 1899-1940
X.E.172-176   Casablanca 1913-1940
XI.E.177-192   Elksar 1878-1939
XII.E.193-211   Fez 1911-1939
XIII.E.212-225   Fez 1883-1939
XIV.E.226-237   Fez 1890-1939
XV.E.238-247   Fez 1909-1940
XVI.E.248-254   Fez 1902-1940
XVII.E.255-285   Fez 1904-1939

XVIII.E.286–302   Fez 1889–1939
XIX.E.303–313   Fez 1902–1938
XX.E.314–324   Larache 1873–1932
XXI.E.325–338   Larache 1903–1931
XXII.E.339–358   Larache 1898–1932
XXIII.E.359–384   Marrakesh 1909–1940
XXIV.E.385–393   Marrakesh 1906–1938
XXV.E.394–397   Marrakesh 1910–1940
XXVI.E.398–416   Marrakesh 1904–1940
XXVII.E.417–442   Marrakesh 1900–1939
XXVIII.E.443–470   Marrakesh 1890–1940
XXIX.E.471–483   Mazagan 1906–1939
XXX.E.484–509   Mazagan 1896–1940
XXXI.E.510–543   Meknes 1918–1940
XXXII.E.544–562   Meknes 1901–1940
XXXIII.E.563–565   Midelt 1928–1932
XXXIII.E.566–582   Mogador 1865–1934
XXXIV.E.583–601   Mogador 1865–1939
XXXV.E.602–620   Mogador 1886–1939
XXXVI.E.621–627   Mogador 1903–1938
XXXVII.E.628–657   Mogador 1903–1939
XXXVII.E.bis.no file number   Mogador 1909–1915
XXXVIII.E.658–685   Mogador 1902–1938
XXXIX.E.667–685   Rabat 1902–1939
XL.E.685–695   Rabat 1911–1939
XLI.E.696–716   Rabat 1910–1939
XLII.E.717(a-c)   Rabat 1926–1933
XLIII.E.717(d-f)   Rabat 1933–1934
XLIV.E.717(g-i)   Rabat 1935–1936
XLV.E.717(j-l)   Rabat 1936–1937
XLVI.E.717(m-o)   Rabat 1938–1939
XLVII.E.717(p-z)   Rabat 1939–1940
XLVII.E.718–719   Rabat 1920–1936
XLVIII.E.720–740   Safi 1868–1940
XLVIII.E.741–757   Safi 1907–1939
XLVIX.E.758–783   Safi 1905–1940
L.E.784–801   Safi 1909–1940
LI.E.802–822   Tangier 1872–1939
LI.E.822 bis–838   Tangier 1867–1936
LII.E.839–867   Tangier 1873–1937
LIII.E.868–884   Tangier 1883–1939
LIV.E.885–897   Tangier 1869–1930
LV.E.897(c)–913   Tangier 1864–1940
LVI.E.914–934(a)   Tangier 1881–1939
LVII.E.935(b-d)   Tangier 1895–1904
LVIII.E.935(e)–943(a)   Tangier 1900–1939
LIX.E.943(b-d)   Tangier 1930–1935
LX.E.943(e)–945(a)   Tangier 1905–1940
LXI.E.946(b-d)   Tangier 1914–1924
LXII.E.946(e)–953   Tangier 1910–1940
LXIII.E.954–971   Tetuan 1884–1940

LXIV.E.972–982   Tetuan 1871–1924
LXV.E.983–1000   Tetuan 1865–1927
LXVI.E.1001–1018   Tetuan 1863–1933
LXVIII.E.1019–1029   Tetuan 1884–1932
LXVIII.E.1030(a-c)   Tetuan 1905–1932
LXIX.E.1031–1035   Tetuan 1892–1932
LXX.E.1036–1044(a)   Tetuan 1867–1910

III. Archives of the Alliance Israélite Universelle. Part III. Material separated from the other files and unclassified

LXII.E.   Fez, Kasba-Tadla, Kenitra
LXXIII.E.   Larache, Mazagan, Oujda, Oued-Zem
LXXIV.E.   Ouezzan, Rabat
LXXV.E.   Safi, Salé
LXXVI.E.   Sefrou, Settat, Taourirt, Taroudant
LXXVII.E.   Tetuan, Tiznit

IV. Archives of the Alliance Israélite Universelle. Part IV. The Leven-Lyautey Correspondence.

*I.J.2Maroc: Lyautey 1912–1919

Archival Sources - B

I. Archives of the Quai d'Orsay. Part I. Public Education

A.E. Maroc.I.403.   Enseignement Public
Reports of Henri Regnault   1908–1909
   Reports of Fernand Couget   1914
   Reports of Saint-Aulaire   1909
   Reports of M. Malpertuy   1910

II. Archives of the Quai d'Orsay. Part II. Cultural and Religious Affairs

A.E. Maroc.I.405. Questions Culturelles et Réligieuses
   Reports of G. Saint-René-Taillandier   1902–1903

III. Archives of the Quai d'Orsay. Part III. The Alliance Israélite

A.E. Serie Administrative-C.142dr2. Alliance Israélite Universelle
   Reports of the French ambassador to Berlin (M. Cambon)
      on the Jews of Morocco   1897–1907
   Reports of Jacques Bigart about the Jews of Morocco   1897–1907

Archival Sources - C

I. The Central Archives for the History of the Jewish People (Jerusalem)

The Proceedings of the Jewish Community Council in Casablanca under the Presidency of Yahya Zagoury
   1907–1915, book I (in French)
   1916–1927, book II (in French)

Archival Sources - D

I. *The Zionist Archives of Jerusalem*

Z1 – Zionist Office in Vienna (Correspondence)
Z2 – Zionist Office in Cologne (Correspondence)
Z4 – The Central Headquarters of the World Zionist Organization in London (Correspondence)
S5 – Zionist Organization Department (Correspondence)
S6 – Emigration (Correspondence)

Archival Sources - E

I. *The Archives of the American Jewish Joint Distribution Committee*

JDC/9(c) 10(a), 10(b): Correspondence and Memoranda concerning Jewish Organizations subsidized by the JDC.
JDC/232(b) 233(a): Correspondence regarding JDC Activities
JDC/247(b): Correspondence regarding the activities of the AIU.
JDC/263(b): Correspondence regarding the activities of the OSE.
JDC/330(a), 330(b): Correspondence and Memoranda regarding the work of the JDC, the AIU, and JDC directors' reports.
JDC/402(b): JDC reports.
JDC/420(c): JDC reports.
JDC/421(a): JDC reports.

Manuscripts

Coidan, Etienne. *Le sionisme au Maroc.* (Rabat, 1946). Collection of the Ben-Zvi Institute in Jerusalem.
"Department of Middle Eastern Jewry," in *Proceedings of the 1948 Zionist Congress.* (Jerusalem, 1951).
Hamet, Charles. *La communauté israélite de Tanger.* (Tanger, 1951). Collection of CHEAM.
Memorandum V: For the Establishment of Hebrew Religious Schools by Osār ha-Tōra and the Improvement of its Existing Educational Institutions. Osār ha-Tōra (Circular, 1949.)
Montagne, A. *Etudes sur l'utilisation à la guerre des israélites marocains.* Rabat, (octobre 17, 1939). Collection of the Ben-Zvi Institute.
M.Y., R.S., R.B. *L'application du statut des juifs et des dispositions racial à la population juive du Maroc.* (février 1943). Collection of the Ben-Zvi Institute.
Nollet, Captaine. *Les juifs du Maroc et l'occident.* (décembre 1953) Collection of CHEAM.
Nouvel, M. *L'évolution du judaïsme marocain.* (mai 22, 1947). Collection of CHEAM.

Official Documents and Pamphlets

Ecole Normale Hébraïque de Casablanca: horaires hebdomadaires des matières enseignées avant 1956.

Ecole Professionnelle Agricole de l'AIU Marrakesh: programmes et horaires des divers enseignements et travaux.

Gouvernement Chérifien: Service central des statistiques: Recensement général de la population en 1951-52. Volume III. La population musulman; Volume IV. *La population israélite.*

Ministerio de Trabajos Dirección general de estadistica: III. Administración local. 1942. Zona de Protectorado y de los territorios de España. Madrid, 1943.

O.R.T. Union (Morocco). A Statistical Analysis and Historical Survey of O.R.T. Activities in Morocco between 1946 and 1963.

Presidencia de Gobierno: Instituto nacional de estadistica: zona de Protectorado y de territorios de soberanïa de España el Norte de Africa. Anuario Estadistica 1948. Madrid. 1949.

Presidencia del Gobierno: Instituto Nacional de estadistica zona de Protectorado y de territorios de soberanïa de España en el Norte de Africa. Anuario Estadistica 1951. Madrid, 1953.

Rabat. Service central des statistiques, recensement démographique. Juin 1960. Population égale du Maroc. Rabat, 1961.

Wizārat al-Ta'līm: Barnāmij al-Lugha al'Arabīyya. Results of the 1956–57 educational reforms.

Wizārat al-Ta'līm: al-Mamlaka al-Maghribīyya. Wizārat al-Ta'līm wa al-Funūn al-Jamīla: Barnāmaj durūs al-Ta'rīkh Lil Madāris al-Ibtid'īyya. Results of the 1956–57 educational reforms.

Wizārat al-Ta'līm: al-Mamlaka al-Maghribīyya. Wizārat al-Ta'līm wa al-Funūn al-Jamīla: Maslahat al-Ta'līm al-Awwalī. Results of the 1956–57 educational reforms.

Taped Interviews

Ben-Ami, Issachar. March 8, 1976, in Jerusalem. Graduate of the AIU school in Casablanca, former instructor at the Ecole Normale Hébräique. Former director of Misgav Yerūshālayīm, a research center on the study of Oriental and Sephardi Jewry.

Braunschvig, Jules. February 8, 1976, in Jerusalem. Former vice-president of the AIU, now serving as that organization's president. A member of the AIU Central Committee since 1932, Jules Braunschvig lived in Morocco for many years and was instrumental in carrying out reforms in Jewish education for the schools of the AIU.

Chouraqui, André. March 5, 1976, in Jerusalem. Born and raised in Algeria, Chouraque served as deputy mayor of Jerusalem and as advisor to former Israeli Prime Minister David Ben-Gurion on Jewish communal integration.

Dahan, Hanania. January 26, 1976, in Bat-Yam, Israel. Graduate of the *Alliance* boys' school in Salé. He is the representative of the Israeli Labor Party in Bat-Yam, Israel.

Ovadia, Rabbi David. February 16, 1976, in Jerusalem. The last in the chain of Sefrou's spiritual rabbis.

Rouche, Rabbi Ishāq. February 9, 1976, in Jerusalem. The first director of the *Ecole Normale Hébraïque* of Casablanca.

Soussan, Mordechai. March 1, 1976, in Jerusalem. Graduate of the AIU in Fez. Currently he is a Ph.D. candidate at the Hebrew University of Jerusalem.

Zafrani, Haïm. May 17, 1976 (interview Part I) and September 20, 1976 (interview Part II), in Paris. Graduate of the AIU and Franco-Jewish schools of Mogador. He continued his studies at the ENIO and served as AIU school director in Boujad, as inspector of Arabic language and culture, and as deputy-delegate of the AIU, together with Elias Harrus after Tajouri's death in 1960 and until 1962 when he left Morocco and settled in France. He was in charge of Hebrew education at the *Ecole National de la Langues Orientales Vivantes* from 1962 until 1966; and conducted research through the *Centre National de la Recherche Scientifique* between 1966 and 1969. Currently he is professor and director of Hebrew language and civilization at the University of Paris VIII. Zafrani is the author of six books and some sixty articles on Jewish-Hebraic studies, Judeo-Arabic and Judeo-Berber.

Books in Arabic and Hebrew

Bar-Asher, Shalom, ed. *The Taqanot of the Jews of Morocco*. Zalman Shazar Center, Jerusalem, 1977. In Hebrew.

Grinker, Yehuda. *The Emigration of Atlas Jewry to Israel*. Tel Aviv, Association of Moroccan Immigrants in Israel, 1973. In Hebrew.

Hirschberg, H.Z. *A History of the Jews in North Africa*. Jerusalem, Mossad Bialik: 1965. Two Volumes. Volume I, English translation, Leiden: Brill, 1974.

— —. *Me-Eres Mēvō ha-Shēmēsh* (The Land of the Sunset). Jerusalem, Goldberg Press, 1957.

Makāryūs, Shāhīn. *Ta'rīkh al-Isrā'īliyyīn* Cairo: (History of the Jews). Matba'at al-Muqtataf, 1904.

Ovadia, Rabbi David. *The Jewish Community of Sefrou*. Center for the Research on the Jewish Communities of Morocco, Jerusalem: 1974–75. Three volumes, in Hebrew.

Books in Western Languages

Abitbol, Michael, ed. *Judaïsme d'Afrique du Nord aux xixe et xxe siècles*. Jerusalem: Institut Ben-Zvi, 1980. A most important work based on papers delivered at the *Ben-Zvi Institute*, (Center for the Study of North African Jewry) in April 1977, which dealt with the social, cultural, and political history of this group.

Adam, André. *Casablanca: Essai sur la transformation de la société marocaine au contact de l'occident*. Paris: Editions du Centre Nationale de la Recherche Scientifique, 1968. Two volumes.

Attal, Robert, *Les juifs d'Afrique du Nord: Bibliographie*. Jerusalem: Institut Ben-Zvi et Université Hébraïque, 1973.

Benech, José. *Essai d'explication d'un mellah*. Marrakesh, 1940.

Bidwell, Robin. Morocco Under Colonial Rule: 1912–1956. London: Frank Cass, 1973.

Bowie, Leland Louis. "The Protégé System in Morocco: 1880–1904." Ph.D dissertation, Ohio State University, 1970.

Brown, Kenneth Lewis. *People of Salé: Tradition and Change in a Moroccan City: 1830–1930*. Cambridge, Mass.: Harvard University Press, 1976.

Burke, Edmund III. *Prelude to the Protectorate in Morocco: 1860–1912*. Chicago: University of Chicago Press, 1976.

Chouraqui, André. *La condition juridique de l'israélite marocain.* Paris, 1950. Alliance Israélite Universelle and Presses du Livre Français.

— —. *L'alliance israélite universelle et la renaissance juive contemporaine, 1860–1960.* Paris: Presses Universitaires de France, 1965.

— —. *Between East and West: A History of the Jews of North Africa.* Philadelphia: The Jewish Publication Society of America, 1968.

Corcos, David. *The History of the Jews of Morocco.* Jerusalem: 1976.

Damis, John James. "The Free School Movement in Morocco: 1919–1970." Ph.D dissertation, Tufts University, Fletcher School of Diplomacy, 1970.

Donath, Doris Bensimon. *L'évolution de la Femme israélite à Fès.* Aix-en Provence: Faculté des Lettres, no. 25, 1962.

— —. *Evolution du judaïsme marocain sous le protectorat français: 1912–1956* Paris: Mouton and Co., 1968.

— —. *Immigrants d'Afrique du Nord en Israël.* Paris: Editions Anthropos, 1970.

Flamand, Pierre. *Diaspora en terre d'Islam: les communautés israélites du sud marocain.* Casablanca: Imprimeries réunies, 1959.

Gaudefroy-Demombynes, Roger, *L-oeuvre française en matière d'enseignement au Maroc.* Paris: Paul Geuthner, 1928.

Gerber, Jane. *Jewish Society in Fez: Studies in Communal and Economic Life.* Leiden: Brill, 1980.

Goitein, S. D. *A Mediterranean Society.* Berkeley and Los Angeles: University of California Press. Volume I, 1967; Volume II, 1971.

Goulven, J. C. *Les mellahs de Rabat-Salé.* Paris: Paul Geuthner, 1927.

Guillen, Pierre. *L'Allemagne et le Maroc.* Paris: Presses Universitaires de France, 1967.

Leven, Narcisse. *Cinquante ans d'histoire: l'alliance israélite universelle.* Paris: Librarie Félix Alcan, 1911–1920. Two volumes.

Le Tourneau, Roger. *Fès avant le protectorat.* Casablanca, 1949.

Miège, Jean-Louis. *Le Maroc et l'Europe: 1830–1894.* Paris: Presses Universitaires de France, 1961–1963. Four volumes.

Montagne, Robert *Les berbères et le makhzan dans le sud du Maroc.* Paris, 1930.

Ortega, Manuel. *Los Hebreos en Marruecos.* Madrid, 1934.

Roland, Joan Gardner. "The Alliance Israélite Universelle and French Policy in North Africa: 1860–1918." Ph.D. Dissertation, Columbia University, 1969.

Silberman, Paul. "An Investigation into the Schools of the *Alliance Israélite Universelle*: 1862–1940." Ph.D. Dissertation, New York University, 1973.

Stillman, Norman. *The Jews of Arab Lands.* Philadelphia: The Jewish Publication Society of America, 1979.

Waterbury, John. *The Commander of the Faithful.* New York: Columbia University Press, 1970.

Zafrani, Haïm. *Pédagogie juive en terre d'Islam: l'enseignement traditionnel de l'hébreu et du judaïsme au Maroc.* Paris: Paul Geuthner, 1969.

— —. *Poésie juive en occident musulman.* Paul Geuthner, 1977–1979, two volumes.

Articles

Abitbol, Michael. "Zionist Activity in North Africa Up to the End of the Second World War." *Pe'amim* 2 (1979): 65–91. In Hebrew.

Adam, André. "Sur l'action du Gaililée à Casablanca en août." *Revue de l'Occident Musulman et de la Mediterranée* 6 (1969): 9–21.

Abramovitch, Stanley. "Jewish Education in Morocco." *Jewish Education* 43, no. 1 (Fall 1973): 23–28.

Benabdallah, Abdelkader. "La politique coloniale française à l'égard des juifs marocains." *L'Opinion*, août 15, 1976.

— —. "La politique française à l'égard des juifs marocains." *L'Opinion*, août 29, 1976.

Benchimol, Isaac. "Les juifs de Tetuan, leurs moeurs et coutumes réligieuses." *Bulletin de l'Alliance Israélite Universelle*, semestriel, 1888: 82–100.

Bensimhon, Charles. "La mission de l'instituteur marocain de l'alliance." *Les Cahiers de l'Alliance Israélite Universelle*, no. 111, septembre-octobre 1957: 57–64.

Bigart, Jacques. "Une mission au Maroc." *Paix et Droit*, 6e année, no. 3, mensuel, mars 1936: 3–6. (Part I)

— —. "Une mission au Maroc." *Paix et Droit*, 6e année, no. 4, mensuel, avril 1926: 14–19. (Part II).

Blandin, "La population de Tanger en 1940." *Revue Africaine* 88 (1944): 89–115.

Bowie, Leland Louis. "An Aspect of Muslim-Jewish Relations in Late Nineteenth Century Morocco: A European Diplomatic View." *International Journal of Middle Eastern Studies* 7 (1976): 3–19.

Brown, Kenneth L. "Mellah and Madina: A Moroccan City and its Jewish Quarter (Salé 1880–1930)." *Pe'amim* 4 (1980): 39–60. In Hebrew.

Caron, Louis. "Où en est le judaïsme marocain?" *L'Afrique et l'Asie*, 2e trimestre, 1951: 4–11.

Cazès, David. "Rapport sur les écoles de l'Alliance de Tanger et de Tétuan." *Bulletin de l'Alliance Israélite Universelle*, semestriel, 1884–1885: 42–53.

Corcos, David. "The Jews of Morocco Under the Merinids." *Jewish Quarterly Review* 55 (1964): 76–141.

Dahan, Jacques. "Le judaïsme marocain en 1954." *Les Cahiers de l'Alliance Israélite Universelle*, no. 85, juillet-août 1954: 35–45.

— —. "Les communautés israélites du Maroc." *Les Cahiers de l'Alliance Israélite Universelle*, no. 91, juin-juillet 1955: 8–14.

"Ecole profesionnelle israélite de Casablanca." *Bulletin d'Information du Maroc, no. 7, avril 15, 1949: 37–49.*

Elmaleh, Amram. "Israélites du Maroc: Fès." *Bulletin de l'Alliance Israélite Universelle*, nos. 7-8-9, mensuel, juillet-août-septembre 1913: 74–84.

— —. "Ecoles: La vie religieuse." *Bulletin de l'Alliance Israélite Universelle*, nos. 10-11-12, mensuel, octobre-novembre-décembre 1910: 248–255.

Gaillard, Henri. "Le sionisme et la question juive dans l'Afrique du Nord." *Renseignements Coloniaux*, nos. 1–3, supplément à l'*Afrique Française* de janvier-février-mars 1918: 3–7.

Halévy, Jospeh. "Rapport sur l'état des écoles dans les communautés juives au Maroc." *Bulletin de l'Alliance Israélite Universelle*, semestriel, 1877: 44–69.

Halstead, C. R. and C. J. Halstead. "Aborted Imperialism: Spain's Occupation of Tangier, 1940-1945." *Iberian Studies* 2 (1978): 53–71.

Hirsch, Samuel. "Rapport sur les écoles et les communautés du Maroc," *Bulletin de l'Alliance Israélite Universelle*, semestriel, 1873: 139–149.

Joly, A. "L'industrie à Tétuan." *Archives Marocaines* 11, no. 1 (1907): 361–393.

— —. "L'industrie à Tétuan." *Archives Marocaines* 18, no. 2 (1912): 187–256.

Laskier, Michael M. "Moïse Nahon: un intellectuel juif marocain." *Les Nouveaux Cahiers*, no. 61, eté 1980: 19–24.

– –, "Jewish Education in Morocco." *Pe'amim* 9 (1981): 78–99. In Hebrew.

– –, "The Jews of Morocco and the *Alliance Israélite Universelle*: Selected Documents and Analysis," *East and Maghreb* 3, ed. S. Schwarzfuchs, Ramat-Gan: Bar-Ilan University Press, 1981: 7–23.

– –, "The *Alliance Israélite Universelle* and the Struggle for Recognition within Moroccan Jewish Society: 1862–1912." In Issachar Ben-Ami, ed. *The Sephardi and Oriental Jewish Heritage*. Jerusalem: The Magnes Press, 1982, pp. 191–212.

– –, "Aspects of Change and Modernization in Morocco's Bled." Michael Abitbol, ed. *Communautés juives des marges sahariennes* (Jerusalem: Institut Ben-Zvi, 1982) pp. 329–364.

Leibovici, Sarah. "Tétuan: une communauté éclatée." *Les Nouveaux Cahiers*, no. 59, hiver 1979–80: 11–22.

Littman, David. "Jews under Muslim Rule, Part I, Morocco, 1903–1912." *The Wiener Library Bulletin* 29, n.s., nos. 37/38 (1976): 3–19.

Miège, Jean-Louis. "Journaux et journalistes à Tanger au xixe siècle." *Hespéris*, 1er & 2e semestres, année tome xli, 1954: 171–232.

– –. "Les missions protestantes au Maroc: 1875–1905." *Hespéris* 43 (1955): 153–192.

Morabia, Alfred. "About Relations between Judaism and Islam." Part one: *Alliance Review* 48, Fall 1978, pp. 13–19; part two: *Alliance Review* 49, Fall 1980, pp. 9–13.

Nahon, Moïse. "Les israélites du Maroc." *Revue des Etudes Ethnographiques et Sociologique*, 2 (1909): 258–279.

Prague, H. "La France au Maroc." *Archives Israelites* 16, 21 avril 1904: 121–123.

Salmon, Georges. "Le commerce indigène et le marche de Tanger." *Archives Marocaines* 1, no. 1 (1904): 38–55.

Sebban, Emile. "L'education juive dans les écoles de l'A.I.U. du Maroc." *Les Cahiers de l'Alliance Israélite Universelle*, no. 91, juin-juillet 1955: 23–32.

Sémach, Yomtov D. "Charles de Foucauld et les juifs." *Bulletin de l'Enseignement Public*, 26e année, no. 163, janvier-février 1939: 3–12.

– –. "L'avenir des israélites marocains." *Paix et Droit*, 7e année, no. 6, mensuel, juin 1927: 9–10 (Part I).

– –. "L'avenir des israélites marocains." *Paix et Droit*, 8e année, no. 6, mensuel, juin 1928: 4–6 (Part II).

– –. "Les israélites au Maroc." *La Revue Française de Tanger*, 1er année, no. 4, 15 mars 1918: 3–7 (Part I).

– –. "Les Israélites au Maroc." *La Revue Française de Tanger*, 1er année, no. 5, 15 avril 1918: 9–13 (Part II).

– –. "Les israélites au Maroc." *La Revue Française de Tanger*, 1er année, no. 12, 15 novembre 1918: 3–7 (Part III).

Shokeid, Moshe. "Jewish Existence in a Berber Environment." *Pe'amim* 4(1980): 60–71. In Hebrew.

Tajouri, Reuben. "Les élèves israélites des écoles du Maroc." *Bulletin de l Enseignement Public*, 10e année, no. 54, décembre 1923: 88–98.

Thabault, Roger. "Le Maroc à l'heure du vichysme." *Les Nouveaux Cahiers*, no. 43, hiver, 1975–76: 16–20.

Weill, Georges. "Emancipation et humanisme: Le discours idéologique de *l'alliance israélite universelle* aux xixe siècle." *Les Nouveaux Cahiers*, no. 52, printemps 1978: 1–20.

Index

'Abd al-'Azīz, Sultan Mawlāy (d.1943), 40, 42–43
'Abd al-Hafīz, Sultan Mawlāy (d.1937), 43–43, 57–58, 153
'Abd al-Krīm, 286, 301
'Abd al-Qādir, Amir, 38
'Abd al-Rahmān, Sultan Mawlāy (d.1859), 37–39
Abdalla, Hadj, 35
Aben Danan, Rabbi Shlomo, 119, 198
Abensur, Moses, 177
Abensur, Rabbi Mordechai, 119, 198
Abikssera, Haïm, 235–36
Abramovitch, Stanley, 245, 247, 326, 347
Abūhseīra, Ysrā'ēl, 270
Abulafia, Rabbi Joseph Samuel, 86
Abūtām, Moses, 19
Action du Peuple, L', 168–69, 210
Administration. *See* French protectorate; Spanish and International zones
Administrative employees, 140. *See* French protectorate; Spanish and International zones
Agricultural training, 106, 128–29, 261–65
Ahad Haam, 244
Ahavat-Sion (Safi), 197
Aide scolaire, 180–234, 294
Alawids, 16
Algeciras: act of, 41–42
Algeria: abrogation of Crémieux decree, 179; French occupation of, 37–38
'Alī, Muhammad, 32
Alliance Française, 66, 72–73, 107, 130
Allied invasion of North Africa (November 1942), 180
Almohads, 14
Alphonso XIII, King, 172
Alumni associations of the AIU, 129–30; in Casablanca, 130; in Fez, 130; in Tangier, 129–30; in Salé, 218
Amade, General d', 42, 68

Amar, David, 343
American Jewish Committee, 184–8; collaboration with the AIU, 186–88
American Jewish Joint Distribution Committee (JDC): 161–62, 178, 182, 184–85, 187, 216–17, 226–32, 247, 251, 261, 277, 282, 284, 294, 326, 328–30, 332, 334, 351; C.I.R.E. project, 231, 330; food and clothing program, 228, 329; kindergarten-nursary school programs, 229–30, 329–30; summer camps, 230; summary of income of JDC-subventioned programs, 229
Anglo-French Accord of 1904, 41, 67, 72, 117
Anglo-Jewish Association, 32, 36, 72, 195; political efforts of, 48–50, 53–54; schools of, 90
Anglo-Jewry, 36, 48–50, 53–54
Anglo-Moroccan commercial treaty of 1856, 38–39, 41, 49, 53, 139
Aquin, Aymé d', 45, 62, 64–65
Arab-Berber-Jewish solidarity. *See* Nationalists
Arab-Israeli wars, 214, 216, 321, 340–42
Arabic education, 101–102, 104, 253–54, 322–23
Arabization of AIU program, 321–23, 330–34
Archives Israélites (Paris), 70, 165
Arkadia, 70
A'shāsh, 'Abd al-Rahmān al-, 17
Asociacíon Hebreo-Español, 172
Asseraf Robert, 343
Association des anciens élèves de l'alliance israélite universelle. See alumni associations of the AIU
Ataturk, Kemal, 290
Avant Garde, L', 331
Avenir Illustré, L' (Casablanca), 203–204, 207, 289